Primary Education in Ireland, 1897–1990

RETHINKING EDUCATION

VOLUME 12

Series Editors:

Dr Marie Martin

Dr Gerry Gaden

Dr Judith Harford

PETER LANG

Oxford · Bern · Berlin · Bruxelles · Frankfurt am Main · New York · Wien

Thomas Walsh

Primary Education in Ireland, 1897–1990

Curriculum and Context

PETER LANG

Oxford · Bern · Berlin · Bruxelles · Frankfurt am Main · New York · Wien

Bibliographic information published by Die Deutsche Nationalbibliothek.
Die Deutsche Nationalbibliothek lists this publication in the Deutsche
Nationalbibliografie; detailed bibliographic data is available on the Internet
at http://dnb.d-nb.de.

A catalogue record for this book is available from the British Library.

Library of Congress Cataloging-in-Publication Data:

Walsh, Thomas, 1976-
  Primary education in Ireland, 1897-1990 : curriculum and context /
Thomas Walsh.
    p. cm.
  Includes bibliographical references and index.
  ISBN 978-3-0343-0751-2 (alk. paper)
  1. Education, Primary--Ireland--History. I. Title.
  LA669.62.W36 2012
  372.9415--dc23

                                    2012002259

Cover picture: Boys from De La Salle School Waterford in Classroom
(1902) – Courtesy of the National Library of Ireland

ISSN 1662-9949
ISBN 978-3-0343-0751-2

© Peter Lang AG, International Academic Publishers, Bern 2012
Hochfeldstrasse 32, CH-3012 Bern, Switzerland
info@peterlang.com, www.peterlang.com, www.peterlang.net

Printed in Germany

To mum and dad
Le grá agus le buíochas ó chroí

Contents

List of Tables

List of Acronyms

B.Ed – Bachelor of Education

CEB – Curriculum and Examinations Board

CEC – Central Executive Committee

CLÁR – Committee on Irish Language Attitudes Research

CMPI – Commission on Manual and Practical Instruction

CNEI – Commissioners of National Education in Ireland

CSO – Central Statistics Office

DATI – Department of Agriculture and Technical Instruction

EEC – European Economic Community

ERC – Educational Research Centre

ESAI – Educational Studies Association of Ireland

GAA – Gaelic Athletic Association

GNP – Gross National Product

INTO – Irish National Teachers' Organisation

JAM – Junior Assistant Mistress

MRBI – Market Research Bureau of Ireland

n.d. – No date

NESC – National Economic and Social Council

NIEC – National Industrial and Economic Council

NPC-P – National Parents' Council Primary

OECD – Organisation for Economic Co-operation and Development

RTÉ – Raidió Teilifís Éireann

T.D. – Teachta Dála (Irish member of parliament)

UNESCO – United Nations Educational, Scientific and Cultural
Organisation

List of Irish Terms Used

Aireacht na Gaeilge – Ministry of Irish

An Gúm – Publications branch of the Department of Education

An Chomhchoiste um Oideachas sa Ghaeltacht – Joint Committee on Education in the Gaeltacht

An Roinn Oideachais – Department of Education

Ard Teastas – Higher Certificate

Breac-Ghaeltacht – Partly Irish-speaking area

Bunreacht na hÉireann – The Constitution of Ireland

Coimisiún na Gaeltachta – Commission on the Gaeltacht

Cumann Dhá Theangach na hÉireann – All Ireland Bilingual Society

Fíor-Ghaeltacht – Fully Irish-speaking area

Gaeilge – Irish

Gaelscoil(eanna) – Irish-medium school(s)

Gaeltacht – Irish-speaking area

Galltacht – English-speaking area

Institiúid Teangeolaíochta Éireann – Linguistics Institute of Ireland

Saorstát Éireann – Irish Free State

Taoiseach – Prime Minister in Irish government

Timirí – Irish language organisers

Tuarascáil – Report

Tuarascáil Staitistiúil – Statistical report

Acknowledgements

It is with great pleasure that I record here publically my sincere gratitude to a large number of individuals for their support and encouragement in the writing of this book. Its completion has only been made possible through the interest, camaraderie, generosity and expertise of many friends, colleagues and professionals. First and foremost, I would like to acknowledge the significant input of Professor Emeritus John Coolahan, both as an inspiring PhD supervisor and for his discerning comments on an earlier draft of this book. I feel privileged that he has given so generously of his encouragement and expertise to guide me. His work, and that of other pioneers of the history of education, provided the springboard and inspiration for this book.

The input of a number of colleagues, family members and friends who provided enlightening critiques, sound advice and pertinent direction on earlier iterations of this book is also gratefully acknowledged, especially that of Mary Walsh, Jacqueline Fallon and Dr Rory McDaid. The scholarly insight, forbearance and commitment of Dr Adrian Kelly to the completion of this book merits particular commendation – for this Adrian, and for so much more, you know that I am eternally indebted.

My former colleagues at the Centre for Early Childhood Development and Education are heartily acknowledged for their support while undertaking my doctoral studies. I would like to thank most sincerely my current colleagues in the Inspectorate for their ongoing support and friendship. I mention in particular Mary Dunne, Dr Brian Mac Giolla Phádraig and John Mescal for their advice, guidance and camaraderie that proved invaluable in sustaining my motivation, and perhaps my sanity at times, while writing this book. Dr Maura O'Connor has been a constant source of professional and personal support and this book has been informed by both our formal and informal discussions on the history of education.

A special word of thanks is due to my personal friends who have sustained me through this process by virtue of their good humour, kindness and friendship. While displaying a tentative interest in my research, their unwavering support has been humbling and for this I continue to be most grateful. They are too numerous to mention individually – you know who you are and how you have inspired me in your own individual way as we have journeyed through life together.

The vast array of research material accessed and analysed would not have been possible without the direct support of a number of organisations and individuals. The library staff in St Patrick's College of Education, the Educational Research Centre, the National University of Ireland Maynooth, University College Dublin (UCD) and Trinity College Dublin deserve special praise. Staff in the National Library of Ireland, the UCD Archives, the archives of the Irish National Teachers' Organisation, the archives section of the Department of Education and Skills and the National Archives of Ireland provided timely assistance to me and for this I am most grateful. Moreover, many individuals have been most generous in sharing with me personal collections of educational materials, and I would like to note particularly the contributions of Professor Emeritus John Coolahan and Professor Áine Hyland in this regard.

The staff at Peter Lang International Academic Publishers and the editors of the *Rethinking Education* series are acknowledged for their professional support. Particular thanks is extended to Christabel Scaife, Commissioning Editor for Ireland, for her professional support and efficient work in guiding the publication of this book.

Last, but certainly not least, I come to my family, whose love throughout my life has been consistent and generous in all its manifestations. Dad and mum have been unconditional in their support for me and their steadfast love has made this book, and so much more, possible. My brother and sister, Tim and Mary, and their respective spouses, Lisa and Andy, are a constant source of support and encouragement to me. My late sister Cathy was, and continues to be, a remarkable inspiration to me in all facets of my life. In recent times, my nephews, Adam, Jamie, Luke, Cian and Ethan and my niece Sophia, never cease to amaze me in all facets of their lives and learning. The camaraderie of family and the richness of life have been enhanced through the arrival of this new generation and their presence provides a new insight and depth to life. Humbly, I dedicate this book to my parents, Tom and Catherine, and to my family in gratitude for their love and inspiration.

Foreword

This book is the first comprehensive historical analysis of curriculum policy, development and implementation in Irish primary schools, over the century from the 1890s to the 1990s. Up to recent decades, primary schooling was the only exposure to formal education for the great majority of the people. This adds a particular significance to the study. The curriculum and its implementation form the core features of pupils' schooling experience. This detailed study of what was taught, why it was taught, and how it was taught provides a very informative insight into the nature of the primary education experience of many generations. However, because of the approach taken by the author, as well as being a history of the curriculum, it is also a very informative history of Irish primary education shaped by the political, religious, social and economic changes in Irish society over this eventful century.

The book is very well structured. The body of the text comprises three main sections, each with three chapters. In each section the author researches and analyses key epochs of curricular change: – 1897 to 1922; 1922 to 1971; 1971 to 1990. During the first period, Ireland was still under British rule. The turn of the twentieth century was a most lively time in European educational thinking and this had a major impact on the reform effort. It was also an exciting period in the Irish cultural revival movement. The author captures all the currents of thought and aspirations very well. The second era deals with curriculum policy in post-independent Ireland. The policy is very dominated by the cultural nationalists' concern for the revival of the Irish language. Following much policy activity in the difficult early years of the new state, the schooling system experienced a period of stagnation. The final section focuses on the changing Ireland of the 1960s, leading to the radically new curriculum policy of 1971, with its strong child-centred emphasis.

The treatment of each era follows an organised pattern whereby the first chapter examines the political, socio-economic, religious and economic forces at play in society, at the time. The next chapter is devoted to a detailed treatment of the ideological influences, the planning processes and the shaping of the content of the curriculum policy. The third chapter is devoted to examining the levels of implementation, the problems encountered, and the progress experienced with the curriculum innovation. The three sections are framed by an informative introduction and insightful conclusion.

The book is distinguished by the range and depth of the sources consulted. Many of the sources are unpublished and a large number are drawn upon for the first time. The author's indefatigable search for all relevant source material gives a very authoritative tone to his treatment of the issues. The extensive reference notes and very comprehensive bibliography will be of major benefit to other students of the period.

The author manages to incorporate a richness of detail in his exposition of developments without allowing this to clog the narrative. His analysis and evaluations of the actions of key agencies and plenipotentiaries are insightful and reflective of wide-reading in curriculum literature. His judgements are forceful, but are well balanced and substantiated.

Each of the three eras under review represented a radical change of policy from that which preceded it. Revolutionary rather than gradual, incremental change was the order of the day in each case. While the author acknowledges the aspirations and ideals of curriculum policy formulators, a clear message emerges of the inadequacies in their thinking and planning in each instance. There is much to admire in many of the efforts made but, it is by no means, a noble story. Many opportunities to realise more of the potential of curriculum change were missed. In particular, the study demonstrates that inadequate or non-existent planning for implementation did much to undermine the curriculum reforms envisaged. Too much reliance was placed on the design and dissemination of the curriculum policy, and far too little on the implementation of the policy and the evaluation of its progress. A lack of pro-active remedial or supportive policy by officialdom in the light of emerging difficulties comes across as a significant weakness.

In his succinct and thoughtful conclusion the author highlights a number of lessons which should be of benefit to curriculum policy into the future. As curriculum policy should always be a live area of concern and subject to regular review, this book should be of great interest to all students of Irish education and, in particular, to those with a responsibility for curriculum policy, evaluation and implementation. The comprehensive and well-arranged bibliography will be a boon to researchers in the field.

Professor Emeritus John Coolahan
September 2011

Introduction

This book critically examines the context, origins, development and implementation of successive primary school curricula in Ireland between 1897 and 1990. In particular, it focuses on the three major policy changes during the period, introduced in 1900, 1922/1926 and 1971. It analyses these changes within the complex web of wider societal and educational factors that impacted on the devising and implementation of successive curricula. It documents the philosophy of education underpinning each curriculum and details the range of subjects included. Following an examination of the policy development process, the successes and shortcoming in the implementation of each curriculum is detailed. The concluding chapter distils a number of key themes that emerge from reviewing a century of curriculum development and implementation and highlights important considerations for curriculum innovation in the contemporary context.

The primary school curriculum was particularly important in the formation and education of pupils through the largest part of the period under review, representing, as it did, the only formal education available to the majority of pupils. The successful design and implementation of curricula impacted not only on the quality of educational experiences for individual children at any particular time but also had important implications for the future well being of citizens and for society as a whole. One of the chief aims of establishing the national system of education in 1831 was to socialise the Irish population into certain norms and to provide for basic literacy and numeracy. This endeavour continued, albeit with different and contradictory emphases, until 1990. The school is one of the key institutions through which society endeavours to preserve and transmit the values, knowledge, attitudes and skills which it believes to be important in order to prepare citizens for future living. Curricula evolve in line with societal developments, catalysed by events such as social and political change and advances in knowledge.

This study† uses the holistic definition of the curriculum cited in the White Paper on Education, *Charting our Education Future* (1995):

> The term 'curriculum' encompasses the content, structure and processes of teaching and learning, which the school provides in accordance with its educational objectives and values. It includes specific and implicit elements. The specific elements are those concepts, skills, areas of knowledge and attitudes which children learn at school as part of their personal and social development. The implicit elements are those factors that make up the ethos and general environment of the school. The curriculum in schools is concerned, not only with the subjects taught, but also with how and why they are taught and with the outcomes of this activity for the learner.[1]

This broad definition of curriculum emphasises that there are two forms of curriculum in operation – the official or formal curriculum that is deliberately planned and organised and all other forms of incidental or unintentional learning within schools. Combined, these two elements form the curriculum as analysed in this study, looking not only at the devised curriculum but how the curriculum was implemented at school level. As will become apparent, what happens in practice can vary significantly from the aspirations and intentions of policymakers.

A broad understanding of societal developments, including changes in political, social, economic, cultural and religious terms, provides the context to examine critically curriculum provision in any era. Curriculum changes do not occur in isolation from the wider context; rather they reflect the societal context and milieu of the day. In this way, an understanding of the circumstances, context, motivation and aspirations of the curriculum planners at various junctures throughout the last century tempers conclusions drawn from a modern day perspective. It also sheds light on the ideology and dispositions of the people involved in devising curricula and the reasons for the radical shifts in ideology throughout the century.

---

†   This book is a restructured and abbreviated version of a PhD thesis, *A Critical Analysis of Curricular Policy in Irish Primary Schools, 1897–1990*, and the reader is referred to this source for further exposition (Walsh, T. (2006). *A Critical Analysis of Curricular Policy in Irish Primary Schools, 1897–1990*. PhD Thesis. Kildare: National University of Ireland, Maynooth).

Changes in the political, social, cultural and economic circumstances in Ireland had a significant impact on the curriculum for primary schools, leading to attempts at sudden changes in philosophy and content which the education system was not always able to deliver.

By viewing the curriculum as a continuum, it can shed light on the perennial problem of effecting curriculum change by identifying recurrent themes in relation to development and implementation. An awareness of earlier traditions and practice has much to offer regarding curriculum planning in the present. Their similarity to, and contrast with, modern day innovations regarding context, philosophy, process of devising, content and implementation provide a perspective and framework within which to contextualise current day endeavours. The history of education teaches us that at certain stages in the development of the education system, only certain things are possible and these are delimited by a multiplicity of factors within the social and educational milieu.

This book is documented chronologically and is divided into three distinct sections, each representing an era of curriculum development and implementation. These three eras are distinctive by virtue of their chronology, their philosophy of education, the content of the curriculum, the methodologies employed and the concept of the child inherent in the curriculum. The first section, comprising chapters one to three, relates to the period 1897 to 1922, during which the *Revised Programme of Instruction* (1900) was devised and implemented. The second section, consisting of chapters four to six, encompasses the curricula that were introduced following the achievement of independence in 1922 and the modifications undertaken up to 1971. The third section, comprising chapters seven to nine, documents curriculum developments in the period from 1971 to 1990. Within each section, the three chapters have distinct purposes. The first chapter in each section examines the societal context and educational milieu in which the curriculum was initially devised and into which it was subsequently implemented. The second chapter is dedicated to documenting the process by which the programme or curriculum was devised and to delineating its philosophy and content. The third chapter reviews the implementation of the curriculum during the period and draws conclusions in relation to aspects that were introduced successfully and facets that were not implemented on a widespread basis.

The first section of this book documents curriculum provision from the establishment of the Commission on Manual and Practical Instruction in 1897 until the advent of political independence in 1922. It details the context for the introduction of the *Revised Programme of Instruction* (1900) from the nineteenth century, including the political, social, economic, cultural, religious and international factors that impacted upon the reform. It examines the process of gathering evidence and developing the programme between 1896 and 1898, and the relationship between the evidence collated and the content of the programme in 1900. The programme introduced in 1900, based largely on the findings of the aforementioned Commission, represented a radical shift from its predecessor, the system of payment by results. It was child-centred in nature, comprising a broad range of literary and practical subjects and advocated the use of heuristic methodologies. The school curriculum was seen to serve the needs and interests of the pupils and schools were envisaged as humane and interesting places to be. It was introduced in a period characterised by poor socio-economic conditions in Ireland, where budgetary contractions in relation to public spending impacted on education. In this context, the implementation of the vision and content of the programme was never fully realised in practice.

The second section relates to the curriculum in operation between 1922 and the introduction of the *Primary School Curriculum* (1971). This curriculum was framed close to the attainment of political independence in 1922 and apart from some minor modifications in 1926, 1934 and 1948, the essence of this programme remained the keystone of curriculum provision for close to fifty years. Among the most important societal influences was the cultural nationalist revival, which reached its zenith around 1920. Owing to the circumstances in which political freedom was achieved, it was somewhat inevitable that the programme in national schools would be characterised by an emphasis on establishing Ireland as an independent nation. While there was some level of involvement of interested parties in devising the programme, many of the participants were of the same ideological position as to the role of schools, especially in relation to the revival of the Irish language. Once again, the curriculum introduced signified a fundamental departure from its predecessor, based on cultural nationalist ideology and focusing on a narrow range of subjects. Moreover, a pre-eminent position was afforded to the Irish language, both as a subject and as a medium of instruction, and many of the remaining subjects were curtailed to facilitate this focus. Although the burden of evidence during the period pointed to the need for reform of curriculum and methodologies, it was implemented, practically unchanged, from 1922 until the late 1960s. One hiatus in the period was the introduction of the *Revised Programme for Infants* in 1948 which, in line with the *Revised Programme of Instruction* (1900), was child-centred and discovery-based in orientation. However, owing to resource implications and other factors, its provisions were not implemented universally. Nevertheless, its introduction was an augury of further developments of a similar manner for all classes in 1971.

The third section relates to the period leading to the devising of the *Primary School Curriculum* (1971) in the late 1960s and its subsequent implementation between 1971 and 1990. The societal context into which the curriculum was introduced and the educational milieu into which it was implemented are detailed. The Inspectorate of the Department of Education was primarily responsible for devising this curriculum and the initial draft changed little following consultation with a limited range of stakeholders. For the third time in as many curricula, it proved to be a dramatic swing of the pendulum from its predecessor of fifty years earlier, returning to the child-centred and holistic educational principles of the 1900 programme. While the content of the curriculum changed substantially to include a wider range of subjects, the greatest shift was within its underlying principles and methodologies. Such a dramatic change in direction and the paucity of provisions and resources to implement the curriculum in practice led to problems in implementing its provisions. The Primary Education Review Body[2] and the Review Body on the Primary Curriculum[3] produced reports in 1990 and these provided a catalyst for educational and curriculum reforms in the 1990s.

Each chapter and section comprehensively summarises and draws conclusions in relation to curriculum development and implementation in the periods examined. The concluding chapter is reserved to document three key themes which emerge following this analysis and looks at implications

for contemporary and future curriculum policy development and implementation. These themes relate to the impact of wider societal factors, the
radical nature of reforms and the inadequate focus placed on curriculum
implementation.

A note on terminology is desirable at the outset. In the earlier part of the
twentieth century, the curriculum followed in schools was referred to as
the 'programme' or 'programme of instruction'. It was only towards the
1950s that the term curriculum became common currency in Irish educational terminology. Therefore, both programme and curriculum are used,
sometimes interchangeably, in the book. The terms 'primary' and 'national'
are used interchangeably when referring to schools throughout the book.
Owing to the historical nature of the research, throughout the vast majority
of the period in question, documents used the masculine pronoun 'he/him'.
This book follows this convention when quoting and directly referencing
primary source documentation.

   As the study spans the period before and after political independence,
the term 'Ireland' or 'Irish' represents different geographical and political entities at various times. Consequently, in the first phase and in any
references to the period prior to 1922, Ireland represents the entire island
of Ireland. Following independence, the Irish Free State (subsequently
Republic) refers to the twenty-six counties that incorporated the South
of Ireland. The six-county jurisdiction is referred to as 'Northern Ireland'
or the 'North'.

Societal and Educational Context for Curriculum Provision 1897–1921

1.1 Introduction

This chapter details the broader societal and educational context within which the *Revised Programme of Instruction* (1900) was devised and implemented. This is largely framed in the period 1831 to 1922, representing the timescale within which the national system of education was introduced until the advent of independence, at which time an alternative programme was devised. A particular focus is placed on the later period following 1890, detailing the salient societal events in Ireland that ultimately had an impact on educational provision between 1897 and 1922. This provides a broad understanding of the effect that various individuals and groups, and national and international factors, had on the development and implementation of educational policies in Ireland.

The key societal features examined are the political, socio-economic, cultural and religious factors that occupied a sphere of influence on education. An analysis of the impact of international influences on the development of the primary school programme is provided as international factors were particularly influential considering the position of Ireland as a colonial state of the British Empire. Having established the wider context, a detailed analysis of the education system in Ireland ensues. This provides the context in which the *Revised Programme* of 1900 was devised, introduced and implemented.

1.2 Societal Context for Programme Development

1.2.1 Political Context

Ireland entered the nineteenth century in a politically dejected state, whereby from 1801, political decisions regarding Ireland were determined at Westminster. In tandem with the nationalist desire for independence, there was an aspiration among the Unionist population for the retention and strengthening of the link to Britain. Thus, Ireland remained divided throughout the nineteenth century along political, religious, ethnic, economic, linguistic and cultural lines. There was a shift in focus from militant means to constitutional nationalism towards the end of the century, as the movement for Home Rule gathered pace from the 1870s under Charles Stewart Parnell. The Conservative Party policy of 'Killing Home Rule with Kindness' had many beneficial effects for Ireland, most notably great strides in solving the Land Question by the turn of the twentieth century. Attempts to grant Home Rule to Ireland were made by various governments in this period, with Home Rule Bills failing to be ratified in 1886 and 1893 for various reasons. A Home Rule Act was passed in 1912 but its implementation, planned for 1914, was postponed at the outbreak of World War One.

The main influences on Irish educational affairs at Westminster were the Irish Parliamentary Party and the churches, especially the Catholic Church. The Irish Parliamentary Party was generally supported by teachers and it thus represented their views in Parliament. There were periods when there was a conciliatory attitude to Irish affairs and this was accentuated when Irish delegates held the balance of power in Westminster at various times from the 1880s. However, the split within the Irish Parliamentary Party in the 1890s weakened its influence until its reunification in 1900 under John Redmond. The power vacuum created by this split, allied to a number of other issues, led to a gradual rise once again of militant nationalism with the advent of the Sinn Féin party in 1905. Sinn Féin grew in strength and popularity, advocating political and economic self-sufficiency. Furthermore, the Irish Republican Brotherhood was regenerated in the early 1900s, characterised by a militant nationalistic focus. This organisation played a central role in the organisation of the 1916 Rising. Although a failure in military terms, the outrage caused by the execution of its leaders made Ireland's quest for political independence from Great Britain more determined.

Following the general election of 1918, the political landscape in Ireland altered radically. Subsequently, Dáil Éireann was established by Sinn Féin in 1919 as an abstentionist assembly, with no Unionist or Irish Parliamentary Party representation, while many of the Sinn Féin delegates were jailed or on the run. The War of Independence ensued and after a long period of bloodshed, a truce was called in July 1921. Subsequently, a Treaty was negotiated, which maintained the partition of Ireland as introduced under the Government of Ireland Act 1920. Sinn Féin split on the question of acceptance of the Anglo-Irish Treaty, and despite a majority acceptance in the Dáil and by the Irish people, a Civil War followed.

1.2.2 Socio-economic Context

The Penal Laws of the eighteenth century reduced Ireland, both economically and socially, to one of its lowest ebbs by 1800. Education was seen as a vital agent to cultural survival and the Hedge Schools proved popular despite the fact they were fee-paying and illegal. The Irish Poor Laws were introduced in the early nineteenth century to address social instability due to widespread poverty and these provided for the establishment of a nationwide network of Workhouses. Despite some recovery in the early part of the century, the Great Famine of 1845–1847 was cataclysmic for the Irish people. The population reduced from 6,528,799 in 1841 to 3,139,688 by 1911.[1] Those who found work or farmed in Ireland laboured under difficult conditions and for little money. The population remaining in Ireland also benefited from money sent home by emigrants.

The Irish Agricultural Organisation Society was established in 1894 in an attempt to assist farmers to help themselves in modernising their techniques and systems, and in progressing their respective lots collectively as opposed to individually. The Department of Agriculture and

Technical Instruction (DATI), instituted in Ireland in 1899, provided a focus on co-ordination within agriculture and established an infrastructure for training and education in technical instruction. Horace Plunkett, the Vice-President of the DATI, was interested in education in so far as it promoted self-reliance and prepared pupils for their future careers. He believed that the Irish system of education around 1900 was turning out 'a generation of second rate clerks'[2] with distaste for industrial or productive occupation. He advocated a focus on manual and practical instruction within the primary schools to form the foundation for later instruction in technical education.

Reforms towards the end of the nineteenth century had a positive impact on the socio-economic situation. The return of ownership of the land, by means of a number of Land Acts from the 1880s, and the initiation of the Co-operative Movement had a profound effect, not only on the economic status of the people, but also on the national psyche. These reforms were important considering Ireland's economy was largely agrarian-based, employing close to 57 per cent of the population in 1911.[3] The agricultural boom experienced after the Great Famine receded in the 1880s with increased foreign competition and this focused the education system on the need for manual and practical instruction to ensure competitiveness internationally.[4] There was a return to boom time prices around World War One, followed by a decline in prices after the War and during the turbulent and disturbed times of the War of Independence and the Civil War.

The establishment of the Congested Districts Board in 1891 greatly benefited Ireland's infrastructure and boosted employment in the poorest districts of the country. The Local Government (Ireland) Act 1898 was also a positive step in improving the social and economic circumstances of Ireland. Conditions in the towns and cities were often deplorable, with widespread malnutrition, overcrowding in tenement housing and endemic diseases, such as tuberculosis. Social provisions were virtually absent and there was a high percentage of infant mortality and illness. Marriage and fertility rates were high with an average family size of in excess of five children in 1911.[5] The battle to achieve better working and pay conditions led to the Great Lockout of 1913, which laid the foundations for the improvement of workers' rights into the future.

1.2.3   Cultural Context

Ireland witnessed a great cultural revival towards the end of the nineteenth century. This movement was instigated following a century in which the Irish language and culture had declined rapidly and there were fears of its ultimate extinction. Throughout the nineteenth century, the Irish language became increasingly synonymous with poverty, disaffection, defeat and ignorance.[6] The decline of the Irish language was a complex phenomenon, involving a multiplicity of interrelated factors, including the greater use of English within the Catholic Church and by activists such as Michael Davitt and Daniel O'Connell.[7] The exclusion of the Irish language from primary schools under the national system aided and abetted this decline, although it cannot be viewed as the sole reason for the demise of the language. The Great Famine was a major catalyst in this regard, leading to the removal of the strongest pockets and proponents of the language through emigration and death. This led to a situation whereby in 1852, 23 per cent of people could speak Irish while in 1912, this had reduced to 12 per cent, largely concentrated along the Western seaboard.[8] Increasingly, newspapers in English became available in Ireland and further advanced the use of English in daily life. The transfer in vernacular from Irish to English occurred with the relative apathy or even support of the people, who increasingly saw English as the language of the pulpit, commerce, prosperity and emigration.

Towards the end of the century, in tandem with national awakenings and consciousness in a number of areas, there was a move to revive the Irish language and culture. This cultural movement began with the Society for the Preservation of the Irish Language in 1876. The Gaelic Athletic Association (GAA) was established in 1884 to promote Irish sports for Irish people, while the Gaelic Literary Society (1892) initiated a revival of Irish literary works and pursuits. However, it was the Gaelic League, founded in 1893 to preserve Irish as the national language of Ireland and to extend its use as a spoken language, that proved the most successful in capturing the hearts and imagination of the nationalist population and which played the greatest part in the revival of the language and culture. Pádraig Pearse, as editor of the Gaelic League's journal, *An Claidheamh Soluis*, ensured that education remained to the fore of the language revival. Through his prolific writings and his intimate knowledge of both the national and international educational context, the influence of the League and its stance on education spread to wider spheres of association such as politicians, teachers and historians.[9] Furthermore, the League was successful in involving the public in the campaign by linking the Irish language to the question of independence.[10] In 1901 alone, the League issued twenty-seven pamphlets on the question of Irish in national schools.[11] From 1900, the League expanded rapidly from 120 branches in 1901 to 593 branches (with in excess of 50,000 members nationally) by 1904.[12] It achieved this expansion by becoming a popular organisation with all social classes, all religious denominations and all political parties, ensuring a broad base of support and financial assistance. Its popularity was enhanced by the publication of O'Growney's *Simple Lessons in Irish* and the appointment of organisers to establish new branches. Despite the League's efforts, between 1891 and 1926, the heyday of the Gaelic League, the number of Irish speakers dropped by 18 per cent, with the most significant decline in the Gaeltacht (Irish-speaking areas).[13]

In educational terms, the Gaelic League sought that where Irish was the home language, pupils should be taught to read and write Irish and be taught English through the medium of Irish. Where Irish was not the home language, it fought for it to be taught as a remunerated subject within school hours.[14] The League had a major issue with the non-Irish character of education in national schools, with the programme and texts perceived as existing in a cultural vacuum. The League was successful in campaigning for the introduction of the *Bilingual Programme*, which was introduced into schools in 1904 (see chapter 3).

These cultural societies and associations served to unite and create networks across a scattered people and to promote a distinct Irish culture. Initially, the movement related to cultural endeavours but ultimately assisted in creating the context for seeking Home Rule, and became intermingled with the militant nationalist movements in the quest for political independence. The increasing popularity of the bicycle as a mode of transport increased the mobility of the people and geographical limitations became less of a hindrance. The Irish National Teachers' Organisation (INTO) was closely affiliated to these organisations and many teachers played instrumental roles in their local organisation and administration.

1.2.4 Religious Context

The Catholic Church in 1800 was in a weakened and vulnerable position following the Penal Laws of the eighteenth century. It began to reform and reorganise itself and to mobilise the support of the vast majority of the population, who were Catholic. One of its first victories was its campaign for Catholic Emancipation, which was granted in 1829. Powerful figures within the Catholic Church such as Bishops Murray and Crolly in the early nineteenth century, Cardinal Cullen mid-century and Archbishop Walsh towards the advent of the twentieth century, catalysed these reforms and built a strong and unified Catholic Church in Ireland. Conversely in 1800, the Protestant Church of Ireland was the Established Church, in receipt of state endowments and patronage, and it enjoyed elaborate spheres of influence in educational, political and social terms. However, the rise of the Catholic Church was mirrored by the demise of the Church of Ireland, which was dealt a severe blow by its disestablishment in 1869. There was much inter-denominational distrust, suspicion and hostility owing to the deep-seated historical animosities between the religious persuasions.

The rise in power of the Catholic Church in Ireland in the nineteenth century is largely attributed to its involvement in educational issues.[15] As patrons and managers of the vast majority of schools in the country, the Catholic Church gained a presence and control over the population. In the absence of a cohesive political force or a powerful middle class, the Catholic Church became the spokesperson for the people on educational issues. Westminster gradually realised the need for Catholic Church support if reforms or innovations were to be successful. This led to a somewhat symbiotic relationship between the Catholic Church and the state, whereby the state would support the Catholic Church on educational issues, while the Catholic Church would support the state to remain in control by constitutional rules.[16] As the main focus of the government was on moral training within schools, the Catholic Church proved the natural partner in order to reach the majority of the target children of Ireland for this purpose. In turn, this had the effect of ordering the time and space of adults also, who were bound to assist their children to attend, to be punctual and to be mannerly, thus spreading a uniformity of behaviour nationally.[17]

In the early part of the nineteenth century, a multiplicity of agencies, denominational leaders, associated church bodies, educational societies and political groups had been involved in the formulation of education policy. The philosophy of the national system was that children of all denominations were to be enrolled in the same school, while applications from mixed denominations for state aid would be favourably prioritised. This ideal was never fully realised and was contested by all denominations. Following 1831, Catholic Church involvement was increased due to the necessity to provide sites for schools and to organise local funding. Involvement at this key stage ensured the reins of power were in clerical hands, to the exclusion of lay, popular and parental control. By 1901, due to religious, demographic, geographic, economic and social reasons, nearly 65 per cent of schools were denominationally homogeneous. These were managed by a total of 2,963 managers; 598 lay and 2,365 clerical.[18] In addition to denominational education, the Catholic Church insisted on segregated education for boys and girls, and this impacted greatly on the multiplicity of small schools in the country. In a Pastoral Letter issued following the Synod of 1900, the satisfaction of the Catholic hierarchy was evident, stating that the education system was 'as denominational almost as we could desire. In most of its schools there is no mixed education whatsoever.'[19]

The denominational system became increasingly synonymous with clerics; the vast majority of schools were vested in diocesan trustees, had the local Bishop as their patron and were clerically managed. Such a structured control at all levels afforded the Catholic Church considerable power and influence over the appointment of teachers and the dissemination of funding. This structure permeated the entire country as the national schools, numbering close to 9,000 by 1900, provided a network for the power and influence of the Catholic Church to pervade all regions and strata of Irish society. The Catholic Church was opposed to any popular control or local lay involvement in education which would undermine its autonomy. By 1900, the Catholic Church in Ireland had become strong, dominant and influential in all spheres of life, from ordinary homes, to the chambers of Westminster, to the Vatican in Rome. The dominant power it had built in the nineteenth century was vehemently guarded and entrenched in the twentieth century.

1.3 International Context

The domestic affairs of Ireland, including its educational provision, were subject to a number of international influences. Ireland, ruled from Westminster, was directly and indirectly affected by progress and developments impacting on England and the rest of the British Empire. This was especially true around the turn of the twentieth century under the Conservative government, which was attempting to 'Kill Home Rule with Kindness' by means of conciliation. Educational reforms, such as the abolition of payment by results in England and Scotland in 1890, permeated Irish educational circles and there were calls for parity in Ireland as a colony of the British Empire. In addition, the growth of the Industrial Revolution led to an economic argument for the inclusion of manual and practical subjects.

The quest for reform in England was catalysed by its declining commercial and industrial strength *vis-à-vis* its international counterparts such as Germany and Prussia. The Royal Commission on Technical Instruction (1884)[20] led to an increased focus on manual and practical instruction in England in an attempt to emulate the successful policies of other countries. There had been developments in relation to the introduction of manual and practical subjects in many countries by the 1890s, including the United States, France, Germany and the Scandinavian countries.

Around this time, the New Education Movement was gaining popularity in Europe. This was a diverse grouping of educationalists with varying ideals for education. It was influenced by the thinking of philosophers and theorists such as Pestalozzi, Herbart, Froebel and Dewey. It was comprised of seven main groups, namely the Practical Educationalists, the Social Reformers, the Naturalists, the Herbartians, the Scientific Educationalists, the Moral Educationalists and the Child-centred Educationalists. Although it was not a homogeneous school of thought, it was united in its discontent with the overemphasis on literary instruction and the curriculum-centred as opposed to child-centred education on offer. It wanted to place education in line with real life, whereby the child was not a miniature adult but a person in the process of formation. The Movement acted as a catalyst in the reform of the existing system by offering multiple, and sometimes contradictory, solutions. As Selleck stated:

> Some wanted the older order restored, others wanted it abolished altogether; some wanted a physically-fit nation, others would not rest until it was morally regenerated; for some the moral regeneration involved religion, for others it meant the supplanting of religion; some were perturbed that industries were failing, some that the army was failing, some that the church was failing, some that the home was failing.[21]

The New Education Movement was characterised by a lack of unity on fundamental issues such as the role of the teacher, child-centred education, religious education and methodologies. Its philosophies penetrated the Irish educational scene through journals and publications, through the Sloyd[†] movement in Europe (notably the Sloyd Association of Great Britain and Ireland) and by virtue of the Commission on Manual and Practical Instruction (CMPI), which will be examined in chapter 2.

1.4 Educational Context for Programme Development

In educational terms, policy was determined externally at Westminster up to 1921, thus resulting in an impact of British educational thinking on the Irish programme. The Penal Laws, denying Catholics the right to be educated, interrupted a long tradition of educational provision originating in the Middle Ages. However, the denial of this basic right whetted the appetite of the Irish for education and the Hedge Schools accommodated the vast majority of the Irish population, while schools were also established on the Continent, most notably in Italy, Belgium and France, to provide for further Catholic education.

---

†   Sloyd is a term for educational training in any material.

After the repeal of the Penal Laws and fearing the growing revolutionary tendencies and ideals in Europe, the British authorities took steps to prevent their importation by the Irish being educated on the Continent. These developments occurred in tandem with changes in the conceptualisation of children and childhood, as advanced by the Romantic Movement. In the early nineteenth century, the government funded certain societies, such as the Kildare Place Society, to provide education for children in Ireland. Other societies, largely affiliated to the Established Church of Ireland, provided education that was not subsidised by the state, but this was not acceptable to Catholics due to the fear of proselytising. In addition, this period witnessed the emergence of schooling by a number of Catholic teaching orders, including the Presentation Sisters (1791), the Irish Christian Brothers (1802) and the Mercy Sisters (1828).

1.4.1 *The National System of Education 1831–1922*

The national system of education established in 1831 provided a framework for the operation of the primary education system. Owing to Catholic complaints against societies such as the Kildare Place Society in the 1820s, the British government sanctioned, by virtue of the Stanley Letter, a national system of education in Ireland in 1831. A Board of National Education or National Board was instituted, presided over by the Duke of Leinster, and composed of twenty Commissioners of National Education, comprising both lay and clerical denominational interests. The national system was planned to be multi-denominational, whereby children of all religious persuasions would receive combined secular instruction:

> The object of the system of National Education is to afford combined literary and moral, and separate religious instruction, to children of all persuasions, as far as possible, in the same school, upon the fundamental principle that no attempt shall be made to interfere with the peculiar religious tenets of any description of Christian pupils.[22]

However, this separation of secular and religious instruction proved highly contentious for all denominations, which viewed religious and secular education as being interrelated and inseparable.

The creation of a national system of education in 1831 was notable for a number of reasons. The state had paid little attention to actively supporting education in Ireland and there was a general mistrust of such involvement. The system of national education in Ireland was granted before such a system was established in England in 1872 or in many other European countries. Moreover, the purpose of the system was not to prepare children for careers or to supply manpower for the economy but for religious, moral and intellectual instruction.[23] An equal emphasis was placed on the participation of both boys and girls. The subjects studied up to the introduction of payment by results in 1872 were literary in nature and included reading, writing, spelling and explanation, dictation, grammar, arithmetic (and its various subsets), geography and needlework for girls.[24]

However, the provision of such a national system was not for completely altruistic reasons. Ireland was often used to test experiments for Britain and the establishment of the national system could be considered as a testing ground for similar developments in England.[25] More importantly, Westminster hoped to create greater unity in Ireland and by retaining full control over programme content, to imbue in Irish children a sense of identity with the British Empire. It was also hoped that education would reduce poverty and instil civility in the Irish population and make it more governable. Both the British government and the Catholic Church were fearful of the alleged morally dissolute and politically subversive influence of the Hedge Schools, a system over which they exercised no control or influence, as well as the secular and revolutionary ideals on the Continent. Thus, education could serve as an agent of socialisation, assimilation and politicisation. Despite the ambitious and commendable ideals to bring about societal harmony and local cohesion through education, the provisions were unworkable and ultimately did not succeed in achieving interdenominational education.[26]

In Britain, a climate of accountability stemmed from the reign of W.E. Gladstone as Chancellor of the Exchequer in the 1850s, with his insistence on efficiency and economy in the public service. The greater scrutiny of the

Treasury in Westminster significantly reduced the autonomy of the Board of National Education in Ireland in relation to expenditure. The Powis Commission (1868)[27] was established in this climate of greater efficiency and led to the introduction of a system of payment by results in Ireland in 1872, as had been introduced in England previously. This saw a basic salary for teachers based on a classification system plus a bonus based on the results of pupils' individual examinations. The programme underwent a radical transformation, largely devised by Sir Patrick Keenan, who was later to serve as Resident Commissioner between 1871 and 1894. The obligatory subjects were reading, writing, spelling and arithmetic for all grades, while grammar, geography, needlework for girls and agriculture for boys were added from third class onwards. A vast array of optional subjects was also available, including vocal music and book-keeping[28] (see appendix 1). While the new system had an initial impact of increasing attendance and improving the promotion of pupils through the classes, it ultimately led to a narrowing of the programme and its delivery in a more didactic and mechanical fashion. Rates of illiteracy declined following the inception of the national system, from close to 53 per cent of the population over the age of five who could not read or write in 1841 to 14 per cent by 1901.[29]

The structure of the National Board was quite complex and reforms were often slow to be implemented owing to this complexity. By 1900, it consisted of ten Catholic and ten Protestant members, while a Protestant and a Catholic filled the position of Resident Commissioner alternately. The influence of the churches, political parties, managers, teachers and other interested parties had to feed upwards through the Inspectorate and Secretariat of the National Board, through to the Resident Commissioner and finally to the Commissioners of National Education. The Board liaised directly with the Chief Secretary and Lord Lieutenant of Ireland, who subsequently communicated with the Parliament and Treasury in London. Ultimately, it was the Parliament that made decisions in relation to education, yet between the National Board and Parliament lay the Treasury. Thus, the Board did not deal directly with the Treasury and the Chief Secretary was constrained by the decisions of the Treasury. This led to an ambiguity on many occasions as to whether it was the Chief Secretary or the Treasury that had denied initiatives or proposals. In reality, Treasury funding for education in Ireland during this period remained higher by up to 60 per cent than for the system in England due to the absence of local rates and support.[30]

The sanctioning of textbooks was an important function of the Commissioners, who endeavoured to provide affordable books that were moral and socialising in character and acceptable to all denominations. In addition, by retaining control over textbooks, the Commissioners gained control over the content of education, ensuring there was a de-emphasis on separate linguistic, cultural and religious identity as the books were largely devoid of material focusing on Ireland's heritage, language, landscape and traditions.[31]

The Local Government Act 1898 provided the infrastructure for the collection of money locally and for the devolution of educational responsibility. In addition, numerous reports and individuals proposed local rate aid around this time, including the Report of School Buildings (1902), the Dale Report (1904), Wyndham (1904), Birrell with the Irish Council Bill 1907 and the Education (Ireland) Bill 1919. The Irish Parliamentary Party successfully supported the Catholic Church in its rejection of the proposed reforms in 1904 and 1907.

The Education (Ireland) Bill 1919, commonly known as the MacPherson Bill, incorporated recommendations around the establishment of County Education Committees for maintaining schools, regulating compulsory attendance for children aged six to fourteen years of age, repairing and equipping national schools, the introduction of local taxation for education and the co-ordination of the education system under a centralised department. National reaction to the 1919 Bill was swift and bitterly divided along political and religious allegiances, with the Catholic Church vehemently opposed to it. However, the INTO and the majority of Protestant interests supported the Bill owing to the salary increment and the rectification of many of the long-standing issues they had campaigned for in the previous decades. The 1919 Bill was introduced on the eve of the War of Independence and there were hopes that a more amenable resolution, to the favour of the Catholic Church, could be achieved under a native government. In this context, the Bill was withdrawn in December 1920.

Teachers had successfully followed their pay claims outside the terms of the Bill and were awarded a substantial rise ten days before a pay freeze on wages was introduced in November 1920.[32]

The defeat of the Bill in December 1920 ensured that many of the issues that had previously marred Irish education were inherited by the Free State, including the lack of co-ordination between the various Boards and Departments, the deficiency of local interest due to lack of popular control and low attendance rates. It also represented a significant landmark victory for the Catholic Church, emphasising the power it could exercise on education policy.

1.4.2 Progress of the National System

The growth of the national system of education was phenomenal in the first seventy years of its existence. It saw an increase in the number of children attending the national system of education from 107,042 in 1833[33] to 770,622 in 1900.[34] The number of schools under the National Board increased to 8,684 in 1900[35] and reduced to 7,947 by 1919.[36] This provided a significant and important broad-based infrastructure of educational provision for Ireland into the twentieth century.

The low rate of attendance within the education system remained an issue throughout the nineteenth century. Attempts to introduce some form of compulsory attendance in the 1870s, when attendance languished at 36 per cent,[37] were successfully resisted by the Catholic Church as an infringement on parental rights. In contrast, Protestants and Presbyterians welcomed such compulsion and called for its implementation in all areas of the country. In 1892, an Education Act was passed enforcing some form of compulsory education for children aged six to fourteen years of age, largely in urban areas.[38] However, there were many caveats within the Act permitting non-attendance and its provisions were not well enforced. As table 1.1 illustrates, attendance did not rise greatly following implementation of the Act.

Table 1.1 Pupil Attendance in National Schools 1888–1904

Year	1888	1890	1892	1894	1896	1898	1900	1902	1904
Percentage of Pupils Attending	58.3	59.0	60.7	63.1	65.6	64.2	62.0	65.1	65.7

Source: Commissioners of National Education in Ireland [CNEI] (1905). *71st Report ... for 1904*, p. 28.

1.4.3 *Participation in the National System*

Churches

The Catholic Church was largely supportive of the system of education introduced in 1831 as it was morally safe and financially favourable, viewing it as a platform to the achievement of a church-controlled, state-financed arrangement. The system provided the finance to educate the poor children of Ireland that the Catholic Church alone could not afford, while it also allowed the Catholic Church a position of power and influence over the administration of the system.

The Christian Brothers found it impossible to reconcile its core ideals and principles with that of the national system, seeing religion as an extension of pastoral care and penetrating all aspects of life and education. Subsequently, their schools remained aloof from the national system until after independence. This allowed their schools to remain imbued with a nationalistic and religious spirit, and for the permeation of this spirit within the programme of instruction. The Presentation Sisters and Mercy Sisters remained loyal proponents of the system.

The Church of Ireland participated in the system initially but had irreconcilable issues with the separation of secular and religious instruction and the fear of the promotion of 'popery' in state schools. It split from the national system in 1839, forming the Church Education Society, thus reinforcing the denominational nature of the national system. The Church

Education Society was liberally financed in the early years, but there was a gradual demise in the position of the Established Church until its disestablishment in 1869. The majority of the Church Education Society schools had returned to the national system by the end of the century. Presbyterians objected to a number of the characteristics of the national system and by 1840 had achieved the necessary conditions for it to remain proponents of the system, namely that non-vested schools were eligible for state support, that clergymen could not visit schools in an official capacity and that religion could be taught during school hours providing advance notice was given.[39] Thus, all denominations remained apart from or etched away at the underlying principles and carved the system into a *de facto* denominational system by the end of the century.

Teachers

Teacher training remained a contentious issue throughout most of the nineteenth century. The churches and state feared the political affiliation and moral character of teachers under the Hedge School system and there were numerous attempts to ensure they were properly trained. The Stanley Letter contained provision for a central training college in Marlborough Street, which operated between 1834 and 1922. The growth of the District Model Schools from 1843, which served as non-denominational training colleges attached to schools, was a source of deep-seated concern to the Catholic Church. Owing to the mixed environment (gender and denominations) and the absence of control over the recruitment and dismissal of teachers, a ban on attending Model School training colleges was imposed by the Catholic Church from 1863.

The Catholic Church favoured no training for teachers as opposed to non-denominational training. The consequence of this stance was that by the 1870s, only 34 per cent of teachers were trained, the proportion being less in Catholic schools (73 per cent of Catholic teachers were untrained as opposed to 48 per cent of Protestant teachers).[40] The hierarchy realised that ownership of schools alone was insufficient; they needed to control the daily interactions in the classroom, which were governed by teacher affiliation and disposition. Although the teachers were paid by the state, they were the employees of the managers who exercised great control over their hiring, activities and dismissal.[41] Following the recommendations of the Powis Commission (1868), denominational training colleges were established in the 1870s.[42] In 1883, the state agreed to support the training colleges under certain conditions and a course of study based on the national programme was introduced in 1884. Courses were extended to two years in duration, with seven denominational colleges operational by 1900. However, by 1900, only half of the teachers were trained, and this percentage was still less for Catholic teachers who had been forbidden to attend the non-denominational Model School training colleges.[43]

The status of the primary school teacher was a serious concern throughout the nineteenth century. Teachers were regulated by an elaborate code of conduct, an inspection system and the delineation of the programme through the strict control of textbooks.[44] The Irish National Teachers' Association (subsequently known as the INTO) was founded in 1868 to promote education in Ireland and to elevate the social and intellectual position of teachers. The INTOs most pressing issue was the question of pay and conditions for teachers, and such demands were often met with hostility by the majority of clerical school managers, fearing the threat to the existing *status quo* and power structure. At the turn of the century, a number of associations were formed to protect and promote managerial interests within the sphere of education.

Inspectorate

From the outset, an Inspectorate became an integral element of the national system, starting with four inspectors in 1831–1832 and growing to seventy by 1859.[45] The men appointed – they were all male until after 1900 – were of high educational attainment and considerable social standing, while experience of teaching or educational administration was not seen as a prerequisite of appointment. The higher salary afforded to inspectors in comparison to teachers gave a clear indication of the relative status differential between the two occupations in the nineteenth century. Each inspector was allocated approximately 100 schools and the role of the Inspectorate was to determine the extent of learning and the quality of instruction, as well as the general order of schools, with a focus on regulation and inspection as opposed to advice.[46] From the mid-nineteenth century, however, a number of teachers were appointed to the Inspectorate, whereby in 1913, of the seventy-six inspectors, twenty-two had been practising teachers.[47]

1.4.4 *The Move towards Programme Reform*

The *Royal Commission on Technical Instruction* (1884) was conducted in Britain and Ireland in 1883 to provide a comparative analysis between technical instruction undertaken by industrial classes of a selection of foreign countries and in the United Kingdom. Relevant findings for the Irish context included its underdevelopment in industrial terms, the lack of preparation for further technical education in national schools and the centralised and unresponsive nature of the Department of Science and Art.[48] The overall finding of the Commission was that technical instruction could not develop or prosper until that aspect of primary education was improved. In addition to the requests from the Treasury for the reform of Irish education, there were calls for the modification of the system from the Catholic Church, which wanted to see a revision of the textbooks in use and increased denominational recognition. By the 1890s, the annual reports of the Commissioners of National Education showed growing concern regarding the suitability of the programme in use within schools. This included the subjects on offer, the effect of payment by results on the quality of instruction and methodologies, and issues such as the provision of school buildings and finance.

By the 1890s, teachers and inspectors expressed widespread dissatisfaction with the system in relation to the content, nature and method of primary education. The main calls were for the abolition of the payment-by-results system and the widening of the programme to include subjects of a more practical nature. This was advocated by the Commissioners of National Education, who were also anxious for some alteration to the system and the framing of a programme more aligned to the needs of the Irish population. In addition, educationalists such as Dr Joyce, principal of the Marlborough Street Training College from 1874 to 1893, were

calling for reform of the imbalanced programme and cited that the time was ripe and long overdue for reform.[49] Prominent educationalists such as Archbishop Walsh had long called for a revision of the programme to include a more practical focus, not the teaching of trades, but education to cultivate observation, accuracy, and neatness.[50]

The inspectors' reports 1890–1898 reveal a number of concerns with the existing system of education. Inspectors noted the neglect of infants in schools and their introduction from a very early age to formal reading, writing and arithmetic. The rigidity of the teaching was a regular element of complaint among inspectors, with a disregard for general training and intelligence.[51] In senior classes, teaching exclusively for the examination became more prominent as it was in these classes that the highest fees were payable and where the highest number of failures were recorded, as indicated in table 1.2.

Table 1.2 Percentage Passes of Each Class under Payment-by-Results Examinations 1897–1898

Class	Infants	First	Second	Third	Fourth	Fifth	Sixth
Percentage Passed	93.0	86.4	78.5	76.6	69.8	68.9	69.1

Source: CNEI (1899). *65th Report … for 1898–1899*, p. 33.

The narrow range of subjects taught beyond the core areas of literacy and numeracy featured prominently in the inspectors' reports. An increased reference to the necessity to include subjects of a more manual and practical nature in primary schools was evident in inspectors' reports from the 1890s. The quality of reading was frequently criticised for the lack of emphasis on explanation and intonation.[52] The introduction of 'Explanation' as an element in the reading examination in 1898 was applauded, believing it would greatly enhance the subject.[53]

In 1895, all inspectors were invited to submit 'a full and unreserved statement of his views as to the present system of examination for results'[54] to the Board of National Education. This was to include the effects of the examination system on teaching, the inspection of the system as well as possible modifications, such as the omission of certain subject areas, a change of some obligatory subjects to optional and the use of class as opposed to individual examinations. While some praised the positive short-term effects of payment by results, the majority felt the system had long out-lived its usefulness and there were many calls for a system of class as opposed to individual examination and for an increased emphasis on inspection as opposed to examination.[55] Most inspectors called for a widening of the programme studied to incorporate more practical subjects to ensure pupils were prepared for all walks of life after schooling, including emigration. Other reforms sought included a greater focus on thinking and reasoning through the improved use of methodologies and a revision of the books in use.[56]

1.5 Summary and Conclusion

This chapter has provided the historical backdrop and the societal and educational context and milieu for an analysis of programme provision in Ireland from 1897 to 1922. The national school system that developed following 1831 was a direct product of the wider societal influences that impacted on its progress. It was a political response to the difficulties of the British Empire in controlling its closest colony and was envisaged as a means to socialise the Irish people and strengthen the link with the Empire. It was a social and economic response to the widespread poverty and the quest for education evident in Ireland, with the intention that basic literacy and numeracy would improve the position of Ireland's citizens in the coming generations. It was also a product of the endeavours of the various religious denominations within Ireland to use the education system to imbue the upcoming generations with their particular religious beliefs and ensure the survival of their faith. There were also attempts to use the education system as a means of transmitting the Irish language and culture, an endeavour largely resisted by the Commissioners of National

Education up to 1922. An important factor was that all social classes in Ireland valued education and this contributed to the exponential growth of the national system of education.

Having entered the nineteenth century in a fragile position in political, social, economic, cultural and religious terms, Ireland made great strides in the turbulent times of the nineteenth century (most notably the Great Famine in the middle of the century) to emerge in 1900 in a more dominant and assertive tone. The INTO was gaining strength in educational terms, prominent figures such as Archbishop Walsh were ensuring education remained on the political agenda, while the policy of 'Killing Home Rule with Kindness' was capitalised upon in Ireland. The British government placed great faith in education to improve the social and economic conditions of the Irish people, realising that living in such poor circumstances, Ireland would never be at peace.

The Catholic Church evolved into a persuasive and powerful organisation, becoming the dominant spokesperson of the people on education. Its status was bolstered by the power it held in the form of ownership and management of schools. The constitutional nationalist movement was gaining momentum, while there was an awakening of cultural identity catalysed by the cultural nationalists. Improved social and economic conditions allowed time and energy for cultural pursuits. The growing awareness and pride in Irish culture became focused on the need for an apposite education system that reflected and cultivated the cultural identity of Irish children. The increased emphasis on agriculture and industry also prompted the questioning of the appropriateness of the education system in preparing children for their future roles in society.

The controversies and difficulties that manifested themselves in the birth and growth of the national school system should not occlude its many achievements and feats in the first seventy years. By 1900, it comprised a network of close to 9,000 schools, catering for the education of in excess of 750,000 pupils in every village and townland in Ireland.[57] The major religious denominations etched away the initial intentions of the Stanley Letter for a mixed denominational education system, achieving separate schools for the religious denominations where feasible, and separate schools for boys and girls in many instances. The training of teachers had been

resolved through the initiation of state-supported denominational training colleges in the 1880s, leading to a growing professional identity among
teachers. The Commissioners of National Education retained control
over the programme in operation in schools and evaluated the quality of
education through a nationwide network of inspectors. In international
comparative terms, Ireland had an extensive and impressive educational
infrastructure by 1900, while the vast majority of Irish children and adults
had attained at least a rudimentary education.

The 1890s became a period of programme reform for a number of
reasons. First, the system of payment by results had been in operation since
1872 and despite evident improvements in national literacy, there was a
general feeling that the system had outlived its purpose. It had resulted in
a narrow range of subjects being taught in national schools, primarily of
a literary nature, with little provision for other aspects such as physical or
creative development. Second, through Ireland's association with England,
there was an awareness of an international trend to place a greater focus
on the holistic development of the child by incorporating manual and
practical subjects in school curricula. Such developments had been introduced in England and Scotland and there were calls for similar reforms
in Ireland. Third, contemporary thinking was informed and catalysed
by wider international influences of the diverse groupings comprising
the New Education Movement, which was united in its campaign for a
reform of the school programme. Fourth, many of the other issues such as
teacher training and attendance legislation, which had remained contentious issues following 1831, had been resolved to some degree by the early
1890s, allowing a focus to be placed on the content of the primary school
programme. Fifth, the physical growth of the system was nearing its end
and there was an opportunity to focus on the content and quality of the
education provided. Finally, there was practically universal support from the
Catholic Church and other churches, the Inspectorate, the Commissioners
of National Education and prominent Irish educationalists for a revision
of the programme to incorporate more practical subjects. These domestic
influences, allied to international influences, instigated a period of intense
educational reform during which a more liberal, flexible and balanced
programme was devised and implemented.

Planning and Content of the *Revised Programme of Instruction* (1900)

2.1 Introduction

Having outlined the societal and educational context for the period 1831–1922, this chapter examines the process by which the *Revised Programme of Instruction* (1900) was devised and is framed largely within the period 1896 to 1900. It begins by analysing the process that led to the establishment of the Commission on Manual and Practical Instruction (CMPI). It details the terms of reference of the Commission and the work it undertook to produce its report in 1898. A specific focus is placed on the final report of the Commission in relation to its recommendations for the national school programme, as it formed the basis for the subsequent *Revised Programme*. The process undertaken to devise the *Revised Programme* between 1898 and 1900 is traced. The various drafts of the programme, culminating in the publication of the *Revised Programme* in September 1900, are documented.

2.2 Origins of the Commission on Manual and Practical Instruction (CMPI)

There was a widespread acceptance of the need for a reform of the education system by the mid 1890s. The Board of National Education had the immediate responsibility for primary education in Ireland and it accepted that a fundamental modification was required. The Commissioners pondered on their responsibility and although they held the power to reform the programme, they concluded that an independent Commission of Enquiry into the primary school programme would carry far greater weight. This was an expedient move as their membership of the Commission placed them in a position to steer its deliberations, while it retained the prestige of a Vice-regal Commission.

On 26 July 1896, the Commissioners issued a memorandum stating their concern with the lack of technical instruction in schools in Ireland and outlining the positive benefits of introducing manual and practical instruction into schools.[1] It also delineated the status of manual and practical instruction in other countries and the Commissioners proposed that before any amendments in this regard were made in Ireland, there was need for greater clarity around the issue and for interested parties to submit their suggestions. Members of the National Board met the Lord Lieutenant in August 1896 and set forth a detailed proposition for the introduction of subjects relating to manual and practical instruction. The Board's request for a Vice-regal Commission was granted and the CMPI was instituted in January 1897. The Commission was comprised of fourteen members, ten of whom were Commissioners of the Board of National Education. It was chaired by the Earl of Cadogan (Lord Belmore) and also included an inspector from England, Captain Shaw, and an inspector from Scotland, Mr Struthers.

The CMPI placed an emphasis on consultation with managers and teachers in order to gain from their expertise. Furthermore, views and opinions were sought from wider circles of individuals and groups with an interest or expertise in education, both domestically and internationally.[2] Another aim of the Commission was to impart the rationale for reform to these key participants in the system for future implementation as their reaction would have a crucial impact on parental and popular perception of the revisions in their localities. One of the primary reasons cited for such a public investigation was the need for clarity around the language and concept of manual and practical instruction. Specifically, the Commission was charged with investigating the necessary changes within the programme to make room for new subjects, the training of teachers, the need for peripatetic teachers, the provision of materials and equipment and the development of night schools.[3]

2.3 Work of the Commission

The purpose of the CMPI was to enquire and to report with a view 'to determining how far, and in what form, manual and practical instruction should be included in the Educational System of the Primary Schools under the Board of National Education in Ireland.'[4] These terms may appear limited but it is evident that the Commission interpreted its task to relate to all non-literary or non-mathematical subjects, thus ensuring a comprehensive investigation. The Commission set earnestly and assiduously about its task. It held ninety-three public meetings, at fifty-seven of which evidence was taken, from 186 witnesses. These witnesses were chosen from a wide array of educationalists such as teachers, managers, inspectors and training college personnel, but also included non-educationalists to ascertain the views of people working in agriculture and industry. In the process of conducting the investigation, 119 schools were visited in Ireland, England, Scotland, Germany, Holland, Switzerland and Denmark.

In addition to the oral evidence collected and collated, in excess of sixty documents were gathered and analysed by the Commission and included as a book of appendices to the report. Many of the appendices related to the teaching of manual and practical subjects in Ireland, England and Scotland. In addition, four Assistants were appointed by the Commission to review and document aspects of manual and practical instruction in France, Germany, Belgium and Holland. Collectively, these represented a vast anthology of policy and practice in relation to manual and practical instruction in Ireland and internationally at the turn of the century and provided a solid evidence-base for the Commission in the drafting of the final report. The Commission published four interim reports with appendices prior to the publication of the final report in June 1898.

2.4 Report of the CMPI

The final report of the CMPI was a synthesis of the voluminous information gathered in the course of the eighteen-month investigation. It made radical proposals *vis-à-vis* the existing system of national education, both educationally and philosophically, favouring strongly the introduction of subjects of a more manual and practical nature. Its overriding and unanimous conclusion was that:

> We may at once express our strong conviction that Manual and Practical Instruction ought to be introduced, as far as possible, into all schools where it does not at present exist, and that, in those schools where it does exist, it ought to be largely developed and extended.[5]

The report emphasised that its conclusions in relation to introducing subjects of a more manual and practical nature were based on educational principles and to redress the imbalance in the existing programme. The proposed range of skills that the study of such subjects provided included the intelligent observation of the world around pupils, training in reasoning and developing manual dexterity. Commission witnesses were confident that, not only would the introduction of new subjects not impact negatively on the existing programme, but conversely, it would help to enhance pupils' experience of the literary subjects, quicken their intelligence and prepare them for their future lives.[6] Furthermore, the final report cited from the testimonies of witnesses that there had been no desire for a return to a literary-focused programme where manual and practical subjects had been introduced, while many jurisdictions continued to extend this aspect of their system.[7] The Commission believed there was a widespread national desire to augment the practical character of national schools in order to strengthen the system of technical instruction in subsequent years, and consequently strengthen national industry. It stressed that subjects of a manual and practical nature should become inherent elements of the programme, rather than being added 'as subsidiary subjects, to be taken in such fragments of time as can be spared from instruction in the "three R's."'[8]

The final report was unanimous and was signed by all members of the Commission, apart from Lord Belmore, who was ill, and Baron Plunket, who had died in the course of the investigation. It was accepted and endorsed by the Board of National Education. The National Board concluded that 'a radical change in the curriculum, in the methods of payment to teachers, in the methods of inspection of schools, and in the methods of official administration in the Central Department were absolutely essential.'[9] Much of the final report was devoted to a detailed exposition of the proposed subjects to be introduced into the programme of national schools.

2.4.1 *Programme proposed by the CMPI*

Kindergarten

The final report of the CMPI recommended the introduction of the general principles and methods of Kindergarten in all schools attended by infant children, not in its purest form, but in conjunction with instruction in the traditional infant subjects. The principles of Kindergarten included the development of all the powers of the child (body, mind and spirit), the inculcation of spontaneity by providing opportunities and materials in a graded and harmonious manner and tailoring the instruction to the disposition, capacity and development of each individual child. It was acknowledged that many of these principles were in direct contrast with the realities for many children in infant classes, where 'the original idea too often was to instruct young children as rapidly as possible in the elements of reading, writing, and arithmetic.'[10]

A detailed exposition of Froebel's concept of Kindergarten was provided within the report, outlining the principles and strategies for its implementation through the gifts and occupations, among other materials. Models of the integration of the traditional subjects and Kindergarten principles were also provided within the final report. It advocated the exclusive use of Kindergarten methods for children less than seven years of age, after which time reading, writing and arithmetic would form the core of instruction. The practical application of information was to be kept in mind from the start of imparting knowledge, pointing out the need for the transmission of the purpose of learning to young children. It was hoped and expected that these principles would underpin the education of children as they progressed from infant classes throughout the rest of their schooling, providing the basis for educational handwork, drawing and elementary science in senior classes. Subject integration and crossover was also advocated and Kindergarten principles were seen as a unifying factor in this regard. The Commission was cognisant of the challenges of introducing such an approach in small schools, proposing the application of Kindergarten approaches across all classes and a greater concentration on junior classes in the morning, followed by their early dismissal to allow a subsequent focus on senior classes.[11]

The emphasis placed on Kindergarten in the final report focused educators on infant classes of primary schools as never before. The proposals were practical in nature, advocating a melange of traditional subjects and Kindergarten methods to improve the educational experiences of young pupils. As O'Connor posited, the status of infants within the education system was greatly enhanced following its publication.[12]

Educational Handwork – Hand and Eye Training/ Woodwork

The final report was confident in its recommendation for the immediate introduction of hand and eye training, stating that the evidence was 'absolutely unanimous and, as we think, entirely conclusive.'[13] The educational handwork proposed was comprised of two main areas, hand and eye training in middle classes (including paper folding, cardboard work, wire work, brick laying, clay modelling) and instruction in the education principles of woodwork in senior classes. The Commission cited the main benefits of studying educational handwork to be the acquisition of general manual dexterity and mental and moral development, asserting the latter to be of most importance.

Extensive detail was provided in the report on the aims and content of educational handwork considering its lack of prominence within the existing programme, with the subject occupying approximately one-third of the report. It proposed dedicating one-and-a-half to two hours per week to the subject. The Commission did not propose making hand and eye training or woodwork compulsory, as there were many issues such as the training of teachers and the provision of grants for buildings, equipment and materials to be settled before widespread introduction. The final report recommended that the National Board provide a free grant of requisites for the various subjects as schools introduced them to ensure that a lack of the necessary materials and resources did not hinder implementation.

While proposing ordinary teachers as opposed to artisans to teach woodwork, the report recommended not allowing unqualified, unmotivated or unskilled teachers to undertake the subject in order to earn additional grants. Woodwork in senior classes would extend hand and eye training, requiring greater manipulation and gradation and utilising skills in drawing. These provisions were seen as relevant for all pupils, but especially to the majority who 'will have to earn their bread by the work of their hands.'[14] The cost of providing suitable facilities and the ongoing provision of materials was noted as being considerable by the Commission, yet the capacity to introduce the subject using makeshift facilities in the interim was outlined. It proposed that grants be paid, not based on the reproduction of exercises at an examination, but on the 'intelligence and skill which the teacher brings to bear upon the work.'[15] The Commission acknowledged the difficulty of achieving congruence between the philosophy of the system of payment by results and the focus on the process advocated for educational handwork, proposing a revision of the system by which grants were allocated for the subject. The report recognised the need to employ experienced organisers to frame a suitable programme and to assist in its implementation, while still allowing schools to submit alternative programmes for sanction by the National Board.

Drawing

A practical and graded course in drawing from infants was proposed, providing mental and manual training in the process. The focus of the subject was to be placed on 'not so much the completion of a drawing, as the mental and manual training involved in its execution.'[16] It proposed that teachers did not need a certificate of ability to teach drawing and that

opportunities for formal training should be made available to all teachers. Proposals were also included for linking the subject to other related
aspects of the programme, such as hand and eye training, woodwork and
elementary science. Drawing was one of the subjects that was somewhat
well established in schools in 1898 (see table 2.1) and witnesses were almost
unanimous in their recommendation for its inclusion.

Elementary Science

Where teachers were proficient to impart instruction, the final report recommended that elementary science would be a compulsory subject in schools.
The subject involved object lessons (observation lessons) in junior classes
and experiments in senior classes, varying according to the needs and circumstances of the locality and character and conditions of schools. The
main focus of object lessons was anticipated to be the intellectual training
derived from the systematic observation and recording of such observations.
In senior classes, it was envisaged that pupils would actively participate in
experiments. A particular focus was placed on inculcating a spirit of enquiry
and research, of imparting self-reliance, of conveying accuracy of thinking
and expression, rather than the digestion and imparting of knowledge on
the part of the teacher. The report recommended that a number of specimen
courses be prepared that could be adapted to the needs of individual school
contexts, while grants for equipment were proposed so the introduction of
the subject required no monetary outlay by teachers. The appointment of
organisers to assist the preparation of courses at individual school level was
recommended, as was a modification in the inspection system to ensure it
evaluated 'the methods of instruction employed by the teacher, and by observ-
ing his success in interesting the pupils and awakening their intelligence.'[17]

Agriculture

The final report of the Commission concluded that:

> We do not think that Agriculture as an art, that is to say practical farming, is a subject
> that properly belongs to elementary education.[18]

In its place, the Commission recommended a course in the elements of the natural and physical sciences relating to agriculture as part of elementary science for boys in rural schools. It further proposed the maintenance and extension of gardens in all schools to illustrate these practical principles, but did not envisage the maintenance of school farms as belonging to the remit of the National Board. Moreover, it proposed ceding control of the agricultural colleges to the DATI, with an arrangement for the training of teachers within the new structures.

Cookery, Laundry Work and Domestic Science

Cookery was regarded as one of the most important practical subjects for girls and the report recommended the teaching of both practical and theoretical elements using simple apparatus as would be available in pupils' homes. The provision of training for teachers was recommended, while the subject could be taught at Centres used by clusters of schools or within separate schools. Cookery was envisaged as an important education to ensure the economical and careful preparation of food:

> It is of special importance in Ireland where the labouring and Artisan classes are sadly ignorant of the art of cookery, their food in consequence being seldom prepared in as economical or nutritious a manner as it might be.[19]

The final report recommended the encouragement and extension of laundry work within schools, along the same principles as cookery. The Commission advocated a more practical focus to domestic science and hygiene through experimental observation, involving the active participation of pupils.

Needlework

The Commission advocated that needlework should continue to form an important element in all girls' schools, but a reduction from five to three hours per week was proposed to allow time for the introduction of other subjects. Furthermore, a greater emphasis was to be placed on its educational elements, rather than on routine and mechanical aspects. Needlework was now to commence in Kindergarten, and continue throughout schooling as part of hand and eye training.

Singing

The use of the tonic sol-fa method for music was endorsed by the report.[20] It was recommended that singing as a subject be brought within the reach of all children in national schools, having a cultivating and refining influence and furnishing a source of permanent enjoyment. Instruction was to begin in infant classes and extend through all classes, while the report asserted that inspection should not be applied to individual children in this subject and should recognise the validity of singing by ear.

Drill and Physical Exercises

Various kinds of drill and physical exercises were proposed within the report, to be introduced as an extension of simple Kindergarten exercises. The Commission cited many reasons for introducing this programme, including the contribution to health, the promotion of posture and orderliness, increased organisation in movements around the school and in class, enhanced regularity, obedience and efficiency and the uplifting of the spirits and general well being of pupils.

2.4.2 *Alterations Needed Within the Existing Programme*

The report of the CMPI was a synthesis and distillation of the evidence presented by key witnesses. Overall, it concluded that the Irish system of education, with its literary bias, was in need of fundamental reform. It recommended a wider range of practical subjects, an emphasis on infant classes, an alternative method of examining practical subjects other than individual examination, and that schools would become more interesting and enjoyable places. It attempted to redress the serious imbalance within the programme in favour of literary subjects by introducing subjects of a more manual and practical nature. The CMPI proposed the inclusion of

Kindergarten, educational handwork, drawing, elementary science, cookery, laundry and domestic science, singing, drill and physical exercise. This more than doubled the range of subjects to be taught in primary schools. However, the majority of these proposed subjects were not taught widely at the time and the vast majority of teachers held no qualifications to impart such subjects. Table 2.1 summarises the lack of established status many of these subjects had within the approximate 8,600 national schools in the late 1890s.

Table 2.1 Extent to which Additional Subjects were being Taught in National Schools in 1896

Subject	No. of Schools (%)
Kindergarten	364 (4%)
Handicraft	15 (0.2%)
Drawing	1,515 (18%)
Cookery	83 (1%)
Laundry	1 (0.1%)
Domestic Science	151 (2%)
Hygiene	28 (0.3%)
Singing	1,217 (14%)

Source: Commissioners of National Education in Ireland [CNEI] (1897). *63rd Report ... for 1896–1897*, p. 32.

The introduction of this multitude of new subjects required alterations to the existing primary school programme in order to accommodate them. Many witnesses, both national and international, suggested an array of modifications that could be made to the existing school programme to enable the inclusion of subjects of a more manual and practical nature. These included a lengthening of the school day and reducing the time allocated to existing subjects to ensure adequate time for the new subjects.[21] In addition to programme changes, evidence to the CMPI proposed alterations to the system of inspection in operation. The system of payment by results was cited by many witnesses as being incongruent with the new subjects proposed and with the achievement of the overall tone of education advised by the Commission.[22]

During the work of the Commission, inspectors were invited in February 1897 to submit ideas for the release of time within the existing programme to introduce the new subjects. Most felt that all of the existing subjects were necessary but that time allocations could be altered. In general, the proposals included making geography and grammar optional, reducing the time for needlework, abolishing agriculture, lengthening the school day and using Saturdays for instruction.[23]

An allocation of approximately four hours per week was considered necessary to introduce the new subjects. The report did not propose any major alterations to the existing programme; instead the time would be attained by making some compulsory subjects optional, by grouping related subjects and by reducing the requirements in some subjects. The modifications proposed gaining two hours from the reduced time allocation for needlework and additional time from the removal of agriculture. Additionally, the report proposed making subjects such as grammar and geography optional in some of the classes, reducing the programme requirements in grammar, geography and arithmetic, and grouping interrelated subjects rather than allocating separate time slots. It was believed that the introduction of practical subjects would complement the existing literary subjects and thus not prove too great a burden for teachers and pupils in their introduction, stressing the connectivity of literary and practical education.

A revision of the system regarding the use of individual examination for assessing the work of teachers in relation to subjects of a manual and practical nature was recommended by the final report. Instead, a system was proposed whereby the grants awarded to the teacher 'should largely depend on the general evidence of his own zeal and industry, on the efficacy of his method of teaching, and on his power to arrest and hold the attention of his class.'[24] The report recommended a more flexible inspection system as essential to the introduction of practical subjects, whereby individual examination would be replaced by a flexible system of incidental visits and class inspections. A 'Centre System' was advocated for schools in large towns and cities, whereby schools in a locality would use a centralised equipped room on a rota basis for instruction in certain subjects such as woodwork and domestic science. In rural districts, the Commission advocated the organisation of a system of peripatetic teachers in schools where teachers were not proficient to teach subjects. These peripatetic teachers would visit schools in turn and demonstrate correct use of the necessary equipment to teach the subjects in question.

The Commission was aware that the proposed changes would have an impact on financing but remained confident that the Treasury would realise the importance of investment in primary education. It was also cognisant of the challenges such a radical change in the syllabus of primary schools would entail. It thus proposed that such modifications be introduced 'not all at once, but gradually and tentatively', starting in the towns and cities.[25] The report also recommended the establishment of School Manager Associations to assist in the development of manual and practical instruction, by facilitating networking, the dissemination of ideas and the promotion of local interest. It concluded by stating that the deficiencies within the existing system could be rectified by the implementation of the proposals, without any detrimental consequences for the advantageous elements therein:

> not disturb what is good in the present system, but only supply what is wanting. It will quicken the intelligence of children, brighten the tone of school life, and make school-work generally more interesting and attractive.[26]

Interestingly, the provisions within the Commission's report relating to the practicalities of providing time and equipment for the new subjects in ordinary schools received a mere four pages. It is arguable that this was insufficient to deal with the magnitude of the changes contained within the report for the introduction of a range of new subjects, which took fifty pages to detail. It did not delineate a precise strategy for implementation, exact time allocations for various subjects or provide mechanisms for the funding of facilities or equipment. Many witnesses brought to the attention of the Commission a multiplicity of practical challenges to implementing the new subjects, which were not adequately addressed within the final report. This impacted negatively on the subsequent *Revised Programme* (1900), which also neglected to develop a detailed implementation strategy based on the realities of schools in Ireland at the time.

2.4.3 Teacher Training

The winds of educational change had already reached the training colleges, whereby the programme was revised in 1896 to incorporate a greater variety of subjects. These included reading, penmanship, spelling and punctuation, grammar, composition, English, geography, literature, arithmetic, theory of method, practice of teaching, needlework, drawing and book-keeping as obligatory subjects. Male students also studied agriculture and an extended programme in mathematics. In addition, all students undertook one of a possible twenty-one optional subjects. There was also an increased emphasis on the science and art of teaching, with these aspects receiving a greater proportion of the marks in examinations.[27] A number of witnesses to the Commission working within the training colleges noted the rudimentary knowledge of the students on entry as being a major barrier to progress. As a result, much time and energy was expended on the basics of education.[28]

The Commission recognised the necessity of further extending the course of studies followed in the training colleges to prepare students in the new subjects. In addition to the aforementioned subjects undertaken in these colleges, the CMPI also recommended hand and eye training, education in Kindergarten principles, physical drill, elementary science, object lessons and singing for both men and women. Woodwork was proposed for men while cookery and laundry work were anticipated for women. Time was also proposed to be allocated to the implementation of these subjects in the practising schools affiliated to the training colleges. The Commission correctly viewed the training colleges as one avenue for the training of teachers. However, there were approximately 12,000 practising teachers at this time, of which 55 per cent were untrained.[29] Many of

these, due to age and circumstance, would never attend training col
and even at full capacity, the colleges were not producing enough teachers
to replace those leaving the service annually. Trained teachers were also in
need of in-service education in the new programme subjects and methods.
The final report recommended a dual approach, catering for some practising teachers within the training colleges and the remainder by organisers
providing courses locally on Saturdays. The Commission stressed that
teachers should not bear any expense in attending these courses, while the
organisers could be employed as peripatetic teachers providing practical
demonstrations and advising teachers on weekdays.

The final report of the Commission proposed ways in which time could
be created for these subjects within the training colleges, including a lightening in the requirements of the programme in certain subjects, a reduction
in the number of subjects that had to be passed individually, a decrease in
the number of compulsory subjects and a change in assessment from mere
knowledge of subjects to testing students' capacity for the work of teaching.
These additions put great strain on the students and staff in the colleges,
resulting in a highly structured timetable and continuous examinations.[30]
With such an array of subjects to cover, depth of instruction was more
difficult to achieve and teaching remained practical in nature. Cramming
was a feature of these conditions, leading to little time for assimilation of
new knowledge or for wider personal reading. In this period, there was a
shift towards thinking of teaching as an art with guiding principles and a
theoretical framework, and this led to the introduction of subjects such
as theory of method, practice of teaching and science of teaching. Over
the years, these subjects were awarded more marks and became necessary
to pass the overall course. The examinations in these subjects also evolved,
requiring reflective and higher-order thinking as opposed to direct factual
answers. From 1900, newly appointed principals required formal training,
the one-year training course was abolished in 1910 and a third year was
added for the 'most competent' students.[31]

The challenges facing the programme devisers regarding teacher training were numerous and complex. Approximately half of the teachers were
formally trained, and that was under a system with an altogether different
philosophy of education. It effectively needed to provide training for 12,000

 y 9,000 schools in a context where transport
͟underdeveloped and expensive. While the report
͟ perform this function, they were inadequate rela-
͟isted at the time. The onus placed on the training
͟truction in the additional subjects, in the absence of
͟s in funding for personnel and equipment, was unreal-
is͟   ͟on that a handful of organisers could impart new syllabi,
provide ͟   ͟ demonstrations and assist schools in the framing of programmes appropriate for individual school contexts on a nationwide basis,
was also impractical. In any case, subsequent implementation of knowledge
acquired was often compromised by the dearth of suitable facilities and
materials. Furthermore, over-reliance on the training colleges seriously
impacted on the timescale for adopting many of the reforms. The inadequate
strategy for the training of teachers in the philosophy of the new system
and in the content of the new subjects proved to be a major challenge in
the implementation of the *Revised Programme* following 1900.

2.5 Planning of the *Revised Programme* (1900)

2.5.1 *Devising the Revised Programme*

A Committee of the National Board was appointed in October 1898 to
consider the final report of the Commission and to devise a scheme to give
effect to its recommendations. On 17 November 1898, an interim report
was produced by this Committee, accepting in principle the recommendations of the Commission.[32]

A subsequent draft of this interim report was forwarded to the Lord
Lieutenant on 20 December 1898, entitled *A Preliminary Scheme for the
Introduction of Subjects of Manual and Practical Instruction into the National
Schools of Ireland*.[33] While skeletal in nature, it was a well evolved draft of
the subsequent programme and contained twenty-two proposals for the

implementation of the recommendations of the CMPI. Many ᵣₑ ommendations within this preliminary report were included in the *Reviseₗₗ Programme*, including the appointment of organisers for new subjects, a reduction in the number of additional subjects and the introduction of Kindergarten, manual instruction, elementary science and drawing. The Scheme also advocated that teachers who obtained training in any of the new subjects would subsequently be obliged to teach that subject. The Committee estimated the extra costs would amount to £14,410 per annum, including £5,500 for twenty-two Local Organisers, £2,040 for three Head Organisers and £3,000 for Equipment Grants. The allocation of £3,000 for equipment was particularly paltry to cater for approximately 9,000 schools.

The planning of the programme was interrupted by the death of the Rt. Hon. C.T. Redington, the Resident Commissioner, in February 1899. He was replaced by Dr W.J.M. Starkie, a Greek scholar who was President of Queen's University, Galway. In evidence to the Dill Inquiry (instituted to enquire into the inspection system following 1900), Dr Starkie asserted that the draft plans for the *Revised Programme* (1900) devised in November and December 1898 formed the basis of further developments and were out of his control, as some proposals had been 'unanimously adopted by the Board'.[34]

On 28 March 1899, Dr Starkie and Professor FitzGerald were appointed to prepare a *Working Scheme on Manual and Practical Instruction* for consideration by the Board.[35] Although the individual Commissioners of National Education were heavily involved in the CMPI, they were not afforded the same contribution in the devising of the *Revised Programme* for schools. Dr Starkie and Professor FitzGerald elaborated on the aforementioned Preliminary Scheme and, in July 1899, the *Report of the Board of National Education, made for the Information of his Excellency the Lord Lieutenant, in reference to the recommendations of the Commission on Manual and Practical Instruction* was forwarded to the Lord Lieutenant.[36] It contained an overview of the implementation of the recommendations of the CMPI and an individual section on each of the subjects proposed. It differentiated schools into three categories – schools capable of carrying out all changes, some changes and no changes.

The report acknowledged that there were few schools in the first category and proposed training for teachers, initially in the second category, in local centres. In the third category of school, it was recognised that 'no immediate steps can be taken to introduce Manual and Practical Instruction, as a considerable time must elapse before the teachers can be prepared for it.'[37] It proposed proceeding tentatively with the training of teachers, extending provision gradually until all eligible teachers were trained in some of the new subjects. The report advised affording latitude to schools regarding the rate and nature of the subjects introduced, based on the advice of inspectors and organisers, citing from international experience the 'unwisdom of trying to impose any uniform scheme upon all the national schools of the country.'[38] The second part of the report related to the actions necessary for the various new subjects to be introduced. These largely revolved around the appointment of organisers in the various subjects to impart training, the provision of grants for materials and equipment and the organisation of equipped 'Centres' in urban areas that could be used by a cluster of schools.

Further drafts were submitted to the Chief Secretary in August and October 1899, with acceptance of a draft produced in November 1899.[39] These iterations differed greatly in scope from the July proposal, insofar as they allowed for the complete abolition of payment by results, an alteration of the method of paying and promoting teachers and the reorganisation of the Inspectorate. It also increased the speed and universality of implementation, with little accommodation for the various categories of schools identified in earlier drafts. The range of subjects proposed (reading, writing, arithmetic, Kindergarten and manual instruction, drawing, elementary science, cookery and laundry, needlework, singing, school discipline and physical drill) was congruent with those proposed by the CMPI. However, the draft report proposed that following a reorganisation of schools, 'all should be made compulsory in every Primary School attended by girls, and all except Needlework, Cookery and Laundry Work, in schools attended by boys'.[40] It further proposed the abolition of home lessons (homework) to make school life more enjoyable and the compilation of a timetable for each school. In addition, a change in methodologies was proposed to ensure 'every child would be under instruction in the same subject at the same time', rather than the Bipartite, Tripartite or Quadripartite system popular at the time.[41] Further recommendations included the provision of a seat for each child, the establishment of a library system, grouping all pupils into four standards, improved heating, lighting and ventilation, the appointment of subject organisers, the preparation of an annual report on teachers by the manager and initiating a system of school prizes. It would appear that the chief architect of this draft, save some specific input from Professor FitzGerald, was Dr Starkie, who had assumed a leadership role in driving the development of the programme.

Inspectors had little input in the *Revised Programme* beyond the evidence submitted by some in the course of the CMPI and when their views were sought about specific matters in 1895 and 1897. This broke the tradition of consultation with senior inspectors, which had been a feature of the practice of preceding Resident Commissioners. Starkie's evidence to the Dill Inquiry reveals the particularly acrimonious relationship he had with the two Chief Inspectors, Mr Downing and Mr Purser, in the period following 1900.[42] Consequently, an invaluable source of knowledge and insight was not harnessed that could perhaps have better tempered the programme to the reality of schools.

While Dr Starkie may have consciously chosen to work alone on the drafting of the programme, there is evidence that he consulted with key agents as the programme neared completion in 1900. Mr Lemass, at the Dill Inquiry, stated that the draft completed in July 1900 was circulated to the heads of the training colleges, the two Chief Inspectors, the twenty-two senior inspectors and a number of other prominent educationalists, such as Dr Joyce and Sir Joshua Fitch.[43] It was also submitted to a number of international experts, including Mr Struthers, a school inspector in Scotland.[44] However, given the late stage of the dissemination of the programme, it is arguable that this was more by way of informing them as opposed to affording meaningful consultation. Feedback submitted at this time by respondents such as Mr Struthers and Mr Fitch was largely ignored. Inspectors Downing and Purser also returned feedback, stating that the programme 'was much too extensive, probably quite beyond what would be possible even in the most favourably conditioned National School ... and quite unattainable in the Ordinary National Schools with one or two teachers'.[45]

They urged a revision of the language and content, with a view to omitting certain elements and simplifying the newly introduced subjects, especially in junior classes. Furthermore, they listed the extensive equipment, facilities and apparatus required for the various subjects, concluding that 'we cannot believe the large amount of money needed for the new subjects will be immediately forthcoming.'[46] Such revisions were not incorporated as Dr Starkie asserted that because the programme was to be promulgated tentatively, such revisions could be implemented at any time.

2.5.2 Content of the Revised Programme (1900)

September 1900 was chosen as the date for the introduction of the *Revised Programme*. Notification ensued to schools that '[T]he Results Programme is abolished. The Revised Programme is substituted therefor.'[47] The programme involved the introduction of the new subjects as well as a change in the methodologies employed:

> The Revised Programme not merely prescribes certain new subjects and excludes some old ones; but also involves some radical changes in the methods of instruction.[48]

The *Revised Programme* of instruction spanned thirty pages and outlined the requirements for each subject, existing and new. The introduction spanned three pages and provided little of a theoretical, philosophical or ideological framework on which the programme was based. No mention was made of the report of the CMPI which formed the basis for its content. It stated its aim was to cultivate the intelligence of children of all abilities by focusing on all aspects of development. From an analysis, the philosophy of the *Revised Programme* was child-centred and liberal relative to its predecessor. It placed an emphasis on the active participation of children in learning and proposed a wide range of subjects of a manual and practical character to redress the previous literary bias inherent in the programme. The programme was to cater for the needs and abilities of all children by being flexible and balanced to support all aspects of development. It stressed that the programme was the maximum to be expected and that it was to be introduced gradually:

It is promulgated provisionally and tentatively, and Managers should understand that there is no obligation on them at present to adopt it in its entirety. The Programme may be taken as representing the maximum of requirements under the various heads.[49]

It also acknowledged that the entirety of the programme would not be feasible in small schools and noted 'the intention of the Commissioners to issue an Alternative Programme for small schools as soon as possible.'[50] This alternative programme was not provided until 1904, at which time the provisions of the *Revised Programme* had been reduced owing to difficulties in implementation.

The programme did not detail guidelines in relation to the practical implementation of each subject but outlined key aspects to be addressed in each class. Separate timetables were proffered for boys' and girls' schools. The time afforded to the traditional core subjects was reduced to four-sevenths of the time they once held to accommodate the range of new subjects. The Commissioners of National Education in their report for 1900 stressed the balanced nature of the *Revised Programme*, putting emphasis on both literary and practical subjects.[51]

English was cited as one of the most important elements of the programme and was to be treated as one integrated subject comprising of both spoken and written language, 'and not as an agglomeration of many heterogeneous subjects.'[52] In addition, a focus was to be placed on clear pronunciation and intonation. The status of grammar and spelling was reduced and there was a fresh emphasis placed on oral and silent reading, in which comprehension was of primary importance. A focus on reading a variety of books provided or approved by the Board, as opposed to the rigidity of a class text, was also advocated.

Arithmetic was to have a more practical and realistic focus, with a wider applicability of skills:

In all the standards the Teachers should endeavour to make clear to the pupils the utility of the arithmetical processes by their application to concrete objects and the ordinary affairs of business.[53]

A focus on mental arithmetic was proposed, as was the provision of appropriate materials for practical instruction in aspects such as length, weight and capacity.

It was envisaged that Kindergarten principles and the heuristic method would permeate the entire workings of the primary school, particularly manual instruction and elementary science. The influence of Froebel on the programme is evident, with specific mention made of the gifts in the description of activities in the various classes. The programme stressed that the purpose of manual instruction was not a preparation for trades but 'rather to train the intelligence and observation, and to produce habits of neatness, dexterity, and carefulness in the child.'[54] The universal application of drawing in all walks of life and its importance from an early age was extolled in the programme. It proposed that the main function of the subject was to engender a taste for the subject and to express ideas rather than the creation of artists. The absence of equipment in many schools was noted and teachers were encouraged to make great use of the blackboard and to display artistic endeavours to brighten up classrooms. The programme issued a specific alert that teachers unqualified in manual instruction and drawing should only attempt rudimentary aspects of the subjects, with between one and two hours per week allocated to the two subjects.

In schools without a female teacher, a special Workmistress or Manual Instructress was to be employed to 'combine the functions of teachers of Needlework, Kindergarten, and Manual Instruction.'[55] In 1904, Dale asserted that teacher assistants and teachers working with junior classes or providing instruction in needlework did not necessarily need 'a high standard of proficiency in the ordinary subjects of examination ... A liking for little children, patience, animation, and natural quickness of mind are much more indispensable.'[56] This provision was formalised from 1 July 1906 whereby schools with an average attendance of between thirty-five and sixty pupils became entitled to a Junior Assistant Mistress (JAM) in addition to the principal teacher. By 1911 there were 2,454 JAMs, who focused largely on the instruction of infants.[57]

The programme provided courses in object lessons and elementary science, while schools were at liberty to submit alternative programmes to suit their particular contexts. The primary purpose of elementary science was to 'produce accurate habits of thought and work' rather than attaining information.[58] Similarly with object lessons, the emphasis was to be on what the child could discover directly, using heuristic methods. The programme also proposed the establishment of school museums and school gardens, as well as excursions to museums and places of local interest. Singing was posited as being a refining, intellectual and uplifting pursuit in all schools. The tonic sol-fa method was proposed as being universally applicable for all teachers, while experienced teachers could employ the staff notation method in senior classes. Physical drill became compulsory for all classes, with positive benefits listed including improved health, reduced monotony, better posture and alertness for learning. It was advised that teachers, prior to receiving training in these subjects, should only attempt their most rudimentary components. Cookery and laundry were compulsory in girls' schools where teachers were competent and suitable appliances were available. The programme focused teachers on general principles in these subjects rather than preparing pupils for particular occupations. It acknowledged that the programme would not be feasible in many schools immediately owing to the absence of space and equipment but encouraged schools to start with the basics and investigate the possibility of using a 'Centre' for a designated number of schools in a particular area. Needlework was compulsory for all girls with female teachers or Workmistresses, with three hours per week allocated to the subject. A practical focus was also advocated for the subject, including the repair of clothes from pupils' homes.

The list of extra subjects was greatly reduced to include Latin, French, mathematics, Irish and instrumental music. These could now be taught in the course of the school day, 'provided the adequacy of the course of instruction in the usual Day School subjects is not impaired or hampered thereby.'[59] The programme alerted teachers not to place too much pressure on pupils by engaging in an excess number of additional subjects and that the 'school should be made a pleasant place in every possible way.'[60] Irish could be used 'as an aid to the elucidation of English', while history and geography were to be introduced 'by the alternative use of Literary, Geographical, and Historical reading Books.'[61] The process of individual examination was abolished and replaced with a general system of inspection. The methods of instruction in use were also to be modified, replacing the didactic with a more child-centred, heuristic approach, 'by which children are enabled to find out things for themselves, by being placed, so to speak, in the position of discoverers, instead of being merely told about things.'[62]

The *Revised Programme* incorporated the recommendations of the CMPI, including the subjects it proposed, its suggestions for allocating time to these subjects, the abolition of payment by results and the system of training teachers in the new subjects. It introduced Kindergarten, manual instruction, drawing, singing, object lessons, elementary science, physical education, cookery and laundry as obligatory subjects, and proposed greater integration of subject areas. It placed a special emphasis on the education of young children, advocating the basing of education on the local environment and proposing that schools should be interesting and humane places. It also allowed flexibility within the programme, encouraging schools to adapt provisions to suit their individual contexts. Instead of subjects in manual and practical instruction being introduced as distinct elements, it was envisaged that they would be integrated aspects of the programme. However, it did not differentiate in its provisions for the various types of schools whose circumstances and contexts would impact on their ability to introduce its provisions.

2.5.3 *Modifications to the Inspectorate and Teachers' Salaries*

The introduction of the *Revised Programme* was accompanied by a number of fundamental changes to the existing administrative and inspection systems. This involved the reorganisation of the Inspectorate in line with the new demands of the *Revised Programme*, where individual examination was replaced by general inspection, effectively abolishing the system of payment by results.[63] This involved reform at all levels of the Inspectorate, and the administrative roles of the Chief Inspectors were now transformed into fieldwork in the schools with the other inspectors. Starkie reduced the inspection districts from sixty to twenty-five, with each division catered for by one senior inspector and two junior inspectors. This reorganisation 'precipitated dissension and disaffection at senior level'[64] and two senior inspectors were dismissed temporarily for their hostility to the reforms in 1900.[65]

The era was also characterised by much contention and unrest as the INTO became increasingly vocal and militant regarding teachers' rights under the new rating system.[66] Teachers were now classified into three grades, with a quota on the number in each grade, and a fixed minimum and maximum salary. In this system, promotion, regardless of ability, rested on the availability of a space in the next grade, thus in effect meaning many teachers received a 'paper promotion.' The maximum salary was to be achieved through triennial increments awarded according to the inspectors' reports, assigned by virtue of Merit Marks, which determined the payment of increments and the promotional prospects of teachers within grades.[67] Starkie organised the Inspectorate on a rotational basis, so that no one inspector would be responsible for the promotion or demotion in grades of a teacher.

The modifications to the Inspectorate and teacher salary payments further exacerbated the state of flux in Irish education in 1900. Not only did teachers have to contend with a radically different programme in schools and a revised system of inspection, but much of their energies and attention were directed on their personal material circumstances as affected by the new rating system. This further reduced their welcome for or acceptance of the *Revised Programme* and occupied the energies of the INTO and individual teachers in seeking an amelioration in the system, thus reducing their focus on implementing the programme's provisions.

2.6 Reactions to the *Revised Programme*

The *Revised Programme* received widespread applause from the press in general for the freedom it afforded to teachers and managers:

> the cast-iron and red tape seem to have been flung through the windows of Tyrone House [offices of the Commissioners of National Education] in the most determined way.[68]

The Central Executive Committee (CEC) of the INTO welcomed an end to the era of payment by results.[69] Overall, teachers noted the inherent qualities of the programme and lauded its underlying educational philosophy. However, at the INTO Congress in 1901, teachers expressed anger at not having been 'taken into the confidence of those who were planning the new methods of training.'[70] They questioned the practicalities of implementing such a radical programme in the existing Irish context, asserting it was 'so overloaded with requirements as to be absolutely impracticable.'[71] In September 1900, a new educational journal, *The Irish School Monthly*, was launched to assist teachers in the implementation of the *Revised Programme*. It commented on the radical changes the implementation of the programme involved, whereby 'here all is new and strange; the change is sudden and complete.'[72]

The support of school managers was seen as critical to the ultimate success of implementing the programme. As they were responsible for the maintenance of schools, the Commissioners anticipated they would provide, from local funds, the requisite equipment and materials for the new subjects being introduced. However, relations were often poor between teachers and managers and local funds were not always forthcoming for such resources, owing to the lack of popular interest or control over education in schools that were predominantly clerically managed. The relationship between the National Board and managers reached a low ebb in 1902 when Dr Starkie admonished managers for the poor physical conditions of schools.[73] This attack impacted negatively on managers' co-operation with the implementation of the *Revised Programme* and the provision of additional resources.

2.7 Summary and Conclusion

The *Revised Programme* (1900) was based on a comprehensive review of national and international best policy and practice in relation to the teaching of subjects of a manual and practical nature. The work of the CMPI was impressive in its speed, range and depth, documenting and publishing its oral evidence and reports garnered on the Irish context and other jurisdictions. The Commission captured much of the desire and quest for redressing the literary imbalance within the programme for primary schools and concluded, in line with the evidence submitted, that a radical revision of the primary school programme was both necessary and desirable. The final report of the Commission distilled the essence of the four volumes of evidence and appendices, and proposed the inclusion of a wide array of practical subjects, including Kindergarten; educational handwork/hand and eye training; drawing; elementary science; agriculture; cookery, laundry and domestic science; needlework; singing; and drill and physical exercise. This was a radical departure from a programme that focused primarily on literacy and numeracy. Furthermore, the final report advocated a fundamental shift in the system of inspection of schools from a focus on individual children to evaluating the performance of the class as a whole. Additional proposals related to the provision of time within the school programme to allow for the inclusion of these additional subjects and strategies to impart necessary skills to both practising teachers and student teachers within the training colleges.

However, despite the comprehensive nature of the report, it failed to address adequately practical issues in relation to implementation. First, the issue of financing the additional subjects in the form of providing physical spaces, equipment and ongoing materials was not given sufficient attention. It was naïve to think that managers and localities would provide such resources considering the tradition of centralised financing for education in Ireland. Second, while the provisions of the final report were radical for large schools, they were unrealistic in small schools, in a context where in excess of 60 per cent of schools were staffed by one teacher in 1900.[74] This teacher dealt with an age-range of pupils spanning between four and fourteen years of age, often accommodated within a one-room school. To implement the recommendations of the Commission in such a context was unfeasible owing to the lack of space, expertise on the part of the teacher in all the new subjects, the wide age range and ability levels of the pupils and the difficulty of providing or even accommodating all of the required equipment.

The process of translating the vision of the CMPIs final report into the reality of practice was undertaken over a two-year period between October 1898 and September 1900. A sub-committee of the National Board completed the initial draft of the *Revised Programme* and this was subsequently developed and extended by the newly-appointed Resident Commissioner, Dr Starkie. Provision was also made for the revision of the inspection system and the payment of teachers. While the National Board ratified ongoing drafts of the programme, they were afforded little input in its devising. The content of the *Revised Programme* reflected closely the recommendations of the CMPI. However, similar to the Commission, the *Revised Programme* failed to address adequately the practicalities of implementation, such as the finance for facilities and equipment and the inherent difficulty of introducing such a range of new subjects in small schools. Despite the fact that Dr Starkie consulted on later drafts of the programme, available evidence suggests little action was taken based on the feedback returned.

Dr Starkie was a formidable character and even in the early days in his position of Resident Commissioner, he managed to alienate and antagonise the key influences in the implementation of the *Revised Programme*, most notably the teachers, managers and inspectors. This occurred at a crucial time in the introduction of the programme and certainly impacted negatively upon its successful implementation.

> The closing months of the 19th century witnessed the opening of a new chapter in the history of primary education in Ireland ... a very serious leap has been taken, and that something of an educational revolution has occurred in our midst.[75]

These aspirational words of Mr Goodman in 1900 were perhaps premature, as the devising of the programme was but the first step – implementation in practice proved a more demanding and arduous 'revolution' to achieve. Chapter 3 examines the implementation of the *Revised Programme* until independence in 1922.

CHAPTER 3

Implementation of the *Revised Programme of Instruction* 1900–1921

3.1 Introduction

> In modern history of Education, there is probably in no country such an example of complete change both in administration and methods of instruction as has recently occurred in Ireland; whether we shall in the future be justified in substituting the word reform for the word change time alone can show.[1]

This chapter examines the question posed by Mr Heller, Head Organiser of Science Instruction to the Commissioners of National Education, in relation to the changes that occurred during the implementation of the *Revised Programme*. This delineation documents the progress in the various subject areas within the programme by drawing on evidence from inspectors' reports in the period. The report of Mr F.H. Dale on primary schools, the only major evaluation of the system in this period, is documented. The role of the major educational interests in the implementation process, most notably the teachers, inspectors and organisers, is examined. A detailed analysis of the challenges that beset the implementation of the *Revised Programme* ensues. The growing influence of the Irish language revival movement in the period and its impact on schools is also examined, focusing primarily on the *Bilingual Programme* introduced in 1904.

3.2 Progress of the *Revised Programme*

3.2.1 *Implementation of Subjects*

Evidence from Inspectors' Reports

The *Revised Programme of Instruction* was introduced into schools in September 1900. The core established subjects of reading, writing, spelling and arithmetic were implemented in all schools.[2] Table 3.1 outlines the number of schools teaching the core and additional subjects introduced by the *Revised Programme*, both prior to and following their official introduction. It is important to remember the conditions of schools in Ireland at this time whereby 64 per cent of the 8,700 schools were one-teacher schools, attendance rates rested at approximately 60 per cent, in excess of half of the 12,000 teachers had no formal training and the average pupil-teacher ratio rested at in excess of 60:1. As is evident, great progress was recorded in each subject area on an incremental basis from 1900 until 1904. Particularly high levels of implementation are evident in drawing and object lessons, subjects that did not require high levels of additional resources in the form of facilities or materials. Vocal music and needlework were also implemented widely, undertaken in approximately three-quarters of all schools. The introduction of Kindergarten, elementary science and cookery languished behind, arguably due to the necessity of specialist equipment, facilities and training for their implementation. The reduced number of schools implementing Kindergarten and cookery after 1904 can be explained due to programme revisions introduced in that year, making manual instruction optional beyond infant classes and restricting the teaching of cookery to fifth and sixth class pupils. Despite the large increase in ordinary school subjects, the additional subjects also experienced improved popularity, most notably a large increase in the number of schools teaching the Irish language.

Table 3.1 Number of Schools in which Core and Additional Subjects were Undertaken in the Primary Schools from 1899 to 1904

Core Subjects	1899	1900	1901	1902	1903	1904
Vocal Music	1,475	3,963	6,032	6,439	6,550	6,683
Drawing	2,146	5,942	8,349	8,532	8,601	8,614
Kindergarten*	448	1,293	1,954	2,656	2,165	2,138
Cookery	125	263	409	631	727	362
Object Lessons	–	3,096	7,673	8,189	8,281	8,392
Elementary Science	–		1,745	2,623	2,499	2,217
Needlework	**	***1,700	5,851	5,985	6,140	6,207

*　No specific mention is made of manual instruction within the table and it is assumed the statistics for that subject are subsumed within those for Kindergarten, as it was common practice within the inspectors' reports to group both subjects.
**　No Return for needlework; 172,337 pupils were examined.
***　Revised Programme of needlework.

Additional Subjects	1899	1900	1901	1902	1903	1904
Irish	105	88	1,198	1,586	2,018	1,983
French	89	24	188	179	193	205
Latin	28	6	74	81	109	101
Instrumental Music	180	31	324	333	358	306

Source: Commissioners of National Education in Ireland [CNEI] (1905). *71st Report … for 1904*, p. 53.

These statistics paint a very positive image of implementation in the early years of the programme's introduction. However, these numbers do not elaborate on the range or depth of implementation of the various subject areas. Moreover, although these subjects were offered or taught in schools, it does not necessarily mean they were taught in line with the *Revised Programme*'s recommendations. An analysis of the inspectors' reports and educational debate at the time provides an insight into actual implementation. While commentators were generally praising of the overall thrust of introducing the new subjects and the philosophy of the *Revised Programme*, many noted difficulties in implementation.

Reading was generally regarded to have improved under the new system,[3] especially by virtue of the introduction of story readers as opposed to class textbooks. Instruction in writing and composition was also generally regarded to have ameliorated following 1900.[4] Fears were expressed from 1900 that the standard in arithmetic had fallen following the introduction of the *Revised Programme*, causing much disquiet among inspectors.[5] The work in physical drill was seen to be of a high quality and was introduced quite widely in schools.[6] Needlework was not seen to have unduly suffered due to the reduced time allowance.[7] Drawing was popular from the outset, yet inspectors noted the tendency to focus on the product as opposed to the process of drawing.[8] Singing became a popular subject in schools and was largely considered to be well taught.[9] There was a gradual improvement in the teaching of object lessons and elementary science, which were criticised as being poorly taught in the early days of implementation.[10] The teaching of history and geography through readers was not perceived to be successful by the majority of inspectors.[11] Cookery and laundry increased in popularity, yet were largely confined to Model and convent schools that had the necessary facilities to implement the subjects successfully.[12]

Kindergarten proved popular in most schools, yet many inspectors noted it was taught more as a subject than used as an approach in infant classes.[13] Manual instruction, the chief focus of the CMPI, enjoyed the least popularity of all the subjects. Inspectors' reports were almost unanimous in asserting the low uptake of the programme's provisions and the poor work accomplished where it was attempted.[14] There had been persistent calls from teachers for its abolition in senior classes and repeated complaints about the waste of time bending sticks and wire in school entailed, viewed as unbecoming to the educational content of the primary school.[15] The envisaged woodwork in senior classes did not materialise in most schools owing to the absence of facilities and the expense of equipment.

Many inspectors noted the general improvement in the teaching and learning process under the *Revised Programme*.[16] As Mr M'Elwaine, Senior Inspector, asserted in 1914:

> Speaking broadly, education in our schools is on a higher plane than in the old days. The pupils are brighter, more intelligent, and, I believe, more resourceful. There is less cramming and more teaching.[17]

This was particularly emphasised in relation to the brighter and more pleasant environment the school had become owing to the variety of subjects studied.[18] However, the suggestions within the programme for the grouping of classes and other policies relating to school organisation were not undertaken widely. While there was some grouping in subjects such as drawing and singing, it did not transfer to the other areas, especially the core traditional subjects.[19] A circular was issued to inspectors in 1907 stating 'it would appear that the intentions of the Commissioners as regards the methods of teaching the courses of instruction in national schools are not yet fully comprehended.'[20] It reminded inspectors of the intention to allow integration between and within various subjects, while outlining the more salient features to be stressed in the various subjects of the programme. Hyland conducted an analysis of the senior inspectors' reports from 1902–1904 and in each year, the majority of schools were reported to be improving, while none was registered as having disimproved.[21]

Evidence from the Dale Report

Following three years of implementation, an English inspector, Mr F.H. Dale, was commissioned to conduct an evaluation of the Irish school system. His terms of reference were 'to enquire and report how typical Irish Elementary day schools compare with similarly circumstanced Public Elementary Schools in England as regards premises, equipment, staffing, and instruction; and to what causes differences in economy and efficiency appear to be chiefly due.'[22] He visited eighty-seven schools and issued his report in 1904.

Dale found that the standard of efficiency was lower in Ireland due to public apathy regarding education and the poor provision of materials and equipment. He regarded the greatest innovation to have occurred in the new subjects introduced, while the subjects with the strongest tradition and most familiarity were the slowest to change. He showed his understanding of the complexity of introducing educational change when he stated that 'the habits and traditions of a system which has remained practically unchanged for nearly thirty years are not easily abandoned.'[23] The Dale Report also asserted that the methods of instruction in the schools in 1904 had altered little from those utilised in the payment-by-results era, with a focus remaining on mechanical accuracy as opposed to practical and age-appropriate instruction. Despite the provisions in the *Revised Programme*, Dale found the education of pupils in infant classes to be one of the weakest points of the system.

Dale identified four main factors that reduced the quality of work in schools, namely the multiplication of small schools, the poor attendance rates, the lack of local interest in education and the uneven distribution of teachers across schools. However, the overall thrust of the report was that while instruction in Irish schools compared favourably with English schools, it was inferior in relation to its method and aim. Dale attributed this to the residual effects of the payment-by-results system and called for the elimination of manual and practical instruction in schools and guidance for teachers in the methods of teaching infants and in arithmetic, history and geography. To support teachers and managers in the implementation of the new subjects and methods, Dale recommended the production of a specimen programme for various categories of schools in each subject area.

Evidence from the Dill Inquiry

The Dill Inquiry (1913) was instituted to enquire into the inspection system following 1900. It heard evidence from a vast array of inspectors, managers and teachers, and also provided an insight into the progress of the various subject areas following 1900. Mr Hynes, retired Chief Inspector, concluded that education after 1900 was more beneficial to pupils than under the results system as it was more practical for their lives.[24] The subjects most commonly mentioned as having deteriorated were arithmetic, spellings and geography.[25] Mr Dilworth, Secretary to the Board of National Education, commented on the improvement in schools since 1900, paying particular attention to the alertness of the pupils, the brightness of the classrooms, the proficiency in mental arithmetic and the improved results attained in new subjects such as singing, drawing, cookery, Kindergarten, elementary science and physical drill.[26] Mr Bonaparte Wyse, an inspector and personal Secretary to Dr Starkie, was emphatic that pupils were much better educated since 1900 in all subjects and acknowledged that the depth of knowledge in certain subjects such as grammar and geography might not be as great.[27] In his evidence to the Dill Inquiry, Mr Dale noted that despite evidence of mechanical teaching still in operation, teachers and inspectors were welcoming of the new system and even by 1903, it was percolating well throughout the country.[28]

Collectively, the evidence from the inspection reports, the Dale Report, the Dill Inquiry and other contemporary commentators point in the main to an improved education for children after 1900. This relates to a better atmosphere for learning, a greater variety of subjects being studied and improved methods for the teaching of reading and writing. The evidence also points to a deterioration in the standards of some of the traditional subjects, most notably arithmetic, grammar and geography. However, many commented that this disimprovement related to mechanical accuracy and memorisation, rather than in understanding and interest as advocated by the *Revised Programme*. It is apparent that great efforts were made to introduce the range of new subjects prescribed in 1900, while those requiring least teacher expertise or expensive facilities and equipment enjoyed most widespread implementation. Manual instruction enjoyed least popularity among parents, teachers and inspectors, and was largely perceived to be unsuited to primary schools. It is arguable that the aims of this subject were misunderstood by many, focusing on the practical outcomes rather than the mental and educational processes involved. While the extent of implementation may have languished behind expectation, it is evident that the new subjects and methods permeated the system to some extent.

Indeed, the greatest progress in implementing the provisions of the *Revised Programme* were achieved in the newly introduced subjects, highlighting the difficulty of effecting educational change in traditional and well-established subjects and practices.

3.2.2 *Work of the Teachers*

The annual report of the Commissioners for 1900 applauded the efforts of the teachers and managers in introducing the *Revised Programme*, with the overwhelming majority of schools having made some attempt at introducing elements of the programme by 1901. Inspectors were almost universal in their praise for the efforts of teachers in embracing the programme in the early years of implementation.[29] Despite this general praise for the zealous work of teachers, a minority of inspectors lamented the slow progress of adaptation, especially among older teachers.[30]

The *Revised Programme* allowed managers and teachers to devise programmes of instruction congruent with the individual needs of their schools and locality for approval by the Board. This gave considerable freedom to teachers and managers to prioritise the new subjects to be introduced and to frame the programme to local needs. The freedom and flexibility of school organisation and planning was never fully utilised by teachers and managers, who invariably adopted the specimen programmes of the National Board.[31] This process of programme adaptation was a role for which there was little support and for which teachers and managers had little experience or knowledge of after the period of payment by results.

Table 3.2 elucidates the high percentage of teachers who attended training in the new subjects, largely provided by the subject organisers appointed. In the first five years of implementing the *Revised Programme*, in excess of 50 per cent of teachers had attended a course in singing, while approximately 40 per cent had received training in needlework, manual instruction and elementary science. However, it must be borne in mind that the majority of these courses were of short duration and many of the teachers attending did not have the benefit of formal training in the wider principles or theories of education.

Table 3.2 Courses attended by Teachers between 1900 and 1904

Subject	No. of Teachers
Singing	6,400
Needlework	4,500
Cookery and Laundry	3,548
Manual Instruction – Part 1	5,260
Manual Instruction – Part 2	2,200
Elementary Science – Part 1	4,100
Elementary Science – Part 2	550

Source: CNEI (1905). *71st Report ... for 1904*, pp. 3–7.

Some teachers complained that the courses were insufficient to prepare teachers for introducing the syllabus and that they did not necessarily lead to the introduction of the new subjects.[32] Moreover, the onus was placed on teachers to travel at their own expense to attend the courses of organisers and subsequently to attempt implementation, often in the absence of the necessary materials and equipment.

Relations between teachers and inspectors deteriorated after the introduction of the *Revised Programme*, owing to the new grading and promotion system, leaving the remuneration prospects of teachers entirely in the hands of inspectors. From 1909, relations between the INTO and the Resident Commissioner declined further over the deputation involving Miss Mahon and the ensuing controversy.[33] The Dill Inquiry (1913) heard evidence from inspectors who felt their status was diminished by the introduction of the *Revised Programme* and who were not convinced of the educational value of the changes. The inquiry found in favour of teachers and noted deficiencies in the organisation of the Inspectorate, the slow rate of promotion and the appeals procedure, making nineteen recommendations to ameliorate the situation.[34]

3.2.3 Work of Inspectors

A set of *Revised Instructions to Inspectors* was issued in 1901 and all inspectors were urged to study them carefully as:

> The method of inspection is likely at all times to influence materially the course of instruction, and it should therefore be so modelled as to give a proper consistent direction to the teaching.[35]

However, inspectors received little advice or training on how to inspect or support the implementation of the new subjects. In 1901–1902, inspectors attended courses in specific subjects but never received general training in the principles of the *Revised Programme*. Between 1900 and 1912, *Revised Instructions to Inspectors* were re-issued regularly and twenty-six circulars on methods of inspection were issued to inspectors.[36] These reiterated the need to test the quality as opposed to the quantity of learning, to focus on the use of heuristic methods, to make a careful consideration where new subjects were not introduced, to allow credit for all progress made, to remember that the new programme was the maximum requirement, to focus on the instruction of infants and to allow for alterations to the needs of individual localities. Moreover, attention was drawn to the emphasis on class as opposed to individual inspection, focusing on how the child was taught as much as the content retained. The Instructions stressed that the overall implementation of the *Revised Programme* would not be a reality in many schools for a long time due to training, infrastructural and financial constraints and that in the interim, 'quality not quantity is the criterion of efficiency.'[37] However, many teachers complained that inspectors' methods did not change in line with the spirit of the *Revised Programme* and that 'the inspection made by certain inspectors is more on the mental storage than mental training.'[38]

3.2.4 Appointment of Organisers

To facilitate implementation of the *Revised Programme*, a number of organisers and assistants were appointed, many of them experts in their respective fields, to assist teachers to understand the new subjects and accompanying methodologies. Courses were provided centrally and these were sometimes followed by visits to schools to support practical implementation. As was stated in the annual report of the Commissioners of National Education in 1904:

> The organisers' classes were the means of perfecting the teachers' knowledge, especially in the case of needlework and singing; while the visits which the organisers paid to school were the means of helping the teachers over the difficulties encountered in the beginning subjects, with the teaching of which they were not familiar.[39]

Mr Heller, a science demonstrator under the London School Board and one of the expert witnesses at the CMPI, was appointed as Head Organiser of Science Instruction by the Commissioners of National Education in Ireland. Heller, and his five assistants, organised six-week courses for teachers in the various branches of science. In rural areas, peripatetic teachers were appointed to provide evening and weekend classes and to visit schools, providing model lessons and practical advice.

Mr Bevis, an influential witness at the CMPI, became the Head Organiser of Hand and Eye Training and Drawing. He started providing courses, with the assistance of four organisers, with nearly 5,000 teachers undertaking training in 1900.[40] The former Examiner in Music to the Board of National Education, Mr Goodman, became the Organiser in Vocal Music, training approximately 300 teachers every six weeks with the help of five assistants.[41]

Miss Prendergast, former Directress of Needlework, aided by five assistants, set about providing courses in needlework and visits to schools to support implementation of the subject. Miss FitzGerald, with the help of eleven assistants, provided training for teachers in cookery and laundry. This was the largest team of organisers as these subjects started from a very low base. A Kindergarten Advisor, Miss Edith O'Farrell, was appointed in 1904 and by 1912, she had six assistants who visited schools and provided courses in Kindergarten throughout the country. From 1908, the Commissioners of National Education employed six organisers to assist with the implementation of Irish by giving Saturday classes, visiting schools and providing model lessons.[42]

By 1912, there were thirty-five organisers employed. In general, the Commissioners were happy with the progress made and the influence of the organisers.[43] However, concerns were raised in the early days of implementation that teachers in many inspection districts were endeavouring to implement the new subjects before they had the opportunity to receive training from the organisers, who were limited in number and were responsible for imparting instruction to 12,000 teachers in 9,000 schools in a context of difficult travel and communication conditions.[44] In addition, there was little support for teachers in the implementation of the existing core subjects, many of which had changed quite considerably in relation to content and methodology.

3.3 Challenges to the Implementation of the *Revised Programme*

A number of issues hindered implementation of the vision of the *Revised Programme* in practice, most notably teacher training, insufficient funding, the physical condition of schools, poor attendance rates and the lack of popular support for the reforms.

3.3.1 *Teacher Training*

As already documented, just over half of teachers in 1900 were trained owing to difficulties in resolving the issue of denominational teacher training colleges. Moreover, these teachers were trained under a system of payment by results, incorporating a narrow programme and a didactic method of teaching. In 1900, the role of the teacher was transformed from being a transmitter of knowledge to a facilitator of learning in classrooms. The overwhelming difference, in the form of an array of additional subjects, accentuated by a shift in methodology, became an obstacle to the successful implementation of the programme. While modifications introduced in 1898 in the training colleges were congruent with the recommendations of the CMPI, they did not go far enough to support the changes as introduced in the *Revised Programme*. Minor revisions in the training colleges in 1901 and 1902 did not alter the programme fundamentally in this regard and the philosophy or methodologies of the *Revised Programme* were not included in the theory of method module. However, the colleges invested heavily in suitable apparatus and staff to introduce the new subjects, despite cuts in their budgets at this time. Thus, while all subjects that a student would eventually teach were covered, it afforded little time for depth of study. This was noted in the General Report on the Training Colleges in 1909:

> The course of study is now too extended (especially for women), hence the students are overburdened for mere examination purposes, leading to some extent to neglect of real training, owing to want of time for thought or for assimilation of what has been learned.[45]

Great strides were made in the period after 1900 to ensure all teachers attended training colleges, so that by 1919, 80 per cent of teachers were formally trained.[46] While the work of the various organisers impacted positively on upskilling teachers in the new subject areas, the short duration of courses, the limited visits to schools to support teachers and the lack of necessary equipment impacted negatively on implementation.

3.3.2 Funding for the Revised Programme

Treasury funding was never as generous as was hoped owing to periods of economic recession in England, particularly surrounding the Boer War in 1900, which coincided with the introduction of the *Revised Programme*. The Treasury became reluctant to increase spending on education in Ireland, having accepted the programme proposals in 1900 as long as they cost nothing in addition to the existing grant, and insisted that expenses for equipment and materials would have to be defrayed locally as opposed to centrally.[47] Owing to public apathy towards education, the poor socio-economic circumstances of the majority of the people and the lack of appreciation of subjects of a practical character, such support was not readily forthcoming. A circular from the National Board in 1901 placed the onus on the manager and locality to defray the cost of any necessary equipment, save in exceptional circumstances where some grants would be forthcoming.[48] Dr Starkie had an acrimonious relationship with school managers and there was little desire among them to fund the provisions requested by the Resident Commissioner and the National Board. Dr Starkie's relationship with Chief Secretary Birrell was also strained and this limited the support of this key official for the programme of reform desired in Irish education.[49] Thus, the Board found itself caught between the Treasury, managers and other funding agencies and it became increasingly difficult to obtain funding from any source.

Table 3.3 outlines the Treasury grant to Irish education in the first years of the implementation of the *Revised Programme*. Between 1901 and 1904, funding remained stable or reduced slightly, when additional finance was crucial for the provision of training and equipment to introduce the new subjects.

Table 3.3 Treasury Grant for National Education in Ireland 1900–1906

Year	Grant (£)
1900–1901	1,387,503
1901–1902	1,305,771
1902–1903	1,333,748
1903–1904	1,376,501
1904–1905	1,393,625
1905–1906	1,391,721

Source: *Reports of the CNEI 1900–1906*, figures taken from the annual financial statements.

3.3.3 *The Physical Condition of Schools*

In 1904, 60 per cent of schools were one-teacher schools and in such a context, the conditions were not favourable to the introduction of subjects of a more practical nature. Dr Starkie attacked school managers publicly for the poor material condition of schools and isolated them from a process for which their support was essential. In 1903, the National Board issued a circular to all managers pointing out such deficiencies and urging immediate alleviation of the problem:

> The Commissioners of National Education wish to direct the earnest and immediate attention of Managers generally to the extremely unsatisfactory condition of many of the National Schoolhouses in regard to repair and cleanliness, and particularly to the disgraceful state of the out-offices, which in numerous instances have been reported to be in such a state of filth as to constitute a grave menace to the health of the children attending the schools in question. Broken and dilapidated doors and windows, damaged roofs, dirty walls, and damp floors are not calculated to make the schools attractive to the children.[50]

A Committee was established in 1902 to investigate the cost of providing school accommodation in the Irish context and to ascertain any required modifications to keep in line with modern educational requirements. It found many deficiencies in the Irish system, most notably the absence of individual rooms for each class, an inadequate number of desks and chairs for each child in attendance and a low allocation of space per child in classrooms.[51]

The report of Mr Dale further evidenced the poor material condition of schools in 1904. He witnessed many schools that were overcrowded, lacking playgrounds and often in poor sanitary condition. In the urban situation, he found great overcrowding in many classrooms, some catering for up to 300 pupils, which was inherently incompatible with the introduction of many of the subjects of the *Revised Programme*. Dale also noted the equipment available in many schools to be substandard, including basic requisites such as a desk and chair for each pupil. He found the books of pupils in Ireland to be of inferior quality, while classroom equipment was often frugal and dilapidated. While country schools were found to be less crowded and were serviced with better play facilities, Dale found them to be often dirty and unsanitary. He reported little evidence of the existence of school libraries and museums as advocated by the *Revised Programme*, while the stark bareness of the majority of classrooms did nothing to nurture the educational process.[52]

3.3.4 School Attendance

Attendance continued to be sporadic, with particularly low attendance rates in autumn and spring. Attendance dropped off significantly in senior classes as pupils completed their formal education early, many after fourth class.[53] In 1901, more than 30 per cent of pupils were in attendance for less than 100 days.[54] Dale cited that the average attendance in Ireland was 65 per cent as opposed to nearly 84 per cent in England.[55] He asserted that with absenteeism at this rate, progress was impossible and children were retained in lower grades, unsuited to their age. Moreover, attendance rates disimproved further after 1900, as the mandatory 100 days' attendance that had previously been required to present for examinations was abolished. This figure improved little in the years after, with attendance languishing at just above 66 per cent in 1908.[56]

3.3.5 Lack of Popular Support for the Programme

The alienation of the key stakeholders in the education system, most notably parents, teachers and managers, did little to enamour them to the task of implementing a programme they did not identify with and had little participation in devising. Many inspectors recorded dissatisfaction among parents with the provisions of the *Revised Programme*, who favoured a more literary education. Thus, some teachers were found to be curtailing implementation in line with parental wishes for a focus on literacy and numeracy in preparation for respectable professions and emigration.[57] The Board did little by way of information sharing or public relations to display the positive and advantageous elements of the new system so that parents would better support its provisions by encouraging their children to attend or by providing financial support to schools. The Catholic Church was not a firm proponent of child-centred education, which conflicted with its underlying approval for didactic and content-centred programmes.

Public apathy regarding education was also cited by Dale as a major disadvantage in the Irish context, leading to the lack of financial support and irregular attendance. This neglect in public interest stretched from parents to local manufacturers, tradesmen and landowners, who had little interest in or impact on the organisation of the programme followed in schools.

Thus, a number of impediments hampered the successful implementation of the *Revised Programme* of 1900. The programme was a radical departure from its predecessor in terms of content and methodology and instead of taking an evolutionary approach, the revolution demanded for its introduction was not forthcoming. The inadequate arrangements within the training colleges led to the output of teachers who were not equipped to deliver the provisions of the *Revised Programme*. Adequate financing for the professional development of teachers, the supply of the requisite equipment and materials and the provision of facilities never materialised from the Treasury or local funds. The key educational stakeholders felt alienated and had little ownership of the reforms. Parents were ill informed about the underlying philosophies and rationale for the introduction of practical subjects and still favoured the literary focus of schooling. The absence of wider public interest in and support for education further militated against implementation.

3.4 Programme Revisions 1904

Following the introduction of the *Revised Programme* in 1900, a process of revision began in 1903 through consultation with teacher representative groups and senior inspectors. This was significantly advanced by the commissioning of the Dale Report. In June 1903, Chief Inspectors Downing and Purser were asked for a statement of their views regarding the *Revised Programme* in relation to breaking the programme up into seven standards in large schools, the best arrangement for combining standards in small schools and the modification of the programme so as to suit different types of schools.[58] In addition, subject organisers were invited to a conference with teacher representatives. The recommendations made by teachers, inspectors, Mr Dale and others collectively led to a number of revisions of the *Revised Programme* being implemented from 1904.

The programme revisions involved the discontinuance of manual instruction in senior classes.[59] The course in arithmetic was revised owing to complaints that standards had disimproved and now included more concrete work and reasoning. The syllabus in cookery was revised and now applied only to fifth and sixth classes, while geography was restored to its former status as a subject. A particular emphasis was placed on Kindergarten and frequent changes of occupation were recommended with time allowances for rest and play in infant classes. Temperance was introduced as a subject from 1906 for moral and material reasons, while a programme in nature study was introduced in 1907. History was afforded the status of a separate subject in 1908, yet owing to the difficulty in agreeing upon a textbook amenable to all traditions on the island, no specific programme was provided. Rural science and gardening were taught as optional subjects from 1911.[60] However, the underlying philosophy of the *Revised Programme* remained unchanged, still based on a heuristic and discovery-learning ideal and allowing a wide degree of freedom to teachers.

These revisions were significant considering the aim and contents of the *Revised Programme*. The programme had been based on the recommendation of a comprehensive and unanimous report by the CMPI. The main thrust of the report was the inclusion of subjects of a more practical character in schools and manual instruction formed the core of the set of subjects introduced. The removal of manual instruction from the programme beyond infant classes just four years after its introduction was an acceptance that it was not being successfully implemented. The subject had failed to enjoy widespread popularity with parents, managers, teachers or inspectors. It is arguable that a modification of the programme and an earnest attempt to provide the necessary equipment, training and resources could have enabled the continuation of the subject in an altered format but the desire for its inclusion had dissipated at this point. As already detailed, many of the impracticalities of the programme that were removed in 1904 had been highlighted by teachers and the Inspectorate and could have been addressed prior to the implementation of the programme.

A set of *Notes for Teachers* was issued in April 1904. These outlined the new subject areas and provided further direction for the grouping of pupils in various sized schools – schools with three or more teachers, schools with two teachers, schools with one teacher and infant schools. These programmes reiterated that the programme was to be implemented tentatively, advising managers and teachers of the desirability of devising syllabi suited to the needs of individual school contexts. Their aim was not to prescribe a fixed programme but to provide 'examples of school organisation which the managers are at liberty to adopt or modify according as the circumstances of their schools may render necessary.'[61] While the provision of these *Notes* in 1904 was a positive step, their absence for the first four years of implementation, arguably the most critical period, created a vacuum of supports for teachers endeavouring to introduce the new subjects. The revisions in 1904 went a long way to assuage the demands of teachers in their complaints about the impracticalities relating to the *Revised Programme*.

3.5 The Position of the Irish language

The school programme in operation since 1831 had neglected the distinctively Irish aspects of children's culture and promoted the cultural assimilation of Ireland as an integral element of Great Britain.[62] Some concessions for the Irish language were granted towards the end of the nineteenth century. From 1879, Irish could be taught as an extra subject from second class upwards, but this was not undertaken with any vigour, being taught in only eighty-three schools in 1898.[63] From 1883, Irish could be used as an aid to the elucidation of English in Gaeltacht areas. With the introduction of the *Revised Programme* in 1900, Irish could be taught as an extra subject to all classes or during school hours, so long as it did not interfere with other subjects.[64] The Gaelic League was at pains to elucidate that the teaching of Irish during the school day to pupils was not contravening the rules of the National Board and worked earnestly to ensure that schools used this concession by distributing specimen programmes and other aids to the teaching of Irish.[65] Supported by the Gaelic League, the number of schools teaching Irish as an extra subject grew exponentially after 1900 (see table 3.4).

The Gaelic League lobbied the National Board and campaigned publicly during the drafting of the *Revised Programme* for the inclusion of Irish from third class upwards, where Irish was the child's vernacular. However, there were many opponents of the Irish language among the Commissioners of National Education and the Board refused to accede to the League's demands. This led to a public campaign, supported by the Catholic hierarchy, John Redmond of the Irish Parliamentary Party and prominent figures such as W.B. Yeats and Lady Gregory. In addition, Chief Secretaries Balfour and Wyndham, Dr Starkie, Sir Patrick Keenan and Archbishop Walsh expressed their support for a bilingual programme.[66] The support of such powerful and representative figures was pivotal in the campaign for the introduction of the *Bilingual Programme* in 1904.

3.5.1 The Bilingual Programme (1904)

Persistent calls and the long campaign by the Gaelic League came to fruition with the introduction of the *Bilingual Programme* in 1904. The *Bilingual Programme* was sanctioned in schools where the majority of children were from Irish-speaking backgrounds and where there was a teacher competent to teach the Irish language. Instruction focused primarily on the development of literacy in Irish and English, while all other subjects were taught bilingually.[67] The Board provided a specimen programme for schools, which could submit alternatives for approval. It was mainly left to teachers to develop bilingual methods and regional associations of bilingual teachers were established to collect technical terms, protect bilingual teachers' interests and to share information in relation to textbooks, materials and resources. This led to the creation of an All Ireland Bilingual Society (Cumann Dhá Theangach na hÉireann) in 1909.

The growth of the teaching of Irish is evident in table 3.4, which shows the increase in the number of schools teaching Irish as an extra subject and operating the *Bilingual Programme* between 1900 and 1921.

Table 3.4 Number of Schools and Fees Paid for Teaching Irish as an Extra Subject and within the Bilingual Programme 1900–1921

Year	Teaching Irish as Extra Subject	Teaching *Bilingual Programme*	Extra Subject Fees	Bilingual Fees	Total Fees
1900–1901	109	–	£955	–	£955
1910–1911	1,448	172	£9,164	£2,903	£12,009
1920–1921	1,560	237	£16,265	£6,224	£27,445

Source: *Statistics relative to the Position of Irish in the National Schools (prior to 1922)*. National Archives, Box 367, File 17511.

In Gaeltacht districts, there was general support for the *Bilingual Programme* from teachers, parents and managers. However, there was some resistance from parents, particularly in districts on the outskirts of the Gaeltacht, who withdrew their children and sent them to non-bilingual schools or who refused to buy Irish books or encourage the practice of Irish in the home.[68] Mr Mangan, Examiner and Inspector of Irish, recorded the rate of progress in the teaching of Irish as disappointing in 1909 for a number of reasons, including the poor methods of teaching employed, the lack of earnestness and knowledge on the part of teachers, the distaste on the part of pupils for the language, the lack of textbooks and the lack of co-operation from parents.[69]

There was a shortage of fluent, qualified teachers to undertake teaching roles in the bilingual schools. In addition, fluency in the Irish language and general teacher training did not mean competency to teach bilingually, which required specific methodologies and resources.[70] Irish was introduced as an optional subject in the training colleges in 1897 but did not prove popular, with only fifty-seven of the 700 students between 1897 and 1900 presenting for the examination.[71] Despite Gaelic League pressure, Irish was never elevated beyond the status of an optional subject in the training colleges prior to 1922. From 1906, a certificate in Irish was needed for a permanent appointment in a bilingual school and schools were prevented from following the *Bilingual Programme* unless there was a teacher present who was qualified and competent in Irish.

The growth of Irish language teaching in the period 1900 to 1922 reflected the increasing power and prominence of the cultural revival movement, most particularly the Gaelic League. Following seventy years of resistance, progress was made in these two decades in the attainment of concessions from the National Board for the teaching of Irish in national schools and the training of teachers for this purpose. However, by 1922, of the 12,000 teachers, only 9 per cent had the Bilingual Certificate, 24 per cent had the Ordinary Certificate while 8 per cent had a Temporary Certificate to teach Irish.[72] This was a significant achievement but did not amount to a critical mass that was capable of undertaking the ambitious plans of the Free State government regarding the inclusion of Irish in the programme following independence.

3.6 Summary and Conclusion

The period 1898 to 1922 was an era of reform and innovation regarding the programme of primary schools. The child-centred concept as portrayed within the *Revised Programme* (1900) was at variance with the conceptualisation of children in earlier programmes. The programme was progressive and enlightened in its philosophy and sought to redress the imbalance in favour of literary subjects within primary education. In fact, the language and content of the *Revised Programme* is re-echoed in many later curricula in Ireland, including the *Primary School Curriculum* (1971) (see chapters 7–9) and in the *Primary School Curriculum* (1999). It was this progressive nature, certainly more revolutionary than evolutionary in its approach, that proved to be one of the major challenges to its implementation in the contemporary context.

The *Revised Programme* fell short of the educational revolution it had aspired to invoke. However, much was achieved in a short period of time and it was perhaps the ambitious expectations that led to this feeling of failure. The report of the CMPI was based on a comprehensive study of the national and international context of best policy and practice and sought the advice and input of eminent educationalists and experts. The diligent work of the Commission drew upon the latest innovations in relation to education and aspired to provide the best education for the needs of all children.

The *Revised Programme* went further and faster than proposed by the CMPI. Important elements of the *Revised Programme* included highlighting the importance of infant education, the introduction of a greater variety of subjects, a reduced emphasis on individual examinations and an increased focus on heuristic methodologies. A *Bilingual Programme* was introduced in 1904 to cater better for pupils whose vernacular was Irish. The *Revised Programme* was innovative in that it allowed flexibility to managers and teachers to align the programme as appropriate with the needs of individual schools and localities. It broke the curriculum mould of schools that had been in operation for thirty years and breathed new life into the system in the form of a broad and varied programme with enlightened methodologies. The evidence points to the fact that the majority of teachers provided a better quality of education under the new system and that although there was some loss in mechanical accuracy, it was compensated for by improved understanding, greater enjoyment of schooling and improved powers of expression. The programme remained wide and teaching methods improved, emanating from a child-centred perspective. Its provisions were in line with European educational thinking, placing an emphasis on scientific, practical and literary education in line with the report of the CMPI.

One of the major failures of the *Revised Programme* was the insufficient attention it paid to the reality of implementation. The school programme exists within the wider political, social, religious, economic, cultural and educational milieu and any proposed changes will be tempered by these wider influences. Programme development must be viewed as an evolutionary process, where gradual change and modernisation prove more steadfast than revolutionary transformations. In short, it was the right programme but not for the societal and educational context of Ireland in 1900. Despite the annual reports of the Commissioners highlighting the many challenges facing the education system such as low attendance rates, the prevalence of small schools, the material condition of the national schools, the lack of basic equipment, the absence of local support and financial assistance for education and the low rate of teacher training, the *Revised Programme* neglected to address these fundamental issues in tandem with the reform of the programme.

Teachers, many of whom were inadequately trained, did not have the confidence, initiative or indeed ability to adapt and implement the programme in the absence of comprehensive supports. Training in the new subjects and methodologies was a prerequisite for success and efforts were required to ensure that this training was provided as soon as possible following the introduction of the programme. As the programme stipulated the maximum of requirements, many teachers felt in awe and unable to enact such radical changes within the context of their daily reality. There was no gradual roll out as proposed by the CMPI from urban to rural areas. There was little ownership of the change on the ground among parents, teachers and managers and many remained dubious about the educational value of the reform. Financial constrictions from the Treasury also marred the introduction of the *Revised Programme*. The supports put in place, in the form of specimen programmes, organisers, small grants for equipment and *Notes for Teachers* were not adequate to invoke such an educational revolution. The small number of organisers, approximately one per 400 teachers, was insufficient to disseminate the content and methodologies of the new subjects, in a context where travel was difficult and many teachers were untrained. In addition, no support was provided in the traditional subjects, whose content and methodologies had also changed in 1900. Moreover, the specimen programmes were not issued until 1904, four years after the introduction of the *Revised Programme*.

The radical nature of the change, the poor relations between the key policy developers and the infrastructural issues in the school system militated against the successful implementation of the *Revised Programme*. In the devising of a programme, it is advisable that stakeholders who are responsible for implementing, resourcing and inspecting the programme play an integral role in its formulation and feel an ownership and understanding of the need for change. Such characteristics were not a feature of the *Revised Programme*. It was an error not to keep such key personnel informed and instilled with a sense of ownership of the changes, as they were the means to translate the theory of the programme into a practical reality. The personality of Dr Starkie as Resident Commissioner also impacted upon programme development and implementation in this period. His zealous appetite for reform led to the alienation of many of the key personnel such as teachers, managers and inspectors, whose support and ownership were pivotal to reform, both during the devising stage and, subsequently, during its implementation. Supports need to be in place before the introduction of a new programme to ensure that success can be achieved. It is also advisable that implementation be incremental, aided by supports, and the introduction of new facets spread over a reasonable period of time for individual elements of the programme to be embedded successfully. In addition, it is not wise to introduce all changes at once, either all the programme changes or certainly not in tandem with administrative and inspection changes. The result in 1900 was that the whole system was placed in a state of flux where everything was new and unfamiliar.

In general, while conceptually well devised, the *Revised Programme* lacked a strategic implementation policy tempered to the societal and educational context of the day, and failed to provide an appropriate support infrastructure to ensure successful implementation. Despite the many shortcomings of the *Revised Programme*, these should not occlude its many positive attributes and the evidence points to an improved education for pupils after 1900, incorporating a wider array of subjects, improved methodologies and an increased focus on making schools more enjoyable and interesting. The process of implementing the *Revised Programme* ended in the early 1920s with the onset of independence and the devising of a new programme for schools.

Societal and Educational Context for Curriculum Provision 1922–1971

4.1 Introduction

This chapter examines the societal and educational context and milieu in which the curriculum changes introduced in 1922 were devised and implemented. First, it analyses key political, social, economic, cultural and religious developments in the period 1922 to 1971. The chapter then addresses the wider educational developments in the period, including a focus on school statistics, the introduction of the Primary Certificate Examination, the provision and management of school buildings and the challenge of providing suitable textbooks. The Irish language was a central element of the school curriculum in the period 1922–1971 and its position, role and impact in wider society is discussed. Owing to the pivotal role of teachers in the process of implementing the curriculum, a special focus is placed on their training and work. The role of the Inspectorate in the inspection and evaluation of schools is delineated. The dearth of educational research and information on the operation of the system is documented. Provision for children with special educational needs is outlined. The chapter concludes by analysing developments in the 1960s and their impact on subsequent curriculum reform.

4.2 Societal Context for Curriculum Development 1922–1971

4.2.1 Political Context

Following the general election in 1918, the First Dáil sat from 21 January 1919 until 10 May 1921. It is noteworthy that there was no Minister for Education in this First Dáil and that education policy was subsumed within Aireacht na Gaeilge (Ministry of Irish), highlighting the association between the education system and the revival of the Irish language and culture even before the advent of the Free State. The absence of a Department of Education until 1924 is significant considering the commitment to provide all children 'with the means and facilities requisite for their proper education and training as citizens of a free and Gaelic Ireland'[1] within the Democratic Programme issued by the First Dáil.

Following independence, the new government inherited the administrative structures and the vast majority of the personnel of the education system.[2] This acted as an inhibitor to a major transformation in the administration of Irish education and led to a continuity of administrative practices and procedures. In this context, it is perhaps unsurprising that there was no fundamental appraisal of the structural elements of the education system upon independence. From the outset, there were many calls for the inception of a Council of Education to act as an advisory body for the Minister and these continued throughout the period.[3] In May 1924, a memorandum was prepared in relation to establishing an Advisory Council 'for the purpose of advising the Department of Education on educational matters.'[4] However, its recommendations were not enacted. It became evident that politicians feared a comprehensive evaluation of the system as time progressed, especially regarding the data that might have been generated in relation to the progress of the Irish language revival. Akenson held that the Catholic Church and the state were united in this regard, as neither wanted a body of citizens sitting to examine, and perhaps criticise, its work.[5] This fear was still evident in the assertions of Bishop Gilmartin of Tuam in 1938 that such a Council would be a 'highly dangerous and objectionable experiment' as it 'might prescribe tests and courses to which the Church as representing Catholic parents and Christ would not agree.'[6]

Following the War of Independence, the Dáil, and subsequently the electorate, ratified the Anglo-Irish Treaty in 1922, which accepted the partition of Ireland under the Government of Ireland Act 1920. During this time, a Constitution was drafted and the Irish Free State came into being on 6 December 1922.[7] The Civil War followed between the pro- and anti-Treatyites, lasting until May 1923, when Cumann na nGaedheal (a pro-Treaty party) retained power.[8] It was against this state of societal flux that the first National Programme Conference on primary education, which will be examined in chapter 5, was operating between January 1921 and January 1922. Cumann na nGaedheal maintained power until 1932, a conservative government that attracted the support of those who wanted peace and stability in Ireland.[9] Eoin MacNeill, a Gaelic League enthusiast, followed by John Marcus O'Sullivan, held the position of Minister for Education up to 1932. Their favourable policies towards the Irish language were supported by the Secretary of the Department of Education, Mr J.J. O'Neill, and by the Minister for Finance, Ernest Blythe.[10]

Fianna Fáil was founded in May 1926 by Eamon de Valera and the anti-Treatyites. The Programme of Fianna Fáil was adopted at its first Ard-Fheis and contained strong commitments in relation to the restoration of the Irish language, especially through the school system.[11] De Valera and Fianna Fáil held power from 1932 until 1948. This was followed by a number of short-lived coalition and Fianna Fáil governments, while Fianna Fáil again assumed power between 1957 and 1973. The defeat of Fianna Fáil at the 1948 election was partially attributed to a bitter teacher strike in 1946, when many teachers and teacher sympathisers switched allegiance to Clann na Poblachta.[12] It is noteworthy that the language revival was an integral policy of all political parties, fearing opposition would lead to the accusation of being anti-nationalist. The continuity of power on the part of Fianna Fáil ensured a high level of consistency in education policy in the era, especially in the earlier period when Thomas Derrig was Minister for Education for sixteen years. Derrig was an active member of the Gaelic League and the policies followed throughout his tenure were largely conservative, focusing primarily on the curriculum, and within that, largely on the issue of the revival of the Irish language. Moreover, continuity was assured as between 1923 and 1968, just four men occupied the position of Secretary of the Department.[13] Peillon argued that the influence of senior civil servants in the Department, emanating largely from middle-class, urban homes and educated in a conservative way, impacted on the unadventurous nature of education policy in independent Ireland.[14] Furthermore, de Valera, a teacher by profession, was Taoiseach throughout a large proportion of this period and undoubtedly had a major influence on Ministers and Department officials. Similar to Derrig, he espoused a conservative view of the role of education, advocating a focus on the core essentials and on imparting large volumes of knowledge through didactic instruction:

> What I am afraid of is ... that teachers are thinking all the time of making subjects interesting and attractive, and that if they spend all their time at that sort of thing the mechanical routine which is necessary to go through a subject as a whole cannot be carried out. It is useless for anybody to think that good work can be done in a national school, or in any school without a good deal of hard mechanical routine work.[15]

Bunreacht na hÉireann, the Irish Constitution, was introduced in 1937. In relation to education, the Constitution was written based on Catholic social thinking, outlining the respective roles of the state, the family, the Catholic Church and the child. De Valera, as chief architect of the Constitution, was inherently loyal to the Catholic Church and was anxious to appease the hierarchy, consulting his personal friend, Rev. John Charles McQuaid, Archbishop of Dublin, on earlier drafts.[16] Three Articles of the Constitution are of particular importance for the education of children, namely Article 41 on the Family, Article 42 on Education and Article 44 on Religion.[17] The Constitution stressed the predominant rights of parents in relation to education and emphasised the subsidiary role of the state, a position that was endorsed by successive Ministers throughout this period. For example, in 1956, Minister Mulcahy stated that he did not see it as the role of the Minister to philosophise on education or to give a view on educational practices:

You have your teachers, your managers and your Churches and I regard the position as Minister in the Department of Education as a kind of dungaree man, the plumber who will make the satisfactory communications and streamline the forces and potentialities of educational workers and educational management in this country. He will take the knock out of the pipes and will link up everything.[18]

De Valera resigned as leader of Fianna Fáil in 1958 and was replaced by Seán Lemass. His dynamic leadership coincided with buoyant external trading conditions and many of the politicians in the 1960s at ministerial level were young, enthusiastic and empathised with the popular mood for educational reform.[19] By the 1960s, the sensitivity towards the Catholic Church in relation to educational reform had abated somewhat. Following decades of denying responsibility for policy formulation and asserting the integral role of the Catholic Church in education, a new Minister for Education, Dr Patrick Hillery, began to affirm his right in this regard.[20] There was also more open questioning of the Irish language revival methods. The boundaries of education had moved beyond the traditional wrangles regarding the Irish language and politicians began to interpret education reform in economic terms, seeking a return for both the individual and the nation.

The state retained strict control over the curriculum during the period 1922–1971 and J.J. O'Kelly, Minister for Education in the second Dáil, stated that teachers were 'servants of the nation' and that 'the nation that employs and pays them must have the right to specify the nature of that work which they are to do.'[21] As well as maintaining control of the curriculum, the Department also drew up the rules and regulations for primary schools. Furthermore, it sanctioned textbooks and monitored implementation of the curriculum through the Inspectorate. It also funded the denominational training colleges and maintained some control by examining the teaching practice of final year students. While government may have determined the curriculum centrally, the Catholic Church through its management and ownership of schools retained a large degree of control around its interpretation and the teachers appointed to implement it.

4.2.2 Social Context

In the decades following independence, the population of Ireland was predominantly rurally based, religious and conservative in nature. However, increased urbanisation was a feature of the period and by 1966, half of the population lived in towns and cities.[22] In 1926, approximately 93 per cent of the population was Catholic rising to 95 per cent by the 1960s.[23] Between 1922 and 1971, infant mortality reduced marginally and life expectancy increased for both men and women.[24] The participation of women in the workforce remained consistently low, owing to the high rate of unemployment and the perception that 'a mother's place was in the home', reinforced by de Valera's Constitution of 1937. There was a greater focus on tax reduction as opposed to increased social spending throughout the period. In such conditions, sectors such as health, housing and unemployment were often prioritised above improving or expanding educational provision.

During and after World War Two, there was a push for reform in relation to social services across Europe but the same thrust for reform was not as immediate in Ireland, which 'had less to re-build, [and] tended to carry on longer in the pre-war educational groove.'[25] The elected isolation from world developments may have protected Ireland from the ravages of World War Two, but it also served to isolate the country from world developments and progress in relation to many aspects, including educational thinking and philosophy. There was little evidence in Irish educational developments prior to the 1960s of the influence of educational philosophers such as Dewey or Montessori, whose thinking was influential internationally at this time. This increased insularity from international influences and the inward looking nature of the Irish state impeded its educational progress in the decades following independence, with little flow of information inwards to Ireland.

The agrarian-based economy affected school attendance as children were often kept at home for prolonged periods of time or on a seasonal basis to help on the farm. There was large-scale emigration and many fathers worked abroad during the peak agricultural season. There was often the absence of an educational environment within the home and the basic requisites of schoolbooks proved a heavy financial burden for many parents.

Biographies from this era paint a dismal picture of school life in the opening decades of the Free State, where children were scared of attending school, authoritarian teacher-pupil relationships were common and use of corporal punishment was prevalent.[26]

The 1950s were characterised by a deep pessimism in social and economic terms and commentators at the time feared the extinction of the Irish people through 'an implosion upon a central vacuity.'[27] In contrast, the 1960s were characterised by dramatic social changes in Ireland, and in no place was this expansion and initiative more evident than in the education system. Following a gradual decline in population from the 1920s, the small increase in the population in the 1960s had a profound psychological impact on the Irish people. This was owing to increased employment opportunities and reduced emigration. Trends in relation to marriage and fertility also began to correspond closer with European norms, with earlier incidence of marriage and decreased family size. Increased economic prosperity called for greater participation in the workforce and, increasingly, parents began to avail of paid childcare services outside the family home.[28]

The increasing availability of communication media, most notably the creation of Raidió Teilifís Éireann (RTÉ) in 1961, heralded a new era in communications and the widespread distribution of ideas and information from all over the world through television. Increased availability of air travel opened Ireland to a larger world, leading to a questioning of the pillars of Irish society such as Roman Catholicism and Irish nationalism.[29] This served to break the insularity and isolationist stance of Irish society for the first time since independence. Censorship and authoritarian control were no longer seen as sufficient to stem the influx of thoughts and materials into Ireland.

Curtin outlined three main functions for children prior to the 1960s; those of ensuring generational continuity, of providing a cheap source of labour and providing security for parents into old age.[30] These functions led to a subordinate position for children in society, with a strict control of children's time and space, an emphasis on passivity and the liberal use of corporal punishment.[31] This conceptualisation was reinforced within a Catholic ideology of the need for strict socialisation to combat original sin and on the need for adherence to rules and regulations. Education became part of this process of normalisation, within a nationalist and Catholic frame of reference. The Constitution concretised the power of the family over the state in relation to children, and the *laissez-faire* policy of the state reduced the visibility of children as a group in society.[32] This view of children evolved gradually by the 1960s, catalysing the educational reforms towards a more child-centred curriculum in the late 1960s.

4.2.3 Cultural Context

The cultural revolution in relation to the Irish language, sports and literature reached a high point around the time of independence. Associations such as the Gaelic League and the GAA had a comprehensive national network and united Irish people in sporting and cultural pursuits. The Gaelic League played a powerful and prominent role in devising the various programmes for primary schools in the 1920s, an influence that impacted on curriculum provision in Ireland up to the 1960s. The language revival movement had widespread support in Ireland from individuals and organisations such as teachers, the Catholic Church, political parties, the GAA and Sinn Féin. However, following independence, there was a rapid demise of the Gaelic League as people felt the language revival had been achieved.[33] The Civil War led to disunity within the Gaelic League and the number of branches plummeted from 819 to 139 between 1922 and 1924, rising slowly to 200 branches by 1970.[34]

In the period 1922–1960, Ireland underwent what Akenson described as a 'cultural implosion.'[35] A number of factors, including political, religious, cultural and economic influences came together simultaneously to remove Ireland from the sphere of influence of the international arena. Ireland adopted an insular policy *vis-à-vis* foreign jurisdictions, feeling under constant threat from the omnipresent English language and culture. As a reaction to independence, 'Irishness' became associated with everything that was 'not English.' The effect of partition was to reinforce mono-cultural societies, both North and South, allowing the creation of separate states through cultural policies. In both jurisdictions, the values of the majority cultures were transmitted in primary schools, with little consideration or respect for the minority traditions.

4.2.4 Economic Context

Ireland's economy was largely agrarian based between 1922 and 1971. Employment and unemployment rates remained somewhat constant throughout the period, with a gradual decline in the number employed in agriculture.[36] Economic policy in the 1920s was based on limited intervention, tariff protection was infrequent and moderate duties were imposed on trade. Taxes and state expenditure on items such as education remained low.[37] In addition, the government of the Free State followed policies of deflation and general retrenchment in relation to all social spending, which impacted on provisions for education.[38] The world depression in the 1930s and the Economic War with Britain further impacted negatively on Ireland's economy. De Valera advocated a policy of self-sufficiency, introducing protective tariffs and instituting a policy of economic nationalism, with a view to each family being self-sufficient and industrious.[39]

During World War Two, the economy remained stagnant owing to reduced exports and the increased cost of imports. Emigration became a persistent problem, whereby between 1945 and 1961, 500,000 people left the country.[40] Ireland did not prosper after World War Two, unlike many other European nations, due in the main to its isolationist stance before and during the war and its focus on agriculture, while the international recovery was based on industry.[41] Ireland reached a nadir in economic terms in the mid-1950s, a period characterised by deep pessimism and a sense of failure and defeatism.

Following the pessimism of the 1950s, the 1960s became a decade of economic renewal and reform, when the Irish state emerged from the doldrums of previous decades. A senior civil servant at the Department of Finance, T.K. Whitaker, produced and published a seminal paper on *Economic Development* in 1958. The proposals were conservative in relation to education, emphasising the need to alter the curriculum to introduce rural and agricultural studies in primary schools.[42] *Economic Development* was followed by three Programmes for Economic Expansion. The first programme (1958) made no specific mention of primary education in relation to economic revival but the general framework involved education playing an important role.[43] The *Second Programme for Economic Expansion* (1964) placed a greater emphasis on primary education. Objectives of the programme included the expansion of the curriculum 'to ensure that the content and scope of primary education are raised to a level consistent with national needs',[44] improving methodologies, the reduction of pupil-teacher ratios, the improvement of teacher training, the provision of increased equipment and resources and raising the school leaving age to fifteen by 1970. The third programme, *Economic and Social Development 1969–1972*, placed an even greater focus on education than its predecessors, setting out to reduce pupil-teacher ratios and to broaden the curriculum to include subjects such as civics, art, environmental studies and physical education.[45]

A number of factors coalesced to improve the economic situation so that between 1958 and 1962, there had been annual growth of 4 per cent in the economy, unemployment fell to less than 5 per cent in 1961 and there was a tangible positive psychological effect evident.[46] Overall, this led to a situation whereby the economy expanded three times as fast between 1959 and 1969 than it had between 1949 and 1959.[47] These developments led to a significant change in the economic status of Ireland in the 1960s, whereby 'total GNP nearly doubled, the decline in population was arrested, living standards increased markedly, the structure of the economy was transformed, and entry to the EEC in 1973 signalled the final stage of the reopening of the economy.'[48] One of the main effects of the economic programmes was to boost morale and provide a vision of what was possible for the Irish economy to achieve. Moreover, it provided the monetary resources to catalyse a period of reform in Irish education and to loosen the straitjacket within which the entire system had become encapsulated.

As table 4.1 evidences, there was a near continuous decline in spending on education as a percentage of the public sector budget, highlighting the decreasing priority placed on education within overall state expenditure. Moreover, there was a significant decline in the proportion of this budget allocated to primary education, reducing from 80 per cent in 1926 to

59 per cent in 1961. Economic investment in education was also low in international terms, especially when one takes into account the relative poverty of Ireland in relation to other jurisdictions and our consequent low Gross National Product (GNP).

Table 4.1   Expenditure on Education in Ireland 1926–1961

Year	Total Expenditure (£'000s)	GNP (£ mil)	% of GNP	% of Public Sector Budget	% Spent on Primary Education
1926	4,798	154.1	3.1	14.1	80.3
1931	5,151	156.2	3.3	16.1	*
1936	5,513	151.5	3.6	13	73.9
1941	5,929	184	3.2	12.1	*
1946	6,781	283.6	2.4	10.4	68
1951	10,999	357.9	3.1	9.3	67.6
1956	15,674	485.1	3.2	9	*
1961	20,385	585.3	3.5	9.5	58.8

*   No data provided for these years.

Source: Department of Education (1965). *Investment in Education – Report of the Survey Team appointed by the Minister for Education in October 1962*. Dublin: The Stationery Office, p. 304; ... (1965). *Investment in Education – Report of the Survey Team appointed by the Minister for Education in October 1962 – Annexes and Appendices ...*, p. 353.

Increased interest and reform led to a sharp rise in the amount of money spent on Irish education in the 1960s. As the Minister for Education, Donagh O'Malley, asserted in 1967, Ireland 'as a small and poor country cannot afford not to spend more on education than a richer one.'[49] On primary education alone, this increased from £10.5 million in 1960–1[50] to £28 million by 1970,[51] representing an increase from approximately

3 per cent to nearly 5.5 per cent of GNP.[52] Tussing argued that this increase in expenditure was only feasible considering the changed perspective of education as an investment in the economy and society, as opposed to the traditional view that the purpose of education was for 'moral, intellectual, and religious objectives.'[53] However, an analysis of the overall expenditure on education in the period led Akenson to this conclusion:

> If one assumes that a people spend their money on things they care about, then notes the chronic pattern of under-investment in education, one is led to the conclusion that Ireland as a nation placed a surprisingly low priority on the educational welfare of its children.[54]

4.2.5 Religious Context

The acrimonious relationship between the British authorities and the Catholic Church which characterised much of the previous century was replaced by a symbiotic and pragmatic union of Catholic Church and state in independent Ireland.[55] The state accepted the pivotal position of the Catholic Church and facilitated its authority in matters such as education. In 1926, the Department of Education described the education system as being semi-state, with power shared between the state and the managers.[56] In return, the Catholic Church denounced the opposition and legitimised the power of the new government, ensuring that the loyal and deferent Catholic population would follow accordingly in the wake of the lawlessness invoked by the War of Independence and the Civil War. By the 1930s, the Catholic Church had become an omnipresent and triumphant force in Irish society as it celebrated the centenary of Catholic Emancipation in 1929 and hosted the Eucharistic Congress in 1932.

There was increasing societal concern in relation to the alleged decline in moral standards, especially sexual morality, from the 1920s. The Catholic Church continued to espouse the ideal of single-sex education at all levels of the system in order to inculcate the separation of the sexes from an early age. The declining population meant that such a policy, in addition to the requirement of denominational education facilities, was highly uneconomical in a climate of limited resources for education. Outside the education system, there were many initiatives to promote morality and to protect Catholic moral values in the 1920s, including legislation on censorship, alcohol consumption and divorce. This led to a paternal and protectionist ethos in Ireland and the increasing institutionalisation of Catholicism within Irish society.

The Catholic Church assumed a dominant role in educational affairs, which allowed it to propagate a denominational education system that was state financed but religiously owned and managed. As Drudy and Lynch stressed, the majority of politicians in independent Ireland had been educated by and remained deferent to the Catholic Church, while the state 'neither had the political will nor the financial resources to challenge the power of the Churches in education.'[57] Successive Ministers for Education were conservative in nature and shared the vision of the Catholic Church for a subsidiary state role in education.[58] In such a climate, there was great sensitivity to state initiative or structural reform in education. The Catholic Church increasingly asserted its role in education following independence, and owing to its power base, it was personally and politically inexpedient for politicians to challenge these assertions. As the Catholic Church stated in 1921 upon the advent of independence:

> And, in view of pending changes in Irish education, we wish to assert that the only satisfactory system of education for Catholics is one wherein Catholic children are taught in Catholic schools by Catholic teachers under Catholic control.[59]

Titley argued that the schools became the main vehicle for the inordinate success of the Catholic Church in Irish society, providing a rich supply of vocations and producing a loyal and faithful laity.[60] Through the schools, Inglis held that the Catholic Church not only influenced the child but also facilitated the extension of its power into the homes of Ireland.[61] The Catholic Church maintained this control by asserting the rights of parents in relation to education, and subsequently affirming its right to decree what an appropriate education entailed. As Archbishop McQuaid stated:

Only the Church is competent to declare what is a fully Catholic upbringing ... Accordingly, in the education of Catholics every branch of human training is subject to the guidance of the Church, and those schools alone which the church approves are capable of providing a fully Catholic education.[62]

Both the Catholic Church and the state were strikingly suspicious of and hostile towards the direct involvement of the community in educational matters, despite the loyalty, devotion and financial support of the laity. Any semblance of democratic planning was replaced by centralised control by the 1930s, with a concomitant removal of the input and rights of parents and other interested parties.

By the 1960s, there were increasing moves towards ecumenism and this led to optimism that religious divides would no longer be so pervasive in the Irish context. The advent of Vatican II (1962–1965) had a profound effect on the Catholic population, relaxing and liberalising the rules of the Catholic Church once so vehemently enforced in the Irish context. It produced policies on education and on the role of the laity, reiterating the pivotal role of parents in education and stating unequivocally the centrality of the laity within the Catholic Church.[63] According to some commentators, this transformed the Catholic Church from being triumphant and monolithic to being more open minded and self questioning.[64]

In independent Ireland, the Protestant population declined from 7.5 per cent in 1926 to 5 per cent in 1956, representing just 2.5 per cent of the school population by 1965.[65] This small minority was under constant threat as a cultural group in an increasingly homogeneous Catholic society, where the Catholic worldview was implicitly inherent in government decisions and actions. The majority of the Protestant population had not supported the quest for independence and as a minority group, it felt isolated in an increasingly Catholic and Gaelic Ireland. While the Irish government upheld the right of the minority to practise its religion, and largely to denominational education, this represented the limit of the concessions. Overall, the Protestant population lacked cohesion and influence politically and did not play a significant role in the affairs of the state following independence.[66]

4.3 Educational Context in Ireland 1922–1971

4.3.1 Establishment of Educational Structures

The Commissioners of National Education were officially relieved of their duties on 31 January 1922, at which point they were informed they would be retained as advisors to the new government. However, they were fully relieved of their duties in June 1923, having not come together as a Board in the interim.[67] This move effectively concentrated power within the Department of Education in the hands of civil servants, as opposed to an independent board as under the previous administration. Pádraic Ó Brolcháin, Executive Officer to the Minister, cited the aim of the government as follows:

> it is the intention of the new government to work with all its might for the strengthening of the national fibre by giving the language, history, music and tradition of Ireland their natural place in the life of Irish schools.[68]

In June 1924, the New Ministers and Secretaries Act 1924 was passed, creating eleven state Departments. Within the Department of Education, three branches were created; primary, secondary and tertiary. The Minister for Education was the 'corporation sole' of the Department, meaning the Minister was the legal personality and the Department was an extension of that personality.[69]

4.3.2 School Statistics 1922–1971

Table 4.2 outlines the number of schools, pupils and teachers, and the average daily attendance between 1925 and 1965. This shows a decline of approximately 800 schools in the period, owing to amalgamations and a decreasing population. The number of teachers fluctuated little until the 1960s, when there was an increase in line with the population and the effort to reduce pupil-teacher ratios. The average pupil-teacher ratio reduced from

39:1 to 35:1 in the period. From the 1960s, there was an improvement in the progression of pupils through the classes in primary schools, but still in 1965–1966, 26.5 per cent of pupils were retained for a year and 10 per cent were retained in classes for two years or more. Circular 10/67 was issued instructing that pupils should normally be progressed to the next class at the end of the academic year, regardless of ability or aptitude.[70]

Table 4.2 Number of Schools, Teachers and Average Daily Attendance 1925–1965

	1925–1927	1935–1936	1945–1946	1955–1956	1965–1966
No. of Schools	5,648	5,243	4,957	4,871	4,797
No. of Pupils on Rolls	518,002	484,601	451,820	486,634	506,225
No. of Teachers	13,257	13,487	12,791	13,262	14,614
Average Daily Attendance	77.0%	83.5%	82.1%	86.0%	88.0%

Source: Department of Education Annual Reports (1928, p. 98; 1937, p. 138; 1947, p. 94; 1957, p. 52; 1968, p. 3).

In 1922, 80 per cent of national schools were one- and two-teacher schools.[71] The Department issued revised rules and regulations relating to amalgamations in 1929 but these had little effect due to the insistence of the Catholic Church for separate education for each denomination and gender.[72] A renewed vigour regarding school amalgamations re-emerged in the late 1960s, owing largely to the need for larger schools to implement the range of subjects envisaged by the curriculum planners, to ensure optimum use was made of available resources, to reduce the incidence of multi-class teaching and the existence of the school transport system.[73] This decision was catalysed by the *Investment in Education* report of 1965, which evidenced the inequitable distribution of educational resources in favour of smaller schools and the poorer range and quality of education they provided. In particular, pupil-teacher ratios ranged from an average of 18:1 in one-teacher schools to 45:1 in larger schools.[74] By the 1960s, the policy of amalgamation was supported in general by the Catholic Church and the INTO, yet it met with much resistance at local level from communities which viewed the school as the locus of the community.[75] The scheme succeeded in reducing the number of schools from 4,797 in 1965–1966 to 4,117 by 1969–1970.[76] This was an important reform in preparation for the introduction of the *Primary School Curriculum* (1971).

Attendance rates remained low following independence, languishing at 77 per cent in 1925 (see table 4.2). A new School Attendance Act was enshrined in legislation in 1926 and became operational nationwide in 1927.[77] The Act established School Attendance Committees in eight large urban areas and the use of An Garda Síochána (national police service) in all other contexts for implementation. While the requirements were more stringent than in the 1892 Act, a clause allowed ten days absence in spring and a further ten days in autumn to facilitate the sowing and harvesting of crops. However, it had a gradual positive effect on attendance rates, which rose to 88 per cent by 1965. The School Attendance (Amendment) Act 1967 revised and updated the legislation introduced in 1926, which allowed the serving of a warning notice on parents of children absent from school and raised the maximum fines under the 1926 Act.[78]

A system of scholarships for sixth class pupils to attend secondary schools was introduced under the Local Government (Temporary Provisions) Act 1923.[79] Approximately 2 to 3 per cent of the age cohort availed of scholarships between 1922 and 1960 and the overall percentage of pupils transferring to second-level education remained low throughout this period (see table 4.6). From 1961, the number of educational scholarships to post-primary schools was increased significantly to 1,739, yet these benefited a minimal proportion of the approximate 60,000 eligible pupils.[80]

4.3.3 *The Primary Certificate Examination*

The Primary Certificate Examination was introduced in 1929 on a voluntary basis to testify to the satisfactory completion by pupils of sixth class.[81] The examination contained written, oral and practical elements. As well as examining the core subjects of Irish, English, arithmetic, history, geography and needlework for girls, pupils could also present for examination in additional subjects. This was a positive element in the examination as it did not focus only on the core subjects and was not entirely literary based. By the mid-1930s, the Department expressed concern that only 16 per cent of schools presented pupils and that less than 20 per cent of eligible pupils sat the examination.[82] The Primary Certificate Examination was introduced on a compulsory basis for all pupils in sixth standard and higher from June 1943.[83] From this time, the examination was based on written papers in Irish, English and arithmetic. This had the effect of narrowing the curriculum, placing an emphasis on the written aspects of the core subjects. This had a particularly negative impact on the promotion of oral Irish. Naturally, the compulsory nature of the examination from 1943 greatly improved participation, as table 4.3 outlines.

Table 4.3 Participation and Success Rates in the Primary Certificate Examination 1930–1966

Year	No. of Pupils in 6th Class	No. of Pupils Presenting	No. of Pupils that Passed	Overall % of Pupils Passing
1929–1930	36,591	10,007	7,427	74%
1935–1936	46,353	10,947	8,141	74%
1945–1946	39,890	27,888	20,851	75%
1955–1956	44,488	35,650	28,213	79%
1965–1966	51,904	45,389	37,834	83%

Source: Department of Education Annual Reports (1931, p. 20 and 128; 1937, p. 28 and 152; 1947, p. 20 and 114; 1957, p. 9 and 69; 1967, p. 29).

The Primary Certificate Examination was abolished in October 1967 following protracted negotiations between the Department, the INTO and the managerial associations.[84] Its abolition was seen as a prerequisite to the reform and development of the curriculum at primary level.

4.3.4 School Buildings and Management

Throughout this period, the majority of schools were managed by local Catholic clergymen, who were responsible for the maintenance and upkeep of schools. They also had authority over the appointment and dismissal of teachers, while the state paid teachers' salaries. Inspectors' reports in the 1920s provided a bleak picture of the material conditions of schools, when many were dilapidated, lacking heat and with few educational resources.[85] A census of primary school buildings conducted by the Department in 1926–1927 revealed the need for the construction, extension or repair of close to 1,800 schools.[86] While 343 schools were built between 1922 and 1933,[87] subsequent annual reports highlighted the consistently large number of schools in need of reconstruction and repair. The programme changes in 1922 impacted on school design with the dropping of manual and practical subjects, whereby moveable partitions were replaced with permanent walls and the practice of providing one classroom per teacher was established.[88] While the INTO was initially supportive of the churches ownership of schools, it often publicised the antiquated and dilapidated condition of many primary schools and called for increased state support.[89]

The quality of school buildings had become a major problem by the 1960s, owing to decades of neglect, the managerial arrangements, the age of many schools built in the early nineteenth century and demographic decline. By 1965, 22 per cent of schools had been declared obsolete and 40 per cent to be non-effective by the Office of Public Works.[90] Between 1958 and 1968, the Department made a major effort in this regard, with 867 new schools constructed and a further 1,025 enlarged.[91] New designs were developed and greater space was afforded in the building of new classrooms from 1960. In the 1965 edition of *Rules for National Schools*, an increase in the allowance to fifteen square feet per child was granted to provide for the increased emphasis on mobility for pupils.[92] The local contribution to be provided was reduced significantly, with the state paying the vast majority of the building costs from the 1960s.[93] While the period witnessed increased state support for the building and maintenance of schools, the churches conceded little in relation to their ownership or management until the 1970s. However, it is clear that many pupils were educated in substandard physical environments during this period and lacked many of the material resources that would have enhanced the quality of their educational experience.

4.3.5 The Provision of Suitable Textbooks

Coiste na Leabhar, or An Gúm (the publications branch of the Department of Education), was established in 1926 with a primary aim of producing suitable textbooks for schools and producing literature in the Irish language that would not have been profitable for publishers to generate unaided.[94] By 1951, An Gúm had produced 599 books in Irish and had translated a further 407. However, only forty-eight of the books produced and eighty-nine of those translated were suitable for primary school children.[95] In addition, of the 203,400 books printed by An Gúm up to 1955, 91,250 had been distributed for use and 96,350 had been sold as waste paper.[96] This was a spectacular waste of resources in a climate of such under-resourcing of primary education and considering the need for quality books in the absence of a range of other materials and resources.

The school library system was neglected from the 1920s, with little official attention to the concept or little provision in practical terms.[97] A school reference library scheme was introduced in autumn 1963 to improve the stock of available books to pupils in an attempt to improve literacy skills in Irish primary schools, funded by an annual grant of £35,000.[98] An allocation of eighteen reference books was proposed for each school, as was a list of 200 optional books, which were to be provided for as resources became available.[99] However, the proposed funding was not made available and the library scheme was restricted to five counties. In 1967, a scheme of free books to necessitous children was introduced, allocating £1 per needy child in second to sixth class.[100]

Bennett conducted an analysis of the textbooks in use in schools after 1922 and invariably found them to be insular in nature and to associate 'Irishness' with Catholicism. Furthermore, themes of patriotism, militarism and anti-Englishness were pervasive and served to marginalise non-Catholics in independent Ireland.[101] Ireland was a central theme of many of these books, focusing on its glorious and spiritual past, with little mention of the world beyond. As time progressed, Bennett noted that textbooks appeared to be 'trapped in a type of time warp,'[102] ignoring the evolutionary nature of modernisation. From the 1960s, a change in emphasis became apparent and the gradual inclusion of more international themes and topics was evident.

4.3.6 The Irish Language in Irish Society

An examination of curriculum policy following independence necessitates a focus on the Irish language, the revival of which was declared to be the primary purpose and *raison d'être* of primary education. The main focus of the Irish language revivalists rested on the education system, most particularly primary schools. In this way, the Irish language was transformed from an optional subject with a relatively low status to the keystone of the primary school programme, with the Minister for Education, Eoin MacNeill, asserting in 1925 that the 'chief function of Irish educational policy is to conserve and develop Irish nationality.'[103] The language revivalists were overcome with optimism and a desire to revive the Irish language upon independence, which obscured careful planning and consideration of the details of the revival. It is apparent that insufficient consideration was given to the complexity of reviving a minority language and of the need to develop the language incrementally.

The aim of the Gaelic League was to make Irish the vernacular of Ireland, believing that language and nationhood were synonymous, and that one without the other was meaningless.[104] This fixation on the interrelationship of the Irish language and nationality grew in popularity in the

1930s and 1940s, advocated by many prominent politicians, particularly the Taoiseach Eamon de Valera:

> we cannot fulfil our destiny as a nation unless we are an Irish nation – and we can only be truly that if we are an Irish-speaking nation.[105]

The end result was a difficulty in disentangling the Irish language education question from wider issues of nationalism and patriotism. Furthermore, it made rational debate on the issue of methods difficult as any questioning of the revival policy was often characterised as an attack on the language, on the government and on the Irish nation as a whole. In this context, the revival question remained entangled with questions of nationalism and patriotism as opposed to linguistics and pedagogy. In 1958, O'Doherty stated that 'our present pseudo-bilingual policy is based on emotional, political and historical factors, to the neglect of pedagogical, psychological and social considerations.'[106] The majority of the population and Irish institutions remained apathetic to the language movement and did little to learn or support the language beyond expressing a tacit support for its restoration. Kelly asserted that the main reason for the failure of the revival was the focus on the ideological as opposed to practical issues, whereby ideology outpaced pragmatic requirements of training, textbooks and standardisation. An evolutionary approach, which would have allowed support structures to be put in place, was not considered in the midst of the optimism and buoyancy of independence.[107]

There was a dual approach to the language revival: to preserve the language in Gaeltacht areas and to revive and extend its use in the Breac-Ghaeltacht (partly Irish-speaking area) and Galltacht (English-speaking area). As table 4.4 evidences, the period was characterised by a contracting population in the Gaeltacht with the number of Irish speakers in the Fíor-Ghaeltacht (fully Irish-speaking area) declining by 35 per cent and in the Breac-Ghaeltacht by 30 per cent between 1926 and 1971. This offers a good barometer of Irish language usage as it was arguably in these areas that the language was spoken on a consistent basis.

Table 4.4 Number of Irish Speakers in the Fíor-Ghaeltacht and the Breac-Ghaeltacht
1926–1961

	Fíor-Ghaeltacht	Breac-Ghaeltacht	Total
1926	128,440	116,464	244,904
1936	123,125	115,213	238,338
1946	104,449	89,125	193,574
1961	83,145	81,084	164,229

Source: Department of Industry and Commerce (1949). *Statistical Abstract 1947–1948*. Dublin: The Stationery Office, p. 32; Central Statistics Office [CSO] (1967). *Statistical Abstract of Ireland 1967*. Dublin: The Stationery Office, p. 55.

One of the major aspects neglected within the revival movement was the failure to institute a systematic range of complementary strategies in wider society to support and extend the work in schools, leaving children alone to carry the burden of the revival. There were few initiatives to enable adults to learn the language in order to assist their children or to provide opportunities or motivation to use, reinforce or enjoy the Irish learned in school. The Catholic Church and state paid token homage to the language but it did not occupy a pivotal position in the affairs of either. One initiative to incentivise the use of Irish in the home from 1933 involved the payment of a £2 grant (subsequently £5) to parents of children aged six to fourteen years of age in Gaeltacht and Breac-Ghaeltacht areas if they could speak Irish and it was their home language.[108] Another 'incentive' to learning the Irish language was its necessity to attain a job within the civil service, a highly coveted permanent and pensionable employment at the time. In addition, Timirí were employed through the Vocational Education Committees to provide Irish language classes to the general population in the 1940s, an initiative that declined considerably by the 1950s. Little pragmatic action was taken to implement the recommendations of Coimisiún na Gaeltachta[109] (Commission on the Gaeltacht) (1926) and Coimisiún um Athbheocan na Gaeilge[110] (Commission on the Restoration of the

Irish Language) (1963) in relation to promoting a holistic approach to the revival efforts.

The lack of agreement on standardised spellings and grammar within the Irish language and the typeface (Gaelic or Roman characters) posed challenges until the 1940s. In 1943, a Committee was established to examine the question of standardised spelling and grammar. It provided new standards for publishers, *Litriú na Gaeilge: An Caighdeán Oifigiúil*.[111] In the 1950s, further progress was achieved in relation to standardising Irish grammar and following consultation, the Department issued its official policy in 1958, *Gramadach na Gaeilge agus Litriú na Gaeilge*. This was followed by de Bhaldraithe's dictionary in 1959, another milestone in the standardisation of the language.[112] However, for decades prior to this, teachers and publishers were left to their own devices and pupils were subjected to various versions depending on their teacher and textbook.

One corollary of the focus on the Irish language within the education system was a decreased emphasis on and even negativity towards the English language. In a Gaelic League Pamphlet of 1936, *You may Revive the Irish Language – The Problem and the State*, the eradication of English was proposed:

> so must the change back to an Irish-speaking Ireland make the ultimate destruction of English in Ireland inevitable ... English came, Irish went. If Irish is to come, English must go.[113]

The linking of the restoration of Irish to dispensing with English caused much unease, particularly among parents, who saw the social and economic necessity of high attainment in the English language. In 1941, a Department circular expressed the fear in government circles of the omnipresence and potency of the English language, with Ireland 'isolated between two English-speaking countries which are pouring on to us an ocean of English speech and thought.'[114] To this end, children were urged not to be 'soldiers on the side of English in the war it is waging against the Irish language.'[115] However, increased emigration, trade, tourism and media presence ensured English remained the prominent language in Irish society and within the education system.

The Irish language education policy had a particular effect on the minority Protestant population in Ireland. Among this group, there were few enthusiasts for the Irish language and education policy was generally in conflict with their educational and cultural principles. The subordination of English within the curriculum, which they regarded as part of their cultural inheritance, was also an anathema to the Protestant population. Furthermore, there were fears in relation to proselytising using the Irish language, owing to its long, historic and implicit associations with Catholicism.[116] In general, Protestants attempted to erode the more radical elements of the Irish language policy and many sent their children to be educated outside independent Ireland to avoid such problems. The issue of textbooks, most notably their religious and nationalistic content and overtones, also remained a contentious issue for Protestants. There was little effort or action by successive Ministers for Education at the time to assuage Protestant concerns regarding the programme.

4.3.7 Teachers in the System

Teachers' satisfaction with the pay scales introduced in 1920 was short lived as the Free State government reduced salaries by 10 per cent in November 1923[117] and by a further 6 to 9 per cent (depending on grades) in April 1933.[118] While the later cut was somewhat softened by the introduction of a non-contributory pension scheme, pay cuts for teachers were retrospective, unlike the case of civil servants.[119] The early cuts caused an abrupt anti-climax to the high expectations of teachers for their treatment under a native government. The fight to maintain or improve salaries exhausted much of the energy of teachers in the 1920s and 1930s, which arguably deflected energies from the implementation of the new programme developed in the early 1920s. In 1938, teachers received their first pay rise of 5 per cent under a native government, the value of which was largely eroded by wartime inflation.

During the period, the vast majority of lay principals and assistant teachers were qualified; a small proportion of the JAMs were formally trained, while approximately half of the religious teachers had formal training.[120] There was no further recruitment of untrained teachers into the education system after 1958. By 1971, only 6 per cent of the teaching force remained untrained.[121]

Entry to Teacher Training Colleges

In December 1924, an internal departmental committee, established to examine teacher training, recommended the abolition of the monitorial scheme and a revision of the pupil-teacher scheme.[122] The recommendations were accepted and implemented, as at this time, the quotas for the various teacher training colleges were not being filled and the imminent legislation on school attendance would require a larger number of teachers and improved qualifications for those teaching older pupils. A new source of students with better education and training was needed, especially native Irish speakers to advance the language revival. A preparatory school model had been advocated by Rev. Timothy Corcoran S.J., Professor of Education at University College Dublin and an influential educationalist in independent Ireland.[123] It was introduced in 1925 to provide an education 'for those clever boys and girls of the Irish-speaking districts who desire to become teachers, and for other clever boys and girls from all parts of the country who are highly qualified in Irish.'[124]

Seven preparatory colleges were established throughout the country to meet the denominational and gender needs of students, including a Protestant college. The majority of the preparatory colleges were located in Gaeltacht regions to accommodate candidates from these areas, to place the pupils in an atmosphere where the Irish language and traditions were still alive and to provide second-level educational opportunities in areas where very limited provision was available. Entry to the preparatory colleges was by means of competitive examinations, with 50 per cent of places reserved for the Gaeltacht population. A number of concessions was introduced to increase the percentage of Gaeltacht entrants in the early 1930s, including increased grants, revised age requirements and bonus marks for those completing examinations through Irish.[125] Students from preparatory colleges who met the requirements were given automatic places in the teacher training colleges. The curriculum offered in the preparatory colleges included Irish, English, mathematics, history and geography, while this was extended in 1933 to incorporate rural science, drawing, music, domestic science for girls and manual work for boys. By 1936, close to half of all students entering the training colleges originated in the preparatory colleges.[126]

The numbers in the preparatory colleges peaked in the 1930s at approximately 600. Owing to the multiple routes into the teaching profession and the decrease in the school-going population, there was an over-supply of teachers by the mid-1930s. To address this, a number of preparatory and training colleges were closed on a temporary basis and the intake was reduced in others. In addition, a 'marriage bar' was operated between 1934 and 1958 which required women to leave their teaching post on getting married, the pupil-teacher scheme was abolished in 1936, teachers who qualified outside Ireland were no longer eligible for recognition to teach in schools and early retirement was enforced for women between 1938 and 1948.

Collectively, the reform of the pupil-teacher scheme and the inception of the preparatory colleges led to increased competition and a higher calibre of entrant to the teaching profession. While the calibre of entrants improved during the period, it was quite a restricted selection process with a major emphasis placed on proficiency in the Irish language. Furthermore, candidates had to decide on a career in teaching at the outset of their secondary schooling. This narrow pool of potential candidates and the subsequent training provided produced cohorts of teachers that tended to be conservative in character. In 1958, Minister Jack Lynch announced that entry to the training colleges would be on merit, based on the Leaving Certificate Examination, oral Irish interview and suitability interview.[127] In May 1960, the new Minister, Dr Hillery, announced the closure of the preparatory colleges (except for the Protestant college) and their replacement by a secondary school scholarship scheme for Gaeltacht students.[128] This dealt a severe blow to the revival cause as this channel had ensured a consistent cohort of native and fluent speakers entering the teaching profession on an annual basis to implement and support the provisions of the programme.

The Training of Teachers

Upon independence, there were five recognised teacher training colleges
in the Free State. The *Programme for Students in Training 1923–1924* was
restructured to accommodate changes to the primary school programme.
Proficiency in the Irish language became an entry requirement and Irish
was an obligatory subject of the course from 1923.[129] Owing to the alarm-
ing rate of failures in the Irish exam in 1924, a lower and higher course was
introduced. Gradually, the majority of students proceeded to sit the higher
course, until the lower course was abolished in 1930.[130] An increasingly
Gaelic atmosphere was promoted and achieved within the training colleges, with approximately 50 per cent of staff capable of delivering instruction through the medium of Irish by 1930.[131] The enhanced focus on Irish
in the preparation of candidates for, and within, the training colleges led
to the increased prominence of the language and by 1930, the majority of
students completed their examinations through Irish.[132] The Church of
Ireland Training College was much smaller after independence and had to
accept the new political and educational reality, especially regarding the
Irish language. The college had not previously taught Irish and now it was
expected to produce bilingual students, even though most students had no
knowledge of the language on entry.[133] The low number of entrants to the
Protestant preparatory college in the first few years owing to the requirements in Irish led to problems attracting and retaining teachers to staff the
approximate 800 Protestant schools from the 1920s.

Following the successful completion of the training programme, teachers were granted recognition to teach in national schools and received a
teaching diploma after two years of satisfactory teaching service. Students
from the training colleges could apply to undertake a third year of training in affiliated universities but this option was not undertaken widely.[134]
Owing to the higher calibre of entrants, a further review of the training
programme was undertaken in 1932 to focus more time on the theory and
practice of education, as opposed to rudimentary elements of training.
This divided the course into three sections: a professional course, a general
education course and an optional course.[135] This placed great strain on
timetables and there was little opportunity for assimilation of information

by students. Moreover, training colleges remained denominational, single-sex, regimented and closed off from other institutions until the 1960s. The culture inculcated in the colleges with crowded timetables and didactic teaching styles afforded little time for personal research or developing self-reliance. Subsequently, this culture was carried into the classrooms and few teachers engaged in further research or study.

There were many changes in the system and content of teacher training in the 1960s. From 1962, training colleges were given greater autonomy to set and correct their examinations and to restructure their courses. Additionally, colleges became less closed as institutions and there was increased freedom afforded to students.[136] Many of the colleges became co-educational and the entry of more mature students, university graduates and students from an urban background changed the traditional composition of teacher graduates.[137] A revision of the syllabus in 1963–1964 placed a greater focus on academic subjects and on a theoretical underpinning to training. Increased emphasis was also placed on teaching methodologies and owing to growing enrolments to cater for a rising population, the hiring of staff with specific expertise was possible. There was also a greater emphasis placed on the use of seminars, tutorials and workshops to provide a more applied dimension to education.

Irish Courses for Teachers

Upon independence, a low percentage of the existing teaching force had the competence or qualifications in the Irish language to implement the requirements of the primary school programme developed in the early 1920s. As is evident in table 4.5, less than 20 per cent of teachers had a Bilingual Certificate or higher in 1924, which was considered necessary to use Irish as a medium of instruction. This effectively meant the majority of teachers could not speak the Irish language, never mind have an adequate proficiency to implement the challenging provisions of the programme. Undoubtedly, such an unpropitious start hampered the revival in the early days and resulted in poor teaching, but more importantly, created a sense of failure among many teachers that proved difficult to overcome in later years. Between 1924 and 1960, the number of teachers without qualifications in

Irish reduced from 59 per cent in 1924 to 4 per cent in 1960. However, a considerable minority failed to achieve the Bilingual Certificate or higher throughout the period which impacted on their competence to implement the programme's provisions.

Table 4.5 Qualifications in Irish of all Teachers serving in National Schools 1924–1960

School Year	No Certificate in Irish	Ordinary Certificate	Bilingual Certificate	Ard Teastas
1924	59.2	20.7	17.6	2.5
1930–1931	27.2	33.4	33.4	6
1940–1941	11.1	24.5	57.6	6.8
1949–1950	8.3	16.9	68.6	6.2
1960–1961	4	6.6	85.1	4.3

Source: Deputy McGilligan (1925). *Dáil Debates*, 2 June 1925, Volume 12, Column 2; Department of Education Annual Reports (1931, p. 139; 1941, p. 9; 1951, p. 107; 1961, p. 89).

The first summer courses for existing teachers 'to develop their teaching on bilingual lines' became operational in 1922.[138] These were organised in nineteen Irish Colleges and an additional 100 centres nationwide established for the purpose.[139] The courses were compulsory for teachers under the age of forty-five between 1922 and 1925 and became optional in 1926. The length of the course was reduced from eight weeks in 1922, to five weeks in 1923 and to four weeks in subsequent years.[140] The courses were well attended; for example, 11,050 teachers attended the summer courses in 1925, dropping to 6,500 in 1927 when attendance became voluntary.[141] There was a major incentive for teachers to attend the courses as the inspector's grading was based increasingly on proficiency in the Irish language. In the first five years, success rates in the examinations for the Ordinary Certificate, the Bilingual Certificate and the Ard Teastas (Higher Certificate) remained low, fluctuating between 17 and 37 per cent.[142] This evidences the low levels of Irish among practising teachers at this time and the inadequacy of the summer courses to raise these standards in such a short period of time. This provision may have been satisfactory to augment competence in a language but was entirely insufficient to furnish 12,000 teachers with the ability to use the Irish language as a medium of instruction in schools.

In 1928, the Department issued a circular entitled *Teachers' Qualifications in Irish*, outlining the requirements for various schools and areas in relation to Irish and urging teachers who had not attained proficiency and qualifications in the language to give it their 'earnest attention.'[143] In September 1931, a further circular was issued regarding the qualifications required of all teachers for recognition, with varying qualifications required by teachers based on their rank, position inside and outside the Gaeltacht and their age.[144] Moreover, the Department forewarned teachers in 1930 that an Ordinary Certificate would be required from 30 June 1932 and a Bilingual Certificate from 30 June 1935 for the payment of increments for all teachers who were under the age of thirty in 1922.[145] The Department had a naïve understanding of the complexity of equipping 12,000 teachers with proficiency to use Irish as a medium of instruction in 1922, considering the vast majority could not even speak the language. It was improbable that teachers could gain such competency in a language in a short summer course, especially when such learning was not reinforced by further provision or usage in wider society.

4.3.8 Inspection and Evaluation

Teachers' work was closely regulated by both the Department through the Inspectorate and the manager at local level.[146] In November 1922, a circular was issued to the Inspectorate owing to the difficulties many teachers were experiencing implementing the programme. It urged inspectors to be considerate owing to the late commencement of the school year, the general unrest in the country and the difficulties many teachers would have in using Irish as a medium of instruction in infant classes. In this context, judgements were to be based on the teacher's preparation, methods and interest rather than on the formal testing of pupils. Furthermore, ratings were not to be altered downwards 'unless for grave reasons clearly established.'[147] The challenge of ensuring inspectors were proficient in the language was also a priority of the Department and those remaining in the service were trained to improve their fluency if necessary, while all new recruits had to prove competence in the language.[148]

In February 1924, a circular informed inspectors that a good grading in Irish and mathematics was necessary for a teacher to grade well overall, where a 'very good' in oral Irish counted 'as two Very Goods.'[149] It further reiterated the necessity of introducing Irish as the medium of instruction as quickly as possible and that 'teachers may be assured that, if they employ Irish as the medium of instruction, their failure to cover the whole syllabus in History and in Geography will not entail a reduction of their marks in the Efficiency Table.'[150] Therefore, the focus from the outset, despite the low numbers of teachers proficient in the language, was to press ahead not only with teaching Irish as a subject, but also with its use as a medium of instruction.

There were many complaints from teachers regarding the Inspectorate in the early 1920s and its effect on the interpretation of the programme. An investigation into the system of inspection in primary schools reported in 1927, paying particular attention to the award of merit marks.[151] The report asserted that the role of the Inspectorate was two-fold and that 'attention should be directed not merely to its controlling function, but also to its function as a guiding and inspiring influence.'[152] It proposed a Board of Appeals for Reports of General Inspections, which was accepted and implemented through three circulars issued in March 1928.[153] Other reforms provided for increased numbers of incidental visits to support teachers and a reduced number of general inspections.[154]

In July 1929, a further circular was issued to inspectors relating to the ratings of teachers. This placed particular emphasis on teachers' work in oral Irish, especially in infant classes.[155] The requirements for the teaching of Irish were further elucidated in Circular 11/31, *Teaching Through the Medium of Irish*. This circular reinforced the rule that the Irish language should only be used as a medium of instruction where both teachers and pupils were competent in the language and that transitional steps should be used to achieve this ultimate goal.[156] However, it was promptly followed by Circular 12/31 in relation to ratings of teachers, outlining the necessity of success in Irish for the attainment of 'efficient' and 'highly efficient' ratings and the condoning of lower standards in other subjects if Irish was progressing well.[157] In 1949, the ratings 'highly efficient,' 'efficient' and 'non-efficient' were removed and replaced with two ratings, 'satisfactory' and 'non-satisfactory,' which were removed in 1958.[158]

The relationship between the Inspectorate and teachers appears to have been strained for much of this period, with much dissatisfaction in relation to low ratings and quotas within each ranking. By linking the pay and promotion of teachers to performance in the Irish language, much of the goodwill inherent in the early years of independent Ireland dissipated. The power of individual inspectors in this regard led to much animosity and distrust from teachers and the increasing link between salary and competence in the Irish language caused much resentment, as well as a tarnishing of the enthusiasm for the revival among teachers.

4.3.9 Information on Education and Educational Research

The period 1922 to 1971 was characterised by a dearth of documented and published information and statistics relating to the education system. Following an epoch of detailed annual reports and published commissions and investigations in relation to education, the Department of Education became increasingly sparse with the quantity and quality of the information it made available.[159] Inspectors' reports were no longer published in full and while extracts were included in annual reports until 1931, they were discontinued from this point. Annual reports became shorter and less detailed and they were eventually discontinued from 1964. Statistical reports replaced the annual reports in the 1960s, which offered little insight into activities within the education system. Moreover, reports were often published long after their content would be of any practical use. The promised triennial reports on the working of the system never materialised and the *Rules for National Schools* were no longer published after 1965. While the majority of commissions that sat in the period did issue reports, it was rare for the background evidence and submissions that informed them to be published.

This practice at a departmental level was mirrored in a general lethargy regarding education in wider society. There were few educational publications, there was an absence of educational journals beyond the teacher journals, there was a dearth of general research relating to education and there were no education correspondents for the newspapers.[160] Moreover, much of the research produced was philosophical and historical in nature, with little empirical evidence generated on the system. The tradition of establishing unwieldy councils and committees to deliberate on educational issues did little to instigate reform as invariably they 'either play safe by opting for the *status quo*, or have any new recommendations so hedged about by qualifications and reservations that their impact is considerably diminished.'[161] This culture negatively affected the generation of evaluations and the documentation of practice regarding the implementation of the primary school programme up to the 1960s.

A number of factors coalesced to revitalise Irish educational research in the 1960s, including renewed linkages to international policy and practice, the production of a myriad of reports, increased academic autonomy within the training colleges, the establishment of the Educational Research Centre (ERC) in 1966 and the availability of postgraduate courses.[162] The Department also began publishing *Oideas*, an educational journal, in 1968. This increased interest in, financing of and participation in educational research during the 1960s revitalised Irish education and began to provide the data needed to substantiate the calls for curriculum reform.

4.3.10 Special Educational Needs Provision

During this period, it is probable that many pupils with mild learning disabilities or special educational needs were accommodated in ordinary schools owing to poor detection and screening systems and a lack of alternative facilities. The 1950s and 1960s witnessed an increased emphasis by the state on and consideration for children who were affected by 'handicap' or disadvantage. Internationally, there was increased attention to the issue of providing an appropriate education and in 1959, Principle 5 of the UN Declaration on the Rights of the Child stated that 'the child who is physically, mentally, or socially handicapped shall be given the special treatment, education and care required by his or her particular condition.'[163] Important investigations such as *The Problem of the Mentally Handicapped* (1960) and the *Report of the Commission of Inquiry on Mental Handicap* (1965) produced seminal recommendations that delineated the course of special education in the following decades.[164] This changing context led to the establishment of a number of schools catering for children with special educational needs, with little incidence of integration with the mainstream system.

The provision of remedial education also became a feature in larger schools from the 1960s, as part of the recognition of the needs of children with learning difficulties. Following the first appointment in 1961, seventy-six remedial teachers worked in the system by 1970.[165] In addition, an emphasis was placed on children suffering from social and economic disadvantage within the education system from the 1960s, through initiatives such as the Rutland Street Project.

The Commission on Itinerancy was established to enquire into the needs of the Traveller community, with a specific focus on education. Its report in 1963 noted that only 160 pupils of the age cohort of six- to fourteen-year-olds were enrolled in any school, attributing this to a lack of interest in education among Traveller parents.[166] The Commission proposed that a special curriculum with an emphasis on practical subjects be prepared. The report viewed the advantages of education in relation to its potential to assimilate and integrate the Traveller population into mainstream society. Following the report, a Committee on the Provision of Educational Facilities for the Children of Itinerants was established to mediate the report from the Department's perspective. This Committee cited the main aim of the Department to be the integration of Traveller children in ordinary classes or special classes in ordinary schools, where they would have the experience of an ordinary school atmosphere and exposure to the discipline of school life.[167] Overall, state policy at this time showed an active disregard for the unique cultural heritage of the Traveller community and aimed at assimilating Traveller culture into mainstream society.

4.3.11 Developments in the 1960s

Following decades of stagnation, lethargy, inaction and under-investment in the education system, a number of national and international factors coalesced to raise the status and prominence of education in the 1960s. There was increased public and political interest in education in the early 1960s as a vehicle to ensure Ireland would not be left behind its European counterparts. Improved economic and social circumstances accentuated the desire for improved social mobility for future generations. In tandem, the traditional role of schools as purveyors of cultural and moral instruction was transformed and education was increasingly viewed as a preparation for life and as an investment in the individual and in society. As the National Industrial and Economic Council (NIEC) stated in 1966:

> Education increases the general capacity of an economy to adapt to changing circumstances: we have no doubt, for example, that if education, greater in extent and more suitable in content, had been offered two or three decades ago, the problem of adapting for freer trade would now be very much less.[168]

From the 1960s, there were increased calls for parental involvement in the management and organisation of education, supported by the provisions of Vatican II, which called for greater lay involvement in schools.

A number of new fora to facilitate debate on educational and other issues were prominent in the 1960s. Tuairim, established in 1954 to awaken public opinion and interest in relation to Irish affairs, drew attention to the lack of leadership and initiative in the Department of Education.[169] The Language Freedom Movement, founded in 1965, called for a rational debate on the revival of Irish. The Movement added to the concern regarding the position of the revival within schools and provided a further platform for the airing of grievances pertaining to education. In 1969, the INTO established an Education Committee to conduct educational research and investigate educational matters.[170] Increasingly, the media recognised the powerful and widespread interest in educational discussion. Television was a new medium and greatly assisted the wider inclusion of the public in debate and acted as an agent of social change and influence on Irish society.[171] Furthermore, the advent of television led to an interactive style of dialogue and debate, and a new frankness of discussion, where press releases and statements were replaced by interviews and cross-questioning.[172]

Politicians were quick to note this growing interest and demand for education and began to abandon the *laissez-faire* policy towards education that was a characteristic of successive governments since independence. As Akenson stated, from the 1960s:

> the Republic's politicians discovered education. Almost overnight the schools were changed from legislative orphans to a topic of continual public interest and debate.[173]

Political policies on education fuelled debate and placed further pressure on the government to reform education in line with the demands of voters. However, while there were differences in emphases in the policies of the different parties in the 1960s, their overriding principles were virtually indistinguishable from one another. In curriculum terms, both Fine Gael and Labour called for a widening of the curriculum and a reduced emphasis on examinations.[174] Fine Gael also issued a policy on the preservation of the Irish language in 1966, with the aim being to preserve the language by securing the support of the people for a more realistic and non-compulsory policy.[175] Fianna Fáil, the party in power, was the only political party not to produce a comprehensive education policy in the 1960s.

By the late 1950s, Ireland was moving away from its elected position of isolation and insularity *vis-à-vis* the rest of Europe and the world. By 1961, Ireland was a member of the Organisation for Economic Co-operation and Development (OECD), the United Nations, the Council of Europe and the United Nations Educational, Scientific and Cultural Organisation (UNESCO), and was aspiring to become a member of the European Economic Community (EEC). These organisations advocated the need for educational reform to ensure pupils were prepared for their lives as future citizens. Additionally, there was a considerable improvement in North-South relations and co-operation, which prospered further under the leadership of Taoiseach Seán Lemass.[176] Such a situation led to a context for the sharing of ideas and information, and Irish politicians and senior civil servants were introduced to alternative and more modern social and

economic policies. Dr Patrick Hillery, Minister for Education, formalised
this as Department policy when he stated in 1962:

> Closer contact with the Continent should, as its first effect, redeem us from a cer-
> tain provincialism which hangs heavily over the Irish mind. It is bad for us to have
> our intellectual, educational, literary, artistic and other horizons confined to these
> islands, with only a very occasional glance over the hedge at what is going on in the
> rest of Europe.[177]

Expansion of Educational Provision

At this time, the majority of the 557 secondary schools were small, offered
a narrow curriculum and were single-sex.[178] In May 1963, Minister Hillery
announced his proposals for the extension of post-primary education,
including the planned comprehensive schools.[179] This was followed in
September 1966 by the introduction of a scheme of free education at post-
primary level by the Minister for Education, Donagh O'Malley. It involved
the abolition of fees, the provision of school transport and the allocation of
schoolbooks to needy pupils.[180] Table 4.6 outlines the rapid growth in enrolments in secondary and vocational schools from the mid-1960s following
the announcement of the scheme of free education. Within these changed
circumstances, a reform of the primary curriculum was considered necessary as pupils would be transferring at an earlier age than previously.

Table 4.6 Number of Pupils Enrolled in Secondary and Vocational Schools 1940–1970

No. of Pupils Enrolled	1939–1940	1949–1950	1959–1960	1964–1965	1969–1970
Secondary Schools	37,670	47,065	73,431	92,989	144,425
Vocational Schools	6,430	6,739	25,608	33,383	50,853

Source: Department of Education Annual Reports (1941, p. 16 and 56; 1951, p. 115 and
146; 1961, p. 102 and 118; 1966, p. 39 and 54; 1974, p. 26 and 58).

Investment in Education (1965) and the OECD Report (1969)

Ireland agreed to take part in an OECD review of its education system under the *Education Investment Programme for Developed European Countries* in 1961. The background report produced, *Investment in Education*, was fact-finding and analytical in character and was evidence-based and objective. It was researched and written from an economic viewpoint and made projections for future lines of development of the system.[181] It differed from previous reports in Ireland in that it remained detached from the intangibles such as culture and nationality, it devised systems to collect and accumulate a mass of baseline data and empirical evidence, it had a theoretical underpinning and used original methods to explore uncharted territory in relation to Irish education. The report had a seismic effect on Irish education and offered many signposts for educational reform. One of the most important effects was to progress attitudes in relation to education as an investment in the individual and the nation, as opposed to a social expense.

The four main areas addressed within the report were manpower, participation, curricula and the use of resources. The report raised four main concerns in relation to the curriculum, namely, the amount of time devoted to the teaching of Irish, the lack of emphasis on mathematics, teaching methodologies that did not take account of individual differences between pupils and the length of the school week. The composition and relevance of the curriculum for the future lives and careers of many of the pupils was questioned. Overall, the report highlighted that the education system was not meeting human needs and it analysed the social inequalities inherent in the system, such as social class, socio-economic and geographical factors. The bleak picture showed a pyramid effect in relation to education in the 1960s, documenting that 20 per cent of pupils were failing to attain even the Primary Certificate, 32 per cent had ceased education at the end of primary school, while only 9 per cent sat the Leaving Certificate and 4 per cent attended university.[182] This impacted upon the economic prosperity of the nation as the majority of citizens lacked the education to foster economic growth, while the basic education many had bore little relevance to their daily lives or future careers.

The report put forward one main recommendation: the establishment of a Development Unit in the Department to initiate long-term planning, compile statistics, evaluate the system, consult with interested parties and be involved in curriculum development. The report concluded that if Ireland was to aspire to join the EEC, there would need to be increased and judicious investment in education, which would in turn lead to increased economic productivity. The empirical and statistical evidence was now at hand to reinforce the long-pronounced assertions for a broader curriculum and for an enhanced quality of education.

The OECD review of education policy in Ireland was published in 1969 and asserted that a thorough reform of the education system was needed.[183] It noted the positive impact of the *Investment in Education* report, which had inspired educational planning and awakened the wider public's interest in education. In relation to the curriculum, the OECD commented on the comparatively short period of instruction in Ireland and the inordinate amount of time expended on the Irish and English languages. It also placed a focus on the importance of teacher education and retraining. Expenditure on education in Ireland was dealt with in detail, highlighting the low level of spending in Ireland relative to other OECD countries, especially considering Ireland's comparatively low rate of GNP *vis-à-vis* other countries internationally. By the time the OECD report was published in 1969, it did not have the same impact as the earlier background report but served to reiterate the earlier findings and locate them in an international context.

4.4 Summary and Conclusion

It is evident that a number of wider societal factors impacted upon educational provision, and thus curriculum innovation, in Ireland in the period 1922–1971. The era was characterised by poor socio-economic conditions. There were low levels of social services and education was a low priority *vis-à-vis* other more pressing considerations such as unemployment and health provisions. The economy remained largely agrarian-based and stagnant for much of this period, with politicians placing an emphasis on self-sufficiency and trade tariffs. There was also a high incidence of emigration, leaving the very old and young to be cared for in independent Ireland. In a traditional, paternalistic society, children were viewed as being the bottom rung of the social ladder and provisions were more generous for the older population as opposed to the young.

The alliance between the Catholic Church and state was an inherent characteristic of education in independent Ireland. This was a symbiotic union: the Catholic Church managed an educational network the state could not afford and this enabled the Catholic Church to retain an integral if not dominant role in education. This stability was important for the political system in the fledgling new state. This power base accentuated the influence and authority of the Catholic Church in Ireland and provided a network to imbue both pupils and parents with Catholic doctrines. Such a close alliance between the Catholic Church and the state heightened the alienation of the Protestant minority in Ireland after independence.

In educational terms, the period was characterised by unpropitious conditions for the implementation of the curriculum provisions introduced in the 1920s. There was a large number of small schools and out-dated school buildings nationwide. The provision of training in the Irish language for existing teachers was inadequate and there were many problems with the production of textbooks, due to issues with spelling, grammar and dialectal differences. Further impediments included large class sizes and low pupil attendance rates. Educational resources were unevenly distributed in favour of smaller schools, which had lower pupil-teacher ratios. Overall, pupil-teacher ratios remained high in the absence of greater investment in the education system, with the majority of pupils attending classes with in excess of thirty pupils throughout the period. While the programme in its entirety was narrow in nature, it was further reduced in practice from the 1940s by the introduction of the compulsory Primary Certificate Examination, which focused on written aspects in the core subjects of Irish, English and arithmetic. In the period, the majority of pupils ceased their formal education after primary school, with some improvement evident following reforms in the 1960s.

While the Irish language formed the core of the school programme following 1922, there was no parallel movement in wider society to support or promote the Irish language outside the education system. The absence of such supports to encourage and build upon the progress achieved within the school system militated against successful implementation. While the public supported the revival movement in abstract terms, few became ardent supporters or active proponents of the endeavours within schools or outside schools to revive the Irish language. The further the language revival became associated with schools, the less part other organisations or the public played in its promotion. It is also apparent that the planners in the 1920s greatly underestimated the task of reviving the Irish language as the vernacular of the people.

In 1922, the vast majority of teachers were not competent to teach Irish or to use it as a medium of instruction. The supports put in place led to a gradual improvement in this regard but the initial enthusiasm and quest for implementation was dissipated before a critical mass was proficient in the language. Owing to the requirements in the Irish language, the pool of candidates from which to choose future teachers reduced dramatically, and led to less heterogeneity than may have been desirable within the profession. A certain level of resentment was created following the linking of ability in Irish to teacher ratings, promotions and salaries and this hostility hardened with time and certainly tainted the spirit with which certain teachers undertook their work. Although the calibre of entrants to the teaching profession improved following reforms in the 1920s, teacher training remained highly structured and controlled until the 1960s. Admittedly, this was apposite to the envisaged role of the teacher at the time to deliver the prepared curriculum to pupils, but it offered little time for personal study or reflection on education and consequently did little to prepare teachers to innovate within their classrooms and schools during the period. Few teachers engaged in further formal training or research and it is arguable that this was a contributory factor to the inertia in Irish education at the time. It is also likely that the large proportion of teachers that remained unqualified between 1922 and 1971 adversely affected the quality of instruction in the period.

Overall, the 1960s were characterised by a willingness to reform Irish education. The wider factors catalysing such a period of reform included increased economic prosperity, links to international agencies and thinking, unprecedented political and public interest in education, the impact of Vatican II reforms and increasing disquiet about the quality of education provided. The inordinate emphasis on the Irish language within the education system also abated somewhat in the 1960s. While it still continued to be debated, there was a more rational and pedagogical basis to dealing with the language question. This widened the education debate from the traditional wrangle on the Irish language to include a wider focus on the curriculum and methodologies. This amalgam of elements ensured the education system was looked at in a whole new light, with an economic lens as well as from the traditional religious, cultural and intellectual perspective. One of the major catalysts was the *Investment in Education* report, which elucidated the impact on productivity that a poorly educated workforce could have and catalysed many educational developments. Chapter 5 examines the curriculum reforms introduced from the achievement of independence in 1922 until 1971.

Planning and Content of the Primary School Curriculum 1922–1971

5.1 Introduction

This chapter examines curriculum provisions in Ireland from the advent of independence until the introduction of the *Primary School Curriculum* (1971). It examines the embryonic stages of development from the Gaelic League programme in 1918, which contained seminal lines influencing later curriculum development. The first and Second National Programme Conferences, which reported in 1922 and 1926 respectively, laid the foundation and set the tone for the curriculum followed between 1922 and 1971. An analysis of their establishment, composition, terms of reference and *modus operandi* is documented. The process undertaken to devise the curricula, the individuals and organisations involved and consulted, and the relationship between the process of devising and the end product, are examined to determine the powerful stakeholders in Irish education in independent Ireland. The chapter documents two further key curriculum developments following the 1920s. The first was a minor modification to the curriculum enacted in 1934, with a view to strengthening further the position of the Irish language within schools. Second, a *Revised Programme for Infants* was introduced in 1948, which represented a hiatus in the philosophy and content of other curriculum traditions in the period.

5.2 The Education Programme of the Gaelic League (1918)

The Gaelic League was aware of the imminence of some form of independence and began to make preparations to ensure schools would be ready to
introduce an education for children more in line with Irish ideals and sensi-
bilities. The reform of education was also a high priority for the increasingly
popular Sinn Féin party, which carried the following motion in relation to
education within its *Programme of Reorganised Sinn Féin* in 1917:

> The reform of Education, to render its basis national and industrial by the compulsory
> teaching of the Irish language, Irish history and Irish agriculture and manufacturing
> potentialities in the primary system.[1]

In 1918, the Education Committee of the Gaelic League began developing a programme for schools, *Gléas Oideachais Gaedhilge i gCóir na Scol.*
This programme contained seminal lines of thought for education policy
within the Free State. It was developed by Máire Ní Chinnéide, assisted
by advisors such as Rev. Timothy Corcoran S.J., J.J. O'Kelly and Micheál
Ó hAodha. These were prominent names in the Irish revival and political
movement and they played an influential role in educational developments in the Irish Free State.[†] This ensured that the Gaelic League played
a prominent and influential role in education at national policy level, as
the most prominent politicians and educationalists shared to some extent
the ideology of Gaelic League cultural nationalism. As Kelly asserted, even
those Ministers in later years who may not have been ardent supporters of
Gaelic League policy dared not challenge it publicly for fear of the wrath
of the powerful Gaelic lobby.[2]

[†]   Máire Ní Chinnéide became the Chairperson of the first National Programme
      Conference; Rev. Timothy Corcoran, a Jesuit priest, was an influential advisor at the
      first and Second National Programme Conferences; J.J. O'Kelly was President of the
      Gaelic League and became Minister for Irish in 1919 and Minister for Education in
      1921; Micheál Ó hAodha was later to Chair the Commission on Secondary Education
      and also become Minister for Education.

Schools were identified by the Gaelic League as being the primary locus for the revival of the Irish language. The Gaelic League programme differentiated requirements between schools in the Gaeltacht, Breac-Ghaeltacht and the Galltacht in relation to introducing the Irish language and culture. In all schools, Irish was to be the official school language, Irish history was to be taught to all pupils and Irish music was to be played as pupils marched from class to class. In the Breac-Ghaeltacht, a bilingual programme was to be used while in English-speaking districts, Irish was to be taught for one hour per day.[3] The programme also contained projections that in two years, grammar, reading and writing would be taught in Irish and English on alternate days to all pupils after the infant standards. In five years, the full bilingual programme would be in force in all schools, except for infants.

The programme was published in 1918 and disseminated for immediate implementation by the Gaelic League, without consulting teachers or other interested parties. While the INTO supported the programme, it became concerned when teachers began to complain of visits from local language enthusiasts demanding the implementation of the programme, 'irrespective of conditions or difficulties.'[4] The Gaelic League and Sinn Féin agreed to suspend implementation of the programme within schools upon the inception of the first National Programme Conference.

5.3 First National Programme Conference

The first National Programme Conference is singularly important as it was framed in the lead up to independence and captured much of the patriotic and nationalist feeling evident in Ireland at this time. It was the first time the Irish people had the opportunity to design their own programme of education and its provisions set the tone for curriculum policy over the next fifty years. The INTO initiated the process of revising the primary school programme, largely as a reaction to the Gaelic League programme and to alter the provisions of the 1900 programme. At the Annual Congress in 1920, the INTO passed a resolution calling for the establishment of a conference 'to frame a programme, or series of programmes, in accordance with Irish ideals and conditions – due regard being given to local needs and views.'[5] The INTO sought to ensure that practical implications of introducing a second language were to the fore and that teachers had an input in policy formulation.

5.3.1 Composition of the First National Programme Conference

The INTO Congress resolution was acted upon and invitations to a number of representative organisations were issued. Owing to the state of flux within Ireland with the War of Independence, and the view that the INTO was not the proper body to convene such a conference, not all of the invitees saw fit to attend. This meant the conference was not well balanced; Protestant representatives refused to attend as they did not see the conference as a legitimate body,[6] the Professors of Education (with the exception of Rev. Corcoran, who acted as an external advisor) did not participate, the Boards of Education were not represented due to the political climate, school management associations did not attend, while the Inspectorate or representatives from the training colleges were not invited. There is little surviving documentation regarding the *modus operandi* and deliberations of the conference between 1921 and 1922.

The conference was chaired by the aforementioned Máire Ní Chinnéide and T.J. O'Connell of the INTO was appointed Secretary to the Conference. There were eleven members in total, consisting of one representative from the Ministry of Education, one from the General Council of County Councils, one from the National Labour Executive, two from the Gaelic League, five from the INTO and one from the Association of Secondary Teachers (Ireland).[7] This was a narrow membership for the production of a national programme of instruction, with 55 per cent of the representation emanating from the teacher unions. One might surmise that such an imbalance would have been a crucial factor in favour of the INTO, but, as will be documented, the power of the Gaelic League and the affiliation of many representatives at the conference to its ideology proved decisive. For example, Cormac Breathnach was an INTO representative at the first National Programme Conference, while he represented the Gaelic League at the Second National Programme Conference. Éinrí Ó Frighil, representative of the General Council of County Councils, recounted the power of the Gaelic League, supported by Frank Fahy (representative of the Ministry of Education) and other conference members, in successfully advancing the position of Irish.[8]

5.3.2   Report of the First National Programme Conference

Terms of Reference of the Conference

At its first meeting on 6 January 1921, its terms of reference were agreed as the adoption of a *minimum* National Programme; to decide on additional subjects and the circumstances under which such additional subjects should be made compulsory; and to consider the question of national and local administration, training facilities, teaching staffs, school premises, attendance and provision of text books.[9]

The programme produced by the conference in January 1922 was not framed within any exposition of a theoretical framework or philosophy of education. The introductory section occupied a mere three pages, which largely summarised the rest of the twenty-five-page booklet and listed the membership. It offered no rationale or curriculum philosophy for the inclusion or exclusion of subjects, documented no research in relation to complaints levelled at the preceding curriculum nor did it provide any methodological guidance. Moreover, no clear vision as to the practical motivation for introducing Irish was provided. The remainder of the booklet was divided in three and delineated the obligatory subjects, the additional subjects and the conditions necessary for implementing the programme. Consequently, little detail was provided as to the exact syllabus in any subject.

The question of national and local administration of education, although clearly within the terms of reference of the first National Programme Conference, was not dealt with in the final report. Coolahan

surmised that even though the INTO and the vast majority of conference
members were in favour of the MacPherson Bill 1919, the lack of inclusion of its proposals in the report showed it was not wise to follow this
line of enquiry in the new political climate, where the Catholic Church
was opposed and there was little public appetite for reform.[10] The failure
to address the administrative structures of education in the infancy of the
Free State resulted in a heightened sensitivity to structural reform in the
following decades.

Subjects in the Programme

The programme in operation prior to independence was perceived to be
out of harmony with Irish ideals and requirements and was criticised by
the conference for the multiplicity of compulsory subjects and the subordinate position of the Irish language. The report provided a brief outline
of the content of each subject. The core subjects of the 1922 programme
were Irish (reading, spelling, writing, composition, grammar), mathematics
(arithmetic, algebra, geometry), English (reading, spelling, writing, composition, grammar), history and geography, singing, needlework and drill.
The work in infant classes was composed of language, drawing, numbers,
Kindergarten gifts and occupations, songs and games. No time allocation
or subject guidelines were provided for various sized schools, with the
requirement that when the full programme was not implementable, 'each
pupil shall receive instruction in Irish for at least one hour per day as an
ordinary school subject.'[11] Teachers were at liberty to submit alternative
programmes framed along the lines of the national programme. It was
iterated that it represented a minimum programme, with higher standards
expected in schools with better resources and staffing. This is interesting as
there was an acknowledgement that the programme was not implementable
in all schools and yet it was still propagated as the minimum acceptable.
It is noteworthy that the only sentence in bold typeface within the entire
programme issued in 1922 related to the rights of parents to veto instruction in either Irish or English within schools:

> It was decided at an early stage of the proceedings that in the case of schools where the majority of the parents of the children object to have either Irish or English taught as an obligatory subject, their wishes should be complied with.[12]

The subject would then be replaced by the inclusion of an additional subject. Akenson asserts that this caveat was included to protect the rights of Protestants who may not have placed such a high value on the Irish language and also to protect teachers from Gaelic League enthusiasts.[13] Moreover, the Treaty had not been ratified at this point and the possibility of educational legislation for a thirty-two-county Ireland was being kept open.[14]

The status of Irish as a subject and as a medium of instruction was raised to a pre-eminent position owing to the fact that 'it was evident the vast majority of the Irish people wished to have [the Irish language] taught to their children.'[15] This assertion was not substantiated by any research within the report. Irish was not only to be a prominent subject but was to permeate all other subjects and be the official school language. Irish language provision for infants became the most contentious issue within the report. While Irish was to be taught in all classes for at least one hour per day, the report stated in relation to infant classes that '[T]he work in the Infant standard is to be entirely in Irish.'[16] As Akenson described, this was the 'shocker' within the programme report.[17] It allowed no teaching of English, not even as a subject, even though 90 per cent of pupils in infant classes spoke English in their homes.[18]

These provisions made the introduction of Irish far more immediate and broad-based than had been proposed by the Gaelic League in 1918. There was no distinction drawn between Gaeltacht and non-Gaeltacht regions or for the varying proficiency of teachers in the Irish language; Irish was obligatory in all schools for all standards and it was to be used as a medium of instruction in infant classes. Perhaps one reason for the proposal and acceptability of such a radical and unrealistic departure at this time was the patriotic fervour inspired by the attainment of independence and the desire to express Ireland's uniqueness as a nation, in an atmosphere where a focus on the reality of implementation was not to the fore. However, even Pádraig Pearse had advised a bilingual approach to education and did not believe in undertaking a child's education through an unknown medium of instruction:

> Irish should be made the language of instruction in districts where it is the home language, and English the 'second language', taught as a school subject ... Where English is the home language it must of necessity be the 'first language' in the schools, but I would have a compulsory 'second language' ...[19]

Within the programme beyond infant classes, it was proposed that the Irish language permeate the teaching of other subjects, including history, geography and singing. Arithmetic was to be taught in relation to the interests and environment of the child by giving 'a local bias to their teaching as will connect the school work of the pupils with their surroundings.'[20] While teaching English grammar, it was advised that 'the terminology of Irish grammar should be used as far as practicable.'[21] In schools that were previously classified as bilingual, Irish was to become 'the sole medium of instruction, English being taught as an ordinary subject.'[22]

A distinct Anglophobia was inherent in the report of the first National Programme Conference.[23] Teachers were directed to use European literature, both ancient and modern, drawing from good translations, while English authors 'should have just the limited place due to English literature among all the European literatures.'[24] It is arguable that the influence of Rev. Corcoran was instrumental in this regard as he perceived the English language to be 'utterly Protestant in core, in tradition, in expression.'[25]

In history, the emphasis on forming national identity was stressed:

> One of the chief aims of the teaching of history should be to develop the best traits of the national character and to inculcate national pride and self-respect. This will not be attained by the cramming of dates and details but rather by showing that the Irish race has fulfilled a great mission in the advancement of civilisation and that, on the whole, the Irish nation has amply justified its existence.[26]

Biographies of outstanding Irish personages were recommended for study in middle classes. In addition, there was to be a greater focus on periods of political division such as the Penal Laws and the land wars, while local history was given little attention. This confrontational focus is perhaps understandable considering the historical context of the War of Independence at the time. The programme prescribed was largely chronological and implied a concept of the child as a passive recipient of facts imparted by the teacher. History and geography were to be taught together as one subject, with formal teaching beginning in fifth class. In history, the years 432–1801 were included in the fifth class syllabus, while the period 1801–1922 was to be taught in sixth class. Within geography, the main emphasis was to be on the geography of Ireland. Needlework was removed as a subject in the lower standards and was to be taught from third class upwards. In singing, the report advocated the use of the staff or sol-fa notation methods, while instruction 'is to be given in the medium of Irish, and all songs are to be in the Irish language.'[27] Drill was to be taught for thirty minutes per week with all instructions to be given in Irish.

From 1922, the following subjects became additional (optional) subjects in primary schools – drawing, advanced algebra, advanced geometry and mensuration, French (or other continental language), Latin, nature study, book-keeping, elementary science, cookery, rural science and school gardening, manual instruction (woodwork) and domestic science. Fees would be paid where one or more of these subjects were taught outside school hours.

Conditions for the Implementation of the Programme

The third section of the first National Programme Conference report made a number of recommendations in relation to the implementation of the programme. This spanned two pages and covered four aspects: teacher training, the acquisition of Irish by teachers, suggestions for schools where the full programme was impractical and school attendance.[28] The report recommended a four-year university degree course for teachers and the provision of facilities to allow practising teachers to attain degrees. While laudable, this provision was unfeasible at this time in Ireland owing to the low levels of educational attainment of many entrants to the training colleges. Courses that did not impact on teachers' leisure time or holidays were proposed in Irish, organised by the Department. In the transition period before the programme was fully implementable, teachers competent in Irish were to be used within schools to ensure all classes received instruction in Irish. Otherwise, the service of an extern teacher was to be employed. The report also called for the implementation of school attendance legislation.

The INTO was concerned regarding the effects and requirements on its members in relation to Irish and presented a resolution from the CEC to the conference in October 1921.[29] This prompted a delegation to attend a meeting with J.J. O'Kelly, Minister for Education, on 5 November 1921 to discuss the implications for teachers who were not able to implement fully the Irish requirements of the programme. O'Kelly assured the delegation that 'there will be no undue hardship or injustice inflicted on any teacher, who, owing to his special circumstances, is unable to fit himself for the teaching in Irish.'[30]

As the drafting of the programme reached a conclusion, it was examined by a Co-ordination Committee to ensure the programme dovetailed with other curricula at second and third level, an innovative measure in the contemporary context. All eleven members signed the final report of the first National Programme Conference on 28 January 1922, days before the Commissioners of National Education were relieved of their duties. A circular was issued in April 1922, stating that the programme of the first National Programme Conference was to be implemented from September of that year.[31]

The programme introduced in 1922 was much narrower than its predecessor, primarily framed along nationalist lines and taking less cognisance of the child's interests and abilities. Not only did the range of subjects become more restricted but the content and focus of many became decidedly Irish in orientation, particularly history and singing. Moreover, there was a gradual exclusion of international content and perspectives, such as in geography where jurisdictions beyond Ireland were only to be included 'to fix the position of Ireland.'[32] The centrality of the Irish language within the programme placed a great strain on many teachers and pupils, even though the programme was characterised as the minimum to be achieved. Not only was the Irish language introduced as a subject but it was envisaged as a medium of instruction for many subjects in the programme, in both Gaeltacht and Galltacht areas. Perhaps owing to the fervour of the achievement of independence, the conference designed an aspirational programme that did not take into account the realities or needs of schools, teachers or pupils at the time. It is arguable that a provisional programme may have been more beneficial as a transitional step for such radical curriculum change, which could have been built on incrementally as capacity developed. Such an incremental approach had been advocated by the Gaelic League in 1918 to accommodate the varying contexts of schools and it is arguable that circumstances had changed little by 1922.

Throughout the process of devising the programme, the CEC and wider membership of the INTO were kept well informed and provided with drafts of the programme as they were developed. A draft was published in the *The Irish School Weekly* on 13 August 1921 to promote discussion and debate and views were sought from members.[33] Such an extensive method of consultation by the INTO was impressive, seeking to reach and include the views of all members through various structures. The positive nature of many of the responses conflicted with the subsequent complaints by teachers about the programme, but it must be remembered that certain elements, including the use of Irish as a teaching medium in infant classes, were not included in the programme at this point. This was a significant later inclusion, which altered fundamentally the provisions of the programme, especially in infant classes.

The INTO played a fundamental role in the first National Programme Conference, from establishing it, providing the Secretary to the Conference and 45 per cent of its membership. In this light, it could be considered surprising that the objectives and ideals of the INTO were not achieved to a greater degree in 1922, especially in relation to the use of Irish as a medium of instruction in infant classes. For the INTO, the programme offered a much-reduced curriculum, a measure of freedom to teachers regarding timetabling and implementation and the prospect of improved conditions in relation to buildings, maintenance and attendance. However, it placed great demands on teachers in relation to its provisions in Irish. One would surmise that the more conciliatory approach of the Gaelic League programme could have been promoted by the INTO as a transitional and incremental solution. However, the prominence and persuasiveness of the Gaelic League had grown exponentially in the intervening years and its expectations for education in an independent Ireland had grown accordingly.

5.4 The Influence of Rev. Timothy Corcoran S.J. on the First and Second National Programme Conferences

The evidence submitted in oral and written form to the first National Programme Conference was never published or documented and it remains difficult to ascertain how much the end product reflected the views and opinions of contributors. Rev. Corcoran S.J., Professor of Education at University College Dublin, had a significant influence on the Gaelic League programme (1918) and acted as an external advisor to both the first and Second National Programme Conferences. His influence is evidenced in the eulogy of Mr J.J. O'Neill, first Secretary at the Department of Education, who was well placed to measure his impact:

> In the reconstruction of the Irish State, he was, from the beginning, the master-builder in Education. The Commissions on Education, set up in 1921, were guided so largely by him that it may be said that the curricula, aims and methods in Primary and Secondary Education which emerged from them were, in the main, the work of his hands.[34]

Rev. Corcoran's prolific writings offer some insights into the philosophy and ideology of this important influence in programme development in the 1920s. He asserted that each child was in the possession of a corrupt nature and weakness of will due to original sin and this corruption could only be driven away by instruction and punishment.[35] Therefore, he espoused a didactic and rigorous method of teaching, imparting the essentials of education in a formal way:

> Interesting teaching is very liable to minimise the essential methods of thorough repetition. Work done from day to day, from week to week, without the hardening influence of revision and of definite testing, is liable to become vague, blurred, and unreliable ... Large masses of facts must be known.[36]

To this end, he castigated the new and progressive educational thinking of philosophers such as Kant, Fichte, Rousseau, Herbart, Pestalozzi, Froebel, Compte, Spencer, James, Dewey and Durkheim, which allowed freedom and initiative to the child, and warned against their adoption in Ireland.[37] Instead he advocated a return to more didactic and formal traditions that had been prominent prior to 1900, placing a focus on memorisation, repetition and the acquisition of a critical mass of knowledge. He did not see any room for joy or pleasure in learning, believing that 'all true education must progressively combine effort with mere interest: it is the effort that enobles and makes worthily human.'[38]

In relation to Irish, Corcoran was adamant that the most effective and efficient way to instigate a language revival was through the schools, particularly infant classes. While not an expert on child psychology or linguistics, or indeed a proficient Irish speaker himself, he forwarded strong opinions and assertions in relation to the Irish language, many of which were simple solutions to complex issues that Irish language enthusiasts were pleased to hear. Corcoran was a proponent of the direct method of teaching, which he asserted negated the necessity to move from the known to the unknown, and thus justified the teaching of infants through a non-vernacular.[39] He cited successful cases of second language learning in the USA and Europe using the direct method.[40] However, these examples related to contexts vastly different to the Irish situation, where the languages in question were already widely spoken and there was a motivation and rationale for their use. From these models, Corcoran concluded that the crucial period for language learning was from the age of three. He proposed establishing Irish language preschools to capture the linguistic assimilation powers of infants:

> The [Irish] language should be the sole aim of that school: if it is, the habit of using the language can be given by one teacher to a hundred children in one year and it can become a permanent possession, a second nature, within the three years ... What about English in such a school? It has no place whatever.[41]

Corcoran asserted that Irish could be transmitted as a vernacular within schools and moreover, '[T]hey can do it even without positive aid from the home.'[42] This would lead to a situation whereby Irish became the dominant language of the country, while English would serve as a 'subordinate' second language. He did not believe in a transitional or incremental

approach to the language as advocated by Pearse, urging all involved to
seize the moment:

> There are too many who are inclined to temporise, to go slow, to make apologies for
> the right policy. Such an attitude makes for defeat on the language front, though the
> path to victory is not so very difficult.[43]

Corcoran's influence carried weight and his convictions were included in
the programme planning in both 1922 and 1926. In many cases, Corcoran
analysed the successful introduction of majority languages, as opposed
to minority languages. While correct in his assertion that the early years
were the language years, he simplified the complexity of introducing Irish
in all primary schools and gave scant regard to factors such as the training
of teachers, parental attitudes and the need for linguistic reinforcement
outside schools. He refused to acknowledge the growing body of knowledge that young children learned best through activity and experiences
as opposed to direct instruction, and as O'Connor argued, his assertions
were highly influential in ensuring the child-centred philosophy of the
1900 programme was not adopted in the Irish Free State.[44]

5.5 Second National Programme Conference

5.5.1 Establishing the Second National Programme Conference

Following two years of implementation of the programme issued by the
first National Programme Conference, the CEC of the INTO officially
called for a second conference to reconsider the programme in May 1924.[45]
It invited by circular previous members of the first National Programme
Conference to attend the review, and while most invitees replied positively,
the Minister refused to send representatives. A deputation from the INTO
met Minister Eoin MacNeill on 1 November 1924 to discuss the lack of
implementation of the recommendations of the first National Programme

Conference, such as the provision of resources, degree training for teachers, improvement of buildings and legislation for school attendance.[46] It also stressed the need for a representative council to modify the programme, referring to the recent modifications made by the Department in mathematics, history, geography, music and needlework. The INTO proposed a conference to examine the programme and argued that it would have more authority if convened by the Minister and consisted of all relevant parties to Irish education.[47] While Minister MacNeill agreed to convene the conference, he asserted it would be an advisory body and he would not be bound by its recommendations.

5.5.2   Composition and Work of the Second National Programme Conference

On 19 May 1925, Minister MacNeill invited a large number of interested parties to attend the Second National Programme Conference. This included a wider array of organisations and interests than attended the first National Programme Conference in 1922. On 4 June 1925, the Second National Programme Conference issued its terms of reference:

> To consider the suitability of the National Programme of Primary Instruction at present in operation in the National Schools, to report to the Minister for Education thereon, and to make recommendations to him as regards any alterations which may seem desirable.[48]

The terms of reference issued to the conference were narrower than in 1922, relating specifically to the programme and with no mention of issues such as school administration or facilities. Rev. Lambert McKenna, a Jesuit priest, chaired the conference. He was a fitting choice of chairman for the Minister as he was a strong proponent of the Irish language and had asserted the positive benefits of studying Irish for the individual and the nation.[49] The Second National Programme Conference consisted of three school manager representatives, five INTO representatives, one representative from the General Council of County Councils, one representative from

the Gaelic League and eleven nominees of the Minister, including politicians and inspectors.

The representation at the Second National Programme Conference
was larger and somewhat wider. However, there was still no direct representation of the training colleges, the Professors of Education, secondary
schools or wider community interests. There were three Protestant representatives at the Second National Programme Conference, a group that was
not represented in 1922. The INTO retained a considerable representation
and while delegates from other organisations were chosen by the Minister,
the INTO was at liberty to choose its own delegates. Most importantly,
the Minister had an inbuilt majority in his eleven nominees.

Correspondence in the National Archives sheds light on this composition. The Department of Education had wished for a wider and larger
number of representatives at the conference, but was discouraged from
doing so by the Department of Finance.[50] The *modus operandi* of the Second
National Programme Conference was impressive and included a sophisti-
cated process of consultation with interested parties and the wider public.
At its first meeting on 9 June 1925, the conference delegated a number of
tasks to a sub-committee. These included drafting a notice for the Press
inviting 'reasoned statements' from interested and knowledgeable parties; preparing and issuing a special letter with questions to individuals
and public bodies whose opinions the conference thought valuable; and
selecting witnesses for oral evidence. The meeting also addressed key questions that had been circulated for consideration relating to the number of
subjects in the programme, provision for teaching Irish and through Irish,
and modifications needed for local conditions.[51]

'Reasoned statements' were received from fifty-four bodies, 150 individuals and 1,260 teachers on summer courses before the deadline of 20 July
1925.[52] A letter requesting statements was issued to a number of organisations not directly represented at the conference. The letter contained eight
sections for consideration and feedback, including the level of detail to be
provided in the programme, the list of obligatory and optional subjects,
views on the teaching of infants, and opinions on the teaching of Irish and
using Irish as a medium of instruction.[53]

The responses received were collated under the eight questions.[54] Throughout 1925 and into 1926, the conference continued to receive correspondence from organisations and individuals relating to the programme. Owing to the expert and representative written responses from interested parties, the conference 'did not think it necessary to summon a large number of witnesses for oral examination.'[55] Subsequently, it interviewed nineteen carefully selected witnesses, including Corcoran, three inspectors and a number of teachers from varying size schools and school contexts. At its second meeting on 22 September 1925, the conference appointed an Examining Sub-committee of twelve members to take evidence from these witnesses.[56] In addition, documents, reports, inspectors' reports, school statistics, syllabi drafted by experts in relation to certain subjects and annotated timetables for European schools were also distributed among conference members to inform their deliberations.[57]

Following the collection and collation of the evidence, the third session of the conference took place from 17 to 26 November 1925 to discuss major aspects of the programme, 'on which, in nearly every instance, we had the great satisfaction of arriving at unanimous decisions.'[58] This included discussion on the level of detail programmes should contain, varying programmes for different sized schools, the list of compulsory and additional subjects, the use of Irish in infant classes and the rights of parents to veto subjects.[59] At that point, two sub-committees were formed, one to draft the programme for schools and the other to draft the report.

5.5.3 *Oral Evidence at the Second National Programme Conference*

Teachers

The evidence presented at the Second National Programme Conference was often polarised and the conference had to tread a careful path to satisfy the exigencies of the various representatives. A number of teachers, all of whom were rated as efficient or higher and had appropriate Irish qualifications, were selected to give evidence, ensuring they represented Gaeltacht,

Breac-Ghaeltacht and English-speaking areas.[60] One overwhelming thread of continuity in the evidence from teachers was the request to issue a definite and detailed programme for all types of schools, including *Notes for Teachers* and specimen timetables.[61] In general, teachers requested a specific focus on oral Irish:

> To save the Irish language I think our first aim at present is to speak it and make Irish speakers of the children.[62]

Máire Ní Ghallachobhair believed it was advantageous to use Irish as a medium in infant classes as pupils gained an ability to assimilate Irish and understand it as a medium in senior classes.[63] However, Cáit Nic Fhlanchuidhe asserted that if the early years were the language years, it too was the time for language development in English.[64] The call to use some English in infant classes was reiterated by many of the teachers.[65] There were also suggestions for Irish to be used as a medium of instruction in the Gaeltacht and English as a subject, with the inverse the case for Galltacht regions.[66] Mr MacEnrí called for three detailed programmes to be devised for various schools; one for the Gaeltacht, one for the Breac-Ghaeltacht and one for the Galltacht, reflecting the programme that the Gaelic League proposed in 1918. A number of witnesses called for a wider curriculum, increasing the number of compulsory subjects proportionate to the number of teachers in the school, retaining only Irish, English, mathematics, and needlework for girls, as the core subjects.[67] The antipathy of parents to Irish was cited by a number of teachers, recalling incidences of parents withdrawing children from schools over its teaching.[68]

Inspectors

Liam Mac Fhachtna, Inspector of Irish, called on teachers to place a greater emphasis on oral Irish and on the teaching methods used, asserting that not all teachers with the Bilingual Certificate were competent to teach through the medium of Irish.[69] Mr Hanly, Inspector of Rural Science, pointed out that rural science as an optional subject had not been successful, as only 112 out of the 1,400 schools with qualified teachers offered the subject.[70]

Inspectors Ó Ceallaigh and O'Tierney called for a broad programme, designed for one-, two- and three-teacher schools, from which teachers would draft annual schemes for approval, with programme requirements depending on the size of school.[71]

An Inspector's Conference on the National Programme in 1925 advocated the increased use of Irish as a medium of instruction in national schools where pupils and teachers were competent, 'until eventually all subjects except English are taught through Irish.'[72] It also proposed that geography and history be taught as separate subjects, that the subject matter in English readers should relate more to Irish life and the inclusion of nature study/ rural science as a subject. A number of individual inspectors also submitted written evidence in relation to education within their districts. Accounts of the implementation of Irish were contradictory; some referring to the progress as being 'undoubtedly disappointing',[73] while others offered general commendation on the success to date:

> The results obtained in Irish are in my opinion encouraging, and if the rate of improvement from year to year is maintained, a large number of the pupils who began their school life a few years ago will be able to speak Irish fluently when they leave the Primary Schools.[74]

Other Stakeholders

In his evidence to the Second National Programme Conference, Rev. Corcoran proposed that the Department issue a general programme, with the detail devised locally by teachers, managers and inspectors. He advocated that subjects such as elementary science, manual instruction, cookery and laundry were unsuited to primary schools.[75] He also called for citizenship to be associated with moral education, for drawing to be linked to mathematics and that physical training be taught to all pupils. In addition, '[M]usic should be entirely re-organised to suit the learning of Irish.'[76] The main thrust of Corcoran's evidence related to the teaching of Irish in infant classes:

The dominant subject in Infant standards, and up to 8 years of age, should be the oral use of Irish. Every part of the curriculum, under 8 years of age, should be annexed to Irish and subserve oral command of it.[77]

Mr Culverwell, Professor of Education at Trinity College Dublin, proposed better adaptation of the programme to the needs of localities. He proposed that Irish be compulsory in infant classes but optional in senior classes, so that it did not interfere with general education.[78] He supported maintaining the veto for parents to object to the teaching of either English or Irish, maintaining that ninety schools had used this right to date. Rev. Phelan, Christian Brothers' Training College, called for the addition of drawing, nature study, manual instruction and domestic economy to the programme, where circumstances permitted.[79] Rev. O'Rahilly, National School Manager, called for a definite and detailed programme, maintaining the core subjects and adding nature study, rural science and citizenship as reading subjects. He proposed the complete exclusion of subjects such as manual instruction, cookery and laundry from primary schools. In addition, he believed that the summer courses in Irish were flawed as they failed to prepare teachers to use Irish as a medium of instruction.[80]

5.5.4 Additional Evidence Collated by the Conference

In addition to oral evidence, the conference collated the submissions received from the public, from organisations and individuals invited to submit proposals and examined documentary evidence. The Catholic Clerical Managers' Association called for the use of both Irish and English in infant classes and for a reduction on the insistence of teaching other subjects through Irish.[81] The Dublin Chamber of Commerce felt that if the programme was to equip children for life, there should be less emphasis on Irish and other subjects should not be taught through Irish.[82] The Association of Training College Teachers called for two periods of fifteen minutes each to be given in infant classes for the teaching of English reading.[83] The submission from Galway County Council advocated the teaching of Irish in schools, but in relation to its use as a teaching medium, it was felt 'that it is not, at present, generally possible to teach the ordinary school programme through the medium of Irish, and that it would probably do great injury to education generally – and to the language itself – to attempt to go too fast in the matter.'[84] The submission from the Defence Forces focused on three particular aspects it thought neglected in the programme; physical culture, hygiene and elements of citizenship.[85] There was much support for the inclusion of civics as a subject in light of the recent achievement of independence.[86]

The Department of Lands and Agriculture and a number of agricultural colleges also forwarded submissions, focusing particularly on defects within the primary curriculum as they related to agricultural education. These included the poor knowledge of arithmetic, defective spelling, poor composition and writing, meagre geographical knowledge, the absence of initiative and a deficiency of general information.[87] It also cautioned against teaching subjects through Irish to pupils who had not learned the language from infant classes, citing it to be 'an additional handicap to the general education of such pupils.'[88]

A number of submissions from Protestant organisations raised the issue of compulsion in relation to Irish and the nationalist leanings of the history programme. The submission from the Protestant Teachers' Union called for a definite programme to be laid down and requested that Irish not be taught below first standard unless it was the vernacular.[89] The Church of Ireland General Synod's Board of Education also raised concerns about compulsory Irish:

> it is in no spirit of hostility to Irish Studies that we feel compelled to enter the strongest protest against the inclusion at the present time of Irish as a compulsory subject at all standards.[90]

Following extensive consultation with members, the INTO submission requested a detailed and definite programme to be issued. While the provision of a wide and varied programme was seen as preferable on educational grounds, it asserted the need for concentration on the essential subjects:

It is too often forgotten that one of the chief aims of the primary school is, or should be, the training of the child in the methods of acquiring knowledge rather than imparting of the actual knowledge itself.[91]

The INTO insisted that if Irish was to retain its compulsory status, there could be no widening of the programme. It was proposed that Irish should not be used as a medium of instruction unless both the teacher and the pupils were competent in the language. The submission also noted the effects that teaching through Irish was having at senior level, where proficiency in subjects such as history and geography could not be achieved while teaching them through the medium of Irish.

A number of discussions were held between the members of the conference in relation to the use of English in infant classes. The Chairman pointed out that the vast majority of the evidence and submissions favoured some use of English.[92] Four main reasons were given for the inclusion of some English: to conciliate parents and gain their goodwill, pupils were often in infant classes until age eight or nine which was too late to start formal learning of English, the difficulty of reading in later standards without a foundation and the need for children to be able to read English to study Catechism. Mr O'Connell argued that all INTO branches wished for the teaching of infants to be in the medium of English unless the children were native Irish speakers. However, some opposed such a development, including Cormac Breathnach, who asserted that 'I will certainly stand by saying that no English of any kind should be allowed for the first two years.'[93]

The Second National Programme Conference made considerable effort and was successful in garnering the considered opinions of a wide array of interested and relevant educational interests in Ireland. It is evident from the foregoing analysis that although certain trends and aspects of consensus were visible, there was much contradictory evidence, particularly relating to the Irish language. The final report distilled the essence of this evidence and through conciliation, negotiation and compromise, framed a programme it aspired would be acceptable to all.

5.6   Report of the Second National Programme Conference

5.6.1   Introduction

The report of the Second National Programme Conference was published on 5 March 1926 and endorsed the programme framed in 1922 as being far superior to its predecessor towards achieving the educational aim of the Irish government. It approved the aims and philosophy of its predecessor, insofar as it strengthened the national fibre by giving the history, language, music and tradition of Ireland their natural place in the life of schools. The 1926 report contained a longer introduction than the 1922 programme, outlining the difficulties in implementing the preceding programme and the proposed solutions. However, it offered no examination of the underlying assumptions, assertions or philosophy of the 1922 report.

The Second National Programme Conference set out the same high purpose for education but differed in that it produced a transitional programme 'being indicative of gradual steps in a steady progress towards an ideal, and being adjustable to the varying circumstances of our schools.'[94] The opt out clause for parents in relation to the teaching of Irish and English prominent in the 1922 programme was formally dropped in the 1926 programme. This clause had protected and offered choice to minority groups in Ireland, such as Protestants, and its omission in 1926 was a serious blow to such interests. The programme issued by the conference was designed primarily for two-teacher schools, which consisted of 71 per cent of schools at that time.

5.6.2   Subjects of the Second National Programme Conference

The 1926 conference issued the following as obligatory subjects: Irish, English, mathematics, geography, history, rural science or nature study, music and needlework for girls. The work in infant classes was identical to that laid out in 1922. The conference acknowledged that the range of compulsory subjects was narrow but justified this for two reasons:

- The efforts to restore Irish as the vernacular, a temporary difficulty, would more than counterbalance such negative effects by the better mental development which the command of two languages conferred on children and;
- The feeling that the previous course had been too extensive and that there was a trend on concentrating on an essential minimum of subjects in other jurisdictions.

The conference provided no evidence as to the 'better mental development' learning two languages provided. Furthermore, the assertion by the conference report that the trend internationally was to concentrate 'on an essential minimum of subjects in recent years'[95] was inaccurate. An examination of evidence gathered by the conference on the curricula of some European countries in the 1920s reveals a broad-based, wide and balanced curriculum in operation.[96]

Irish and English

The requirements in relation to the teaching of Irish were modified somewhat in 1926 to allow greater freedom 'and at the same time serve as a practical discretion and a sympathetic exhortation to those of them who are not as yet fully qualified in Irish.'[97] Most notable of all was that Irish and English were now to be taught in higher and lower courses, depending on the competence of pupils and teachers. The higher course was to be taken in the predominant language of the school and the lower course in the other language, a transitional step until all schools were able to take the higher course in Irish 'as the teachers' qualifications improve.'[98] Initially, only a small number of schools would be capable of the higher course in Irish but it was hoped that practically all would be capable of the lower course. The final report stated clearly that instruction through Irish was only to take place when the teacher was proficient and competent in the language and pupils were able to assimilate the instruction given.

The various subsets of English and Irish comprised conversation, reading, memory work, writing, grammar and composition, graded according to the higher or lower course and the class in question. The rule remained regarding the teaching of infants through Irish, as its benefit had been promulgated through 'authoritative evidence.'[99] This evidence elucidated that by teaching Irish using the direct method for a number of years between the ages of four and eight, it 'would be quite sufficient – given trained and fluent teachers – to impart to children a vernacular power over the language.'[100] It is highly probable that the source of this 'authoritative evidence' was Rev. Corcoran. Furthermore, while the assertion may have carried some truth, the contemporary context certainly could not provide 'trained and fluent teachers' in the Irish language. A compromise was reached regarding the use of English in infant classes, allowing the concession that before 10:30 a.m. and after 2:00 p.m., English could be taught. The practical usefulness of this provision is questionable, considering the late time many schools started and the shorter day for infants, usually terminating around 2:00 p.m.

The conference also recommended that the teaching of infants should be entrusted 'to the best Irish teacher in the school – even if that teacher be the principal of the school.'[101] The Bilingual Certificate was taken as an acceptable qualification but was not a necessity to teach Irish, while teachers who were not entirely competent to teach through Irish were instructed to teach it for one hour per day and to use it as often as possible outside that. An interim solution of hiring temporary teachers to impart instruction in Irish where no teachers were qualified or competent to do so within schools was promulgated in the report.

Mathematics

The mathematics programme was comprised of arithmetic, algebra and geometry. Owing to difficulties in the previous programme, the 1926 conference modified its provisions and asserted additionally that 'the present state of Mathematical knowledge among women-teachers left us no alternative but to suggest that both Algebra and Geometry be optional for all women-teachers.'[102] In addition, algebra and geometry became optional in one-teacher schools. If rural science was taught in a mixed two-teacher school with a male principal, it was then optional to omit either algebra or geometry. Teachers were also urged when teaching mathematics to have regard for 'the actual experience and interests of the pupils.'[103] Attention of teachers was also drawn to the fact that mental work should precede written work, that pupils should be encouraged to discover principles for themselves and to place a greater emphasis on accuracy.

Other Compulsory Subjects

History and geography were reconstituted as separate subjects and prior to their formal introduction, it was advised that simple concepts and interesting information be imparted informally through readers. It was encouraged that a proper perspective be maintained on military and national events:

> Attention should be paid especially to the broader issues of the period, such as the struggle for national independence and religious equality, and to the struggle for the land and the language.[104]

Local history, a previously neglected aspect, was raised in importance by proposing improved supports for teachers to gather information locally. The conference proposed that the information collected could be collated and distributed in each area as a resource for all teachers. The focus in geography was on local and Irish aspects, while important geographical facts of other countries, as they related to Ireland, were to be taught. Both history and geography were to be taught through the medium of Irish, where feasible.

The music programme was to be limited due to the demands on the timetable, with a distinct focus on Irish music. An emphasis was to be placed on singing with purity and tone, with all songs in the Irish language in the lower standards, while some songs 'from non-Irish composers may be admitted, but only those in which the music is of a high standard.'[105] Needlework was a compulsory subject for girls from third class, though smaller schools were not required to complete all of its components. The main aspects of the subject were knitting and sewing, while darning and garment making were added in senior classes.

Either rural science or nature study was added as an obligatory subject depending on the type and size of school. The focus of these subjects was on the educational as opposed to vocational viewpoint:

> they will be of great indirect utility in making our children favourably disposed towards, and prepared for, agriculture, the natural vocation of a large proportion of them, and in interesting all of them in the characteristics and resources of our country.[106]

The criterion of achievement was to be 'the success of the teacher in arousing the children's curiosity and in stimulating their interest in the facts of nature.'[107] The subjects were not compulsory in one-teacher schools or in schools without teachers qualified to teach them.

Optional Subjects

In addition to these compulsory subjects, the following subjects were optional within schools: drawing, domestic science, cookery, laundry, physical training and manual instruction. There was an expectation that physical training would be taught in larger urban schools and the programme outlined the positive effects on deportment and manners as well as 'its excellent effects upon national health and efficiency.'[108] It was considered more appropriate to introduce subjects such as manual instruction and domestic economy at post-primary level, owing to lack of time and facilities. Fees for teachers were recommended for cookery and laundry taught outside school hours.

Religion

The statement within the report of the Second National Programme Conference regarding religion was insightful and elucidated the influence of the Catholic Church, both on the conference and in society generally. No such statement had been included in the 1922 programme and it is quoted in full here to give an accurate sense of its thrust:

; of a school curriculum Religious instruction is by far the most impor-
;ubject matter, God's honour and service, includes the proper use of all
ties, and affords the most powerful inducements to their proper use. We
assume therefore, that Religious Instruction is a fundamental part of the school
course. Though the time allotted to it as a specific subject is necessarily short, a
religious spirit should inform and vivify the whole work of the school. The teacher
– while careful in the presence of children of different religious beliefs, not to
touch on matters of controversy – should constantly inculcate, in connection with
secular subjects the practice of charity, justice, truth, purity, patience, temperance,
obedience to lawful authority and all the other moral virtues. In this way, he will
fulfil the primary duty of an educator, the moulding to perfect form of his pupils'
character, habituating them to observe, in their relations with God and with their
neighbour, the laws which God both directly through the dictates of natural reason
and through Revelation, and indirectly through the ordinance of lawful authority,
imposes on mankind.[109]

Evidently, the statement was carefully phrased so as not to relate specifically to any one religious denomination or alter in any way the mixed
denominational principle underpinning the national system, yet would be
of most benefit to the Catholic Church which owned and managed the
majority of schools. The language of the statement is useful for an analysis
of the curriculum insofar as it elucidated a certain image of the child as
perceived by the conference. The child was conceptualised as an object to
be 'moulded,' as opposed to building on the uniqueness and individuality
of all children. This particular conceptualisation of childhood required a
defined curriculum, delivered through didactical methodologies to ensure
that knowledge was conveyed and assimilated. This was in direct contrast to
the concept of the child inherent in the *Revised Programme* (1900). From
the 1920s, religion was left to the expertise of the churches and therefore no
syllabus was set forth in this area, nor was the Inspectorate to be responsible
for the examination or supervision of the subject. This left religion in a
central but ambiguous position; while it was the central tenet and unifying force within the curriculum, no guidelines on its teaching or content
were included in the final report and the Department retained no control
over its implementation.

5.6.3 Conditions for the Implementation of the Programme

The report of the Second National Programme Conference also issued a number of recommendations it considered necessary to implement the new programme. These included the improvement of the material condition of many schools, the introduction of free school meals in various districts at certain times, the provision of schoolbooks, guidance from the Department to publishers to ensure books were in harmony with departmental policy, the formulation of *Notes for Teachers* detailing the changes to the programme and the advancement of plans to enable teachers to obtain degrees. These recommendations were largely practical in nature and addressed many of the concerns expressed by witnesses and conference members in relation to implementation.

A note of reservation was included by the four signatories from the INTO, while the fifth delegate did not sign the final report. The note of reservation proposed the number of obligatory subjects be reduced to Irish, English, mathematics and needlework, as these core subjects had many subsets that had to be taught in both Irish and English. The INTO further suggested that a list of optional subjects should be issued, and schools could choose from this based on local circumstances, resources and qualifications of staff. While the INTO agreed on most matters within the report, it believed that in the prevailing conditions 'effective work could be done only by concentrating on those subjects which were regarded as absolutely essential.'[110] Following the deliberations of the conference, the Minister for Education accepted the programme of the conference on 7 May 1926, without modification. Furthermore, he agreed to consider its recommendations in relation to the necessary supports for the implementation of the programme.[111] A circular was issued in July 1926 to this effect, while the programme was implemented in schools from September 1926.[112]

The Second National Programme Conference was convened to frame a programme that was attainable as opposed to an ideal. It was felt that a transitional programme was needed to satisfy the demands of enthusiasts and to allay the fears of teachers, while indicating the gradual steps by which the ideals of the 1922 programme might be realised. The formulation of the 1926 programme appears to have been more comprehensive and inclusive than its predecessor, attaining the views and perspectives of the key interests in Irish education. However, like its predecessor, it failed to delineate a theoretical framework as an underpinning for its provisions and to substantiate the rationale for the inclusion or exclusion of various subjects. The final report conveyed an earnest desire to distil the essence of the evidence gathered and to produce a programme amenable to the views of engaged parties. This was a complex task considering the contradictory nature of much of the evidence gathered, with powerful arguments advanced by both opponents and proponents of the Irish language. The resulting programme was less stringent in its provisions for the Irish language, accommodating the various contexts by introducing a higher and lower course and allowing some teaching of English in infant classes. This introduced some level of mediation of the programme and recognised the differing realities of various geographical areas. However, considering the volume of evidence in favour of not using Irish as a medium of instruction, particularly in infant classes, the power of the Gaelic lobby is evident in the minor reforms introduced.

The rest of the 1922 programme remained largely intact, apart from the inclusion of nature study or rural science as an obligatory subject, the removal of drill, the reconstitution of history and geography as separate subjects and minor modifications within other subjects. In spite of many calls for a definite and detailed programme to be delineated, the programme for all compulsory and optional subjects occupied a mere thirty pages. In the absence of the promised *Notes for Teachers* in most subjects until 1933, it provided an inadequate support for teachers in determining the content and methodologies to be employed. The conference represented the final comprehensive public investigation into the primary curriculum for in excess of forty years and its underlying philosophy and provisions remained intact until 1971.

5.7   Provision of *Notes for Teachers*

There was little detail provided on the individual subjects in the programmes issued in 1922 and 1926 and it is arguable that this absence of direct information for teachers before the issuing of Notes adversely affected their capacity to interpret and implement the programme within classrooms and schools. *Notes for Teachers* relating to rural science and nature study were provided in 1927 and between 1933 and 1935, Notes were made available in the remaining subjects. Below is a brief outline of the nature and content of these Notes and an analysis of their usefulness as a resource for teachers implementing the programme introduced in the 1920s.

Notes on Rural Science and Nature Study (1927) espoused the aims of the subject to be the deepening of children's interest in the world around them, to lead to enquiry and to appeal to the senses.[113] Further notes were provided in 1930 in relation to undertaking lessons in these subjects. These advocated the organisation of school plots and stressed the practical nature of the subject, that in 'the education of children things are more effective than words.'[114]

Notes on Irish (1933) reiterated the important role of schools in the restoration of Irish as the vernacular and outlined the various aspects in the junior, middle and senior classes. The perceived extent of teachers' competence in Irish may be illustrated by the fact the *Notes for Teachers* on Irish were written in English. Schools were not only to teach Irish and use it as a medium of instruction, but were also to ensure its use as the official and incidental language of the school. All instruction was to serve the needs and interests of the national linguistic endeavour, for which children were to act as frontline soldiers:

> Its aim is frankly and unequivocally to make Irish speakers of the children of the Galltacht (English-speaking areas), so that by the age of fourteen they may be able to express themselves freely, fully and correctly in the new language ... ensure or preserve the cultural continuity of the nation by putting its youth into possession of the language, literature, history and traditions of the historic Irish people, thus fixing its outlook in the Gaelic mould.[115]

This provides an insight into curriculum thinking at that time. An externalist view of the curriculum is prevalent, whereby each child was to be moulded in the Gaelic outlook, focusing on the needs of the nation as opposed to that of the child. Beyond advocating the direct method of instruction, little advice was furnished on methodology. Furthermore, a greater emphasis was placed on written aspects of the language as opposed to oral, despite the avowed aim to make Irish the vernacular of children.

Notes on English (1933) broke down the number of components that comprised the subject, including reading (oral and silent), explanation of matter, composition, penmanship, spelling and dictation, formal grammar and analysis, paraphrasing, memorisation and recitation of poetry.[116] The Notes on English were particularly short and teachers were advised to consult the *Notes for Teachers* on Irish for a description of teaching methods. Notes on History (1933) cited the subject as being one of the most difficult for teachers to teach but if well taught 'pupils will learn that they are citizens of no mean country, that they belong to a race that has a noble tradition of heroism, and persistent loyalty to ideals.'[117] This was to be portrayed not only by acts of patriotism and self-sacrifice, but also by those who served Ireland in more humble ways. The importance of local history was stressed as was the significance of using the Irish language to impart instruction:

> The Irish language was perhaps the most powerful of the influences that saved our people from defeat and absorption from alien forces in that long struggle. It is still a very powerful influence in preserving national continuity and for this if for no other reason it is most fitting that it should be the language used in our schools to teach our history.[118]

Notes on National Tradition and Folklore (1934) stressed the value of Irish folklore and lamented its lack of prominence in the Irish curriculum.[119] Visits to local areas and ruins were encouraged in the effort to enliven the interest of pupils.

Notes on Physical Training (1933) drew on the system of physical education in operation in Sweden at the time, where the interdependence between the body and mind was stressed.[120] There was also a moral dimension to the training, focusing on obedience and courage. Notes on Geography (1933) outlined a shift in emphasis in 1926 from facts, figures and memorisation to relational and interpretative geography.[121] The aims included the communication of a certain number of geographical facts and principles and the cultivation of the desire and ability to use and interpret these throughout life.

Notes on Music (1933) cited the importance of the subject to all nations as it provided both physical and mental pleasure and when taught as a pleasant and living element, it became 'a vital means of self-expression, a preparation for social life, and a basis for future musical creation.'[122] Music was also seen as an important element of the Gaelic and national renaissance. The Notes on Mathematics (1935) stated that the main focus of the subject was to be on training 'in the art of thinking – consecutively, closely, logically' and applying this in life generally.[123] They called for a focus on the principles of mathematics as opposed to mechanical practice exclusively. The Notes emphasised the importance of relating problems to the actual needs and interests of children.

In general, inspectors who had expertise in particular subject areas compiled each set of Notes. The Notes did not follow the same format or outline; some contained a detailed syllabus for each class while others provided more general and overarching advice. They ranged in length from approximately sixteen pages (English, physical training) to sixty-four pages (Irish). This lack of standardisation, their theoretical nature as 'practical' Notes, their brevity and the absence of details relating to individual classes reduced their value as a practical resource for teachers. The absence of Notes to supplement the limited detail in the programmes for the first decade of their implementation left a vacuum in precise guidance to teachers on content and methods. Subsequently, most Notes were not revised or amended in any way following their publication until 1971.

5.8 *Revised Programme of Primary Instruction* (1934)

There were a number of calls following the implementation of the 1926 programme for a revision of its provisions. Numerous assertions were made at INTO Congress speeches regarding the impossibility of implementing the range of subjects in the programme and the INTO passed resolutions in 1933 and 1934 calling for a curtailment of subjects.[124] In hindsight, it is difficult to understand the assertions of an overloaded curriculum considering the narrow range of subjects taught relative to previous programmes and the wide range of subjects offered in many European countries as elucidated in a departmental report in 1927.[125] If there was an issue with the programme, it is arguable that it lay with the stringent requirements in the Irish language as opposed to the range of subjects.

Fianna Fáil made the revival of the Irish language an election issue in 1932 and promised progress in this regard if elected. Following its success, two meetings between the Fianna Fáil Minister for Education, Thomas Derrig, and the INTO in March and October 1933, discussed the breadth of the programme, the absence of *Notes for Teachers* and the position of Irish in the programme. The INTO remained steadfast in calling for a narrowing of the curriculum rather than reducing the scope of existing subjects to facilitate the revival of the Irish language.[126] Derrig identified schools as the main locus of the language revival and conceded in 1934 that:

> If I am satisfied that by lightening the school programme we can achieve more success in the way of advancing the use of the Irish language and improving the efficiency of the teaching in Irish, ... I certainly shall endeavour to lighten the programme.[127]

The negotiations culminated in a revision of the primary school programme introduced in 1926 and the *Revised Programme of Primary Instruction* was introduced into schools on 1 October 1934. The 1934 programme returned to the rigidity of the 1922 programme, contained no rationale or discussion around the proposed changes or its philosophy and simply stated:

> The Minister of Education has decided on certain modifications in the programme of instruction for Primary schools. They come into operation immediately.[128]

Algebra and geometry were now optional in one- and two-teacher schools, in three-teacher mixed schools and in classes taught by women. In three-teacher boys' schools, either algebra or geometry was to be taught. Rural science and nature study were no longer obligatory. In return, the higher course in Irish was to be adopted in all schools and the lower course in English was to be studied by all pupils outside infant classes. In addition, English was no longer to be taught in infant classes where there was a teacher competent to teach through Irish. Moreover, English became optional in first class. This revoked the concession within the 1926 programme allowing English to be taught before 10:30 a.m. and after 2:00 p.m. in infant classes. The main aim of lightening the programme was to 'make for more rapid progress and more effective work in the teaching of Irish and in the development of teaching through Irish.'[129]

The modifications in 1934 arguably sacrificed the general education of pupils to progress further the Irish language revival. In particular, the status of English was further diminished within schools, in a context where it was the vernacular of the vast majority of pupils.

5.9   *Revised Programme for Infants* (1948)

By the 1940s, training colleges, inspectors and Kindergarten organisers were seeking a reform of infant education.[130] In 1948, Richard Mulcahy of Cumann na nGaedheal became Minister for Education within the new Inter-party government and agreed to a review of infant education. Following exploratory work by the Inspectorate, the *Revised Programme for Infants* was introduced in 1948 and the accompanying *Notes for Teachers* were published in 1951.[131] These were flavoured by the underlying principles and philosophies of the 1900 curriculum, based on child-centred and heuristic ideologies. The language used and the conceptualisation of the child conveyed within the programme contrasted greatly with the provisions within the programmes of 1922, 1926 and 1934. The programme was developed from years of experience by Organising Inspectors such as Eileen Irvine and its tone and content were familiar to many infant teachers who had attended summer courses in Kindergarten in the 1940s.[132] The aim of the infant school was cited as being:

> to provide the atmosphere and background in which the child's whole personality may develop naturally and easily. It should therefore take cognisance of the child's interests, activities and speech needs, and utilise them to the full in aiding and directing such development.[133]

While nationalistic in tone, the needs, interests and abilities of the child were placed at the centre of the learning process. The Irish language was to remain the medium of instruction in infant classes, with an optional thirty minutes of English daily. The infant school aspired to give English-speaking children:

> a vernacular power over Irish at an age when they are most adaptable and imitative and their vocal organs are plastic. Where the teachers are sufficiently qualified the aim should be to reach a stage as early as possible at which Irish can be used as the sole language of the Infant School.[134]

The programme called for a blend of realism and unity in the child's education, ensuring the activities were within the normal experiences of the child.

Notes for Teachers in relation to the teaching of infants were issued in 1951 and shed further light on the philosophy of the programme. These placed an emphasis on the individual needs of the child and the development of a pleasant and stimulating environment was encouraged:

> The purpose of the infant school is to provide for young children the environment, opportunities and activities most favourable to their full development. Infant teaching if it is to be successful, must be based on the young child's instinctive urge to play, to talk, to imitate, to manipulate materials, to make and do things.[135]

Play was cited as an important learning mechanism, with the aim of 'eliminating formalism from the infant school.'[136] Language was seen as central to learning and while all children would learn Irish, it was urged that there was to be no repression of the urge of children to express themselves. Individual, group and class work was encouraged, with inherent flexibility in the timetable allowing frequent intervals and changes of lessons. The Notes offered two approaches to the teaching of Irish to make children competent speakers by the age of eight; the incidental approach and the graded approach. The development of ability in the Irish language was advocated, through songs, dance, listening to music and rhythm. Furthermore, the Notes proposed the 'habit of speaking only Irish in the playground should be gradually established so that the child may associate the speaking of Irish with happy activities.'[137]

The importance of art was stressed as a subject that awakened curiosity and stimulated the imagination. Handwork was seen as important to allow children handle various materials, to investigate, manipulate and experiment. Physical education was advocated for ten to fifteen minutes daily, to promote mental and physical health, and for social and language development. Nature study was seen as ideal for informal conversation and observations and while not a formal subject, could be used to arouse curiosity and interest in the world around pupils.

O'Connor cited the importance of the 1948 programme as it represented the embryonic stages of the progression towards a more child-centred curriculum in the decades ahead:

> The age of rote-recitation of numbers and words was gone, and a new era had dawned. Where the early educators led, others followed in due course.[138]

In many ways, this 1948 modification redrew tentative lines to the *Revised Programme of Instruction* introduced in 1900 by being child-centred and activity-based in nature and provided a foundation for curriculum developments in the 1960s. While the content of the programme was laudable, it was not accompanied by the provision of reduced pupil-teacher ratios, equipment or materials, or perhaps a focus on implementation to ensure the vision became a reality.

5.10 Summary and Conclusion

The 1920s was of critical importance in the development of the curriculum as the reforms introduced following the advent of independence remained steadfast and delineated the path of Irish education for the next half century. These captured the patriotic fervour that was prominent in Ireland at the dawn of independence, when schools were perceived as the keystone to the language revival. The curriculum reforms in 1922 were in essence an attempt to reverse the policies of the National Board regarding the position of the Irish language and Ireland in the programme. They aimed to accentuate the differences between the pre- and post-independence educational policies, focusing on the Irish language and Catholic religion as the main characteristics of this distinct identity. The policy provisions introduced in the 1920s were pursued by all governments, while those who questioned the effects on pupils or showed concern for general educational standards were often castigated. What is surprising is that the patriotic zeal embodied in the 1922 programme remained largely unrevised for close to fifty years, and the evolutionary societal changes in the interim were subsequently not reflected in the programme.

The curriculum introduced in the 1920s was a radical departure from its predecessor. It restricted the range of subjects offered, with a predominant focus placed on the Irish language. Beyond Irish, English, mathematics, religion, history, geography and needlework for girls, the wide-ranging suite of subjects introduced in 1900 was reduced to ensure an increased focus on the Irish language. The narrow range of subjects introduced in 1922 remained fundamentally unaltered for the next fifty years, and if anything, there was a gradual diminution in their range and depth to facilitate an increased focus on the Irish language. While Irish was to be taught to all pupils for one hour per day, the main bone of contention of the provisions for the next forty years was the insistence that Irish be used as the medium of instruction in infant classes. While this resolve was reduced somewhat in 1926, allowing English before 10:30 a.m. and after 2:00 p.m., this was revoked in 1934. From 1948, thirty minutes of English was allowed daily at the manager's discretion.

The first National Programme Conference framed a programme containing seminal lines of thought, although entirely more ambitious, than that outlined by the Gaelic League in 1918. This placed the Irish language and culture at the core of the curriculum and in turn, relegated the status and time afforded to other subjects and areas of the curriculum. One major flaw in the programme in 1922 was that, unlike the Gaelic League programme in 1918, it did not mediate the programme for the various educational contexts in which it was to be implemented. It was naïve to believe that by devising a policy, schools nationwide in Gaeltacht and Galltacht areas would be uniformly capable of introducing its requirements in relation to the Irish language. This oversight created a sense of failure among many teachers in the early years of implementation when they realised the difficulties they were experiencing in introducing a programme that was propagated as the minimum expected.

The programme devisers erroneously believed that schools could instigate a cultural and linguistic reform of the magnitude of changing the vernacular of an entire population, the vast majority of whom spoke English and expressed no active desire to change. There was an insufficient realisation of the scale of the task in 1922, which would have needed planning, motivation, and a commitment to using the language by all citizens, as well as active political support for such a transformation. This was exacerbated by the unreality of the policy goals, undue optimism, incoherent implementation and widespread public apathy for the revival. Although each programme contained a reference to reforms needed for implementation, there was often inaction or certainly lethargy in relation to their enactment. This included failing to instigate adequate strategies to ameliorate the lack of proficiency of teachers in Irish, addressing the provision of appropriate textbooks, materials and equipment and the timely provision of *Notes for Teachers* on the various subject areas. Generally, schools as institutions have been powerless to instigate societal change or foster an alternative identity without the active will and participation of wider society, a commitment that was not present in relation to the revival of the Irish language.

The curricula as laid out by the programme conferences in 1922 and
1926, and the Department in 1934 and 1948, were succinct and contained
little of an accompanying rationale or theoretical framework to underpin
their contents. While a great deal of documentation survives relating to
the operation of the Second National Programme Conference, little exists,
or perhaps ever existed, regarding education policy development in 1922,
1934 and 1948. The terms of reference for the conferences in the 1920s were
generally narrow, precluding an examination of wider structural issues that
impacted on implementation. Even when these were included as in 1922,
the conference failed to address structural issues such as local administration. Moreover, when submissions were invited or evidence gathered, there
was a tradition of not publishing such documents with the final reports. In
this context, it remained, and still remains, difficult to garner the extent to
which reports were evidence-based or representative of interests. However,
it is clear that various participants wielded varying amounts of power and
influence. The prominent status afforded to witnesses such as Rev. Corcoran
and the philosophy of the Gaelic League ensured that their beliefs were
incorporated into the programmes devised in the 1920s and thus permeated curriculum provisions up to the 1970s. This highlights the central
role that an organisation or individual can play in determining education
policy at a particular point in time through a convergence of societal and
educational factors and, more importantly, the lasting impact this can
entail long after the power and presence of that individual or organisation
has diminished. From the 1930s, there was little consultation in relation
to curriculum changes with interested parties, with decisions made and
policies devised at departmental level.

The concept of the child as portrayed within curriculum documentation remained consistent throughout the 1920s and 1930s; a child that
needed to be filled with knowledge, to be moulded into perfection by
strict discipline and the amassing of vast quantities of factual data. During
this period, the curriculum was devised from a political and nationalistic
frame of reference as opposed to a pedagogical or educational approach. It
prioritised national as opposed to individual interests, and consequently,
the content was not based on the needs, interests or abilities of the child.
The focus within the curriculum was on literary as opposed to practical

subjects, whereby the programme became almost void of practical aspects for the majority of pupils. Each successive review of the curriculum, particularly in 1934, was undertaken to increase the emphasis on the Irish language and arguably impacted negatively on the general education of pupils. Moreover, the remaining subjects in the curriculum were largely ignored within reforms, particularly the English language, which was the home language of the vast majority of children.

A break with this conceptualisation of the child was evident in the *Revised Programme for Infants* (1948), which returned, in theory at least, to a more child-centred and heuristic approach. This placed the child's abilities and interests at the centre of the learning process and learning was to be enjoyable and discovery oriented. The extent to which these varying philosophies were realised in practice is now treated in chapter 6, which focuses on curriculum implementation between 1922 and 1971.

Implementation of the Primary School Curriculum 1922–1971

6.1 Introduction

This chapter documents the implementation of successive curricula in the period 1922–1971. The implementation of the programmes emanating from the first and Second National Programme Conferences are analysed concurrently as they were devised within a few years of one another and their content did not differ significantly. The focus on the Irish language revival within schools throughout the period dominated evaluations of the programme and much of the available documentation emphasises the Irish language, to the neglect of many other aspects of implementation. This chapter draws on available sources such as inspectors' reports produced between 1925 and 1930 and the annual reports of the Department of Education published until 1964. In addition, organisations such as the INTO conducted research into the programme, most notably a report in 1941 in relation to the use of Irish as a teaching medium and the *Plan for Education* published in 1947. A number of government commissions and agencies examined curriculum provision at different times in this period and despite the fact that many of their recommendations were not implemented, their reports provide an important barometer for the evolution of thinking regarding curriculum issues.

6.2 Reports of the Department of Education and Inspectors' Reports

The annual reports published by the Department of Education in the period from the 1920s to the 1960s are an important source of information on curriculum implementation. Between 1925 and 1930, these included excerpts of inspectors' reports which provide a rich source of data on the programme in the early years of implementation. Following that, annual reports until 1964 generally contained short sections entitled '*An Obair ins na Scoileanna*' [The Work in the Schools], which was presented consistently in the Irish language. Moreover, the greatest focus of these short sections was placed on the implementation of Irish, while no reference was made to other subjects in certain years. Overall, these reports were insufficient to convey a sense of how the various subject areas were progressing or to communicate the range of experiences in diverse geographical areas. The next sections examine the treatment of the various subject areas in these reports.

6.2.1 Irish

The individual inspector reports included in the annual reports of the Department in this time fluctuated between optimism and pessimism for the revival of the Irish language. Many inspectors noted an improvement in standards facilitated by the introduction of Irish:

> It is agreed that the introduction of the second language has helped to improve the intelligence and self-reliance of the pupils. It has not lowered the proficiency in English, rather has it improved it: for it has given the child new ideas and called upon him to make a better effort at self-expression.[1]

Others noted the revival to be progressing slowly, with greater quality work being achieved by younger and generally better qualified teachers.[2] In 1928, inspectors reported that outside the Gaeltacht, schools had made 'very little attempt at using Irish as a teaching medium, and the complaint is general that Irish is rarely heard except at Irish lessons.'[3] The overemphasis on the written and reading aspects of Irish was criticised and a focus on oral Irish was encouraged.[4]

Progress in composition was cited to be slow in the first years of implementation, with many schools focusing on reading as opposed to writing skills.[5] Compulsory Irish in infant classes was lauded but it was noted that this foundation needed to be built upon in the subsequent classes. As one inspector stated, '[I]f infants learn easily they forget with even greater facility.'[6] Inspectors also noted the lack of opportunity for pupils to use Irish outside the school system:

> the opportunities for either speaking or reading it will be very scant after completion of their school life, and that much of what they carry away from school will soon be lost.[7]

In 1931, a memorandum was prepared on the teaching of Irish based on confidential reports of Divisional Inspectors. It revealed that in Gaeltacht areas, parental preference was for instruction in the English language, while teacher proficiency remained poor in many areas. In Galltacht areas, teacher competence in the language was judged to be of a low standard, with few pupils gaining adequate proficiency to benefit from instruction through Irish or having opportunities to use the language. One problem cited in this regard was the low number of schools with a full cohort of qualified teachers in the Irish language, thus lacking continuity. The inspector for Sligo compared this situation 'to an army where every sound warrior is tied on to a helpless or wounded comrade.'[8] Overall, the situation was considered in need of review as 'a continuance of the present policy can never bring about a Gaelic Ireland.'[9] In Galltacht areas, inspectors reported that despite improvements in teacher qualifications, there was little enthusiasm for the language or extension of its use 'and the consequence is that the language teaching in the schools is not producing speakers.'[10] Other inspectors castigated the teaching of Irish as merely a school subject:

> it is not enlivened by a spirit of enthusiasm; it is simply regarded as a programme subject and is taught in a less or more routine fashion for an hour a day and during the remainder of the day only English is heard.[11]

The 1932–1933 annual report of the Department acknowledged the slow progress in relation to the Irish language, especially in relation to its use as a medium of instruction in the Galltacht, while its use was continuing to recede in the Gaeltacht:

> Níl an Ghaedhilg ag breith buaidhe ar an mBéarla mar ghnáth-chainnt. Is dóigh liom anois go gcaithfear a adhmháil nach bhfuil ag éirighe leis na Scoileanna cainnteoirí Gaedhilge a dhéanamh de na leanbhaí.[12][†]

Annual reports cited the positive effect of the £2 grant, the increasing number of teachers proficient in the Irish language coming into the system, the programme revisions in 1934 and the provision of *Notes for Teachers* on the use and teaching of Irish in Gaeltacht and Breac-Ghaeltacht schools.[13] However, little improvement in Irish was noted in Galltacht areas, where slow progress continued to be reported.[14] Minister Derrig expressed his disappointment in relation to progress at the 1941 INTO Congress, stating that in the Galltacht, not even 5 per cent of classes over third standard did all their work through Irish:

> I confess that I am troubled at the slowness of our progress in that respect. The heart of our Gaelic civilisation is the Irish language. If we do not save Irish we will never again be able to win back the culture of our fathers.[15]

Statistics relating to the use of Irish as a teaching medium and its prevalence of being taught as a subject affords an insight into the number of pupils affected by the Irish language policy. The annual report for 1931 stated that 50,000 infants in the Galltacht were receiving all instruction through Irish, while the remaining 70,000 received most instruction in Irish.[16] Outside infant classes, 41 per cent of schools in the Gaeltacht were providing all instruction through Irish, while this reduced to 1 per cent in both the Breac-Ghaeltacht and Galltacht.[17] Overall, this equated to 228 out of 5,378 schools in the country completing all their work through

---

†   Irish is not gaining victory over English as the vernacular. I am of the opinion now that we must admit the schools are not succeeding in making Irish speakers of the children.

Irish. The Department cited the main reasons for the delay in introducing the language as being the lack of qualifications on the part of teachers and the inability of children to assimilate instruction. At this point in 1931, the Department conceded it would be fifteen to twenty years before the entire work of the primary school would be in Irish, the time needed to replace the 6,000 teachers in the system without proficiency in the Irish language.[18] Given this admission, it would have been wise to revise the policy to fit the contemporary reality, which subsequently could have been amended in line with increasing qualifications.

Table 6.1 documents the number of schools nationwide that used Irish as a medium of instruction between 1935 and 1965. As is evident, the number of schools in the Gaeltacht using Irish as a medium of instruction reduced quite considerably from 363 in 1945 to 231 in 1955, and stabilised at this point into the 1960s. However, the most considerable decline occurred in the Galltacht schools between the 1950s and 1960s, reducing by 52 per cent in the decade. It is likely that the provisions of Circular 11/60, which was one of the first key amendments to the Irish language policy in schools, catalysed this decline. This allowed teachers to decide whether to use Irish as a medium of instruction or as an ordinary school subject.[19]

Table 6.1 Number of Schools Teaching all Subjects through Irish under the Headings Fíor-Ghaeltacht, Gaeltacht, Breac-Ghaeltacht and Galltacht in 1936, 1946, 1956 and 1966

	1935–1936	1945–1946	1955–1956	1965–1966
Fíor-Ghaeltacht	166	177	231 (Gaeltacht)	237 (Gaeltacht)
Gaeltacht	70	75		
Breac-Ghaeltacht	110	111		
Galltacht	266	257	244	117
Total	612	620	475	354

Source: Department of Education Annual Reports (1937, p. 155; 1947, p. 104; 1957, p. 62; 1967, p. 16).

In addition, many other schools taught some of the subjects through Irish. For example, in 1944–1945, ninety-two schools in the Gaeltacht, 316 schools in the Breac-Ghaeltacht and 1,834 schools in the Galltacht taught two or more consecutive classes through the medium of Irish.[20]

From the early 1930s, commentators began to call for an evaluation of the progress made to date and to assess the effects of using Irish as a teaching medium.[21] It is arguable that successive Ministers feared the results a comprehensive analysis of the system would reveal and resisted any attempts to disclose the true situation in relation to the revival.

6.2.2 English

There were mixed views on the implementation of English in inspectors' reports. The introduction of Irish was considered by some inspectors not to have adversely affected the standard in English and other subjects as it had improved pupil's self-expression.[22] A lack of focus on grammar was noted in many annual reports.[23] There were also reports that the distinction between the higher and lower courses in Irish and English was not adequately understood and the textbooks provided in both subjects did not match these requirements.[24] A number of inspectors lamented the lack of emphasis on teaching comprehension and of using material beyond the textbook, such as newspapers and magazines.[25] Others noted serious defects in developing pupils' oral language and expressive skills.[26] Many inspectors commented on the limited availability of school libraries to improve reading in schools.[27]

Following the programme modifications in 1934, a number of annual reports recorded a decline in the standards in English, with less time afforded to the teaching of grammar and composition.[28] Other reports stated that the majority of schools continued to teach English in first class, as this class was invariably grouped with second class in smaller schools.[29] Towards the end of the period in question, inspectors recommended greater flexibility in relation to the methods used to teach reading, including the use of silent reading, grouping, the use of library books and greater discussion of reading matter.[30]

6.2.3 Mathematics

Progress in arithmetic was generally viewed as slow, with an overemphasis on mechanical questions as opposed to problem solving.[31] Arithmetic problems were seen to be poorly understood by pupils and unrelated to their experiences:

> The exercises are too mechanical; there is too much working of dreary sums that have no relation to real life, and the pupils do not even in these develop accuracy of calculation, because the work being uninteresting causes want of concentration.[32]

Other inspectors criticised the fact that teaching was not based on the local environment of the school or pupils.[33] The teaching of algebra and geometry was considered to be weaker than the general teaching of arithmetic.[34] Algebra was seen to be taught in a didactic manner, while younger teachers were starting to use more innovative methods.[35] By the 1960s, annual reports continued to lament the lack of emphasis placed on concrete materials and oral work in mathematics, with the focus still placed on the mechanical and routine aspects of practice.[36]

6.2.4 History and Geography

Inspectors were generally disappointed with progress in history.[37] Local history was seen to be a neglected aspect of the subject, of which many teachers had little knowledge or interest, exacerbated by the 'inaccessibility of authoritative sources of information.'[38] The lack of historical understanding on the part of children and the over-reliance on the textbook were common complaints regarding history in the annual reports.[39] There was encouragement in relation to the teaching of history following the issuing of the Revised Notes in 1962, covering much of the previously neglected twentieth century subject matter. However, an over-dependence on the textbook and a lack of emphasis on local history were still cited as weak points.[40] The teaching of geography was criticised as being often relayed as a series of facts, often relating to Ireland only.[41] Other annual reports lamented that the basic principles of geography were not imparted, weakening other elements of instruction in the subject.[42]

6.2.5 Singing

Singing was largely confined to the teaching of songs in the Irish language and the annual reports expressed disappointment at the low level of proficiency of pupils in general music on leaving primary school.[43] Inspectors criticised the lack of emphasis on voice training and clear enunciation, with many lessons concentrating on the 'mechanical singing of songs.'[44] Others called for more of a focus on musical theory.[45] Music teaching was noted to have improved in the 1960s with the provision of courses for teachers and through participation in local competitive musical festivals. However, inspectors still criticised the standards attained generally in ear-training and sight-reading.[46]

6.2.6 Needlework

Needlework, which was only taught to girls, was rarely commented on within the inspectors' reports or the annual reports. In general, the Department expressed overall satisfaction with instruction in the subject.[47] However, the quality of the work was seen as being somewhat reduced owing to the later age at which instruction commenced.[48]

6.2.7 Rural Science and Nature Study

The introduction of rural science and nature study was viewed positively as a relief from academic learning and a way to stimulate the senses and the power of observation and reasoning.[49] Following their introduction on a compulsory basis from 1926, rural science was taught in 661 schools while nature study was imparted in 2,612 schools in 1932–1933.[50] An innovative mechanism to improve their popularity involved conferences at county level in 1927–1928 between inspectors and teachers.[51] However, there was often disappointment at the rate of progress and availability of the subjects.[52] The method of teaching the subjects in a didactic as opposed to exploratory way was criticised:

> Too often, however, the aim seems to be to convey information, to be accepted on the teacher's authority, rather than to stimulate curiosity and to put the children in the way of satisfying it by personal experiments.[53]

The annual reports after 1934 noted a decline in the number of schools teaching rural science and nature study once they were made optional.[54] By the late 1950s, annual reports noted that the subjects were rarely taught in a formal manner.[55]

6.2.8 Physical Drill

The optional nature of physical drill led to a dramatic reduction in the number of schools offering the subject and it was rarely mentioned in inspectors' reports. This trend continued until the 1960s, when annual reports noted the subject was taught mostly in large urban schools by external teachers, where games were popular in boys' schools and Irish dancing featured prominently in girls' schools.[56]

6.2.9 Teaching of Other Subjects

The omission of domestic economy from the programme was lamented as it 'leaves the girls with a sadly defective practical training for life in a country where primitive household conditions so largely obtain.'[57] Annual reports noted that cookery and laundry became less popular, even in schools with the necessary facilities and equipment.[58] Circulars were issued in 1939[59] and 1943[60] to encourage and promote the teaching of cookery and laundry in primary schools. The absence of other subjects such as manual instruction and drawing was also noted but considered a necessary sacrifice for the language.[61]

6.2.10 Other Issues in the Reports

A number of themes recurred in inspectors' and annual reports throughout the period that related to implementation, although not to specific subject areas. These included the tone of education provided in schools, the treatment of infants within schools and the use of the local environment of the pupil in teaching and learning. Generally, while inspectors were reluctant to commit to an overall endorsement of the programme, there was general positive regard towards it within the inspectors' reports in the 1920s.[62] However, inspectors lamented the fact that the national tone imparted in schools was not ideal, calling for a greater link between the language, history, folklore and literature in order to make 'some more direct call to awaken the feelings of our people to a sense and appreciation of their national heritage.'[63] Furthermore, the programme was criticised as being too detached from the reality of the lives of many children.[64] The lack of focus on the local area was criticised by many inspectors who felt the production of cheap books on localities would prevent a dependency on the popular textbooks, as 'up to the present the mental attitude of indifference to their surroundings one finds among so many teachers is saddening.'[65] In 1962, the annual report criticised the lack of focus many of the younger teachers placed on the local environment of schools, instead over-relying on textbooks 'which cannot possibly give pride of place to local interests.'[66] Other inspectors praised the transformation in ensuring the inclusion of content of a distinctly Irish character within the programme. In the mid-1920s, one inspector stated:

> The greatest change that has been effected so far is this, that a visitor to the schools would readily realise that it is in Ireland he is.[67]

The dearth of equipment in infant classrooms was cited as an ongoing problem,[68] and it was noted that while teachers paid attention to older pupils, 'the infants have to be left largely to themselves.'[69] Other inspectors were more upbeat about the transformation within infant classes, stating that such work had 'flourished' and there was increased incidence of 'sympathetic and motherly treatment of infants.'[70] While a gradual approach was urged in the *Revised Programme for Infants* (1948), the Department commented on the over-zealous nature of some teachers and the ensuing neglect of essential subjects.[71] While some inspectors praised the increased use of active methodologies and group work in infant classes, others lamented the fact that these methods were not more prevalent in senior classes.[72] Even in the 1960s, the teaching of infants was cited as a weak point as teachers still used 'out of date methods when dealing with certain aspects of the programme.'[73] Another defect in the work of schools was noted to be an overemphasis on class teaching, which did not cater for the needs of all pupils, and the need for teaching to have more visual appeal.[74] While compulsory education ended at fourteen years of age, there was a tendency in rural areas for pupils to remain in national schools beyond this. While inspectors found the education provided up to fourteen years of age to be generally positive, it tended to stagnate at this point in the absence of a distinct programme to challenge older pupils:

> there is nothing in the work to stimulate the vigour of their minds, to challenge them to put forth their best efforts, to attract them by its novelty, or please and satisfy them by a sense of progress and achievement.[75]

6.2.11 Summary

The information conveyed within the five years that inspectors' reports were partially published and in the short accounts of the work in the schools published until 1964 indicates that the totality of the programmes as devised in the 1920s and amended in the 1930s and 1940s was not being implemented as envisaged. Moreover, many of the inspectors' comments were contradictory in nature, perhaps owing to various interpretations of the progress achieved or the lack of consistency in implementation. The overwhelming emphasis of the Department was placed on progress in the teaching of Irish and in the use of Irish as a medium of instruction. Year after year, the Department reported slow and unsatisfactory progress in this regard, whereby at the peak, only 12 per cent of schools used Irish as a medium of instruction. Given this knowledge and insight, it is surprising that the Department did not deem a fundamental review of implementation necessary or worthwhile. These data, allied to the statistics relating to teacher qualifications in Irish throughout the period, point to a Department attempting to go too far, too soon, for the contemporary context and an unwillingness to modify, even when there was overwhelming proof of this necessity. The preoccupation with the Irish language is evident by the consequent neglect of the remaining subjects within the annual reports of the Department, with various subject areas receiving no mention for consecutive years. In fact, the trend throughout the period was to focus less time on all subjects except the Irish language. This disregard for the broader education of pupils arguably had a detrimental effect on the general education imparted in the period and did little to prepare pupils for their future lives and careers. Considering the pivotal importance of the English language as the vernacular of the vast majority of pupils in Ireland and its necessity for the significant proportion of the population that emigrated, it appears that it was given insufficient attention in the school system in this period.

The reports of the Department evidence the fact that much of the mathematics teaching remained mechanical and routine in nature, which did little to prepare pupils for practical arithmetic in later life. From the limited data available, it would appear that little emphasis in history and geography was placed on local aspects, with the focus remaining on imparting and memorising facts. Singing and needlework were also afforded a low priority as subjects within the Department reports and their implementation in practice was reported to be basic in nature. Once rural science and nature study became optional subjects in 1934, they were not commonly taught. These were subjects that could have gone some way in preparing pupils for their future lives and occupations in a predominantly agrarian economy. Similarly, physical drill, domestic economy and drawing practically disappeared from the primary school curriculum during this period, a removal that was justified to enable a greater focus on the Irish language.

Notwithstanding the many sacrifices for the revival of Irish, it was abundantly evident from the outset that the methods were not succeeding; yet the solution was more of the same, with increased intensity. While this may have been understandable in the 1920s owing to patriotic fervour and nationalist feeling, it was highly questionable to perpetuate such a system for decades to the detriment of pupils' general education.

6.3 Government Reports

A memorandum of the Minister for Education in April 1927 regarding the activities of the Department since its inception sheds some light on the aspirations and actions of the Department in its first few years. The memorandum was divided in two; relating to the reconstruction of the educational machinery and the gaelicisation and democraticisation of education. In relation to the infrastructure, the memorandum stated:

> there is being constructed and there has already been partially carried into effect a system which will provide an educational highway from the infant school to the University for every boy and girl in Saorstát Éireann who is capable of benefiting from such an education.[76]

The reform of the curriculum was also heralded as a great success as it focused on the essentials and ensured pupils remained interested in the land. It also applauded the revolution within the spirit of education, helping to rebuild Irish nationality and democracy, creating a self-reliant and self-respecting people. The optimism in relation to the language revival was tangible within the memorandum:

> Already the progress is so great that it is certain that unless something most unexpected should happen the coming generation in this country will be bilingual in the next decade and succeeding decades and generations will have restored to them in full the language and the culture they lost through the operation of alien influences in the 19th century.[77]

The assertion in relation to the educational highway appears to have been highly aspirational, as was optimism at the revival of the Irish language considering the reality described in inspectors' reports at the time.

In December 1931, the Department prepared *Education in the Irish Free State – General Statement*.[78] This refuted allegations that Irish education policy was insular in nature and cited the co-operation of educational experts from France, Germany, Sweden and Switzerland in Irish education, as well as consultation with prominent Irish educationalists. Moreover, the reconstruction achieved was of a more practical and radical nature than heretofore as it 'was in effect a widening and deepening of the conception of the meaning of education in the teaching of every subject.'[79] The programme in operation in primary schools was lauded, having been formulated in a consultative and democratic way:

> A new programme which is at once thoroughly modern and thoroughly national has been in operation for several years and is proving a great success.[80]

Some of the assertions within this General Statement are questionable, particularly the involvement of international experts in the devising of Irish education policy and the widening and deepening of the concept of education.

A number of government reports during this period, while not focused primarily on education, provide insights in relation to implementation. The *Report of the Committee on Technical Education* (1927) focused on the primary curriculum in relation to its role in providing a better foundation for further technical training. It drew attention to the goal espoused in 1922 that the education of pupils should relate to their environment, especially in relation to agriculture in the countryside and to industry and trades in the cities.[81] While the report endorsed a concentration on the essential subjects, it recommended the reinstatement of drawing as a compulsory subject up to sixth class and for rural science to be introduced into all schools. To facilitate the extra subjects, the report concluded that the school week should be lengthened from the existing twenty hours in line with international jurisdictions. The report further advanced the introduction of the Primary Certificate Examination by recommending a formal examination for pupils in sixth class.

The Commission on Emigration (1956) noted the crucial nature of primary education and called for a greater focus on practical subjects, such as agriculture for boys and domestic economy for girls, to assist them in their future roles. It also stressed the need for a greater emphasis on citizenship. A call for differentiation within the curriculum for children from rural and urban areas was also made.[82] Two reservations further raised issues relating to education, reiterating the call of the Commission on Youth Unemployment (1951)[83] for an examination of the content of the curriculum, particularly Irish.

6.4 Large Scale Studies into the Education System

6.4.1 INTO Study on the Irish Language (1941)

There was discontent among teachers, managers, principals, parents and Protestant authorities with Irish language policy throughout the 1930s. In the absence of a government or Department enquiry, a resolution was passed at the INTO Congress in 1936 to conduct an investigation into the effects of using Irish as a medium of instruction.[84] While detailed questionnaires were issued to all teachers, replies were requested from teachers only who had taught pupils through the medium of Irish. The 1,347 replies were collated and in 1941, the *Report of Committee of Inquiry into the Use of Irish as a Teaching Medium to Children whose Home Language is English* was published.

Results from the questionnaire indicated that the practice of teaching through the medium of Irish did not support desirable characteristics of infant class teaching. Eighty-two per cent of the infant teachers that responded stated that 'their pupils did not derive benefit from instruction through the medium of Irish equal to that which they would derive were

English the medium used.'[85] Furthermore, 83 per cent of teachers favoured the use of both Irish and English as languages of instruction, given the centrality of language in infant classrooms for both learning and expression. In relation to history, geography and music, the vast majority of teachers replied that instruction in Irish was not of equal benefit to that of English. When asked what subjects could be taught successfully through Irish, 60 per cent of respondents asserted that using Irish as a teaching medium did not benefit the child in any subject. The report concluded by reinforcing the limited impact a school can have on linguistic attainment, as pupils spent the majority of their time with parents and in the community. The pervasive influence of English in the cinema, radio, books and newspapers was also cited as an impediment, as was the lack of standardisation in relation to spelling and grammar.

Minister Derrig castigated the INTO report as 'a challenge clearly to the present policy of teaching infants in Irish or teaching other subjects through Irish in the schools.'[86] Furthermore, he incorrectly asserted that the authors were not cognisant of the conditions in the schools as they were educated through the medium of English,[87] an unreasonable assertion against individuals who were practising teachers who had used Irish as a medium of instruction. In essence, the report embodied the collective views of in excess of 1,300 teachers who had direct experience of using Irish as a medium of instruction in national schools and represented the largest empirical study of the Irish language policy conducted in the period 1922 to 1971. In response to this report, the Department employed a Czechoslovakian educationalist, Dr Johanna Pollak, to investigate the effects of teaching through Irish. Her report was critical of Irish language policy, claiming children viewed Irish as a foreign language, it was restricted to schools and pupils were too young to benefit from such instruction.[88] Furthermore, Pollak noted the problems that lack of standardisation in grammar and spellings posed for the revival and recommended action towards this end. Unsurprisingly, this report was not published but it provided further evidence of the need to reassess language policy, knowledge upon which the Department and Minister for Education did not act at this time.

6.4.2 Church of Ireland Studies on the Irish Language

In 1936, the Church of Ireland adopted a resolution that teaching infants through Irish was 'harmful to the education of the infant and tends to stunt rather than foster infant mental development.'[89] The Board of Education of the General Synod conducted its own investigation in 1938 and concluded that the revival had led to the implementation of a restricted curriculum. Furthermore, the study found that development was retarded by the teaching of and through Irish, that undue strain was placed on teachers trying to deliver the programme, that the salaries of teachers were affected by not having Irish qualifications, that no progress had been made in the promotion of Irish as a vernacular and that many Protestant parents were sending their children to private schools or outside the state to avoid these negative effects.[90] The majority of Protestant schools were small and teachers spent a large proportion of the day teaching Irish to all levels. A further study regarding the use of Irish as a teaching medium in Protestant schools was conducted by a sub-committee of the Board of Education in 1949, *Teaching through the Medium of Irish*. The report concluded that:

> Not to use the home language of the children, be it Irish or English, is a psychological outrage upon the most helpless and inarticulate section of the community.[91]

The report made a number of recommendations, including the teaching of Irish for thirty minutes daily in infant classes, for one hour in senior classes and an examination of the effects of the Irish language requirements on the recruitment of teachers.

6.4.3 Department of Education Investigation into the Education System

Minister Derrig established a departmental committee in March 1945 with wide terms of reference:

> To examine the existing educational system, primary, secondary, technical, vocational and the provision available for university education, and to make recommendations to the Minister as to what changes and reforms, if any, are necessary in order to raise the standard of education generally and to provide greater educational facilities for our people.[92]

A sub-committee of inspectors analysed provision at various levels of the system and examined research and educational statistics. It presented its final report to the Minister on 1 December 1947, but congruent with the air of secrecy that surrounded education, it was not published. Consonant with government policy and public opinion, the centrality of religion within the curriculum was assured. In addition, the pre-eminent position of the Irish language was not questioned:

> The revival of the Irish language and the fostering of the distinctive Irish turn of mind and way of life must continue to be a main aim of the educational system whatever changes may be made within.[93]

The report expressed general satisfaction with the educational standards in the contemporary context of schools, notwithstanding the revival efforts. However, the primary programme was criticised in relation to the lack of focus on practical subjects and the academic and formal approach to teaching. It is noteworthy that the report made no distinct reference to infant education considering the focus of the revival on infant classes and the subsequent reform of infant education in 1948. In any case, to remedy the situation, the report made a number of recommendations to modify the programme to make it more practical and realistic for children. Among these were that:

- Formal algebra, geometry and cookery should be omitted;
- Provision should be made for physical education, nature study and drawing;
- Refresher courses should be provided for teachers in new subject areas;
- Clear programmes for all subjects, old and new, should be drafted, indicating what might be normally attempted.[94]

An appendix to the report provided sample timetables for the inclusion of the new subjects in a variety of schools. Furthermore, the report recommended raising the school-leaving age to fifteen and ultimately to seventeen years of age. The report was never published and when the Fianna Fáil government fell from power in 1948, it was not acted upon by the subsequent government and it had no impact on policy at the time. However, it represented the first significant government review of the education system since the 1920s. The recommendations it made were wide-ranging in nature and, if implemented, would have addressed some of the fundamental limitations that beset the curriculum during this period. It would have widened the range and breadth of the curriculum, provided a definition of what was expected at each class level and enhanced provision for pupils at second level. However, despite significant developments in education internationally in the aftermath of World War Two, neither the political will nor the public appetite had yet been adequately whetted for such reforms to be introduced in Ireland.

6.4.4 INTO Plan for Education (1947)

In September 1943, the INTO undertook 'to prepare a Plan for Education, suitable to the needs and aspirations of our people and which would at the same time, set forth in a general way, the educational ideals of the Organisation.'[95] An examination of the Plan produced is beneficial as it highlights many inadequacies in relation to the programme in operation at the time and provides a barometer on educational thinking in the period. The research was undertaken by Mr David Kelleher, President of the INTO 1945–1946, who was supported by members of the INTO Executive. The Plan was presented as a discussion document as opposed to a blueprint and it hoped to awaken public consciousness in relation to education. It was based on the underlying principle of the child having the right to the fullest education possible within an integrated system, placing the child at the centre of the learning process:

189

:urriculum the needs of the child must take precedence over all
ives or aims. If we build about the child, and for the child, we
96

ee main defects in the contemporary system, namely,
...quality, the academic bias in the programme and the lack of co-ordination. The Plan pointed out that education, which was supposed to prepare people for all aspects of their life, ended for most people at primary school level, 'when the pupil is only on the threshold of mental development.'[97] To this end, the extension of free secondary education to all up to the age of sixteen was called for to prepare children for the complexities of daily living. The Plan called for a more open, integrated and extended system of common professional training for all teachers, linked to the universities. It proposed that the state take over responsibility for maintaining schools from the managers, without changing ownership from the trustees. There was also a call for increased space for play and recreation around schools, for improved health services and the provision of meals for children.

The Plan asserted that the curriculum could not remain static in a world characterised by social, cultural, economic, political and educational change. In relation to Irish, the focus on written as opposed to oral work was criticised as a hindrance to the revival. The Plan recommended that mathematics should relate to ordinary, daily problems, and to this end, greater flexibility within the programme was called for to account for the daily reality of pupils in various areas. Formal algebra and geometry were proposed to be removed from the programme as they were too specialist and had no practical application at primary level. *In lieu*, drawing was proposed as a subject that used reasoning skills in a better way. The programme in history was seen as too extensive, leading to a lack of historical perspective. The Plan proposed that history be taught for three years as opposed to two, with a greater focus on social history, and that there be a greater balance and truth in the historical perspective. A reform of geography was also advocated, focusing on the study of human and social as opposed to physical geography. A greater focus on music appreciation was recommended, as were enhanced linkages to musical organisations in wider society.

The leaning towards academic, intellectual and examinable aspects, with a consequent neglect on practical elements of education, was highlighted as a defect. The value of practical education for all pupils, on a par with academic subjects, was stressed. The neglect of physical training was also castigated within the Plan, with the system demanding 'perpetual immobility.'[98] The introduction of science was proposed if children were going to be educated until the age of sixteen, beginning with rural science and domestic economy. The exclusion of art and craft from the curriculum was also seen as leading to an imbalance in education and to a neglect of certain areas of development. These were interesting assertions on the part of the INTO, considering its vociferous opposition to the introduction of any additional subjects in the 1920s and 1930s, and its campaign to remove rural science and nature study in 1934. Moreover, it was also in direct conflict with subsequent INTO policy as stated in the *Report of the Council of Education* in 1954.

The Plan proposed better and more widespread use of modern teaching aids by embracing new technology. Devices such as the instructional film to assist geography and nature study and the radio to assist the language revival were proposed. The provision of school libraries was recommended to develop a taste for reading for pleasure as opposed to through compulsion. The Primary Certificate Examination was criticised, especially its focus on written as opposed to oral aspects of Irish.

The language revival was afforded much attention within the *Plan for Education*:

> The task is a gigantic one, particularly in modern times and in our geographical position, with the immense resources of the English language, its relentless and unceasing torrent, wireless, propaganda, pictures, continuously sweeping us – and particularly our highly impressionable youth – in the opposite direction.[99]

The Plan blamed the lack of success in the revival on the negative associations with the language and the emphasis on written as opposed to oral aspects. The *Notes for Teachers* were criticised for containing no practical methods for restoring Irish as a vernacular. It proposed a commission to concentrate solely on the co-ordination and acceleration of the revival both within and outside schools. To ensure use of the language after school, the Plan proposed the establishment of a Youth Movement, which would improve character formation, strengthen the national fibre, engender respect for manual labour and the development of civic spirit, all interknitted with the Irish language.

The *Plan for Education* was published in March 1947. However, it was not widely read by teachers or the general public and did not create the platform for educational debate in society as the INTO had wished.[100] While the CEC of the INTO endorsed an early draft of the Plan in 1945, the final report was not mentioned or endorsed following its publication in 1947. However, the editor of *The Irish School Weekly* stated the Plan 'may be regarded as an expression of INTO educational policy, and it reflects and codifies the suggestions that have been put forward at congress after congress for many years.'[101] Furthermore, little mention was made of the *Plan for Education* at INTO Congresses, in INTO journals or in INTO submissions in subsequent years as an expression of INTO policy. In fact, it was in the 1960s, and subsequently, that the Plan was promulgated as INTO policy, at a time when its progressive views had become far more mainstream thinking.

The *Plan for Education*, despite its lack of impact on policy and practice at the time, is important in providing an insight into the shift in educational thinking among a minority in Ireland at this time. It was influenced by international thinking in the post World War Two period in relation to many of its underlying assertions. It proposed a range of solutions to the educational problems of the day and asserted an INTO policy at odds with previous stances regarding the curriculum in the 1920s and 1930s. Its vision and perspective was ahead of its time, a factor that perhaps contributed to its lack of impact in the contemporary context.

6.4.5 Report of the Council of Education (1954)

There were numerous calls for the establishment of a Council of Education from the 1920s. In the run up to the 1948 general election, Fine Gael promised the establishment of a Council of Education if elected. It was established in May 1950 and consisted of twenty-nine members, twenty-six of whom were professional educators and three members represented rural interests.[102]

The Council of Education had two elements within its terms of reference – to examine the function of the primary school and the curriculum to be pursued from the infant age up to twelve years of age.[103] These terms of reference were narrow in nature and it is surprising the review was limited to the curriculum for pupils up to twelve years of age, considering the large number of pupils above this age in primary schools and the lack of provisions for secondary education. Moreover, the terms of reference restricted it to playing an advisory role and served to reinforce the compartmentalisation of education which did not assist curriculum planning. To fulfil this function, the Council invited submissions from interested parties and the general public in February 1951. It received sixty-seven memoranda and a further nine on special subjects.[104] Based on the favourable response rates, and the difficulty envisaged in selecting representative witnesses, it decided not to seek oral evidence.

The Council reported in June 1954 that the function of the primary school was to provide 'a basic education and it prepares the child for further education should he receive it.'[105] This vision was a narrow assertion of the role of education and reflected the conservative nature of the members of the Council. It saw no link between the education system and the economy and in contrast to European trends, reinforced an elitist view of access to education. Unsurprisingly considering there were eleven clergymen of various denominations on the Council, the report endorsed the philosophy of the 1926 programme in relation to religion, that 'it was the soul, the foundation and the crown of the whole educational process, giving value and meaning to every subject in the curriculum.'[106]

The Council advocated that the curriculum was too narrow to prepare pupils for further education and employment, and proposed the inclusion of drawing, nature study and physical training 'which not only give a wider culture, but also serve as aids to the teaching of the fundamental subjects.'[107] To allow for their inclusion in the curriculum, a reduction in the requirements of other subjects was suggested. However, the report asserted that schools already taught between eight and ten compulsory subjects in a twenty-five-hour week and warned that additional aspects could weaken ability in these core subjects. By raising such concerns and inserting so many qualifications, the initial recommendation to include three additional subjects was diluted greatly and lost its impact. The Council recommended detailed programmes be issued to all teachers for all subjects and that optional subjects be omitted as they were rarely undertaken in any case.

The report called for greater emphasis on oral Irish and for an increased focus on the revival outside schools. Furthermore, the report recommended research into bilingualism by a Research and Advisory section within the Department, which would co-ordinate teaching methods, devise aids, provide handbooks, plan syllabi and organise prizes. Beyond these suggestions, no further practical recommendations were made to reform the revival attempts within the education system. Similarly in relation to the infant curriculum, members of the Council agreed that its content was unsuitable. However, its only recommendation was the allocation of thirty minutes for English per day in classes outside the Gaeltacht, which had already been allowed on an optional basis since 1948. Following a four-year analysis of the problem and thirty years of expressed public concern regarding the Irish language, such recommendations lacked the scope and depth required to address the Irish language revival within schools. No evidence was provided to support the recommendations of the Council in this regard, nor was any investigation into the success or failure of the revival movement conducted to warrant a continuation of the existing policy. It did not examine the effects of the language revival on pupils, the impact on other subjects, the degree to which the language was being used or the effect of using Irish as a medium of instruction. The Council of Education paid scant regard to the position of English, recommending an increased emphasis on silent reading. Furthermore, it made no comment on methodologies or on the nature of the books available. The extent to which it was out of tune with the way in which young children learned was evidenced in the recommendation that the use of comics and detective stories for reading be discontinued and be substituted with historical stories.

The Council received many complaints about the unsuitability and unnecessary nature of the Primary Certificate Examination. However, it recommended the maintenance of the examination on the basis that it was 'valuable and necessary, in so far as it imparts to the child a sense of order, enables him to distinguish between values, and exercises his memory and powers of perception.'[108] The Council felt that in the modern world, education beyond primary schooling was necessary to develop the country economically, to reduce emigration and to enable pupils to take their place in the world. However, it did not recommend that the state enhance direct provision of second-level education, proposing instead increased state scholarships. While such scholarships only benefited 5 per cent of the age cohort, the elitist nature of the report is evident in the assertion that fees were generally low and were not charged to poorer pupils at all.

The final report was signed by twenty-five of the twenty-nine members of the Council on 25 May 1954, while two Minority Reports were submitted. The first Minority Report was signed by Canon Harvey Nesbitt, Dr Henry Kennedy and Dr Patrick Moran, representing Protestant interests. It expressed concern that the Council did not adequately address the inordinate amount of time spent on Irish in primary schools, which impacted negatively on educational standards. Given the lack of success of this policy for thirty years, they stated that 'there is no indication that if the policy is pursued in the future, a different result will ensue.'[109]

Two of the three INTO members on the Council signed the final report, although they had been cautioned by the INTO president and the CEC not to do so if it conflicted with INTO policy, especially 'any recommendations aimed at extending the present school programme.'[110] The third member, Liam Forde, ex-President of the INTO, submitted a Minority Report asserting the Council had erred in extending the number of obligatory subjects and in maintaining the Primary Certificate Examination. The INTO Minority Report, which was congruent with the INTO memorandum to the Council,[111] saw the main aim of primary education to be the restoration of the Irish language:

> Either we are in earnest about the revival of Irish, or we are not. If we are in earnest then everything else should be subordinated to this aim and we should be prepared, to sacrifice the teaching of subjects no matter how desirable, and to cut to the barest minimum those other subjects which must be included in the Programme.[112]

These assertions on behalf of the INTO were in firm contrast to the ideals of education promulgated in the INTOs *Plan for Education* (1947), which called for a more balanced and broad curriculum, and represented a reversion to the INTO policy of the 1920s and 1930s.

There was widespread disappointment following the publication of the Council's report, which was perceived to contain little fresh thinking. Fr Birch, a lecturer in Maynooth, criticised the report for its paucity of concrete recommendations and the poor treatment of the question of Irish.[113] Fr Ó Catháin lamented the lack of evidence-base used or generated by the Council and questioned the rationale and excuse provided for not calling witnesses, which would have enhanced the process of investigation within the report and 'have dispelled in this Report that atmosphere of the ivory tower which too often pervades it.'[114] At the INTO Annual Congress in 1955, resolutions were taken deprecating the recommendations of the Council regarding the addition of extra subjects, the continuation of the Primary Certificate Examination and the maintenance of the *status quo* in relation to Irish language methods.[115]

Overall, the *Report of the Council of Education* reflected the sterility in Irish education at the time and despite the many obvious problems within the system, the report largely endorsed the *status quo* and did not see the compelling need for reform. It missed an opportunity to examine critically the provision of the primary school curriculum and to lay the foundations for reform within the system. It contrasted with the curriculum reforms in England and Northern Ireland at the time, which were child-centred and emphasised all domains of development.[116] It was written from a Catholic concept of childhood, stressing limited functions for the school and the need for strict instruction of the child for preparation as a good Christian and citizen. Indeed, in tone and content, it had changed little from the reports of the first and Second National Programme Conferences in the 1920s. Moreover, the research contained in the report was largely historical and philosophical in nature, with a virtual absence of statistical data or examination of the limited range of Irish educational research.

In any case, the recommendations of the report were largely ignored and it had little impact on the education system at this time. Perhaps one development catalysed by the Council's report was Minister Moylan's initiative in 1954 to introduce the 'free half day' scheme to allow 'greater scope and variety to the curriculum so that the whole atmosphere of the school might be vivified.'[117] This allowance was not widely used owing to the demands of the curriculum, with the Department's annual report of 1954–1955 noting 10 per cent of teachers adopted its provisions.[118] While a Department memorandum in October 1956 accepted the recommendations in principle, it stated that it was unfeasible to introduce them immediately owing to the economic climate.[119] A *Programme of Primary Instruction* was published in 1956 but this was not informed by the *Report of the Council of Education* and it reiterated, almost verbatim, the aims and content of primary education from previous programmes.[120]

6.4.6 MacNamara Study (1966)

Fr John MacNamara, a lecturer in St Patrick's Training College, published a study in 1966 on the effects on pupil attainment of using Irish as a medium of instruction. This was one of the first studies to examine the impact on children of learning through the Irish language, rather than focusing on national, cultural or ideological objectives. The study focused on fifth class pupils in 120 schools and included a continuum of schools where arithmetic was taught to all classes through English, through to where all classes were taught through the medium of Irish. The study found that 42 per cent of time in schools was spent on Irish, while an additional 22 per cent was spent on English.[121] In addition, it reported that teaching arithmetic through Irish to English speakers retarded ability by eleven months in problem arithmetic but had no effect on mechanical arithmetic. Moreover, pupils in Ireland were found to be seventeen months behind their British counterparts in English writing. The report pointed to the fact that twice the amount of time was spent on the English language in schools in Britain and on the inadequacy of the English curriculum in schools in Ireland.

Of more interest and consequence was the contrast between children in Ireland from Irish and English speaking backgrounds. While MacNamara found children from Irish-speaking backgrounds to be sixteen months ahead of children from English-speaking areas in Irish, they were behind by seven months in mental arithmetic, by eleven months in problem arithmetic and by thirteen months in English attainment. While this had negative effects on attainment in arithmetic, which was taught through Irish in a small percentage of schools, the most critical outcome was the effect on the English language 'since all Irish national school children whose mother tongue is English (over 96 per cent of national school children) are involved.'[122] This report quantified what many had suspected for years in relation to the negative effects of using Irish as a teaching medium on pupils and on other elements of the curriculum. Despite criticisms of the report (see chapter 7), it created a stimulus for debate of the role of schools in the language revival and undoubtedly influenced subsequent reforms in the late 1960s. As Garrett FitzGerald concluded:

> It would be difficult indeed to read this book with an open mind and to resist the conclusion that a radical review of the curriculum of our national schools is now demanded by common justice to the children whom we have condemned to this system.[123]

6.4.7 Increasing Concerns in the 1960s

Tuairim published a pamphlet in 1962 entitled *Irish Education*, dedicating a full chapter to the issue of curriculum. This castigated the rigidity of the curriculum imposed on all schools regardless of facilities, finance, access to specialist teachers or of the linguistic backgrounds of pupils:

> Because it is considered politically desirable that all primary schoolchildren should be able to read, write and speak two languages, two languages are entrenched in the curricula for all primary children regardless of their intelligence and linguistic ability. Educational aims are thus subordinated to a political one.[124]

Tuairim proposed that the curriculum in each school should be devised locally by the principal, teachers and inspector to ensure it met the needs of individual contexts, guided by a national syllabus. It advocated that in line with international practice, pupils in infant classes should be taught through their home language and that at the teacher's discretion, the second language could be introduced informally. One hour per week each was also proposed for art, music, speech training and drama, physical education and craft. Research by the Teachers' Study Group in 1964 found a twenty-six-month reading age difference between Dublin and British children and a similar gap was reported in 1969.[125] While some differential would be expected owing to the teaching of two languages in Ireland, its size caused some disquiet. Kelly and McGee also highlighted the unfavourable performance of Irish pupils in English reading when compared to their international counterparts.[126] In 1969, Kellaghan *et al.* found that teachers rated the progress of 25 per cent of their pupils across all subjects to be unsatisfactory, while 66 per cent of pupils were judged to have a difficulty with one or more subjects.[127] The main subjects in which pupils were experiencing difficulty were Irish, arithmetic and English.

6.5 Summary and Conclusion

There was a paucity of educational research during the period 1922 to 1971 from both state and non-state sources. Consequently, the delineation of curriculum implementation in this period is less expansive than in the earlier period from 1900 to 1922, or in the later period following 1971. A particular dearth of information relates to the actual practice at school and classroom level owing to the non-publication of inspectors' reports for most of the period and the near absence of research by individual teachers. In general, evaluations and commentary during this period focused on the Irish language revival in schools, perhaps much like the actual curriculum did, to the detriment of the remaining subjects.

In relation to Irish, while many inspectors and politicians extolled the progress being achieved, the general weight of evidence pointed to poor progress in the subject within the school system, particularly its use as a teaching medium. As its zenith in the 1940s, only 12 per cent of schools used Irish as a medium of instruction and this had declined significantly by the 1960s. The national aim to produce Irish speakers was never realised to any degree and most pupils left national schools with a rudimentary grasp of the spoken language. This basic competence in the Irish language came at a high price when one examines the time allocated to Irish within schools during the period, reducing the amount of time available for the study of other subjects and the narrow range of subjects studied. English as a subject received little attention during the period, even though it was the vernacular of the vast majority of pupils and was a *sine qua non* for the future lives and occupations of all, whether in Ireland or abroad.

Evaluations on the implementation of mathematics reported a continued focus on the mechanics of the subject rather than the development of concepts or mathematical thinking. In history and geography, the emphasis remained on the memorisation of facts and the content related largely to Ireland. While singing and needlework remained compulsory subjects, they were rarely commented on and it is arguable that they were not afforded a high status within the programme. Subjects such as physical drill, rural science and nature study, cookery and laundry were rarely taught during the period. Consequently, the curriculum in operation remained narrow and in practice, it was further constrained by the emphasis within the Primary Certificate Examination on the written aspects of Irish, English and mathematics from the 1940s. Such an imbalanced curriculum for much of the period arguably did not meet the interests of many pupils throughout their schooling or their future needs in their subsequent lives and occupations.

A number of lessons can be learned from an analysis of curriculum provision and implementation in this period. On the positive side, the 1920s witnessed some participation of educational stakeholders in the devising of the curriculum, especially in relation to the Second National Programme Conference. The programmes transmitted elements of the national language and culture to new cohorts of children that had been denied to previous generations. It was flexible and allowed for local adaptation, whereby teachers could submit individual programmes to inspectors as long as they were congruent with the national programme.

However, the programme introduced in 1922 was a radical change from its predecessor and curriculum change and implementation works best in an evolutionary as opposed to revolutionary format. The shedding of many of the additional subjects introduced in 1900 was not lamented by the majority of teachers but the radical change in the underlying philosophy and ideology of the programme proved challenging for many teachers. The time and expertise required to implement the programme in both languages proved great and many of the teachers, in the absence of adequate supports, were unable to deliver on this to the degree required by the programme. The general public remained largely apathetic towards the language revival and in the absence of wider movements in society to promote the language or to create a necessity for its use, the effectiveness of efforts in schools was greatly reduced. Schools invariably reflect and consolidate societal norms and in this context, were an inadequate medium to instigate such a fundamental social change in the absence of widespread political and popular support.

While the INTO was involved in devising the programme and teachers were largely supportive of its ideology, teachers were generally unprepared for its implementation. The *Bilingual Programme* had been operational in approximately 5 per cent of schools and less than 10 per cent of the teaching profession were qualified to use Irish as a medium of instruction in 1922. The summer courses provided were short and intensive in nature and were insufficient to transform teachers' ability in Irish. The pressure felt by teachers to hasten the implementation of the programme often led to poor teaching of Irish, souring the taste of both pupils and teachers for the national language. This also led to poor relations for much of this time between teachers and the Department, as the grading of teachers became increasingly linked to competence in the Irish language.

The material condition of schools was also poor, with large classes, poor buildings and equipment, few educational resources and relatively low attendance rates. While the programmes were put into operation immediately, the recommendations in the 1922 and 1926 programmes cited as necessary for implementation were introduced on a piecemeal and haphazard basis over the following decades. There was little action taken on the improvement of school buildings and equipment, it was 1933 before most *Notes for Teachers* in the various subjects were issued, the provision of training opportunities for teachers in universities was not acted upon, while the provision of school books and standardised formats of Irish were not delivered upon by the Department within a reasonable timeframe. Access to the teacher training colleges became increasingly restricted with the inception of the preparatory colleges and the emphasis on recruiting native Irish speakers. Salary cuts in 1923 and 1933 marred the high expectations of teachers for education under native rule.

At a national level, there was a consistent resistance to enquiry or investigation into the workings of the education system, despite the glaringly obvious fact that the provisions of the programme were not being implemented in practice. The dearth of information emanating from the Department on the workings of the system quelled debate and public interest in the system. In the absence of such data, it remained difficult to pinpoint problems or delineate paths of reform for the programme.

The period was characterised by an emphasis on national and cultural influences on the primary school curriculum. The curriculum framed in 1922 was to prove the bedrock of curriculum provision for the next fifty years and the few modifications enacted did not interfere with its underlying ideology or philosophy. Though the participants in the 1922 and 1926 Programme Conferences were largely educationalists, the programme was primarily motivated by political and nationalistic considerations, as opposed to educational aims and principles. These considerations were prominent well in advance of independence and when the opportunity came, the provisions made were more draconian than many had imagined. This was owing to the high pitch of patriotic fervour in Ireland at that time, the link between the Irish language and nationhood and the composition of the particular conferences and politicians involved in education. In analysing the documentation in relation to the introduction of Irish in the national schools, there was little debate or analysis on the effects of the language on the child. It was largely viewed in nationalist terms; that it was vital for the good of the nation and therefore necessary for the child. The programmes did not accommodate the needs or interests of the vast majority of children attending schools, most of whom spoke no Irish in the home. Moreover, it ignored many of the inherent elements of the culture of Irish people that had been assimilated over centuries and made little provision for minority traditions.

The primary focus of education in the period 1922–1971 was on transmitting the national language, history and culture to upcoming generations. The state retained strict control over the determination of the curriculum in this period and the earlier democratic efforts in the form of the programme conferences in the 1920s were replaced by more centralised and secretive processes to determine the school programme. The Free State government had the opportunity in 1922 to reshape the structure of the Irish education system along new lines but no attempt was made to address structural issues. Instead, the curriculum became the main focus of reform and it would appear that once the path of curriculum change was set in motion in 1922, it became an unstoppable force, and successive governments were unwilling to reform or even investigate its successes or shortcomings. Despite the evident problems with methods and the disappointing results obtaining, there was a reluctance to slow down or change direction with the revival; the only response was to provide more of the same, with greater intensity. This attitude led to stagnation in Irish education. While the needs of the society and economy developed in the forty years after independence, the nature of Irish education did not evolve to fit the changing needs of the country.

The unwillingness of successive governments to observe and learn from international jurisdictions in this period is also noteworthy. Upon independence, Ireland veritably became an 'island' in the world, cocooned from international influences and refusing to acknowledge the reality of world developments. The primary reason for this insularity was the fear of the omnipresence of the English language and culture on all shores, an influence that could prove fatal to the national revival of Irish. There was also a fear of increasing secularism and socialism on the Continent, influences that might challenge the authoritarian control of both the Catholic Church and the state if allowed to filter into Irish society.

It was in the late 1950s and early 1960s that politicians began to realise the importance of education to Irish society, and therefore, to the economy. A number of factors coalesced to catalyse this process, including increased calls for a wider curriculum, contact with international jurisdictions, the advent of free post-primary education, the removal of the need to prepare pupils for formal examinations with the abolition of the Primary

Certificate Examination, the advent of developments in communication and technology, increased economic prosperity, a reversal in the trend of emigration, the presence of a young cohort of motivated politicians and the increasing aspiration for the attainment of equality of educational opportunity. There was also a need to align the Irish economy in order to attain membership of the EEC. One of the main influences in this regard was the theory of human capital development, which showed a direct relationship between educational expenditure and economic development, a theory that influenced the decisions of the Department of Finance in relation to investment in education. The deference and sensitivity towards the Catholic Church in education began to wane and politicians began to assert their role in education policy. By the end of the 1960s, the quest for reform was well established and many of the traditional obstacles to change had been surmounted. Chapter 7 examines the ramifications of this and the societal and educational context for the development and implementation of the *Primary School Curriculum* (1971).

Societal and Educational Context for Curriculum Provision 1971–1990

7.1 Introduction

The pace of societal change in the 1960s, as outlined in chapter 4, continued unabated for much of the 1970s and 1980s, with a gradual transformation of all aspects of Irish life evident by 1990. This chapter provides a lens through which educational change, and more particularly curriculum developments introduced in 1971, can be viewed in this period. It documents the significant developments in Irish society, focusing on the political, socio-cultural, economic and religious aspects of change. This is followed by an overview of the educational context in the period which impacted on the development and implementation of the *Primary School Curriculum* (1971).

7.2 Societal Context 1971–1990 for the *Primary School Curriculum* (1971)

7.2.1 Political Context

Following the dominant position of Fianna Fáil from the 1930s, forming fourteen of the eighteen governments between 1932 and 1982, the 1980s witnessed frequent changes of government and a large number of coalition governments. Despite numerous changes of governments and Ministers for Education during the period, there was remarkable stability in educational and curriculum policy and ideology throughout the period, facilitated by the continuity of senior civil servants.[1] An analysis of the policy documents of the main political parties and their election manifestos reveals no great diversity in relation to their ideology regarding curriculum. The challenge of reducing pupil-teacher ratios, especially in the context of increased enrolments, remained to the fore of all policies. Fianna Fáil and Fine Gael further committed themselves to establishing a curriculum council,[2] which was introduced as the Curriculum and Examinations Board (CEB) in 1984. Regarding the curriculum, all political parties committed to a comprehensive review of its implementation,[3] a promise fulfilled by the inception of the Review Body on the Primary Curriculum in 1987. This proved to be a springboard for curriculum reform in the 1990s, leading to the introduction of the *Primary School Curriculum* (1999).

The Department continued to administer all aspects of the education system centrally, with no advisory council or intermediate structures. It is worth noting that its capacity to perform such functions was greatly affected by a reduction from 1,116 staff in 1981 to 816 in 1990.[4] The role of the Development Unit, established following the *Investment in Education* report, was effectively terminated in 1973, while a Primary Education Policy Unit was established to oversee a strategic policy for education in the late 1980s.[5] The Inspectorate of the Department played a central role in the development of the curriculum in 1971.

The 'Troubles' in Northern Ireland became a feature of Irish politics from the late 1960s. In 1973, the Irish people overwhelmingly endorsed Ireland joining the EEC. The lead up to entry led to much questioning of our level of preparation for Free Trade and the importance human capital would play in ensuring Ireland's success within the EEC. In educational terms, Ireland's membership of the EEC did not impact fundamentally on the content or delivery of the curriculum.[6] However, it increased Ireland's cognisance of educational developments in other jurisdictions.

7.2.2 Socio-cultural Context

> Few societies have changed so rapidly and so radically as has the Republic of Ireland since 1960.[7]

The demographic profile of Irish citizens continued to change throughout this period, with a rise in population from 2.978 million in 1971 to 3.526 million in 1991.[8] By the late 1980s, the start of a period of demographic decline was evident within the primary school system, reflecting the decline in annual births from 74,000 in 1980 to 53,000 in 1989.[9] Increased urbanisation assisted the policy of amalgamations and creating larger schools for the implementation of the *Primary School Curriculum* (1971). Economic prosperity in the 1970s led to a reduction in emigration and even witnessed net immigration. However, emigration re-emerged as a perennial problem in the 1980s, with 200,000 people leaving Ireland between 1980 and 1990.[10] In the early 1980s, approximately one-third of the population received a means-tested social welfare payment each week.[11] In this context, child poverty was a major issue and the ability of parents and families to provide funding locally for school equipment and resources was compromised, a feature that impacted negatively on the ability of schools to provide the requisite wherewithal for implementing all aspects of the curriculum.

The conceptualisation of children in society changed greatly from the 1960s, no doubt influencing the introduction of the *Primary School Curriculum* (1971), which in turn catalysed other developments. There was a major shift in focus towards the meeting of individual needs and to a less-authoritarian approach to education. Corporal punishment was abolished from 1 February 1982.[12] This reform was aligned to the concept of child-centredness espoused in the *Primary School Curriculum* (1971) and to the more enlightened conceptualisation of childhood prevalent in wider society. From the 1980s, there was a growing awareness of children's rights in society, yet children's voices were little heard in matters that affected them.[13] Approximately 20 per cent of schools benefited from a scheme of school meals for the needy, provided by the Department of Social Welfare. Grants for schoolbooks were also made available for necessitous pupils.[14]

The issue of women's rights in society came to the fore in the 1970s, with many positive achievements such as employment equality and equal pay. The percentage of women in the workforce also increased greatly in this period, rising from 24 per cent in 1981 to 34 per cent in 1991.[15] However, even by the late 1980s, there was paltry state provision for early childhood care and education services and the majority of parents placed great reliance on extended families and private provision.[16] Child protection also began to emerge as an important issue by the late 1980s, with the Child Abuse Prevention Programme designed for primary schools in 1987 owing to the increase in reported abuse cases.[17]

7.2.3 Economic Context

The 1970s were characterised by a number of booms and recessions, with the oil crisis of the mid-1970s impacting negatively on the Irish economy. Between 1977 and 1982, national debt more than doubled, while inflation in 1982 reached 20 per cent.[18] In the midst of low economic growth, rising unemployment, high inflation and a deficit in the balance of payments, it was difficult to sustain increased expenditure on education or invest in curriculum implementation. Gemma Hussey was Minister for Education from 1982 to 1986 and noted that her entire tenure was a period of agitation against cuts in educational expenditure.[19]

By 1987, Ireland's national debt was £25 billion (1.5 times GNP), unemployment was at 18 per cent and 30,000 people (approximately 1 per cent of the population) were emigrating annually.[20] This situation led to a number of cutbacks in education under the new Minister, Mary O'Rourke, who was appointed when Fianna Fáil returned to power in 1987. Circular 20/87, which aimed at removing 1,300 teaching posts by January 1988, would have led to significant increases in class sizes.[21] The INTO mounted a concerted public campaign, in conjunction with parents and boards of management, and was successful in resisting the implementation of some of the provisions of the circular. By this time, the power of the INTO had increased significantly and it fought battles with the churches that it had avoided historically in relation to issues such as school governance and maintenance.[22] In addition, the INTO attained prominent representation on review committees and bodies to ensure it played a fundamental role in policy development.

While educational expenditure increased dramatically between 1970 and 1990, the majority of the increases were consumed by inflation and in providing for increasing enrolments at all levels. Traditionally, Ireland had operated the education system in a frugal and spartan manner, with low teacher wages and generous input from religious congregations. Developments from the 1970s left Ireland with an extensive and expensive system.[23] The budget in relation to primary education rose from £24 million in 1970 to nearly £470 million in 1990.[24] However, increases in teachers' salaries and inflation consumed the vast majority of this budget and little remained to fund ancillary services or school resources. In general, spending tended to be more favourably weighted towards the second and third-level sectors. For example, in 1989, £850 was spent per primary school pupil, £1,475 was spent per second-level student and £3,150 was allocated per third-level student.[25] Tussing questioned this regressive system of financing education, which ran contrary to the interests of the poor, and called for a redistribution of funds in favour of the primary level which would benefit all pupils.[26]

The National Economic and Social Council (NESC) compared the levels of spending in the Republic with other jurisdictions, asserting that Ireland spent 61 per cent of that spent in Northern Ireland and 58 per cent of what was spent in England on education in 1975.[27] It also estimated in 1972 that the locality financed 79 per cent of non-pay items within schools. The local contribution to the financing of education, as well as money raised through the school, was increasingly required to sustain the basic running of schools. Therefore, the ability of schools, particularly those catering for large cohorts of pupils affected by socio-economic disadvantage, to compensate for the absence of state funding by providing such materials was limited. A survey by the National Parents' Council Primary (NPC-P) in 1990 reported that 59 per cent of funding of primary schools was met through capitation grants, 6 per cent through other Department grants and the remaining 35 per cent through parental and local contributions, with the local element determining the level of resources, equipment and materials available to schools.[28]

There was more equivocation about the value of investing in education in the 1980s, with a feeling that education had not delivered on its investment. There was an increasing demand for a return to focusing on the basics in education (literacy and numeracy) and for accountability for educational expenditure in the economic climate of the 1980s.[29] This was part of an international trend, most notably in the United Kingdom, where a prescribed and instrumental curriculum was implemented to facilitate easier evaluation and central control.[30] This was in direct contrast to the child-centred, process-focused *Primary School Curriculum* (1971), with an emphasis on the affective domains of education. Ultimately, this utilitarian approach to education was avoided in the Irish context and reforms in the 1990s continued along the path of developing a child-centred, process-focused and holistic curriculum.

7.2.4 Religious Context

Ireland remained a largely conservative society in the 1970s, where abortion and divorce were prohibited, contraception was illegal until 1979 and the overwhelming majority of the population were practising Catholics.[31] However, Irish society was gradually becoming more secular and pluralist, with increasing numbers of non-Catholics at successive censuses and increasing tolerance and support for those who deviated from Catholic norms.[32] Less emphasis was placed on adoption and institutionalisation of children born outside marriage and a focus was placed on family support services.

There was a dramatic reduction in vocations to all aspects of religious life from the late 1960s. Table 7.1 evidences the decline in the direct involvement of the religious in the provision of education, representing a decrease from 19 per cent to 5 per cent of the total profession between 1970 and 1990.

Table 7.1 Number of Religious Teachers (Qualified and Unqualified) on 30 June 1970, 1980 and 1990

	No. of Male Religious Teachers		No. of Female Religious Teachers		Total No. of Religious Teachers		
	Qualified	Unqualified	Qualified	Unqualified	Qualified	Unqualified	Total
1970	525	122	2,008	196	2,533	318	2,851
1980	324	1	1,551	34	1,875	35	1,910
1990	156	0	913	0	1,069	0	1,069

Source: An Roinn Oideachais Tuarascáil Staitistiúil (1974, p. 17; 1982, p. 31; 1991, p. 27).

This forced a rethink of Catholic Church policy in relation to involvement in education, realising it would no longer have the personnel to maintain its historical presence within, and control over, schools.[33] Other factors that catalysed the prominent decline of the religious within education included the emergence of other powerful educational interests, such as teacher unions and parent groups, and the growth of pluralism in Irish society.[34] The NPC-P was established in June 1985 and it gained a representative capacity at national level. While the churches and state still held pivotal power in relation to the devising and implementation of education policy, this was increasingly influenced by the myriad of partners involved in Irish education.[35]

In spite of this decline, the expansion of the education system from the 1960s benefited both the Catholic and Protestant Churches, owing to the increased amount of current and capital expenditure flowing through schools. As Drudy and Lynch asserted:

> while the churches' ownership powers are immediately evident (through their control of school sites and buildings), their consultative and administrative powers, though less evident, are equally significant.[36]

There was ongoing pressure for the establishment of more democratic and representative structures for the management of primary schools, particularly following the influence of Vatican II in relation to the involvement of laity in the Catholic Church. Despite the constitutional position, neither churches nor state had afforded parents a prominent role in education. In June 1973, Seán O'Connor, Secretary of the Department, issued a blueprint for democratising education as part of wider intermediate structures for Irish education. Following much negotiation and conciliation, an agreement was reached whereby parents and teachers were afforded representation on a board of management. The agreement was incentivised by the payment of a capitation grant for children attending a school with a board, which replaced previous separate grants for heating, cleaning and decoration.[37] The duties of the board were largely administrative in nature and involved a limited impact on education policy at national or school level. The churches still had a majority on boards and the chairperson was appointed by the patron.

The denominational nature of primary schools became an increasing concern for parents and pupils not subscribing to the Catholic faith after 1971. Following a protracted campaign, the first multi-denominational school was achieved in 1978. It, and the nine other multi-denominational schools established by 1990, were organised on a co-educational, child-centred and democratic basis.[38] These schools operated under the *Rules for National Schools* and implemented the *Primary School Curriculum* (1971), with the religious education element reflective of pupils of all faiths, or none, attending the schools.

7.3 Educational Context and Milieu 1971–1990

7.3.1 *Schools, Pupils and Teachers*

Table 7.2 details the number of schools, pupils and teachers in the system in the period. While the number of schools reduced by approximately 20 per cent, there was an increase of approximately 9 per cent in the number of pupils and of 37 per cent in the number of teachers.

Table 7.2 Number of Schools, Pupils and Teachers in Ordinary Schools on 30 June 1970, 1975, 1980, 1985 and 1990

	1970	1975	1980	1985	1990
No. of Ordinary Schools	4,047	3,497	3,305	3,266	3,242
No. of Pupils in Ordinary Schools	490,039	511,101	537,069	555,083	540,572
No. of Teachers in Ordinary Schools*	14,859	16,718	18,811	20,909	20,296

* Includes non-classroom teachers such as special class teachers, Visiting Teachers, etc.

Source: An Roinn Oideachais Tuarascáil Staitistiúil (1974, p. 8, 14 and 17; 1977, p. 4, 14 and 34; 1982, p. 10, 18 and 29; 1986, p. 2, 7 and 27; 1991, p. 2, 7 and 27).

The policy of amalgamating small primary schools continued in the 1970s as it was considered that the *Primary School Curriculum* (1971) could only be implemented effectively in larger schools. The policy of the Department was not to replace one- and two-teacher schools in order to improve the distribution of teachers and to ensure schools had adequate resources to implement the curriculum. The physical condition of schools continued to improve. For example, the number of schools with piped drinking

water increased from 47 per cent to 70 per cent, with flush toilets from
46 per cent to 81 per cent, with central heating from 20 per cent to 55 per
cent and electric lighting from 63 per cent to 91 per cent between 1965
and 1975.[39]

As table 7.3 displays, the number of schools with 100 pupils or less
reduced by in excess of 50 per cent during the period, while larger school
units grew concomitantly. However, the preponderance of smaller schools
meant that even by the 1980s, approximately 20 per cent of schools had
an administrative principal, with the remainder staffed by teaching
principals.[40]

Table 7.3 Number of Schools Classified by Number of Pupils Attending 1970–1990

	<50 pupils	50–99 pupils	100–199 pupils	200–299 pupils	300–399 pupils	400–499 pupils	500+ pupils
1969–1970	1,336	1,410	721	174	121	97	188
1979–1980*	765	967	879	287	160	128	229
1989–1990	582	834	958	366	502		

*   Including Ordinary and Special Schools

Source: An Roinn Oideachais Tuarascáil Staitistiúil (1974, p. 9; 1982, p. 17; 1991, p. 26).

Table 7.4 offers an insight into pupil-teacher ratios in schools. While
the number of classes with forty pupils or more declined considerably,
in excess of 70 per cent of pupils remained in classes of more than thirty
pupils in the period 1970–1990.

Table 7.4 Pupils Classified According to Class Size 1975 and 1990

	1974–1975	1989–1990
0–19 pupils	20,175	14,828
20–29 pupils	96,249	139,692
30–39 pupils	209,778	361,514
40+ pupils	184,899	24,538

Source: An Roinn Oideachais Tuarascáil Staitistiúil (1977, p. 24; 1991, p. 23).

Between 1970 and 1990, more than 50 per cent of all four-year-olds and nearly all five-year-olds were enrolled in infant classes of primary schools.[41] Table 7.5 illustrates class size at infant level, showing the high proportion of young children in classes of more than thirty pupils. While somewhat improved by 1990, in excess of 70 per cent still remained in classes of thirty or more pupils, while 4 per cent were in classes with in excess of forty pupils. Undeniably, such large class sizes impacted on the ability of infant teachers to employ activity- and discovery-based methodologies and to focus on the individual needs of each child in these formative years of development.

Table 7.5 Class Size at Infant Level 1985 and 1990

Class Size	1984–1985	1989–1990
0–19 pupils	2,071	1,751
20–29 pupils	28,939	29,169
30–39 pupils	83,539	71,320
40+ pupils	9,376	4,186

Source: An Roinn Oideachais Tuarascáil Staitistiúil (1986, p. 20; 1991, p. 20).

The statistics in the above tables can be further disaggregated to reveal a large discrepancy in pupil-teacher ratios in the various schools. In 1989–1990, the average pupil-teacher ratio was close to 31:1, while the average ratio in schools with between fifty and ninety-nine pupils was just over 19:1. This increased to 34:1 for schools with in excess of 300 pupils.[42] This highlights the uneven distribution of teaching personnel in favour of smaller schools. In this way, while larger schools were favoured for implementing the curriculum, they were actually disadvantaged considerably in the number of teachers allocated to them. Conversely, while small schools lacked appropriate levels of resources, equipment and an administrative principal, they benefited from considerably lower pupil-teacher ratios.

Many pupils in smaller schools were located in consecutive-grade classes or multi-class situations. As table 7.6 demonstrates, the number of pupils in single-grade classes remained constant, the number in consecutive classes increased by approximately 40 per cent, while the number in multi-grade classes reduced by 25 per cent during the period. The stress on using activity methods, on providing for individual pupil needs and on using group techniques proved challenging in a context of multi-grade classes and high pupil-teacher ratios.

Table 7.6 Pupils in Single-Grade Classes, Consecutive-Grade Classes and Multi-Grade Classes 1975–1990

	1974–1975	1979–1980	1984–1985	1989–1990
Single Classes	304,418	334,797	368,539	310,845
Consecutive Classes	113,044	124,570	123,308	158,832
Multi-grade Classes	93,639	77,702	63,236	70,895

Source: An Roinn Oideachais Tuarascáil Staitistiúil (1977, p. 23; 1982, p. 21; 1986, p. 18 1991, p. 17).

The retention of pupils in classes became a less common occurrence, with the number of pupils thirteen years of age and above in primary schools reducing from 38,208 in 1964[43] to 6,111 in 1979.[44] School attendance also remained steady at over 90 per cent throughout this period. However, non-attendance remained an issue among certain cohorts of the population, especially those affected by disadvantage and those with learning difficulties.[45]

7.3.2 School Design and Equipment

The design of school buildings evolved, as they had done in earlier periods of curriculum reform, in line with the new educational and philosophical approaches. The space allowance per child within classrooms increased to nineteen square feet by 1974.[46] In addition, the majority of the 500 new schools built in the 1970s had a more homely feel and were equipped with wet areas, textile flooring, moveable furniture, better lighting and display facilities, general purpose rooms and better storage space, which impacted positively on the learning experiences afforded within them. Among the influences on the provision of more space and for the different use of such space were the focus on individual difference, the integration of subjects, the emphasis on play, the redefinition of the role of the teacher, the importance of facilitating group activity and project-work and enabling children to be active agents in their own learning. These developments had a direct impact on the implementation of the *Primary School Curriculum* (1971) within these schools, providing the physical structures that allowed the vision of the curriculum to be implemented in practice. However, this related to a minority of schools, while most pupils attended schools that were characterised by a lower space allowance, cumbersome furniture, an absence of storage and recreational areas and a lack of basic equipment for implementing the curriculum. From 1978, a grant was paid for clerical assistance in schools with seven or more teachers and for caretaking from 1979 in schools with more than sixteen teachers.[47] Given the preponderance of small schools, only 40 per cent of schools had a caretaker and 12 per cent of schools had secretarial staff by the mid-1980s.[48]

One specific design innovation in the 1970s was the creation of shared areas within schools to facilitate greater freedom for teachers in the use of space. In this design, classrooms were paired, whereby each class had a small base room and a combined circulation or shared space between them. By 1981, there were 291 shared areas in 127 schools.[49] Shared areas contained many advantages that would have facilitated the implementation of the curriculum, including allowing children to work alone or in groups, the provision of different areas for various activities, facilitating co-operation with other teachers and accommodating the help of additional and specialist teachers. However, the concept was not popular or widely used and ceased to be provided for by the late 1980s.

In 1970, the Department announced that new books would be required but would not be produced until the curriculum was finalised, with the full range of texts expected by June 1971.[50] De Buitléar noted that a number of subject committees, each under the leadership of an inspector, had been established to facilitate liaison between the Department and publishers of books for the *Primary School Curriculum* (1971).[51] Consequently, teachers were advised to continue using the existing textbooks until the new books came on stream. In 1972, Minister Faulkner acknowledged that a full complement of books was still not available for the curriculum.[52] This produced a vacuum in supports for teachers in the embryonic stages of implementing the curriculum, where new content and approaches were being attempted with traditional textbooks and a dearth of additional resources.

In addition to changes in the physical structure, the tools and resources used within classrooms also altered to include more audio-visual equipment. An Audi-visual Aids Unit was established in the Department in 1968 to develop hardware and software for distribution to schools. In 1971, £250,000 per annum was announced for the provision of teaching requisites and audiovisual aids, and for the equipping of schools and Teachers' Centres.[53] This allowed a £12 grant for a one-teacher school and an extra £10 for each additional teacher to purchase teaching aids, which was to be supplemented by local funds.[54] A further grant was provided to schools with three or more teachers for the purchase of equipment such as projectors, duplicators, tape recorders and film strips, starting at £40 for smaller schools and rising to £100 for schools with more than sixteen teachers. Even in 1970, this was a paltry provision for schools to become equipped to the level expected for the proposed new curriculum, with many schools beginning from a very low base. Minister Faulkner proposed the establishment of local parents' committees to provide financial (and other) aid to schools in obtaining the necessary equipment and materials for implementation.[55] This situation exacerbated inequality within the system considering such provision was largely determined on the socio-economic background of the area, size of school and geographical location. Grants for equipment and materials were cut in the 1970s and their value greatly eroded by the high inflation inherent in the Irish economy. By 1989, the equipment grant had reduced to £80,000.[56]

7.3.3 Teachers in the System

In tandem with the growing school population, the teaching force also increased by 37 per cent in the period 1970 to 1990. This period also witnessed the practical disappearance of untrained teachers. The increasing feminisation of the profession became more prominent, and between 1972 and 1991, the number of male candidates entering the training colleges reduced from 32 per cent to 13 per cent.[57]

Table 7.7 Teaching Workforce on 30 June 1970, 1975, 1980, 1985 and 1990

	Total No. of Teachers	No. of men	No. of Women	Number Trained	Number Untrained
1970	14,859	4,677	10,182	13,819	1,040
1975	16,718	4,838	11,880	16,328	390
1980	18,811	5,045	13,766	18,693	118
1985	20,909	5,125	15,784	20,905	4
1990	20,296	4,863	15,433	20,294	2

Source: An Roinn Oideachais Tuarascáil Staitistiúil (1974, p. 17; 1977, p. 34; 1982, p. 30; 1986, p. 27; 1991, p. 27).

A common salary scale for all teachers was achieved in 1969, with posts of responsibility introduced in primary schools in 1973. These were allocated primarily on seniority, and in the absence of guidelines, there was no uniformity in relation to the duties assigned and posts often became a reward for seniority as opposed to a special duty benefiting the school.[58] A salary increase was achieved in 1980 following direct negotiations with the Minister for Education.[59]

The Higher Education Authority *Report on Teacher Education* in 1970 noted the inadequacy of the two-year training programme for student teachers to become versed in educational developments, to acquire the science and art of teaching and to allow specialist study. It proposed a three-year non-university degree course (Bachelor of Educational Science) for primary teachers.[60] While welcoming the thrust of the report, the INTO[61] and the training colleges[62] rejected non-university degrees for teachers. Following negotiations between the universities, the training colleges and the Department, university degree courses were achieved in 1974. The Bachelor of Education (B.Ed) degree was a professional degree consisting of education and general academic studies pursued concurrently, yet the main focus and percentage of marks remained on the theoretical, practical and methodological aspects of education.[63] The training colleges were renamed 'colleges of education' and became affiliated to various universities for awarding and accreditation purposes. An intensive one-year course for university graduates was also offered, while those qualifying abroad were recognised once they passed the necessary Irish examination. In 1985, courses were introduced for teachers qualified prior to 1974 to upgrade their qualifications to degree level.[64] Entry to the colleges of education remained competitive, and the calibre of entrants remained consistently high in the 1980s, with the average student teacher in the top quartile of entrants to third-level education.[65]

Comhairle na Gaeilge was established in 1969 to advise on how best to further the Irish language and to assist the government in relation to policy formulation. It asserted that the level of proficiency of teachers in Irish qualifying in the training colleges disimproved in the 1970s, owing to the focus on other subjects and the greater diversity in entrants to the profession.[66] Ó Buachalla expressed concern that between 70 and 80 per cent of students followed the professional course in Irish, representing less than two hours contact time per week, arguing that these were often the weakest students in Irish.[67] An evaluation of the B.Ed course conducted by the ERC in 1982 reported that 61 per cent of students' study time was spent on the academic subjects, although only 32 per cent of the contact time was attributed to these.[68] Furthermore, the fact that many theoretical areas were completed in the first two years and did not contribute to degree marks was raised as a concern.

In-service education remained a demand of teachers from the inception of the *Primary School Curriculum* (1971), a demand that went largely unmet throughout the period. Prior to the introduction of the curriculum, a Steering Committee on In-service Education was established in November 1970. Its purpose was to provide induction for 15,000 practising teachers in the new curriculum, including training in the use of new techniques, methods, pedagogical apparatus, assessment, psychology, special educational needs and social problems. The Committee noted the urgent need for systematic in-service provision to introduce the curriculum, asserting that 'it was now time to have a look at in-service training as a continuing process, it was time to begin thinking of such training as a permanent organised feature of our educational system.'[69] The Committee formed a Working Group to investigate various possibilities for the provision of in-service education, and following a number of research visits, proposed the establishment of a network of Teachers' Centres nationwide for the use of teachers at both primary and post-primary levels.[70]

In 1972, twelve Teachers' Centres were established to act as a focal point for teachers to meet, to provide lectures and seminars, to deliver in-service courses and induction programmes, and to provide resources and materials. Among the other functions of Teachers' Centres were to act as a resource centre for teachers to prepare and construct equipment and materials for distribution, to facilitate the display of teachers' and children's work and to enable publishers to hold exhibitions.[71] By 1979, there were twenty-two Teachers' Centres nationwide, yet many areas remained poorly served especially in the Midlands, West and Southwest. In 1985, O'Reilly asserted that the absence of full-time directors and the lack of release time for teachers resulted in poor uptake in their use and that their role in the provision of in-service education 'remains largely unfulfilled.'[72]

While some provision for in-service education at a local level may have existed, there was a vacuum at policy level in relation to planning, co-ordination, resource allocation, evaluation, certification and continuity. This resulted in most in-service education being short-term in nature and attended on a voluntary basis. The oil crisis of 1973–1974 impacted negatively on spending in education and while the £30,000 allocated to in-service training in 1969 had risen to £80,000 in 1974, this reduced to £12,000 in 1975 and remained inadequate for the remainder of the decade.[73] In 1990, the £35,000 spent on in-service education represented an investment of £1.50 per teacher and 0.06 per cent of the total education budget.[74] The lack of investment in in-service education impacted negatively on the dissemination and implementation of the *Primary School Curriculum* (1971), as teachers felt largely unsupported in relation to interpreting its content and methodologies. Attendance at voluntary summer courses remained high throughout the period, arguably incentivised by the allocation of three days personal leave for teachers participating. Approximately 50 per cent of teachers attended summer courses annually by 1990.[75]

In 1980, Minister Wilson established a Committee 'to identify priority areas of in-service training of teachers and to make recommendations to the Department.'[76] The Committee prioritised in-service on curriculum areas and methodologies to ensure adequate implementation and development. However, there was little concerted action in relation to the recommendations. The *Programme for Action in Education* (1984–1987) stated that it would prioritise in-service education, with precedence given to courses on learning difficulties, teaching art, physical education, science and Irish, the elimination of sexism and the introduction of computers.[77] However, there was a lack of commitment to implementation and provision remained *ad hoc* and sporadic in nature. In 1991, the OECD also called for in-service training for teachers to support changes in classroom organisation and methodologies as envisaged by the curriculum.[78]

The responsibility of the principal became increasingly complex, evolving from an administrative role prior to 1971 to a management role in the 1970s and 1980s and through to a leadership role by the 1990s.[79] The

Primary School Curriculum (1971) raised the profile of the school principal both within and outside the school, with increased responsibilities in a wide variety of areas such as boards of management and curriculum implementation, as outlined in Circular 16/73.[80] Many of these developments took place in a climate of little support or training for principals in tasks that were largely unrelated to their pre-service training and teaching experience. The Primary Education Review Body report called for a rational distribution of the multiple responsibilities of the principal to personnel such as the vice principal, holders of posts of responsibility, secretarial and caretaker personnel, with initial management training and ongoing in-service for principals.[81] The OECD called for increased and specialist training for principals and school management to support decision making, resource management, accountability, interpersonal and community relations, and use of middle management structures.[82]

The enthusiasm and optimism within the profession in the 1970s with the advent of university degrees and a growth in intake was replaced in the 1980s by reduced numbers due to demographic decline, limited opportunities for progression, pressure on teacher salaries and greater demands within the role. It also led to the closure and down sizing of colleges of education, with consequent effects on available expertise and staff morale. For example, the annual intake in the two largest colleges of education (St Patrick's College and Mary Immaculate College) fell from 250 to 100 in the late 1980s, while Carysfort College was closed.[83] Career breaks were facilitated by the Department from 1985 in an effort to provide new employment opportunities, with approximately 500–600 teachers using this facility annually in the late 1980s.[84]

7.3.4 Special Educational Needs

Table 7.8 illustrates the large increase in the provision for special education between 1970 and 1990, with a 67 per cent rise in the number of special schools and a 57 per cent increase in the number of pupils attending such schools. The main area of expansion related to schools catering for pupils with mild and moderate 'mental handicap' and emotional disturbance, while provision for physical and sensory disability remained constant. In addition, there were over 3,000 pupils in special classes within ordinary schools in 1990, a provision that did not exist in 1970.

Table 7.8   Number of Schools and Pupils in Special Schools 1970–1990

	1969–1970	1974–1975	1979–1980	1984–1985	1989–1990
No. of Special Schools	70	88	110	116	117
No. of Pupils in Special Schools	5,401	7,198	8,115	8,495	8,491
No. of Pupils in Special Classes	–	1,865	2,247	2,711	3,119

Source: An Roinn Oideachais Tuarascáil Staitistiúil (1974, p. 8; 1977, p. 4 and 14; 1982, p. 2 and 10; 1986, p. 2 and 7; 1991, p. 2 and 7).

The government produced a number of reports between 1970 and 1990 relating to pupils with special educational needs.[85] In general, these recommended increased levels of integration of pupils with special educational needs into ordinary schools. In the period, integration did not impact in any significant way on mainstream classes and was largely confined to special classes. In the absence of special curriculum guidelines, the majority of integrated pupils followed a mediated form of the *Primary School Curriculum* (1971), devised in the main by individual teachers. Approaching the 1990s, there was a realisation that the provision of services for pupils with special educational needs was not a black and white issue between integration and segregation. Instead, owing to the complexity of the issue and the range of needs of children, a continuum of provision was required to cater for all needs.

Remedial education became a feature of provision in larger schools from the 1960s. Remedial teaching at that time invariably involved the withdrawal of pupils from their classrooms in small groups for tuition in basic reading skills. The aim cited by the Department was to close the gap between attainment and ability by specialised teaching in small groups or individually.[86] This supported the focus within the curriculum on meeting the needs of the individual child and provided assistance to the classroom teacher in this regard. Many concerns were raised regarding the effectiveness of the system, including training for remedial teachers, the level of communication between the remedial teacher and the classroom teacher and parents, the long-term benefits of remedial education and the paucity of provision for equipment and resources for remedial teachers.[87] By 1990, there were 890 remedial teachers employed in primary schools.[88]

Although the Department employed a small cohort of psychologists from the mid-1960s, their services were not available to national schools. Such a service was perceived to be increasingly necessary considering the focus on the individual needs of each child within the curriculum and the increased prevalence of integrating pupils with special educational needs in mainstream schools. Despite calls from a myriad of organisations and reports for the introduction of a psychological service to schools,[89] this was not achieved prior to 1990. In 1990, there were twenty-seven Visiting Teachers for pupils with hearing impairment and three for those with visual impairment.[90]

The provision of an appropriate education for Travellers became a special focus of the period following 1971. In this time, Traveller participation rates greatly improved, yet in 1981, only 50 per cent of Traveller children attended school regularly.[91] In 1980, a Curriculum Committee was established to study the particular needs of Travellers and the expectations of Travellers from participation in the education system. The curriculum produced was not detailed on a class-by-class basis but ordered each subject within four broad age-ranges to accommodate the varying ages for entry to schooling, placing a special emphasis on the attainment of literacy and numeracy.[92] In the early 1980s, there were two special schools and approximately seventy special classes for Travellers, using varying degrees of integration with ordinary classes. The *Report of the Review Body of the Travelling People*[93] and the *Programme for Action in Education*[94] proposed a policy of integration for Travellers, with special supports to counteract their disadvantage, such as preschool education, the provision of special classes and a Visiting Teacher Service. By 1990, the majority of Traveller children attending school were either fully or partially integrated in mainstream classes, while approximately 30 per cent attended special classes.[95]

Following the publication of the *Investment in Education* report, a greater focus was placed on tackling inequality within the education system. Minister Faulkner asserted his hope in 1970 that the provisions of the curriculum would cater for the needs of disadvantaged pupils by allowing all pupils to progress and achieve success at their individual level and provide a wide range of experiences and subjects.[96] The 1980s were characterised by an increased awareness and political will towards disadvantage but action was marred by economic crisis and budgetary contractions. Minister Hussey asserted that one of her main priorities as Minister for Education in the 1980s was the concentration of funding on disadvantaged schools and children.[97] She ensured that provisions for disadvantage were a priority within the *Programme for Action in Education* (1984–1987) by introducing a special scheme in approximately 200 disadvantaged schools in 1984. The £500,000 additional funding for the scheme in 1987–1988 provided for additional teaching posts, special improvement and equipment grants, in-service education, developing home-school links, school books and other requisites in targeted schools.

7.3.5 The Irish Language

The number of schools in which Irish was used as the medium of instruction continued to decline in the period 1970–1990, as is evident in table 7.9. The increasing number of Gaelscoileanna (Irish-medium schools) established in the 1970s and 1980s masked the greater decline in teaching through Irish that occurred in both Gaeltacht and Galltacht schools during this period. This decline was particularly acute in schools that previously taught some aspects of the curriculum through Irish. Overall, by 1990, approximately 5 per cent of schools used Irish as a sole medium of instruction.

Table 7.9   Methods of Teaching Irish in Primary Schools 1971–1990

Method of Teaching	1970–1971*		1979–1980		1989–1990	
	Schools	Pupils	Schools	Pupils	Schools	Pupils
Schools/ pupils in which all classes are taught through the medium of Irish	199	14,053	169	16,196	178	20,496
Schools/ pupils in which some classes are taught through the medium of Irish	49	13,709	16	5,332	10	3,119
Schools/ pupils in which some subjects/ activities are taught through the medium of Irish (at least one subject as well as Irish)	1,719	235,366	1,178	213,202	1,164	197,958
Other schools/ pupils	1,890	233,641	1,941	302,339	1,890	319,320

*   Figure relates to September 1971.

Source: An Roinn Oideachais Tuarascáil Staitistiúil (1974, p. 13; 1982, p. 28; 1991, p. 23).

As in previous eras, the debate around the Irish language was characterised by two distinct viewpoints; those who wanted its position to be strengthened and supported in society and those who believed that too much was already being done to bolster the language. The number of declared Irish speakers in the census continued to rise in this period, as was the tendency from 1926. In 1971, 789,429 citizens stated they were Irish speakers, with 1,998,089 declared as non-Irish speakers.[98] This represented 28 per cent of the population declaring itself to be able to speak Irish and appeared to be a high proportion considering the report of the Committee on Irish Language Attitudes Research (CLÁR) reported that only 4 per cent of the population outside the Gaeltacht used Irish frequently and intensively in 1975.[99]

The inception of the Buntús Gaeilge Research Project in 1962 provided great optimism that the learning of Irish would be 'much easier and very much more enjoyable'[100] with the use of new methods. This project studied the vocabulary, structures and syntax patterns of the Irish language, with a view to formulating graded courses using audiovisual aids in primary schools.[101] From this initial research, conversation courses were prepared for schools, as well as handbooks, tapes, pictures, audio-visual aids and carefully graded reading books based on oral work. Starting in junior classes in 1967–1968 and in senior classes from 1969–1970, the graded courses produced were piloted for one year in approximately 150 schools and revisions based on experiences enacted. Short courses were held nationwide by a cohort of 150 trained teachers on the new principles and methods.[102] Teachers and educationalists welcomed the new approach, particularly its structure and the provision of necessary materials.[103] Each series contained forty lessons, each one with five steps, and was designed to last one year.

The Buntús approach formed the core of the Irish language curriculum between 1971 and 1990. However, it was not reviewed and made current on an ongoing basis and by 1990, its dated nature and over-dependence on the audiovisual approach negated many of its benefits. Ó Domhnalláin, one of its devisers, regretted that the pressure to roll out the programme across all classes led to a neglect of conducting research on the effects of implementation at the transition point between both approaches.[104] Mac Aogáin asserted that the Buntús programme was never intended to replace all other methods and argued that an over-reliance on this method had a negative impact on standards in Irish.[105]

There was a movement from the 1970s to establish all-Irish medium schools outside the Gaeltacht as research began to assert there were no negative cognitive effects for children educated through Irish. Following MacNamara's controversial report in 1966 documenting the negative effects on educational progress that instruction through Irish imposed, a number of researchers began to refute such contentions. Cummins reviewed the research evidence and concluded that instruction through the second language did not impact negatively on academic outcomes.[106]

Further research found that pupils in Irish- and English-medium schools did equally well in English at grade three, while those in Irish-medium schools had a greater proficiency in Irish.[107] Ó Ciaráin reported significant positive differences in attainment in Irish and mathematics in Gaelscoileanna.[108] Effectively, Gaelscoileanna were ordinary national schools that followed the *Primary School Curriculum* (1971) and where Irish was the language of instruction and the language of communication amongst teachers and pupils. While the first Gaelscoil was established in 1954, the second did not open until 1969, while following this, the numbers increased quickly from thirteen in 1974 to sixty-eight in 1990.[109] Department policy was supportive of extending the network of Gaelscoileanna, owing to the positive results they were achieving in the Irish language.

7.3.6 *Inspection and Evaluation*

In this period, the Inspectorate continued to be the main liaison personnel between schools and the Department. The Inspectorate evaluated national schools on a cyclical basis, with approximately 700 school inspections undertaken annually.[110] Its work was governed by Circular 12/76 and subsequently Circular 31/82, which outlined the functions of inspection, the responsibilities of inspectors, incidental visits, school reports and general inspections.[111]

A survey of inspectors' work in 1979–1980 revealed the wide-ranging duties inspectors performed, and showed that 42 per cent of their time was allocated to work outside schools. The *Report of the Committee on Primary Schools Inspection* (1981) asserted the need to reorganise the Inspectorate to ensure 'that they can discharge their primary function, which is to inspect schools and advise teachers.'[112] It also stressed the fundamental importance of the advisory role of the Inspectorate as an element of the job profile to be further developed. In 1990, inspectors spent, on average, 51 per cent of their time in schools, with 35 per cent of this time afforded to general/school reports, 44 per cent on advisory and support work and 21 per cent on 'special' work, such as the appointment of teachers, checking enrolments and investigating complaints against teachers.[113]

Despite an increase in the range of duties for the Inspectorate, there was no accompanying increase in personnel and resources. A review of staffing in 1981 recommended a cohort of 129 inspectors to fulfil duties, with an additional inspector to be appointed for each increase of 250 teachers.[114] The cohort of inspectors remained extremely low in the early 1970s, at the time additional support was most necessary to introduce the new curriculum, reducing from sixty-seven inspectors in 1970 to a low of sixty-three in 1974.[115] The effects of this understaffing in the 1980s is evident from table 7.10, which shows a decreasing number of inspectors, spending a reduced amount of time in schools and conducting a diminishing number of general inspections.

Table 7.10 Inspection of National Schools 1982–1988

	1982–1983	1984–1985	1986–1987	1988–1989
No. of Schools	3,390	3,383	3,389	3,363
No. of Teachers	20,435	20,798	20,993	20,514
No. of Inspectors	85 (63)*	80(58)*	77 (55)*	76 (54)*
No. of Days (av.) per Inspector in Schools	136.5	110.3	117.66	108.6
% of Time in School	50	41	43.5	40.6
No. of Full School Inspections	744	605	736	496
No. of General Inspection Reports Furnished	1,884	705	864	466

*   District inspectors only.

Source: Review Body on the Primary Curriculum (1990). *Report of the Review Body on the Primary Curriculum*. Dublin: Department of Education, p. 124.

The structure and format of the *Primary School Curriculum* (1971) led to problems in relation to assessment and accountability as progress was not easily evaluated. Kellaghan, founding director of the ERC, argued the importance of stating educational objectives in terms of pupil behaviours to assist evaluation of the curriculum in 1973.[116] Greaney identified a number of challenges to developing standardised tests in the Irish context, including the identification of objectives owing to the vagueness of the curriculum, the unrealistic targets in many subjects and of developing tests for Irish speakers.[117] There was an increasing availability of standardised tests throughout the period, many emanating from the ERC and the Department's psychological service. The lack of suitable tests to measure implementation limited the ability of curriculum planners and teachers to identify positive and negative aspects of implementation, and consequently to alter policy or practice as a result. The increasing availability of such tests from the 1980s did not impact significantly on practice, owing to a lack of awareness among teachers of their function and purpose.

The CEB and the NPC-P called for a statement of aims and objectives for primary education that could be easily assessed and evaluated. Furthermore, the NPC-P called for the formal assessment of pupils in third and sixth class at its annual meeting in 1987, owing to the perception of falling standards.[118] The INTO consistently opposed the introduction of national examinations for pupils, stating the inspection system already assessed the quality of teaching and learning and that record keeping by teachers and the use of standardised tests sufficed.[119] Throughout the period, there was little use made of standardised tests to inform teachers' practice. While a number of such tests were used to evaluate aspects of implementation at a national level, in general, these did not impact on the practice of individual teachers.

An emphasis on self-evaluation within schools became a focus from the late 1980s, such as looking at aspects of teaching methods, curriculum, parent and community relationships and school operations.[120] This approach evolved in tandem with the development of the School Plan, which became an increasingly integral feature of school planning and evaluation.[121] However, the development of a School Plan or school self-evaluation practices did not become embedded to any appreciable degree in school culture prior to 1990.

7.3.7 Educational Research and Information

Educational research in the period 1971–1990 also witnessed expansion and its nature evolved somewhat from the era of gathering knowledgeable people to form commissions, to the production of factual reports on which deliberations and planning could be based.[122] There was also a great increase in the general public's interest in education and of individual research on all aspects of the system. However, state investment in educational research remained paltry, decreasing marginally from 0.05 per cent of the education budget in 1970[123] to 0.04 per cent in 1980.[124] The *Report of the Committee on Primary Schools Inspection* noted the absence of monitoring standards at a national level, which meant comparative analysis was not available and the report called for 'more concrete evidence' to be gathered in the climate of increasing accountability.[125] Kellaghan criticised the lack of comprehensive research and data on the functioning of the education system, which he described as 'bitty and piecemeal.'[126] The CEB noted a dearth of longitudinal studies, national studies of pupil achievement and research focusing on pupil performance, concluding that:

> Because of the relatively large areas still unresearched, it is difficult to get any over-view of actual practices in classrooms, of national standards of attainment, of teacher effectiveness, or of the suitability of the curriculum.[127]

The Primary Education Review Body report noted the dearth of policy-related research, advocating closer co-operation between researchers and policymakers, the wider dissemination of research findings and a more co-ordinated and systematic approach to research.[128] Furthermore, the impact of research on policy development was also difficult to analyse, as policy making was not always transparent or carried out in the public arena, leading Kellaghan to conclude 'that research rarely has any discern-able impact on the policy-making process.'[129]

Basic degree training for teachers allowed further study at postgraduate level in the form of Masters' and Doctoral programmes, which became available in many of the Irish universities from the 1970s. This led to a situation whereby between 1980 and 1990, more postgraduate theses[130] were produced compared to the entire period from 1911 to 1979.[131] Approximately 13 per cent of these related to the curriculum.[132] In 1976, the Educational Studies Association of Ireland (ESAI) was established to foster and promote co-operation within the burgeoning research community. The Irish Association for Curriculum Development was founded in 1971 and it encouraged and promoted curriculum development through conferences and lectures.[133] However, the Association focused principally on post-primary curricula and its impact on the development or implementation of the *Primary School Curriculum* (1971) was limited. Other developments during the period included the establishment of the Irish Association for Teachers in Special Education in 1969, the Association of Remedial Teachers of Ireland in 1974 and the Reading Association of Ireland in 1975.

Tussing criticised the Department for the dearth of information available on the system, such as organisational and fiscal structures, enrolment and expenditure forecasts and the distribution of expenditure.[134] Moreover, many evaluations of the curriculum conducted by the Department and its agencies were never published or made available to inform practice. *Rules for National Schools* were no longer published after 1965, leading to a situation whereby schools throughout this period, and beyond, were governed by the basic rules of 1965, which had been amended *ad infinitum* in the intervening years by circulars and directives. In 1984, Minister Hussey addressed some of these concerns by publishing *Léas*, an information bulletin issued three times annually by the Department. However, this initiative was short-lived and *Léas* ceased to be circulated following the publication of four bulletins in 1986. The NPC-P issued a quarterly newsletter from spring 1987, *Cúram*, which assisted the dissemination of educational information to parents. Colgan criticised the secretive nature of the operation of the Department in 1991, noting the absence of even an annual report in narrative form since the mid-1960s.[135] This absence of current data on the system hindered policy development and an understanding of the overall operation of the education system.

7.4 Summary and Conclusion

It is evident that the political, socio-cultural, economic and religious context in this period differed greatly from earlier eras. From a political perspective, education remained high on the national agenda and state investment in education continued to increase throughout the period. All political parties had formulated detailed policies on education and election manifestos invariably contained similar strategies. Ireland's entry to the EEC impacted little on the curriculum, yet Irish educational thinking was increasingly flavoured by international developments. The social context was also transformed from earlier eras, with the fabric of Irish society continuing to undergo a metamorphosis that was initiated in the 1960s. Corporal punishment was abolished in 1982 in line with the new conceptualisation of childhood inherent within the *Primary School Curriculum* (1971). There were periods of both emigration and immigration over the two decades from 1971, primarily emigration, and there was a tendency towards increased urbanisation and secularism. Demographically, the period was one of increasing population and this placed pressure on educational institutions to cater for a large increase in participation in schooling. The range of stakeholders with an input in educational matters increased significantly, most notably to include teachers and parents, which altered somewhat the previous binary churches and state power structure.

The economic barometer recorded many changes in the two decades but the overall climate was one of recession and retrenchment. This impacted on the availability of resources for investment in education and consequently on funding for the implementation of the curriculum. Therefore, much of the additional investment in education was absorbed by inflation and to provide for increasing enrolments. This was particularly evident in relation to the attempts to reduce class sizes throughout the period, whereby the majority of pupils were taught in classes of more than thirty pupils, militating against the ideology of the curriculum to cater for individual differences and to enact activity and discovery methods. The economic situation catalysed the calls for a return to basics in education, which threatened the curriculum model implemented in Ireland in 1971 that focused on the holistic development of the child. However, such moves were largely resisted in the Irish context.

While there was a reduction in the number of religious personnel in Ireland between 1970 and 1990, the Catholic Church still maintained a prominent position within the education system through its ownership and management functions. The Irish population remained overwhelmingly Catholic and the Catholic Church retained a powerful position in wider society. School design evolved during this period, the most notable innovation being the inception of shared areas within schools. However, the majority of schools remained unaltered from their traditional design and owing to the absence of funding, were not modernised or equipped to facilitate implementation of the ideology of the 1971 curriculum.

The number of primary teachers increased in tandem with enrolments between 1970 and 1990. The teaching profession was bolstered by the achievement of a degree as a basic qualification in the 1970s, improving the status of teachers and their ability to specialise further within the field of education. The role of the principal also diversified greatly following 1971, consisting of a host of new demands and responsibilities. One of the main demands of teachers throughout this period was for a systematic and comprehensive system of in-service training to ensure teachers were cognisant of modern educational thinking and teaching methodologies. This related largely to ensuring that teachers trained in traditional methods were prepared to implement the *Primary School Curriculum* (1971). Owing to economic difficulties and lack of co-ordination at a national level, this demand was not substantially achieved during this period.

Provision for pupils with special educational needs and those affected by educational disadvantage also received a particular focus from the 1970s. Government policy became increasingly focused on integrating pupils with special educational needs into mainstream schools, where appropriate. The provision of remedial education also increased greatly in the period and supported individual pupils to reach their potential. Disadvantaged groups, including Travellers, became a policy focus, particularly from the 1980s.

The Irish language remained an integral feature of the education system in this period, although the level of controversy and debate was tempered by a number of other emphases and issues within the system. Evidently, the traditional conception of education as being largely for cultural aims was relegated. This reduced the focus on the importance of the Irish language and emphasised aspects of the curriculum that had not been prioritised since independence. The Inspectorate continued to play an integral role in the operation of the education system, primarily through its function as a liaison between the Department and schools and through the inspection of schools. This body was negatively affected by resource deprivation, operating without a full complement of inspectors for much of the period.

The provision for and incidence of educational research improved considerably from the 1970s and this provided a greater insight into the operation of the education system than was previously documented. However, by international comparison, state investment in research remained low and the range and scope of research was consequently constricted. Furthermore, timely data relating to the education system remained difficult to attain.

Against this background, chapter 8 examines the process by which the *Primary School Curriculum* (1971) was devised and the provisions it made for pupils in the period following 1971.

Planning and Content of the *Primary School Curriculum* (1971)

8.1 Introduction

This chapter examines the process of developing the *Primary School Curriculum* (1971) and is presented in three distinct phases. The first is the decision to produce a White Paper on Education in 1966, a task that was undertaken by the Inspectorate. Although *Towards a White Paper on Education* was never completed or published, it was a key document in the production of the 1971 curriculum. It assimilated much national and international thinking on curriculum issues at the time and provided a rationale and structure for the revision and transformation of the curriculum. The second phase in arriving at the *Primary School Curriculum* (1971) was the development of a Working Document in autumn 1968, essentially a first draft of the curriculum. This document developed and extended the section on curriculum within the draft White Paper and judiciously outlined the content in the various subject areas. The third phase related to the production of the Teacher's Handbooks with the content of the curriculum. These were developed by committees of inspectors between 1969 and 1971 and were distributed to all teachers between the spring (Part 1) and autumn (Part 2) of 1971.

8.2 *Towards a White Paper on Education* (1967)

In 1965, the Minister for Education, George Colley, announced a formal review of the curriculum and an examination of lengthening the school day.[1] This was superseded the following year by the new Minister for Education, Donagh O'Malley, who established a Steering Committee within the Department in December 1966 to advise on all aspects relating to primary education for a proposed White Paper. This process was directed by the Assistant Secretary, Mr Ó Conchobhair, and co-ordinated by Deputy Chief Inspector, Mr Ó Foghlú. Mr Ó hUallacháin, Deputy Chief Inspector, had responsibility for the primary section of the White Paper and he was assisted by Mr Ó Muircheartaigh (Secretary), Mr Ó Súilleabháin (Divisional Inspector), Mr Ó Cuilleanáin (Divisional Inspector), Mr Ó Domhnalláin (District Inspector) and Mr de Buitléar (District Inspector). The process was further supported by a number of White Paper sub-committees appointed in January 1967, which were comprised of an additional twenty-five to thirty inspectors.[2] On 13 January 1967, the Secretary of the Department issued a letter to all inspectors inviting any opinions or recommendations to the Committee drafting the White Paper before 31 January 1967. An appendix to the letter contained a list of items inspectors may have wished to address, including subject areas, special education, teacher training, inspection, bilingualism and school management.[3]

The reports of the sub-committees were completed in February 1967 and the final report, *Towards a White Paper on Education*, was subsequently produced weeks later by the Steering Committee. This short turn around was impressive considering the comprehensive nature of the final report. However, the speed at which it was produced also detracted from its integrated nature and authority as a curriculum planning document. Such a timeframe allowed for little if any detailed curriculum research to be undertaken, while the rushed and unco-ordinated nature of its production limited its value as a foundation for subsequent curriculum development. The production of the final report by a myriad of individual sub-committees militated against the production of an 'integrated' curriculum so widely espoused by the Department.

Towards a White Paper on Education spanned some 120 pages and focused primarily on the primary curriculum, containing sections on the Purpose of Primary Education, General Considerations for the Curriculum, Learning and Teaching Methods and Curriculum Content. It also contained many sections as add-ons that were submitted by the various inspector sub-committees, such as pupil attainment, transfer to post-primary schooling, human and material resources, research and development, inspection, school buildings, special education and school management.

In its 'Introduction', *Towards a White Paper* alluded to international educational developments and emphasised that Irish education was static and needed to develop in line with, and learn from, other jurisdictions. However, considering the timescale for its development, it is unlikely that a detailed examination of national or international policy or practice was possible. It provided a limited theoretical underpinning for the *Primary School Curriculum* (1971), a fundamental aspect that had been omitted in previous curricula. This underpinning was derived from a stage model of development and key concepts of individual development. In its intro-duction, the rationale behind a change in curriculum was outlined, while the link to Pearse's vision of education was confirmed with the opening quotation:

> The function of central authority should be to co-ordinate, to maintain a standard, to advise, to inspire, to keep the teachers in touch with educational thought in other lands.[4]

The radical changes in the world in political, technological and social terms, and their effects on the relevance of the curriculum, were noted and the need to reorient education from first principles, rather than make piece-meal changes, was suggested. To this end, an evolutionary as opposed to revolutionary approach to curriculum reform was advocated, with regular review of the progress achieved. This advocacy is somewhat questionable considering the radical nature of the changes proposed. With the advent of free post-primary schooling in 1967, primary education would now provide a foundation for all subsequent education. The rate of advance of knowledge regarding education in the previous decade was acknowledged and the White Paper noted the paucity of scientific data on child behaviour and development available to the Council of Education in 1950–1954. Consequently, in its report, 'more emphasis was generally placed than now seems desirable on teaching rather than learning, on content rather than method, on the "general" child rather than the "individual" child.'⁵ To this end, the Department had sent inspectors to study and observe international models and to report on positive innovations to improve the Irish situation, ensuring development was 'based on research and controlled experimentation.'⁶

The second chapter of the draft White Paper concerned itself with the 'Purpose of Education' and its content was reproduced, practically verbatim, in the published handbooks of 1971. It proposed that the purpose of education should reflect the Christian philosophy of society, with dual hereditary and environmental influences (home, school, churches) on the child. The complexity of individual children was espoused in relation to their physical, emotional, intellectual and spiritual needs and potentialities, and the draft White Paper concluded that the current education system was too narrow to realise these aims.

The centrality of language to learning was emphasised, especially in developing, applying and extending the language of the home. While accepting that there was general support for preserving the Irish language and promoting it as a language of communication, the importance of the English language was also extolled. Such importance included the fact that it represented a common language North and South and therefore 'forms a most potent binding force for national re-integration.'⁷ Furthermore, it was the language of 95 per cent of the population in Ireland and a major world language, 'as well as a repository of a great cultural heritage to which we have made our own special contribution.'⁸ In addition, the second language would be taught for a defined period each day and its use extended as a medium of instruction as competence grew. The draft White Paper stressed the importance of oral language for communication. The need for consistency and continuity in the child's education was also advocated, as was the need for communication between the various levels of the system to ensure the prevention of voids and duplication in the process. The ability of the existing curriculum to meet these needs and objectives was questioned and the need for reform was acknowledged.

The third chapter dealt with the 'Curriculum: General Considerations'. The purpose of primary education in the past was to equip people for life through mastery of the core essentials. This was broadened somewhat to include music, history, geography and some practical subjects, but their role was limited due to time constraints. There was now a need to extend this preparation through the widening of the curriculum. A further reorientation in practice related to the integration of subject areas rather than the discrete compartmentalisation of subjects. The fourth section of the draft White Paper outlined 'Method: Learning and Teaching', focusing specifically on the research findings from modern psychology in relation to child development, suggesting that while 'the sequence is fixed, the rate of progress for individuals is not uniform.'[9] Piaget's stages of development were detailed, with a particular emphasis on the 'phase of intuitive thought', the stage of development most children were experiencing on entry to school. Learning through informal play was a principal means of education at this stage and the need for the provision of appropriate experiences was stressed:

> The senses are the gateways of knowledge and experience, and they need to be stimulated and sharpened if the child's first-hand experiences are to be complete and exciting and worthy of communication.[10]

The use of concrete materials from the environment was also advocated, as was placing emphasis on the understanding of concepts rather than on practice and drill. The importance of developing all aspects of the child was also stressed, including the intellect, the subjective, the creative and the imaginative. The need for parents and teachers to have an understanding of the principles underpinning the new approach was cited and teachers were advised to advance slowly and to be patient for positive results to become evident.

The 'Content of the Curriculum' was addressed in a lengthy section within the draft White Paper. The existing curriculum was criticised for a number of reasons, including that:

> It still tends to treat children as if they were identical, environment as if it were irrelevant and subject content as if it were easily defined. Its greatest fault, perhaps, is that it fails to look on education as a trail of discovery, enrichment and understanding for the growing child, and sees it instead as a logical structure containing conventionally differentiated parts which may be imposed by adults on children.[11]

As a replacement, the keynote for the new curriculum was to be 'purposeful activity, pupil mobility, flexibility of development, freedom, experimentation.'[12] It also posited that children did not learn in the same way as adults, in that in the early stages they learn through informal and imaginative play, and subsequently through purposeful concrete activity. In this context, the teacher's role was to guide the child's learning, ensure adequate materials and organise linguistic, mathematical and artistic experiences. Individual difference and the importance of activity-based learning were not new concepts in the Irish context, as they were an integral element of the *Revised Programme* introduced in 1900. In fact, the provisions and content of this earlier curriculum seem to have eluded curriculum designers in the 1960s, as they made little or no reference to the provisions of the programme that had previously existed in the Irish context in the first two decades of the twentieth century and which bore similarities to the 'new' concept of education being extolled. The centrality of language in the curriculum as the basis for conceptual thought, social communication and the core of human experiences was recognised. The seven areas of the curriculum (religion, language, mathematics, social and environmental studies, art and craft, music and physical education), almost identical to those contained within the *Primary School Curriculum* (1971), were listed and detailed.

A number of additional sections produced by various committees of inspectors were included in the draft White Paper. The unrealistic nature of many of their proposals reflects perhaps the committee approach to their development, with little cognisance taken of the overall implications of recommendations on various aspects of the curriculum. The reform of the assessment of pupils' learning was proposed, linking it to the aims of education and the curriculum, as opposed to the use of terminal examinations or standardised tests alone. Record cards were proposed as a means to record observations, factual data and opinions, added to each year to form a comprehensive picture of progress. Great care was advised in the choice and administration of standardised tests and in the interpretation of results. The devising of tests appropriate to the Irish context was seen as 'a matter of urgency' to allow the monitoring of progress in aspects of the curriculum at national level, with a view to revising the curriculum and textbooks.[13]

The two aspects of school organisation in need of attention were considered to be the preponderance of large classes in the cities and the large number of small schools in rural areas. Amalgamating small schools was posited as a solution to both problems, allowing the re-deployment of teachers to larger schools. The transfer of weak teachers to large schools was suggested, where their influence on pupils was less extensive and protracted. The use of teachers with specialist subject knowledge in large schools, and shared between a number of small schools, was advocated where the 'need may arise.'[14] The initial and in-service training requirements of teachers were not addressed within the draft White Paper, as a special Commission had been established under the Higher Education Authority to investigate this matter. The draft White Paper proposed the establishment of a Diocesan Council in each diocese to address inconsistencies in the performance of managers. The Department would be represented on this Council and administer grants directly to the Council for buildings and maintenance, as well as a range of other functions. Owing to the short duration of the school day in Ireland relative to other jurisdictions, it proposed extending it by thirty minutes daily.

A section on special education dealt with existing provisions and future aspirations for educating children with special educational needs in special schools, hospitals and special classes. While good progress had been achieved in relation to provision for, what was termed at the time, the 'moderately handicapped', the larger numbers and lack of diagnostic and advisory supports for 'mildly handicapped' children made it difficult to distinguish them from those who were 'educationally retarded.' The role of the Department's psychological service as a support to all schools in the detecting, referring and placement of children in special schools was also outlined. The psychologist would also play a role in identifying children with learning difficulties in schools and advising on an appropriate course of remedial action. This was an aspirational recommendation as the psychological service had no function in primary schools at this time and consisted of a small cohort of psychologists working within the Department. The intention of raising the school age to fifteen in 1970 was also noted, resulting in a minimum three-year post-primary cycle for all pupils. In this instance, transfer would need to occur at twelve years of age, so pupil classification and promotion would be based on age into the future as opposed to ability.

Early childhood education provision, particularly for children in areas of high population density and who were socially deprived, was 'believed' to be beneficial for emotional, physical and mental nurture. In addition, the 'desirability' of establishing nursery schools to foster early fluency in the second language was considered.[15] Clearly, the language used in relation to early childhood education was reserved and non-committal. The draft White Paper also stated it would 'welcome' a decision by private schools to become integrated within the national system or to be bound by minimum regulations. Furthermore, with the increasing trend toward ecumenism, it was hoped that all denominations could be educated in the same schools in the future. However, the underlying assumption was that this 'ecumenism' would take place in schools underpinned in the overwhelming majority of cases by a Catholic ethos.

As purposeful activity, pupil mobility, flexibility of deployment, freedom and experimentation were all recurrent themes of the proposed curriculum, the provision of suitable school buildings and resources was seen as a priority and progress in this regard was noted. The draft White Paper asserted that often the structure of schools outlived their functionality in the changing educational and demographic context. To this end, the construction of less expensive and less durable structures was proposed, by using prefabrication and moveable walls. The provision of running water, central heating and flush toilets to all schools was seen as a priority. Verandas and annexes were proposed to facilitate the teaching of small groups. The importance of the school library as an educational resource was not seen to be reflected in the provisions and resources allowed for it to schools. The inadequate provision of equipment or grants for equipment was also noted. It proposed considering leaving the production of textbooks to market forces, with special provisions for Irish language publications.

The need for ongoing research and development in relation to education was seen as an integral element of educational progress. The draft White Paper proposed the establishment of a specialist research section within the Department to make available research from other countries, be responsible for the dissemination of information and build a research library. In addition, it would encourage further research in training colleges, assist special study groups, maintain contact with universities and other researchers and disseminate such research information.

The draft White Paper was never refined or prepared for publication and therefore was never edited into a unified whole. Seán O'Connor, first head of the Development Unit from 1965 and subsequently Secretary of the Department of Education from 1973, attributed the blame for not proceeding with the White Paper to Minister O'Malley, who was interested in progressing things quickly. When O'Malley realised the production of a Green Paper, the ensuing consultation and the publication of a White Paper could take up to four years, he lost interest in the project.[16] Coolahan asserted that the absence of policy statements or White Papers was premeditated as a policy of 'pragmatic gradualism', allowing *ad hoc* planning that could react to ongoing developments.[17] While praiseworthy for many of its proposals, the draft White Paper was written in an aspirational tone, with a preponderance of 'shoulds' and 'coulds' as opposed to 'woulds' and 'wills.' Considering its status as a proposed White Paper on Education, it was non-committal on many key aspects, while many of the aspirations would have been very challenging to achieve or implement in the contemporary context. In the absence of a White Paper, there was a lack of focus on addressing aspects of school and system organisation raised in the draft White Paper that were necessary to implement the curriculum. However, it set the tone for further curriculum development in the Irish context and informed the development process over subsequent years.

8.3 Development of the Working Document (1968)

Some nine months after the preparation of the draft White Paper, a 'New Curriculum Steering Committee' of inspectors was established in December 1967 to produce the first draft of the curriculum. Questions considered at the initial meeting of this Committee on 19 December 1967 included:

- Will the entire curriculum be taught in all schools without delay?
- If not, how can it be introduced gradually?
- What schools are most appropriate to introduce the full curriculum immediately?
- What special training and equipment will teachers need?
- How will the Inspectorate prepare itself to support implementation?
- How will the implementation of the curriculum be inspected and evaluated?
- Will additional officers be needed beyond the Inspectorate to support the implementation of certain subjects, such as art and craft and physical education?
- What time scale is needed for introduction?[18]

The section on curriculum within the draft White Paper formed the basis for the Working Document produced in 1968. This process was assisted once again by a number of 'New Curriculum Sub-committees' established in January 1968. From available documentation, it appears that thirty individual committees of inspectors were formed to address diverse aspects, focusing on the various subject areas and wider educational issues. These contributions were collected and collated by the New Curriculum Steering Committee, whose work was directed by Mr Ó hUallacháin, Deputy Chief Inspector. This Committee continued to work between 1968 and 1971 on devising and preparing the *Primary School Curriculum* (1971) for implementation.

The content of *Primary Education New Curriculum – A Working Document* reflected largely that of the draft White Paper, with less emphasis on the background and rationale and increased detail in relation to the content of each subject area.[19] In essence, the curriculum published in 1971 proved to be a further evolution of the Working Document. The Introduction of the Working Document outlined the two aims of education, which subsequently appeared in the *Primary School Curriculum* (1971), and asserted the need to prepare the child for life in an ever-changing world. The focus on the methods of teaching and on the attitudes, enthusiasm and quality of teachers was cited as more important than the content of the curriculum. The Working Document also asserted the role of education in the transfer of knowledge, culture and attitudes to subsequent generations. The importance of basing education on the child's environment and experiences to ensure education was purposeful and meaningful was stressed. The integrated nature of the subject areas was emphasised owing to the fact the child did not see subject barriers, so therefore the curriculum should not impose them. Beyond a statement of principle on the fundamental role of religion in education, no further detail was provided on religious education in the Working Document.

The centrality of language within the curriculum was emphasised as 'the basis of both conceptual thought and social communication and, as such, is the key to all human experience and the essence of every other subject.'[20] The mathematics section stressed the need for better understanding of concepts and structures. As a transitional measure, two programmes (A and B) were devised in mathematics. While it was intended that Programme A would eventually become the norm, Programme B was advocated for teachers until they were familiar with the new approach to the subject. The subsequent *Primary School Curriculum* (1971) contained one programme in mathematics, with an optional experimental syllabus.

8.4 Consultation on the Working Document

The Department stated from the start of the process of devising the new curriculum that a draft would be submitted to teaching and managerial bodies
for their consideration prior to publication.[21] The Working Document produced by the Committees was presented to the INTO in September 1968
and to managerial bodies and training colleges in October 1968. It is interesting that there was no official consultation with post-primary interests
or with wider educational stakeholders or the general public regarding the
Working Document or the subsequent *Primary School Curriculum* (1971).
At this initial INTO meeting, all delegates expressed a welcome for the
philosophical and psychological thinking underpinning the curriculum,
with 'unanimous approval for the idea of getting away from the rigidity of
the past.'[22] All delegates were asked to submit feedback within two months,
following which the Working Document would be reviewed and regional
conferences for teachers and inspectors organised. In December 1968, *Notes
on the Draft Curriculum for Primary Schools* were added to the October
draft of the Working Document.

Plans for reform were announced and disseminated to the wider public
in *The Irish Times* in December 1968. This pointed out the forthcoming
radical changes in content and methodology and cited primary education
as the 'stepping stone' to further education.[23] A full copy of the Working
Document was published in *An Múinteoir Náisiúnta* on 9 February 1969,
owing to complaints by teachers that they could not access copies.[24] The
Department collated the responses of a large number of organisations
to the Working Document. However, in line with the tradition of the
Department at this time, these responses were not published.

The overall response of the INTO to the Working Document was
that it 'whole-heartedly endorses the aims and principles upon which the
suggested new curriculum is structured.'[25] While the INTO welcomed the
proposals, it believed that aspects of the curriculum content were overly
ambitious but this could be mediated by the provision of the necessary
resources and financial support to ensure the vision of the document became

a reality in practice. The INTO submission represented a dramatic shift from the stance taken in the INTO Minority Report at the Council of Education (1954) and reverted strongly to the aims and principles of its *Plan for Education* (1947). It now welcomed the greater breadth being introduced into primary education in the form of additional subjects and the underlying ideological changes proposed. However, the INTO comments concluded with a warning not to progress too far down the road of child-centredness or progressivism:

> Finally, whilst the ideal of a child-centred curriculum is desirable, it should always be borne in mind that there is no royal road to learning, and that it will still be necessary to engage in some sound teaching and sound learning.[26]

The Teachers' Study Group welcomed the changes the Working Document would bring to the work and atmosphere in schools.[27] The overall response was positive, with the Study Group welcoming the unified curriculum, the reduced emphasis on nationalism, the liberal timetable, the attention to the needs, interests and abilities of each child, the altered pupil-teacher relationship and the freedom afforded to the teacher. While welcoming of the developments proposed, it was acutely cognisant of the implications for implementation. It made many functional and pragmatic suggestions to ensure the successful implementation of the provisions of the curriculum, at both a national level and within individual classrooms. As with the INTO submission, the Teachers' Study Group made the Department aware of many of the difficulties that could impede the practical implementation of the curriculum.

Other organisations that responded, most particularly managerial bodies and training colleges, expressed an overwhelmingly positive attitude to the proposed curriculum changes.[28] A number of themes are evident in these submissions. Overall, there was a significant endorsement of the range of subjects included in the Working Document. Many alerted the Department as to the difficulties inherent in implementing the curriculum and pointed to the need for supports and strategies for teachers in this regard. These included the re-training of teachers, reduced class sizes, a teacher's handbook, the re-education of parents in the new aims, grants for equipment and materials and inspectors/ organisers to assist teachers. Concerns, in general, rested not on the content or methodologies proposed, but with time implications, teacher expertise and the provision of equipment and resources to support implementation. A number of submissions questioned the appropriateness of Programme A in mathematics, concerns that were addressed by omitting it in the *Primary School Curriculum* (1971). A selection of organisations also called for a redrafting of the section on religion following consultation with the appropriate denominations to provide more detail on what was to be taught.

The issue of alignment with post-primary curricula was also raised in many submissions, noting the difficulties the mismatch would entail. The wide scope and ambitious nature of the syllabi in physical education, art and craft and music was addressed by a number of organisations, considering the training of teachers and the facilities available to many schools. While some of these issues were addressed within the *Primary School Curriculum* (1971), the Department did not take cognisance of the difficulties of implementation raised by many of these organisations. Such a failure to temper the curriculum to the reality of the educational context, or to introduce strategies to align the educational context to the needs of the curriculum, was a considerable failing on the part of the curriculum planners and led to implementation difficulties following its introduction.

Reactions in the Press were generally favourable to the Working Document. *The Irish Times* carried a three-part analysis of the Working Document in July 1969, entitled *The End of the Murder Machine?* This commented on the revolutionary nature of the changes, the most important at any level in education since the foundation of the state.[29] In *The Irish Times* Annual Review of 1969, the positive developments in primary education were again applauded, noting the positive reaction of teachers to the innovation. However, it also stressed the importance of investment for implementation to be achieved:

> At the moment it is far from being a system – it is only a piece of paper, an intention, a manifesto. Money needs to be poured into teacher retraining – a critical matter – into new buildings, new equipment, new teaching aids.[30]

Copies of the Working Document were circulated internationally to personal contacts established through inspectors' study visits but there was no formal or structured system of international consultation at the time. One inspector in England found the draft document to be a 'tremendous achievement.'[31] He iterated the need to instil the basic principles of child-centredness and to prepare teachers for the new approaches as:

> It is not just content you are changing, but, aims, attitudes, and philosophies.[32]

8.5 Information Sharing on Curriculum Change

A departure in departmental policy from preceding curricula was that senior Department officials presented and published widely on the proposed curriculum changes as part of a process of consultation with the education sector. These key personnel provided insights into the development of the curriculum, including the rationale, the *modus operandi* for its formulation, its guiding principles and content, which were not necessarily contained within the official documentation or documented in any other way. One major element of this information sharing was a booklet issued by Minister Brian Lenihan to all parents entitled *All Our Children* in 1969, outlining the rationale for and progress in the reform of education. It explained the reasoning behind the abolition of the Primary Certificate Examination and the introduction of Report Cards, the policy of amalgamation, changes to the primary school curriculum, the reform of post-primary education and developments at third level. A brief rationale for and insight into the content of the various subjects was also provided. The changes in content and the introduction of new methodologies were explained and justified as being beneficial to the child:

> The old programme, too, seemed to lay emphasis on *what* the child was taught rather than *how* he was taught, on teaching rather than on learning, on subject-matter rather than on the child himself.[33]

In an article by Mr Ó Floinn, Assistant Secretary of the Department, in *An Múinteoir Náisiúnta*, a rationale for curriculum change was offered. This included the rapidly expanding nature of current knowledge, the absence of modernisation of the curriculum since the 1920s, new insights in child psychology, increased international contact and the prospect of joining the EEC. Ireland's increasing participation on the international stage and improved communication with its international counterparts 'forced us into a comparison of our more or less static educational system with the dynamic changes which have occurred and which are occurring in the United States, in Britain and in Western Europe.'[34] To this end, Ó Floinn admitted that the logical step would have been to begin reforms at primary level and extend them through the system. However, the more immediate need to reform second-level education took precedence, as did the awareness of the magnitude of the reforms needed at primary level, and the greater financial and resource implications at this level. While this may carry some truth, there was no logical reason for a mismatch between the two curricula considering the same Department devised them both and within a similar timeframe. Perhaps this was due to the very separate traditions and operation of the primary and post-primary Inspectorate in the 1960s, with little communication or co-operation between the two.

Furthermore, Ó Floinn outlined the Christian and democratic principles underpinning the curriculum and the need for co-operation between the home, the school and the churches was emphasised:

> the purpose of education in a given society should reflect the philosophy of that society. Ours is a Christian society. We should have no apology to offer then for an educational programme which consistently seeks to inculcate Christian values and principles.[35]

This was further endorsed within the new curriculum, which reinforced the integrated nature of religious and secular education. The practical challenges regarding implementation of the curriculum were also outlined, in a context where 63 per cent of all schools were one- and two-teacher schools, where it was acknowledged that implementation was 'impossible.'[36] This was a surprising statement from the Assistant Secretary of the

Department that it had devised a curriculum that would be impossible to implement in 63 per cent of schools. This was further exacerbated by the fact it was not accompanied by a strategic and well-resourced plan to increase drastically the number of schools in which the curriculum was implementable, or even provide a transitional curriculum for use in these schools in the interim.

Mac Donnchadha, a primary inspector involved in drafting the mathematics curriculum, provided a rationale and outline of the changes in mathematics in *Oideas* in 1969. This involved a review of mathematics education worldwide, concluding that young children were able to deal with more abstract concepts than previously believed, and the fact that constructive thinking could precede analytical thinking, depending on psychological maturity. The role of the teacher in this process was also transformed:

> The new approaches attempt to provide for the child as wide a variety of experiences as possible. The teacher guides the child towards a discovery of basic concepts from which more sophisticated concepts can be derived.[37]

While this would entail greater demands on the teacher in the form of new content and methods, the reward was in the fact that 'the child's enquiring attitude towards his environment and his enthusiasm for mathematics make the teacher's work infinitely more interesting.'[38]

De Buitléar, a primary inspector who played a key role in curriculum development from the late 1960s, extended this exposition in a number of articles written in 1968 and 1969. He observed that the major advances in knowledge and the sciences, especially child psychology and learning processes, had revolutionised education in other countries but had not impacted on Irish education. De Buitléar noted that the curriculum designers had to clarify their own concept of education, as the general philosophy and aims of education would determine its organisation and pedagogical approach. At the outset, the inclusion of additional subjects in the existing curriculum, as recommended by the Council of Education, was rejected. Such an approach was viewed as insufficient to assimilate the psychological and pedagogical advances since the 1920s:

D'oir an seanchlár do ré atá caite; ach tá an oiread sin athruithe taréis teacht ar an saol ó tháinig an dréacht bunúsach de i bhfeidhm sa bhliain 1926 nach n-oiriúnódh sé anois ba chuma cé na leasuithe a dhéanfaí air.[39][†]

Furthermore, there was a realisation that a common curriculum for all schools and pupils was not feasible 'irrespective of native ability and endowment; irrespective of social, cultural or physical environment and of possible future destiny.'[40] Child-centredness enshrined this new educational philosophy as:

> it rejects the idea of a curriculum or a school programme or an educational approach which views knowledge as being divided up into separate water-tight compartments or subjects and which bases its teaching techniques on the successful imparting of specified areas of knowledge to the child by the teacher.[41]

The irony is that what was produced was a subject-based curriculum, with associated exemplars of how integration could be achieved. De Buitléar continued, in language that re-echoed that of the 1900 *Revised Programme*, that this 'new' view of education recognised that the child was an active agent in his own learning, progressing at his own rate and by his own effort, with a stress on the learning as opposed to the teaching process. This has consequences for teaching techniques and methodologies, whereby the emphasis was on doing, on action methods, on exploring and experimenting, under the judicious guidance of the teacher. It was asserted that integration needed to be judiciously planned by the teacher, and between teachers, within the school. De Buitléar stressed that project-work was particularly valuable in this regard as many aspects of the curriculum could be covered in this way. The training of teachers was also seen as an imperative, with the training colleges already addressing the issue for new teachers. A retraining programme for teachers trained in the old system and methods was seen as essential, as were demonstration centres and pilot schools for teachers to see elements of the curriculum in practice.

---

† The old programme suited a bygone era; but so many changes have occurred in life since the basic draft of the curriculum was agreed in 1926 that it would not be suitable whatever alterations were made to it.

To facilitate this, the use of 'blocks of time' as opposed to discrete thirty-minute periods was advised. In 1967, the Department devised time allocations for the various subject areas for selected classes, yet these were never included in the subsequent Teacher's Handbooks. Table 8.1 documents these time allocations, with in excess of 60 per cent of time dedicated to Irish, English and mathematics and the least amount of time afforded to music and physical education. In addition, 2.5 hours per week was allocated to religion in all classes.

Table 8.1 Time Allocations (Hours Per Week) for the Secular Subjects of the Primary School Curriculum (1971)

	Infants (%)	1st–3rd Class (%)	4th–6th Class (%)
Irish	3.5 (23.3%)	5 (25%)	5 (25%)
English	3 (20%)	4 (20%)	4 (20%)
Mathematics	3 (20%)	4 (20%)	3.5 (17.5%)
Social and Environmental Studies	1 (6.66%)	2.5 (12.5%)	3 (15%)
Art and Craft	2.5 (16.66%)	2.5 (12.5%)	2.5 (12.5%)
Music	1 (6.66%)	1 (5%)	1 (5%)
Physical Education	1 (6.66%)	1 (5%)	1 (5%)

Source: *Curaclam do na Bunscoileanna*, December 1967. (Unpublished).

Minister Lenihan outlined the need for a comprehensive review of the curriculum at the INTO Congress in 1969:

> what is envisaged is not merely an adaptation or reshaping of the old Programme of Instruction but the structuring from basic principles of an organic curriculum to meet the challenge and needs of a new era.[42]

The curriculum aimed to develop the child's sense of identity by eliminating the barriers between religious and secular education, by using objective standards of evaluation and judgement and by preparing children for active citizenship. Minister Lenihan further warned that to 'attempt a wholesale changeover involving both content and method without adequate preparation would be disastrous.'[43] Focusing on the lack of preparation in relation to teacher education and in the absence of providing the necessary finances for equipment and resources and ensuring it was aligned with the post-primary curriculum, it could be asserted with some certitude that adequate preparations were not made for the introduction or implementation of the *Primary School Curriculum* (1971). Minister Faulkner provided an extensive exposition of the provisions of the curriculum in the Dáil in April 1970, stating that it was arranged to meet the needs and interests of children. In response to teacher concerns, Minister Faulkner reassured teachers that they would not be asked to implement any aspects they were not comfortable with, advising them to start implementing aspects they were confident with and building from there.[44]

One innovative move was a special closure of all primary schools on 5 November 1971 to enable teachers to discuss the first Teacher's Handbook and plan for implementing the curriculum at school level.[45] While feedback reported in *An Múinteoir Náisiúnta* was largely of a positive nature, it signalled impediments to implementation.[46] A second curriculum day was organised for all teachers on 7 December 1976, five years following implementation. These days were a novel measure at the time to allow teachers to engage with the provisions of the curriculum and to plan for its implementation at school level.

The information provided by Ministers and Department officials during this period provide an insight into the thinking and developmental process that led to the curriculum reforms in 1971. The announcements prepared both teachers and parents for the educational changes that were imminent and enhanced preparation for their implementation. The evolution in their thinking is apparent and it also allowed the curriculum developers to test reactions to new ideas and subsequently to adapt policy and *modus operandi* as needs arose.

8.6 Piloting the Working Document

The Department issued a circular to all schools in 1969 stating that a pilot phase of implementation would precede universal introduction and that the draft curriculum would undergo continuous review in the light of practice:

> the proposed curriculum is not to be regarded as being in any way final or definitive. Whatever shape the agreed curriculum takes, it should be subjected to a trial period of about five years ... It should, therefore, be subjected to a continuous review so that it may benefit from educational research development.[47]

The pilot process was conducted in a representative cross-section of 600 schools between 1968 and 1971.[48] This comprised three schools (Curriculum Centres) for four broad subject areas (language, social and environmental studies and music; mathematics; art and craft; and physical education) in each of the forty-eight inspection divisions. The purpose of these Curriculum Centres was to facilitate trial and evaluation of the teaching materials and methodologies involved in the curriculum and also to provide demonstrations for visiting teachers. Grants for a defined amount of equipment and materials were provided to pilot schools on a priority basis, depending on the subject areas they were piloting.[49] The Department facilitated teachers to visit a Curriculum Centre for one half-day with the consent of the manager of the school and the local inspector. There is no documentary evidence as to the prevalence of teachers' uptake on such visits and it appears that it was not a common practice.

Walsh noted that while the centres were of considerable value, they lacked a support framework beyond the Inspectorate, which was already working to full capacity and operated with depleted numbers in this period.[50] O'Connell claimed in 1979 that Curriculum Centres were selected for their specialist knowledge and commitment to individual subjects, which led to an unrealistic expectation being set for implementation in ordinary primary schools.[51]

It is unfortunate there was no official evaluation of the functioning of the pilot schools or the support role they played in introducing the curriculum by the Department. However, occasional case studies of the *modus operandi* of pilot schools were documented in *Oideas* at the time. Mr Gillespie of St Andrew's in Rialto, Dublin, participated in the piloting of the art and craft element of the *Primary School Curriculum* (1971). He detailed the increased workload on teachers in the form of planning and preparation, as well as the efforts to integrate art and craft with other aspects of the curriculum. The positive effect on the physical layout of the classroom was also detailed:

> Desks lost their old military-precise formation and were dragged into twos and threes here and there; less time was spent on purely academic subjects and art and craft took their rightful place in the schoolroom.[52]

The necessity for increased funding for equipment and materials was also stressed, and while acknowledging the grant from the Department, Gillespie asserted 'it is not meant to be churlish to state that this grant was by no means sufficient and the teachers had to invent and beg and scrape so as to make the scheme possible.'[53] The overall evaluation of the pilot experience was positive, leading to greater initiative and self-reliance on the part of pupils, especially for brighter pupils. Moreover, for slow learners, the school was a happier environment with a much greater variety of work.

A further experience of implementing aspects of the curriculum in Scoil Áine, Raheny, Dublin, was also documented in *Oideas*. The school placed a focus on integrating the various aspects of education through the use of projects and themes chosen by the teachers and children, co-ordinated by the principal. The provisions of the curriculum in this regard were praised as it allowed unity of purpose, involved the wider school community, based learning on the local environment and ensured all aspects of the curriculum were covered.[54] Benefits to the pupils included a wider vocabulary, an increased interest in reading, greater co-operation and self-reliance.

The provisions for informing and retraining teachers included special residential courses for 600 principals of the largest schools in 1969 and for a further 1,370 principals of smaller schools in 1970.[55] The one-week residential course for principals was quite short to deliver the philosophy and content of an entire curriculum, while it was also noted that the entire week was not devoted to curriculum issues.[56] In the October 1969 edition of *An Múinteoir Náisiúnta*, an account was provided of the four-day course for principals in St Patrick's College. This outlined to principals the supports that would be put in place for implementation, including further courses, teacher's handbooks, Curriculum Centres and the provision of necessary equipment, initially to the pilot schools.[57] Principals were further advised that training would be provided for all teachers and that the curriculum would be introduced on a gradual basis, as the principal and teachers saw fit. Between 1968 and 1971, summer courses for 4,000 principals were provided.[58]

In addition, in-service training was made available for principals of smaller schools and teachers in regional centres following pressure from the INTO for such provision. In 1969, 1,000 teachers attended courses in music and 800 attended courses in physical education in 1970.[59] Such in-service was provided by the Department and other agencies, including the INTO, the training colleges and Teachers' Centres. From 1971, the Department granted participants on in-service courses an additional three days personal leave from school for attendance at courses during vacation times.[60] In 1972 and 1973, a three-week residential course in Maynooth was provided in each area of the curriculum for seven teachers from each inspection division (350 teachers in total each year), who in turn relayed their learning to other teachers in the district through study groups, local lectures and other fora.[61] Many study groups were formed nationwide and these oftentimes organised seminars and lectures that were facilitated by inspectors and training college lecturers. Journals such as *An Múinteoir Náisiúnta* carried advice, suggestions and articles in relation to the implementation of the curriculum. In addition, many teachers attended summer courses, some of which related to the curriculum. Overall, the level of provision was un-cordinated and insufficient to prepare all practising teachers for the implementation of the philosophy and content of the curriculum.

Annual financial allocations to each school were promised to fund necessary equipment and resources, but Minister Faulkner asserted that the state would not be able to finance all the possibilities available within the curriculum. To this end, the establishment of local parents' committees was encouraged to ensure parents were involved as well as interested in education, which 'would prove very beneficial in advancing the new curriculum by supplying incidental aid, financial and other, to the schools.'[62] While laudable, it was unrealistic to expect parents and local communities to provide the resources to support the implementation of a curriculum over which they had little ownership.

An analysis of documentation reveals that little fundamental alterations were made to the Working Document based on the consultative process or from the piloting of the curriculum in schools. The philosophy and content of the curriculum remained largely unaltered from the draft White Paper in 1967 and little was undertaken to address the concerns regarding implementation raised by organisations and schools. While commendable in theory, consultation and piloting the curriculum could only have been effective if submissions impacted on subsequent development and if the pilot scheme was formally evaluated to inform policy and practice. In the absence of this approach, the barriers to implementation were not addressed in any systematic way and this impacted negatively on the operation of the curriculum in the years ahead.

8.7 The *Primary School Curriculum* (1971)

Concurrent with the pilot scheme, a committee within the Inspectorate, assisted by a number of sub-committees, was developing Teacher's Handbooks to disseminate the curriculum to all teachers. The *Primary School Curriculum* (1971) was presented in two handbooks; Teacher's Handbook Part 1 was launched in spring 1971 and Teacher's Handbook Part 2 was completed in autumn 1971.[63] These were heralded as a guide for teachers, as opposed to a blueprint, to support implementation. Following years of criticising the subject-based curriculum previously in operation, the new curriculum, while acknowledging the linguistic, mathematical and artistic organisation of the child's experiences were integrated, arranged the curriculum under seven broad subject areas. These were religion; language; mathematics; social and environmental studies; art and craft activities; music; and physical education. Throughout the various subject areas, a limited number of insights and suggestions for integration were offered.

Teacher's Handbook Part 1 presented the Aims and Functions of the Curriculum, its Structure and Organisation, religious education, and outlined the syllabus for Irish, English, mathematics and art and craft. Teacher's Handbook Part 2 continued the detailed elaboration of the syllabus in social and environmental studies, history, civics, geography, music and physical education. Both handbooks were presented bilingually (apart from the section on Gaeilge which was in Irish only), and invariably began with the aims and objectives for the subject. This was followed by advice for the preparation of work, classroom organisation, syllabus content, possibilities for integration and materials to be used. Illustrations were contained throughout the handbooks (apart from in the section on civics and music), including visuals of equipment, children working, examples of written work and products in art and craft. Many of the sections provided glossaries and resources of interest or support to the teacher in implementing the curriculum. Each subject area concluded with a section on the use of Irish within that subject in Galltacht schools. A number of inconsistencies in style and in the way in which the curriculum is presented is obvious to the reader, with different styles and tones used for the various sections, representing the input of the various individuals and committees involved in its devising.

8.7.1 Aims, Functions, Structure and Organisation

The introduction to the Teacher's Handbook Part 1, which detailed the Aims and Functions, Structure and Organisation of the *Primary School Curriculum* (1971), spanned ten pages. This represented a rather inadequate foundation on which to premise the remaining 700-page national curriculum contained within the two handbooks. The Aims and Functions comprised five of these pages. These contained no in-depth analysis or delineation of the philosophy of education on which the curriculum was based. The introductory paragraph was particularly weak and admitted that '[G]eneral statements concerning the purpose of education have a tendency to lose their impact, not because they are false but because they are by their very nature incomplete.'[64] It continued by outlining that there 'are certain guidelines which it ought to follow', reflecting the values of society. In that case, Ireland, as a Christian society, should inculcate Christian values:

> Each human being is created in God's image. He has a life to lead and a soul to be saved. Education is, therefore, concerned not only with life but with the purpose of life.[65]

The two main aims of primary education were stated in terms of the child, as opposed to the previous focus on cultural nationalistic aims. These were:

- To enable the child to live a full life as a child;
- To equip him to avail himself of further education so that he may go on to live a full and useful life as an adult in society.

In order to achieve the first, it was necessary to take two factors into account:

- All children are complex human beings with physical, emotional, intellectual and spiritual needs and potentialities;
- Because each child is an individual, he deserves to be valued for himself, be provided with a range of experiences and opportunities to stimulate and fulfil, 'which will enable him to develop his natural powers at his own rate to his fullest capacity.'[66]

Despite the short nature of this section, a notable proportion was consumed with lengthy quotations from publications by the OECD, the NIEC and UNESCO. Similar to the draft White Paper, the new curriculum talked of child-centredness and viewing the child as an active agent as a recent discovery, making no reference to the child-centred curriculum that operated in Ireland between 1900 and 1922. Furthermore, it is arguable that the generalisation that infant class teachers based their practice on the principles of child-centredness following 1951 was over-stating the reality.

When addressing obstacles to implementation, the handbooks judiciously used the past tense in relation to the existence of unsuitable school buildings, high pupil-teacher ratios and lack of understanding of group-teaching methods. However, insights from the *Investment in Education* report, the Department's annual reports and the subsequent difficulties pertaining to implementation paint an altogether more dismal picture of the physical and pedagogical reality that prevailed and continued to prevail in many schools. While isolated cases of new buildings, ample resources and use of progressive methods no doubt existed, their prevalence was exaggerated as being the norm. It can be concluded that the comments on prevailing school conditions did not represent the reality of the majority of schools at that time.

The section on the Structure of the Curriculum elaborated the traditional way in which subjects were compartmentalised, which it cited to be unnatural for the young child who was not aware of subject barriers. A number of reasons were outlined for introducing an integrated curriculum, rather than just 'graft some additional subjects on to the existing one.'[67] This was followed by the admission that, 'for the purpose of convenience', the curriculum was organised under seven broad subject areas.[68] The reason for its presentation in such a format was more likely to be due to the fact that it was devised by various committees of inspectors on a subject basis. Organisation of the curriculum was proposed through 'blocks of time' as opposed to strict half-hour periods, yet no guidance was provided as to the allocation of time across the various subject areas. The handbooks dedicated eight lines to the issue of evaluation, asserting that the proposals were in no way final or definitive:

> Research and regular evaluation will be necessary if the curriculum is to continue to keep pace with changing conditions.[69]

However, the physical presentation of the curriculum in two hardbound, full colour, illustrated Teacher's Handbooks created an air of permanence about them and it was unlikely that they would be reviewed on an ongoing basis as promised.

The role of the principal teacher in the implementation of the *Primary School Curriculum* (1971) was highlighted as central and critical, a role that required principals to keep abreast of educational thinking and to introduce new ideas and initiate experiments within their schools. A number of onerous responsibilities were allocated to the principal, in addition to the functions already performed. Among others, these included overseeing planning for curriculum implementation, reviewing teachers' planning, ensuring progression in the pupils' learning and co-ordinating the work of each class to ensure progression in learning. The reality of a principal teacher being able to undertake this additional multiplicity of roles was highly questionable in a context where more than 80 per cent were teaching principals. Such an expectation to transform the role from one of administration to one of leadership and management, if it was to be realised, would have required an accompanying set of supports such as training, role development, time allocation and financial incentives, none of which was prioritised in the following years.

A new role for the teacher was also envisaged in this altered teaching and learning context, whereby the teacher was 'no longer regarded as one who merely imparts information but rather as one who provides suitable learning situations and who guides and stimulates the child in his pursuit of knowledge.'[70] The treatment of the role of teachers in the past was somewhat dismissive in nature and their function was characterised as 'that of a medium through whom knowledge was merely transferred to his pupils.'[71] This negative view of the teacher naturally disappointed teachers who had correctly characterised the role and function they performed as more complex prior to 1971. The teacher, although allowed more freedom under new curriculum, also assumed greater responsibility. This included the more careful planning of work, an awareness of the needs of individuals, knowledge of the environment, attendance at in-service courses and participation in study circles. In exchange for the increased responsibility, teachers were promised 'a deeper professional consciousness and a greater opportunity for personal fulfilment.'[72]

While the principles underpinning the curriculum were not explicitly listed, an analysis of the handbooks reveals the five principles to be a focus on individualised instruction, the full and harmonious development of the child, the use of activity and discovery techniques, the integrated nature of the curriculum and the inclusion in the curriculum of material drawn from the child's environment. As is evident, each of the principles was inspired by the child, elucidating the prominence of the child within the curriculum. These aims and principles differed greatly from those implicit in the preceding curriculum. For example, the principle on full and harmonious development stressed the importance of developing the aesthetic, emotional, intellectual, cultural, moral, physical, social and spiritual dimensions of the child, rejecting the previous substantial focus on cognitive development. Furthermore, it was cognisant of meeting 'the needs of children of widely varying natural endowment and cultural background.'[73] The child's own environment provided the most congenial ground to sow and foster the seeds of knowledge, and the forging of strong links between home and school life was advocated. Furthermore, the curriculum endeavoured to prepare children to live in and contribute to an unknown world, owing to the rapid changes in society and technology. Such preparation required a radical shift from the learning methodologies of the past. At this juncture, the handbooks quoted from the NIEC report, which stressed the centrality of teachers in the delivery of the curriculum, as success 'depends less, perhaps, on the actual subject matter that is taught than on the manner of teaching and on the attitudes, quality and enthusiasm of teachers.'[74]

8.7.2 *Religion*

The section on religion spanned three paragraphs and was largely a statement of principle based on the paragraph in the *Rules for National Schools* (1965). Teacher's Handbook Part 1 stated:

> Of all the parts of a school curriculum Religious instruction is by far the most important, as its subject-matter, God's honour and service, includes the proper use of all man's faculties, and affords the most powerful inducements to their proper use.

Religious Instruction is, therefore, a fundamental part of the school course and a religious spirit should inform and vivify the whole work of the school. The teacher should constantly inculcate the practice of charity, justice, truth, purity, patience, temperance, obedience to lawful authority and all the other moral virtues. In this way, he will fulfil the primary duty of an educator, the moulding to perfect form of his pupils' character, habituating them to observe, in their relations with God and with their neighbour, the laws which God both directly through the dictates of natural reason and through Revelation, and indirectly through the ordinance of lawful authority, imposes on mankind.[75]

This paragraph was included, almost verbatim, in the report of the Second National Programme Conference in 1926 but it is interesting that the clause, 'while careful in the presence of children of different religious beliefs, not to touch on matters of controversy', (see section 5.6) present in the 1926 programme had been removed from the *Rules for National Schools* in 1965[76] following a recommendation of the Council of Education (1954) and was also omitted in the 1971 curriculum. This modification gave categorical recognition to the denominational nature of schools and denied the validity of a separation of religious and secular instruction, removing the safeguards for parents of minority faiths for their children not to attend religious classes. This ignored the reality that all schools were not attended by pupils of one (or any) religious denomination and removed the option for parents to allow their children opt-out of religious instruction, nor did it offer any alternative provision to them at this time. Beyond this, the handbook stated that the prescribing, examination and supervision of religious education was outside the competence of the Department.

Discontent was further exacerbated by the statement in the curriculum that religious and secular education were inseparable and that, as part of an integrated curriculum, religious education should illuminate the whole life and atmosphere of the school. This was in line with Catholic Church thinking of the time, as the Vatican II statement on Education insisted upon the integration of Christian education into the whole pattern of human life, as opposed to treating it in isolation.[77] Glendenning questioned the constitutionality of the integration of religious and secular instruction allowed within the curriculum and in the *Rules for National Schools*, stating the provisions broke the spirit, if not the letter, of the Constitution.[78]

Collectively, the changes of 1965 and 1971 created a different situation, whereby the denominational nature of schools was recognised, the requirement to be sensitive in the presence of minorities was withdrawn, educational provision for those who did not want to attend denominational schools was removed and the curriculum offered religious and secular subjects on an integrated basis. This made no accommodation for those in Ireland who did not practice the majority religion, while no additional provision was offered to meet minority needs. The denominational system at primary level was strengthened by the introduction of the *Primary School Curriculum* (1971), whereby religious education permeated secular education in the work of the school.

8.7.3 Language

The teaching of language in the curriculum was divided into four separate sections to distinguish between the various contexts for language learning, namely the teaching of both Irish and English in the Gaeltacht and in the Galltacht.

Gaeilge sa Ghaeltacht

The curriculum stressed the importance of an ability to converse in Irish and to give a firm foundation to develop oral aspects of the language. Guidance was provided for four distinct class groups: junior and senior infants, first and second class, third and fourth class and fifth and sixth class. In infant classes, the emphasis was placed on oral aspects, reading and writing. This was extended in senior classes to include story-telling, poetry, grammar and project-work. The use of puppets, mime and drama was recommended. The creation of a correct atmosphere for the teaching of Irish was stressed to ensure pupils gained an ability to talk about themselves:

B'fhurasta, trí ghníomhachtaí oiriúnacha, imeachtaí an bhaile a athchruthú chun teacht ar chumas na bpáistí chun labhairt faoina saol féin.[79][†]

Gaeilge sa Ghalltacht

A great onus was placed on the principal teacher to promote the use of Irish and to create an Irish atmosphere in Galltacht schools. It was the responsibility of each teacher to prepare a scheme of work to be viewed by the principal, including sections on oral work, reading and writing. Such a scheme of work was to be based on the ability and interests of the child. The benefits of using the new courses and teaching methods in Irish (Buntús) were also listed. The advice in the handbooks was that Irish should be used incidentally within various subjects, depending on the age and ability of the pupils.

English in the Galltacht

The fundamental and central importance of language in learning was acknowledged in the curriculum and was seen as a unification of all areas of learning:

> Language has an important bearing on the mental, emotional and social develop-
> ment of the child: it is the base on which successful teaching and learning in other
> areas must stand, not only at primary, but at all levels of education.[80]

To this end, it was asserted that 'every lesson is a language lesson' and the importance of developing language was stressed, as it not only affected the child's learning, but also 'profoundly affects him in the formation and expression of his thoughts and feelings.'[81] The handbooks acknowledged that oral language development had been a neglected aspect and the aims of oral language were delineated. The role of the school was to supplement and extend the language of the home and to develop and enrich the child's

---

†   It is easy, through appropriate activities, to recreate the events of the home to enable
     children to speak about their own lives.

speech, so that language became an instrument of thought, expression and communication. Particular emphasis was to be focused on children from culturally deprived homes. The multiple aspects of each area of the English curriculum (oral language, reading and writing) were described and elaborated upon.

English in the Gaeltacht

Five pages were allocated to the section on teaching English in the Gaeltacht, as opposed to forty pages dedicated to teaching English in the Galltacht or twenty-three pages afforded to the teaching of Irish in the Galltacht. The handbook stressed the desirability of children in the Gaeltacht learning English to complement mastering their first language. In this regard, the key to second language learning was motivation for use in communication.

8.7.4 Mathematics

> Mathematics is an integral and essential part of any school curriculum, not merely because of its economic utility and its contribution to social life, but especially because of its intrinsic educational value and the personal enjoyment and satisfaction that springs from it.[82]

The aims of mathematics included kindling an interest in the subject, giving children a grasp of mathematical structure and laying the foundation for further work. This replaced the focus on mechanical skills and fact memorisation. Advances in knowledge to support this development included that all children go through certain stages of development and that children develop concepts best through first-hand experiences and in concrete situations. To accommodate these advances in knowledge, the mathematics programme placed an emphasis on learning by doing, through the use of structured activities and materials from the everyday environment. Consonant with this change in emphasis, the role of the teacher was to provide opportunities for exploration and investigation, to act as a guide and consultant, to grade and structure activities:

> His chief responsibility will be to see that the pupils learn through their own dis-
> coveries rather than through information imparted by him.[83]

Traditional compartments of mathematics, such as algebra, geometry and arithmetic, were rejected within the integrated nature of the curriculum. A regular and 'experimental' syllabus for mathematics was offered, both to be taught by guided experimentation. The experimental programme contained extra elements and provided a more challenging programme for brighter children. To facilitate the teaching of the syllabus, class, group and individual instruction was proposed. As the handbook stated:

> However, since guided experimentation, investigation and discovery will form the
> basis for much of the work, the organisation best suited to such an approach will
> generally be on group or individual lines, with less emphasis than heretofore on
> class teaching.[84]

Attainment of materials was to be largely accommodated by making them or sourcing them locally, while other resources such as unifix cubes and Cuisenaire rods could be purchased. However, there was no elaboration on the sourcing of funds for the purchase of such mathematical equipment. Teachers were warned against placing undue emphasis on textbooks, beyond them giving further experience in concepts already explored, stressing that the primary resource was the local environment and that 'the textbook must supplement rather than dictate the teacher's approach.'[85] The centrality of language in learning new concepts and in discussing/ solving mathematical problems was also emphasised.

8.7.5 Art and Craft

Art and craft activities were an entirely new aspect to the curriculum in 1971. A brief rationale for their inclusion was provided in the handbooks, citing their importance as a medium of expression, to investigate materials and objects, as an outlet for creative and artistic ability, as an appreciation of design, pattern, texture and colour, and the pleasure and enjoyment of sensory activities.[86] The syllabus was varied to ensure its adaptability to the needs, interests and aptitudes of all children. A focus was to be placed on the process as opposed to the product in art and craft, cultivating the creative interest and enthusiasm of pupils and placing an emphasis on the active role of the child in this process. Guidance for teachers was provided within the handbooks in the areas of play activities, picture making, pattern and design, construction and creative crafts. To achieve the elements of the art and craft syllabus, a separate room dedicated to this element was recommended. However, it was asserted that through careful planning in the ordinary classroom, success could also be achieved. The expectation of a separate room was quite unrealistic considering the preponderance of small schools, many of which were poorly equipped and maintained.

8.7.6 Social and Environmental Studies

The syllabus in social and environmental studies was primarily concerned with human activity, the child's physical surroundings and natural phenomena. This facilitated children's natural urge to explore the environment and to organise their knowledge to form a concept of their milieu. Owing to the need to adapt this to the individual context and environment of each school, an outline programme as opposed to a syllabus was provided.

The focus in social and environmental studies was on stimulating and fostering children's interest in the world around them. In this way, the focus was not on the quantity of the knowledge conveyed but on the process of acquiring this information through experience, observation and investigation:

> The aim should be, not to convey the maximum amount of factual information, but to arouse and stimulate the child's interest in his environment, to enable him to understand the various aspects of his experience and to cultivate in him an enquiring attitude of mind.[87]

Many advantages to this aspect of education were cited, including the development of a positive attitude towards living things, developing leisure time activities and hobbies and motivation for creative work. The role of the teacher in this situation was to provide the context for such experiences from topics that arose naturally, which demanded preparation and a knowledge of the local environment. The three main determinants of the topics studied were the season, the local environment and the interests of pupils. Integration was also easily facilitated with this subject, owing to the children's innate curiosity in the world around them.

History

A new approach to history was advocated within the curriculum, whereby it was to be 'thought of as a whole range of interrelated activities which uses the historical as the binding factor – an area of interest and activities rather than a subject as such.'[88] In this way, the child would become more personally involved with the subject and it eliminated the strictly chronological approach to history previously practised. In addition, methodologies changed to incorporate the more active involvement of the child as opposed to an over-reliance on memorisation. A greater focus was encouraged on social history and on the lives of ordinary individuals from the past. Furthermore, the handbook stressed that 'the contribution of all creeds and classes to the evolution of modern Ireland' should be represented fairly and that the 'distortion or suppression of any truth which might seem to hurt national pride'[89] should be avoided. This insertion may have been influenced by 'the Troubles' in Northern Ireland at this time.

Another aspect prioritised in the handbook was the study of local history. The local area could comprise any aspect or geographical size and such a study facilitated the integration of many subject areas. This syllabus was to be devised at individual school and classroom level, which rendered the use of textbooks to be of secondary importance as they lacked association with the local environment. To this end, the teacher needed to be able to source local knowledge rather than be an expert on all aspects of the environment. This knowledge was to be achieved by the study of reference books and the locality of the school. Other resources advocated included a reference library, pictures, illustrations and maps, materials for drawing and modelling, projector and slides, televisions, a school museum and visits to museums and libraries.

Civics

Civics had not been included as a separate subject in primary schools prior to 1971. The purpose of the subject was to create awareness for children of their shared membership of various organisations (e.g., family, school, locality, country, etc.) and to develop acceptable social and moral attitudes which took into account the rights of other members of society. This built upon the foundation of experiences in the home and in the wider circles of family and community that influenced the child:

> Civics is that part of school activity which helps the child to become a better member of society and to appreciate his rights and his obligations towards it.[90]

This was to be achieved through developing and cultivating self-discipline and self-responsibility, rather than by authoritarianism. Teachers also acted as role models through their lives, personalities, habits, attitudes and relationships with children and other adults. As a subject, much of the content was to be taught informally and many resources such as films, slides, tapes and records were advocated.

Geography

The primary focus in geography was to be placed on 'the relationship between people and the environment in which they live.'[91] The subject matter was to be based on the interests and enthusiasm of both pupils and teachers. Once again, the focus was to be placed on the local environment of the child 'as the basis from which there is to be an extension outwards to the home county, to the country as a whole, to neighbouring countries and thence to the world at large.'[92] Methodology was also revised to place an emphasis on observation and discovery. This placed an emphasis on the use of field trips, project-work, demonstrative and investigative work. However, the traditional role of the teacher in imparting 'a considerable body of information and explanations' was also advocated, which was an unusual statement within the Teacher's Handbooks:

He will encourage them to find out information for themselves, whenever possible, but he will also realise that over-reliance on the discovery method alone may limit drastically the over-all result.[93]

Integration across a range of subjects was proposed, as was the use of group work. The usefulness of reference books and local libraries was advocated as a source of information and an over-dependence on textbooks was discouraged as it 'will stultify a teacher's whole approach to geographical activity.'[94]

8.7.7 Music

Music was included in the curriculum as a pleasant and living element of school life, as a vital means of self-expression, as a preparation for social life and as a basis for further musical appreciation and creation. Given this wide rationale, it was asserted that:

> No other artistic activity can combine the same physical and mental pleasure that springs from active participation in music-making, can simultaneously engage the powers of so many individuals, can so fully create a sense of unity and disciplined co-operation.[95]

The impact of increased exposure to music through radio and television was welcomed and the curriculum endeavoured to extend pupils' awareness of popular music through song-singing, music making, listening and moving to music. The main purpose of the syllabus was to 'give each child the opportunity of expressing himself creatively in musical terms.'[96] In addition, it allowed experimentation with a range of instruments, the composing of rhythms and the discovery of harmonies.

8.7.8 Physical Education

Physical education was previously included as an optional subject within the curriculum, with an emphasis on physical training. Within the curriculum, physical education was listed as an essential subject for aesthetic, emotional and moral development. In this way, children were enabled to express themselves in movement and general physical activity. The elements of physical education included were gymnastics, dance, games, athletics and swimming. The subject was suitable for both individual and group participation and an emphasis was placed on enjoyment and tailoring the content to each child's individual capacity. The handbook acknowledged the absence of an adequate range of equipment in most schools and recommended improvisation, making use of both indoor and outdoor spaces. In addition, a syllabus in health education was provided for each class, to be integrated with other aspects of the curriculum in order to 'promote the cultivation of good health habits and high standards of hygiene.'[97]

8.8 International Influences on the *Primary School Curriculum* (1971)

Elements of the draft White Paper, Working Document and the subsequent *Primary School Curriculum* (1971), especially the focus on child-centredness, can be traced back to educationalists such as Pestalozzi and Froebel, as well as to the more contemporary influences of Piaget, Montessori, Bruner and Dewey. Collectively, these modern influences instigated a focus on the changing role of the teacher, the emphasis on the need to accommodate individual differences, on the freedom of choice in relation to subject matter, on learning by doing, on basing learning on the child's interests, on focusing on the process as opposed to the product, on the integrated and spiral nature of the curriculum, on the role of the environment in learning and the concept of child-centredness.[98]

However, the curriculum did not rely exclusively on any particular educationalist, instead choosing *à la carte* aspects from a broad spectrum of psychologists, sociologists and philosophers that suited the Irish context at this time. In this way, such theories were tempered for the cultural, social and linguistic reality of practice. This ensured that although the curriculum was revolutionary in nature, it maintained a link with its predecessor in many ways and acted as a bridge from traditional to progressive practice. Examples of contradictions in this transition within the curriculum include the emphasis on child-centredness and the preoccupation of preparing the child for adulthood; the all-round development of the child was emphasised, yet some domains (i.e., cognitive) were more valued than others; the curriculum was presented as an integrated entity but was divided into subjects; and religion occupied a precarious position as the most important subject, yet no syllabus was set forth.

The report of the Central Advisory Council for Education in England (Plowden Report) (1967)[99] was read and discussed widely by Irish educationalists, fuelling the pressure from teachers, training colleges and other educationalists for change to the modern psychological and sociological ideas contained within the report. The Teachers' Study Group facilitated a number of seminars and meetings to discuss the report and even organised for Lady Plowden to visit Dublin to present on its findings.[100] The Plowden Report provided a concise and contemporary summary of educational research and experience, which was highly influential in the Irish context. The characteristics and principles of the curriculum in 1971 were all evident in the Plowden Report of 1967, including the emphasis on individual difference, on flexibility within the curriculum, the interaction of heredity and environmental influences, learning through activity and discovery and the integration of school subjects. The Plowden Report also dealt comprehensively with a number of wider factors impacting on the curriculum such as educational disadvantage, health and social services, preschool education, continuity to second-level education, children with special educational needs, the training of teachers, school buildings and equipment. The language of the 1971 curriculum reflected that of the Plowden Report, especially in relation to the aims of primary education, while the subject areas were also similar in content and presentation.

Evidence of an awareness of developments in Scotland is also apparent. The Scottish curriculum was child-centred, placed an emphasis on the environment, on activity methods, on audio-visual aids, outlined similar subject areas and placed an emphasis on educational research and in-service education for teachers.[101] Furthermore, the approach reflected curriculum developments introduced into Northern Ireland in 1956, which strengthened and extended the child-centred and integrated focus of the curriculum. It sought to address all aspects of the child's development and placed an emphasis on the active participation of the child in learning. The subject areas were identical to those introduced by the *Primary School Curriculum* (1971) in Ireland, with the teachers no longer regarded as mere 'purveyors of knowledge.'[102]

Many of the inspectors involved in drafting the curriculum had travelled and witnessed curricula in operation in the United States, Britain and Europe. However, it is arguable that the structure of the curriculum in 1971 was based on a hybrid of the objectives model prevalent in the United States, and on the process focused, child-centred curriculum that was popular in Britain at this time.[103] This represented a compromise between the two schools of thought, allowing an instrumental view of education in conjunction with ensuring the process was emphasised.

8.9 Summary and Conclusion

The philosophy and content of the *Primary School Curriculum* (1971) represented a seismic shift in state policy and attitude towards the education of children and set the tone for subsequent provision along the lines still delivered in the first decades of the twenty-first century. This chapter has traced the evolution of the curriculum from its genesis in the draft White Paper (1967), through its development as the Working Document (1968) and finally as the finished product as presented in the Teacher's Handbooks in 1971. This development process was focused and concise in nature, facilitated principally through the primary school Inspectorate.

From the outset in 1967, the mould that had encapsulated curriculum development and the conceptualisations of childhood prevalent in Ireland from the 1920s was broken and cast aside. The draft White Paper set the tone and foundation for future development of the curriculum and was a seminal policy document for Irish education. It encapsulated aspects of national and international thinking from a number of fields of expertise, including psychology and curriculum development, to forge a curriculum consonant with Irish ideals and requirements. However, considering the timescale for its development, there was little time to study and synthesise international developments or conduct an in-depth analysis of curriculum theory. Moreover, the principles that guided the work of the curriculum devisers or the research they conducted that provided the evidence-base for reform was never published or made available. This impacted negatively on the theoretical underpinning for the subsequent educational reforms, a feature that had previously been neglected in Irish curriculum policy development. The subject areas identified in the draft White Paper, although largely undeveloped and lacking detail, provided the structure for the curriculum introduced in 1971.

The preparation and publication of the Working Document, a first version of the curriculum based on the draft White Paper, was also a novel move by the Department. The Working Document marked a further development of the curriculum area within the draft White Paper, containing far greater detail on the content of the curriculum for the various subject areas for individual classes. The consultative process facilitated by the Inspectorate was innovative and it allowed for the measured opinion of educationalists and interested parties to be submitted for consideration. Furthermore, the Working Document was shared with INTO members in *An Múinteoir Náisiúnta*, thus widening the breadth of the consultation. This improved teacher familiarity with the nature and content of the curriculum introduced in 1971 and allowed a period of engagement with the ideals underpinning the curriculum in advance of implementation. It is unfortunate that the consultative process was restricted in nature to key interested parties, whereby feedback was not sought from the general public or post-primary interests, which could have further enhanced the quality of the curriculum produced. While much of the feedback was positive in nature, many concerns and comments were included in relation to the practicality of implementation in the contemporary context. Unfortunately, the observations put forward by the various interested parties did not impact significantly on the final product. This neglect weakened the curriculum as it led to a programme that was unrealistic in certain aspects of its implementation, and this subsequently impacted negatively on its rollout.

The inception of pilot schools was also a pioneering initiative in the Irish context. Between 1968 and 1971, approximately 20 per cent of schools nationwide participated in this pilot process in a range of various subjects. This enhanced teacher familiarity with the subjects not only within the schools, but also for neighbouring schools that visited and observed implementation in practice. The dissemination process was further advanced by the establishment of study groups, the organisation of lectures and seminars, and courses organised by a myriad of institutions and organisations. Once again, there is a dearth of official documentation as to the operation of the pilot project in schools and no official review of its implementation was initiated. Consequently, it is difficult to evaluate its effect upon practice or its achievement in relation to preparing teachers for curriculum implementation. Furthermore, it would appear that the experiences of implementing the various subjects in the pilot schools did not impact on the revision of the curriculum, which emerged largely unchanged from the earlier Working Document.

The *Primary School Curriculum* (1971) differed little in ideology or structure from that outlined in the draft White Paper and the subsequent Working Document. It was presented in a detailed and illustrative manner and the Teacher's Handbooks were a significant advance on the Notes previously supplied to teachers. However, its theoretical framework outlined in the introduction was weak and failed to provide a strong foundation on which to build a national curriculum. There were many contradictions inherent within the curriculum, as attempts were made to align aspects of the traditional approach with more progressive thinking. These included the tension between a process and objectives model of education; the focus on the holistic development of the child while the cognitive domain was foregrounded within the curriculum; and the presentation of an integrated curriculum under discrete subject areas. The language used in relation to the role of the teacher was unfortunate, as regardless of the intention, it painted the function of the teacher prior to the 1971 curriculum to be basic in nature, 'merely' an imparter of knowledge. This did little to motivate or endear teachers to the proposed reforms.

The lack of clarity within the Teacher's Handbooks as to the aims and outcomes in each subject created a vacuum in relation to teacher and parental expectations. There was also a lack of cohesion in relation to its content, owing to the fact that a large number of sub-committees were responsible for devising various aspects of the curriculum. The principles underpinning the curriculum were not clearly delineated, the rationale for the inclusion of each subject was not always evident and the syllabus for each subject was not stated in terms of pupil outcomes, thus making evaluation more complex. The physical presentation of the high quality, colour-illustrated, hardbound handbooks evoked a message that these were not temporary documents. There was also an absence of guidance on the time allocation for each subject within the handbooks, causing uncertainty and confusion among teachers as to what was expected of them. Such time allocations had been called for in many submissions of organisations returned on the initial Working Document. Another oversight was the lack of alignment between primary and post-primary curricula, bearing in mind the same Department devised both programmes within a similar time period. This somewhat undermined the philosophy of education underpinning the *Primary School Curriculum* (1971), especially in the senior classes, when a perception arose that it failed to prepare pupils adequately for subsequent post-primary education.

The 1971 curriculum proved to be a radical shift in ideological position, content and methodology from its predecessor. It was underpinned by the ideology of child-centred education, offering a wide range of subjects and encouraging discovery learning methods as an integral element. The curriculum differed from its predecessor by virtue of the fact that it focused on children in the present, valuing the importance of childhood, rather than focusing exclusively on their future lives as adults or citizens. There was also a greater focus on individual and group learning and the use of the environment as a source of learning. The curriculum allowed for greater flexibility in relation to the selection of content and methodologies, empowering decisions to be made at a school level taking into account the school environment, facilities and the interests and stage of development of the pupils. As in the earlier part of the century, a renewed focus was placed on subjects of a more manual and practical nature, once again directed towards the holistic development of the child. While the core subjects of English, Irish, mathematics and religion remained intact, the relative focus on these subjects altered, with a greater emphasis placed on the English language and a reduced emphasis and time allocation for Irish. It represented a broadening in the range and scope of subjects studied by primary school pupils. Furthermore, methodologies evolved in line with modern educational and psychological trends, most notably in relation to mathematics and language learning. The inclusion of additional subjects such as music, art and craft, social and environmental studies and physical education provided for a more balanced approach to the curriculum. While an academic bias was retained, it became tempered and balanced by an emphasis on the aesthetic, physical, creative and emotional aspects of development. This provided for an enlivened educational experience for pupils, where their talents and interests could be developed to some extent by the education system. The provisions of the 1971 curriculum ensured the emphasis on cultural nationalism was firmly replaced with a focus on the needs, interests and abilities of each child. The emphasis on moulding children had been replaced with enabling children to be active agents in their own learning.

The concerns of many of the interest groups that provided feedback on the Working Document proved legitimate in practice. A focus on implementation must be a key component of any initiative, especially a national curriculum, but little or no attention was focused on this in the 700-page handbooks. This resulted in the absence of an explicit commitment to providing the necessary training and resources to ensure the policy became practice in schools. Chapter 9 examines the implementation of the *Primary School Curriculum* (1971) from its introduction until 1990.

Implementation of the *Primary School Curriculum* 1971–1990

9.1 Introduction

This chapter analyses the implementation of the *Primary School Curriculum* (1971) by examining the broad array of evaluations and commentaries on the curriculum between 1971 and 1990. The expansion of the education departments in universities created a growing cohort of academics and researchers with expertise in various aspects of education. These generated data and fuelled debate on educational issues, and the growing number of organisations and conferences provided fora for the dissemination and discussion of research findings. The achievement of a graduate profession for teachers in the mid-1970s opened the possibility of study at postgraduate level and understanding the implementation of the curriculum in this period was enhanced through such postgraduate research. While many of these studies were localised and small-scale in nature, they provide case studies and insights into practice at classroom level and from the perspective of teachers at the frontline of the education system.

At the outset of the chapter, a number of large-scale studies by the Inspectorate, the Conference of Convent Primary Schools, the INTO, the Curriculum Unit, the ERC, the CEB and the Department are documented. The vast array of smaller scale studies by postgraduate researchers and academics are subsequently categorised under the subject areas of the curriculum and by overarching themes.

9.2 Large-scale Studies on Curriculum Implementation

9.2.1 Evaluations by the Inspectorate

In March 1974, following three years of implementation, the Inspectorate issued questionnaires to forty-eight District Inspectors seeking their opinions on the way in which the curriculum was being implemented. In relation to the principles of the *Primary School Curriculum* (1971), inspectors were positive about their influence on practice, especially in relation to catering for individual needs. The second aspect of the study focused on the implementation of the six subject areas (excluding religion) of the curriculum. Great improvements in English were noted, with the exception of spelling and handwriting. Oral Irish was seen to have disimproved, as had written work in both Irish and English. While there was a marked improvement in the understanding of mathematical concepts, a slight deterioration was noted in relation to computation and the memorisation of number facts. In relation to all other subject areas, reasonable progress was regarded as being achieved.[1]

The major obstacles to curriculum implementation were cited as being teacher education and attitudes, followed by large class sizes and inadequate inspection and advisory services. Other factors included the design of classrooms and schools, levels of equipment and resources and the lack of continuity between primary and post-primary curricula. Implementation was seen to be greatest in medium and large schools. The results of this survey were never published and it should be remembered that the study was based on the observations and opinions of inspectors rather than any systematic and structured observational framework.

Following five years of implementation, the Inspectorate evaluated the impact of the Buntús programme in fifth and sixth class by issuing a questionnaire to approximately 500 teachers. The vast majority of respondents were favourable to the teaching of Irish. Most teachers had attended a short training course in the new methods, yet 32 per cent felt inadequately trained in audiovisual methods.[2] This amounted to a significant proportion not entirely confident in using the Buntús programme, the most common programme used for Irish language teaching in schools in the period under review. Instances of using Irish as a medium of instruction for other subjects were rare outside schools in the Gaeltacht, with 80 per cent of schools teaching all other subjects through English. Of respondents, 13 per cent saw no change in the standard of Irish since the new methods were introduced, 39 per cent believed the standards to be better, while 48 per cent reported there had been a disimprovement.

The widespread use of the Buntús programme was evidenced in the fact that 73 per cent of respondents used the programme daily. However, 30 per cent of respondents expressed a preference for traditional methods. Audiovisual methods were praised in relation to providing greater pleasure in learning the language and arousing interest, while traditional methods were seen to provide more vocabulary and lead to greater accuracy in written work. Buntús lessons were criticised in relation to their limited vocabulary, lack of variety in subject matter, lack of focus on girls and their tendency to be boring. Proposed amendments to improve the Buntús programme included placing a greater emphasis on grammar and vocabulary, allowing greater freedom for the teacher in selecting teaching methods, providing improved training for teachers in language teaching methods, ensuring better provision of materials and resources, extending commentary at the expense of dialogue and improving the alignment of primary and post-primary curricula. The spectrum of issues and challenges raised by the Inspectorate in the early 1970s were reiterated throughout the period in many reports, yet little concerted action was taken to address these.

9.2.2 Report of the Conference of Convent Primary Schools

The report of the Conference of Convent Primary Schools was based on a questionnaire to all members in 425 schools in 1974 in order to assess the impact of the new curriculum. Overall, the vast majority expressed a favourable or very favourable attitude towards the curriculum. There was overwhelming agreement that there had been an improvement in relation to all aspects of oral English, reading and writing.[3] Attitudes to mathematics were also favourable, where slower progress was seen to be compensated for by deeper understanding. A total of 87 per cent of respondents reported an improvement in the attainment of concepts but only 48 per cent saw an improvement in computational skills, while 65 per cent witnessed a disimprovement in the memorisation of number facts. The Buntús programme was perceived as beneficial to pupils, with 74 per cent noting an improvement in oral Irish, but progress in written Irish under the new curriculum was viewed as more problematic, with only 58 per cent noting an improvement. Overall, there was agreement on the need to return to a focus on basic skills, such as spelling, tables and penmanship.

The introduction of social and environmental studies was welcomed for awakening pupils' interest in the world around them. However, only 36 per cent of teachers rated themselves as being 'very good' at conducting fieldwork, with 34 per cent giving themselves a rating of 'good' and a further 20 per cent 'fair.' The majority of teachers reported that the inclusion of art and craft had fostered the intellect, imagination, observational skills and creativity of pupils. While 86 per cent believed music appreciation had improved, 76 per cent believed special ability in music was required to teach the syllabus. The role of physical education in developing the shy child was praised.

Other positive benefits of the curriculum were seen to be improved attendance, enhanced communication between pupils, better pupil-teacher relationships and improved relations with visitors to the school. The new teaching methods were also posited by the vast majority to impact positively on pupils to work independently and in groups. An obstacle to implementation was cited as the lack of parental knowledge and awareness of the new approaches, which were qualitatively different to parents' school experiences. The haphazard nature of in-service provision was criticised, as was the limited availability of equipment and large class sizes.

This study was more positive towards the implementation of the curriculum than the Inspectorate study in 1974. It painted an optimistic picture of implementation across all aspects of the curriculum, with a concern that a re-focus on the core and essential elements of education needed to be introduced. It is interesting that certain insights were revealed by the study in relation to implementation. While there was a unanimous welcome for social and environmental studies, few teachers actually engaged in field-work, which was a key aspect of the curriculum. This mismatch between the rhetoric and reality of implementation appears continuously in evaluations up to 1990, many of which looked at teachers' attitudes rather than actual practice in schools. One reason for this may be a 'halo effect', as the new curriculum was generally perceived at the outset to be wholesome and it may have been considered the correct thing to express support for its provisions, in theory at least.

9.2.3 Evaluations of the Irish National Teachers' Organisation (INTO)

Curriculum Questionnaire Analysis (1976)

The CEC of the INTO decided to survey teachers' reactions to the new curriculum in 1975, attaining 7,677 questionnaire responses.[4] The main objectives of the study were to determine teachers' perceptions on the achievement of the aims of the curriculum, to evaluate the effect on pupils and teachers, to ascertain teacher attitudes to the curriculum, to determine difficulties in implementing the curriculum, to gauge the effect of additional subjects and to establish parental difficulties in understanding the curriculum.

In response to ten 'philosophical' questions, teachers indicated a high degree of acceptance in theory for the principles underpinning the curriculum. Respondents reported an overwhelming improvement in English reading, writing and speech, with some concern for progress in spelling. With the exception of Irish reading, teachers reported a disimprovement in all other aspects of Irish. While the understanding of mathematical concepts was seen to have improved significantly, no change was perceived in relation to computational skills or problem solving, while the memorisation of number facts was seen to have disimproved. Furthermore, while subjects were being taught and implemented, a significant proportion of teachers were unhappy or lacked confidence in relation to their progress. For example, just over half of respondents felt they were implementing the art and craft and music curriculum satisfactorily. While 65 per cent of teachers were implementing the physical education curriculum, only 34 per cent believed they were teaching the subject satisfactorily. This was worrying, with approximately half of respondents not feeling confident in their ability to implement core subject areas within the curriculum. Such findings are interesting and provide a barometer of actual implementation, as while the majority of studies focused on teacher attitudes to the curriculum, few questioned the aspects implemented in practice. Discrepancies are evident in the answers provided from respondents, with a mismatch appearing between the theoretical acceptance of the curriculum and its practical implementation as envisaged in the handbooks. This is highlighted forcefully in relation to the elements of subjects implemented and the degree of satisfaction teachers felt with regard to their ability to implement core aspects of the curriculum.

Despite these findings, respondents indicated that the curriculum had a significant effect on classroom practice, as close to 65 per cent reported that they had changed in relation to use of group teaching, 69 per cent in relation to employing project-work, 73 per cent in relation to the use of discovery methods, 91 per cent in relation to providing increased activity for children, 79 per cent in relation to increased use of source materials and 67 per cent in relation to increased use of visual aids. Teachers rated class size to be the greatest barrier to curriculum implementation, as well as unsatisfactory physical environments, poor provision for equipment and materials, and lack of alignment between primary and post-primary curricula. The study also revealed the *ad hoc* nature of in-service provision for the curriculum in the form of summer courses, weekend courses, evening courses and occasional lectures. Aspects cited as most urgent within these professional development courses were classroom management and organisation, methods of teaching, subject matter, child development and dealing with children with learning difficulties. Little action was taken based on the findings of the report, which, consonant with those of the Inspectorate and the Conference of Convent Primary Schools, began to document clearly the action needed to support successful implementation.

The Irish Language in Primary Education (1985)

In 1984, the INTO issued a questionnaire to all members on their attitudes to the Irish language and on the suitability of the syllabus.[5] In relation to the teaching of Irish, 22 per cent of teachers taught entirely through Irish and 75 per cent partially through Irish. However, the majority of respondents believed the results achieved from teaching Irish did not reflect the time and effort expended on the subject or that the expectations set could be met in the limited time available. Most teachers used a combination of Buntús and A.B.C.[†] methods, with 39 per cent relying on the Buntús programme alone. Moreover, many did not follow the guidelines for the Buntús programme, believing the language to be too difficult to stimulate conversations within the time available. Only 25 per cent of teachers believed they succeeded in stimulating their pupils' interest in the language, while 22 per cent of teachers recorded that pupils read books in Irish other than their textbooks.

In relation to perceived ability, 75 per cent of respondents believed their pupils could understand Irish, 53 per cent were happy with reading achievement and 33 per cent were pleased with outcomes in writing. A total of 63 per cent of respondents called for a new syllabus in Irish to be devised by a representative body of teachers, language experts and inspectors, with the majority requesting a greater focus on oral Irish within any revised syllabus. It is interesting that there was least demand for a new syllabus among infant teachers, rising incrementally to 72 per cent of senior class teachers requesting a change. The findings of this INTO survey were closely aligned to those of a Market Research Bureau of Ireland (MRBI) study commissioned by the INTO in 1985.[6]

INTO Study on the Curriculum (1986)

In 1986, the INTO Education Committee conducted a follow-up study in relation to teacher attitudes to the curriculum. Questionnaires were

---

†   The A.B.C. method related to the approach to teaching Irish introduced in the 1920s, focusing on language structure, vocabulary, and fluency and creative conversation.

issued randomly to 1,000 teachers and 789 were returned.[7] Respondents to the 1986 study continued to indicate their considerable support for the principles underpinning the curriculum, with somewhat reduced support for the principle of integration. The INTO proposed that the lower acceptance of the principle of integration may have been owing to the reliance on textbooks by 90 per cent of teachers (as opposed to the handbooks by 60 per cent of teachers), with most textbooks treating subjects individually.

Approximately 50 per cent of teachers grouped children for various aspects of the curriculum; this occurred mostly amongst experienced teachers and in junior classes. However, two-thirds expressed a preference for class teaching and 60 per cent preferred didactic teaching methods, compared to 36 per cent who favoured activity-based methods. Furthermore, only 50 per cent brought their classes on a nature walk once a year. Such findings contradict the strong endorsement of the principle of using activity- and discovery-based methods also recorded in the report. This poses a fundamental question in relation to the validity of findings from attitudinal surveys, which do not offer an accurate reflection of actual practice in schools. Particular concern was expressed regarding the implementation of music, physical education and art and craft. For example, 44 per cent of teachers stated that their music syllabus was taught by another teacher within the school and 9 per cent by a music specialist, a worrying finding considering music was a core subject within the *Primary School Curriculum* (1971). However, fifteen years into its implementation, in excess of 50 per cent of classroom teachers were not, in fact, teaching the subject.

The recommendations of the report reiterated those that had become standard from the 1970s, including a reduction in the pupil-teacher ratio, the provision of comprehensive in-service education, improvements in school and classroom environments, the supply of equipment and books for school libraries, the employment of peripatetic advisers (especially in music, art and craft and physical education), the introduction of remedial and psychological services in all schools for pupils with learning difficulties and greater alignment of primary and post-primary curricula. This report points to the fact that challenges to implementation identified a decade earlier had not been addressed to any significant degree and continued to cause a discrepancy in relation to the curriculum as intended in the handbooks, as endorsed by teachers and as implemented in classrooms.

9.2.4 Educational Research Centre (ERC) Evaluation (1977)

The establishment of the Educational Research Centre (ERC) in 1966 provided an additional mechanism for conducting research in the Irish context. The Department commissioned a study by the ERC in 1977 on curriculum implementation. The ERC issued questionnaires to principals in a representative sample of schools on the implementation of the curriculum and of changes in standards.[8] The study again examined principals' perceptions of change rather than conduct an evaluation of changes in practice. Principals were encouraged to consult teachers in completing the questionnaire, and as approximately 80 per cent of principals were also classroom teachers, the majority had direct experience of practical implementation. The questionnaire was returned by 446 of the 489 principals surveyed.

The principles of the curriculum were endorsed by the majority of respondents, with less support for the integrated nature of the curriculum. However, a high degree of implementation was reported in relation to the integration of subjects which contradicted the earlier lack of endorsement. Higher levels of implementation were noted in middle-sized schools. Overall, trends in standards pointed towards improvement. This was highest for English (with the exception of writing), mathematical concepts and Irish reading. Greatest deterioration in standards was noted in relation to the memorisation of number facts and in the presentation of written work. Principals ranked eight items in terms of contributing to the lack of curriculum implementation, with pupil-teacher ratios, time impediments, the lack of equipment and library facilities, and the lack of continuity between primary and secondary education cited as the main barriers. These constraints echo the findings from earlier studies.

It is interesting that the two evaluations conducted by the Department in the 1970s failed to take into consideration the direct views of those implementing the curriculum on a daily basis, namely the teachers. While the focus in both studies related to the practice of teachers, the methodology employed directed questions to both inspectors and principals.

9.2.5 Reports of the Curriculum Unit of the Department of Education

The Curriculum Unit was established within the Department in 1976 with a brief to co-ordinate, evaluate, diagnose and prescribe the curriculum at both primary and post-primary level. It was staffed primarily by inspectors and as the Inspectorate was the chief architect of the *Primary School Curriculum* (1971), this should be kept in mind when examining the findings of its evaluations. Through the forming of Committees of Inspectors with particular subject-area expertise, it produced individual reports on all aspects of the primary school curriculum between 1979 and 1988. Despite a government commitment,[9] these reports were not published or made available and as a result, contributed little to the understanding of curriculum implementation at this time. The following section treats of the Curriculum Unit evaluations in chronological order.

Physical Education

The Committee to evaluate the progress of physical education in primary schools reported in 1979. Only 35 per cent of inspectors felt the work undertaken in relation to physical education was satisfactory, attributing such a situation to a lack of knowledge and understanding on the part of teachers for the subject, their lack of confidence to teach it and their perception that it was not an important subject.[10] A further issue was that 33 per cent of schools had indoor facilities and 71 per cent had outdoor facilities, while only a minority of schools had adequate apparatus. Games and athletics were the aspects best taught, with swimming, dance and health education most neglected. Recommendations hinged on the provision of in-service courses in order to change attitudes, awaken interest, demonstrate methodology, advise on planning and organisation, demonstrate integration opportunities and provide adequate resources and facilities.

English

The English Committee issued a questionnaire to inspectors (fifty-nine respondents) and teachers (287 respondents) in 1980. It also administered reading tests based on those used in 1972 and found improvement in attainment.[11] Greater scope was proposed in the development of oral skills, as was a more varied approach to poetry, the increased use of dramatic activities in middle and senior classes, a focus on writing and a more complementary relationship between the classroom and remedial teacher. A wide range of separate recommendations was proposed for principals (e.g., better co-ordination of the work of the remedial and classroom teacher, choice of textbooks, etc.) and teachers (e.g., use of group methods, additional attention to writing, etc.) regarding English. The Committee also recommended undertaking national surveys into the teaching of English every five years and an improvement of school library facilities. A third national reading test was administered in 1988 to fifth class pupils, with results showing no significant changes to those obtaining in 1980. This also found that pupils attending all-Irish schools scored significantly higher on English reading ability than pupils in ordinary national schools.[12]

Music

In 1980, a Music Committee issued questionnaires to principals and administered tests on song singing, intervals, sight-reading and ear training to 2,773 pupils in first to sixth class.[13] The study found a good repertoire of songs, the inclusion of Irish songs and correct pitch. However, mastery of intervals was low. Similar disappointing results were recorded for sight-reading, while aural skills were somewhat better. The report called for all schools to have a definite policy on music in the School Plan, to provide increased time for music on a regular basis and to focus on musical literacy. A major expansion of in-service education in music was also recommended. As in previous studies examined, there were many concerns raised regarding the implementation of music, which was perceived to be a complex syllabus for non-specialist teachers.

Social and Environmental Studies

The Social and Environmental Studies Committee issued questionnaires to teachers and District Inspectors. Its report in 1983 found a greater use of the local environment in junior classes than in senior classes.[14] It criticised the over-reliance on textbooks in senior classes, where the teaching of social and environmental studies bore little relationship with the local environment. Civics was also noted to be a neglected subject, as was the inclusion of field trips at all levels. While social and environmental studies were well integrated with other aspects of the curriculum, there was little evidence of linkage within the subjects. Recommendations included the provision of more training at pre-service level, supports for studies on local areas, the provision of quality reference books for libraries and guidelines on the use of the local environment.

Mathematics

In 1977 and 1980, the Curriculum Unit issued tests in mathematics to primary school pupils. The results in 1977 relating to junior and middle classes showed that number facts and computational skills were well mastered, while commutative, associative and distributive properties had been achieved by a minority of pupils.[15] Mastery of various elements disimproved between second and fourth class. The 1980 report was based on the views of inspectors and the results of criterion-referenced tests undertaken by approximately 6,000 pupils in second, fourth and sixth class.[16] Based on these, 52 per cent of inspectors recommended minor modifications to the curriculum. Approximately three-fifths of inspectors believed there was not enough emphasis on oral work or mathematical activities and that there was an over-reliance on the textbook.

In 1984, the Curriculum Unit produced a further report on mathematics achievement, based this time on criterion-referenced tests issued to 2,377 sixth class pupils. There was a high correlation with the results from 1977 and 1980, whereby pupils achieved well in mechanical operations and interpreting graphs and charts. However, there were disappointing results in concept development, metric measures, geometry and problem solving, leading to the conclusion that:

> Efforts to cultivate the implementation of a discovery/ activity approach to the teaching of Mathematics during the past 10/15 years have not been very successful.[17]

The recommendations of this report included the need for a greater emphasis on developing understanding of basic concepts through the use of concrete materials and activity methods, a more structured approach to the teaching of problem solving, the development of mathematical language through oral discussion and an overall review of mathematical content within the curriculum.

Art and Craft

The Art and Craft Committee issued separate questionnaires to teachers (475 returned), principals (532 returned) and inspectors (79 returned) in 1983. A majority of teachers stated that their initial training did not prepare them adequately to teach this subject.[18] Principals and teachers outlined some practical problems with implementation such as the availability of materials and facilities, large class sizes, the absence of running water, space and the storage of materials and equipment. Approximately two-thirds of inspectors believed inadequate time was allowed for art and craft in schools. Furthermore, there were few instances of visits to local galleries or museums and less than half of the suggested art activities were actually attempted, with art appreciation and printing least popular. The recommendations of the Committee included a systematic evaluation of art and craft to be undertaken, an examination of the adequacy of college of education training courses, the delivery of in-service education, the provision of materials and facilities for the subject, and a revision of the syllabus in the handbooks.

Irish

The Curriculum Unit's report on Irish assessed its implementation in Gaeltacht and Galltacht areas, as well as in Gaelscoileanna. The Committee

issued questionnaires to inspectors and studied a research report by Institiúid
Teangeolaíochta Éireann (Linguistics Institute of Ireland) entitled *Spoken
Irish in Primary Schools*.[19] The Curriculum Unit's report in 1985 concluded
that greater unity and clarity was needed between the oral, reading and
written aspects of the syllabus:

> Níl cúntas sách léir i gCuraclam na Bunscoile nó i lámhleabhair na gCúrsaí Comhrá ar
> na cuspóirí atá le baint amach ag an dalta ag na leibhéil eagsúla sa bhunscoil.[20][†]

To this end, the report recommended a redrafting of chapter 5 of the
Teacher's Handbook Part 1, with an increased emphasis on documenting
realisable objectives in oral Irish. Most inspectors expressed satisfaction
regarding the progress of reading in Gaeltacht and Galltacht areas, yet
there was general dissatisfaction with progress in writing. Tests administered found that pupils scored higher on listening as opposed to speaking skills. In addition, teachers in Galltacht areas were encouraged to
make greater use of informal Irish for communication and in teaching
other subjects. In-service courses were recommended, as was an awareness campaign aimed at parents to highlight the importance of their
attitude to the language for their children's learning. In Gaeltacht areas,
the report highlighted the need to demand more from pupils who did
not speak Irish in the home and the need to employ better methodologies for teaching oral language. Among the recommendations for the
teaching of Irish in Gaeltacht areas were the supply of appropriate textbooks and other resources in Irish, as well as in-service for teachers on
'*cúrsaí a leagfadh béim ar Theagasc na Gaeilge agus ar úsáid na Gaeilge
mar mheán teagaisc.*'[21][‡]

---

†   The objectives that the children must achieve at the various levels in the primary
    school are not defined clearly enough in the New Curriculum or in the manuals for
    the Conversation Courses.

‡   ... courses that would emphasise the teaching of Irish and the use of Irish as a medium
    of teaching.

Implementation of the Principles of the Primary School Curriculum

The Committee entrusted with the task of assessing the implementation of the five principles of the curriculum issued a questionnaire to all inspectors and to 1,000 teachers.[22] Overall, there was a high degree of acceptance of these principles, with the full and harmonious development of the child and allowing for individual difference endorsed most widely. However, this endorsement was contradicted by a perception that cognitive development should be prioritised. While a high incidence of group work and use of activity and discovery methods in junior classes was reported, this declined in senior classes, while the environment was rarely used for subjects outside social and environmental studies. Beyond cross-subject approaches, high levels of integration were not commonly reported and some level of integration was only noted by 50 per cent of inspectors, despite its endorsement as a principle by teachers. The report cited five main factors affecting the implementation of the curriculum, including an over-reliance on textbooks, the deficit of equipment and resources, the lack of individual teacher preparation, the impact of large class sizes on using active methods and lack of alignment with post-primary curricula.

Report on Pilot Schemes in Computers and Science

A pilot project in thirty schools regarding the teaching of computers was organised between 1984 and 1986. Its results were positive on the whole, finding that children participating benefited educationally in terms of language, social skills and problem-solving ability.[23] The pilot scheme on science in primary schools operated in senior classes in a selection of schools in Galway and Dublin. Favourable results were reported for participants, including improved observational skills, logical thinking, language ability and manual dexterity.[24]

The picture painted by this suite of evaluations of the various subject areas is one of uneven implementation of the curriculum in practice. While aspects of all subject areas were being implemented, there were fundamental elements that failed to become common practice in the majority of schools.

While some Committees focused on aspects of curriculum implementation in English, mathematics and music, most did not examine implementation of the curriculum in practice. Reliance was placed on questionnaires to inspectors, principals and teachers to garner information. This served to elicit the opinions and judgements of professionals regarding the curriculum, rather than examine in a comprehensive way what was happening in classrooms. The failure to conduct cohesive, empirical research in relation to all aspects of curriculum implementation, focused on actual practice of teachers in classrooms, limited the value of the findings of the various reports. Certain anomalies are apparent within the findings, largely in relation to the reported implementation of certain principles and aspects of the curriculum, as compared to actual implementation. Also, these reports were never published. It is possible that inspectors, in their ongoing work and engagement within schools, imparted the lessons from these evaluations in an informal way. However, in the absence of publishing the reports or formally communicating their recommendations to schools, they consequently had little impact on practice. Furthermore, many of the recommendations for the Department were not implemented, despite an awareness of many of the fundamental impediments to the successful implementation of the curriculum.

9.2.6 Evaluations by the Curriculum and Examinations Board (CEB)

The CEB was established in January 1984 to review and develop the curriculum at primary and post-primary level; to initiate and support research and development in curriculum innovation; and to review legislative, administrative and financial constraints that may impinge on curriculum proposals. The CEB established a number of Committees, including one on primary education. In 1987, the CEB was reconstituted as a non-statutory advisory body, the National Council for Curriculum and Assessment. This section details chronologically a number of reports completed by the CEB on the implementation of individual subjects and two overarching reports which related to the overall implementation of the curriculum.

The Arts in Education

The CEB published a Discussion Paper on *The Arts in Education* (1985), covering music, the visual arts, drama and dance. In general, the implementation of these subjects was seen to be compromised by a number of factors, including teachers' attitudes to the arts, the quality of teacher education, high pupil-teacher ratios, pressure on the timetable and inadequate facilities and materials. The CEB recommended a study regarding the implementation of the various elements of arts education as 'the evidence presented here is unequivocal: existing provision is inadequate and must be improved.'[25] This conclusion resonated well with many studies regarding the poor implementation of art and craft and music during this period.

Language in the Curriculum

The report, *Language in the Curriculum* (1985), endorsed the centrality of language, especially oral language, within the curriculum. To this end, it called for a refocus on the interdependency of oral language and all other aspects of language and learning. The report proposed a greater emphasis on the study of language acquisition in the colleges of education and within in-service education, and more integrated planning for language development at individual school level. The question of introducing modern languages, in light of Ireland's participation in the EEC, was also considered for its cultural and economic benefits. In relation to the Irish language, the report concluded that 'the crisis facing Gaeltacht schools requires immediate attention.'[26] The language-centred approach of the Buntús programme was seen to be in conflict with the child-centred philosophy of the curriculum and also did not accommodate the diverse categories of pupils attending primary schools. The report outlined four possible contexts for language teaching, each of which required appropriate language development courses, reading materials and textbooks. The importance of early learning experiences in relation to a second language was stressed and the methods of teaching language through the direct-method and audiovisual aids were seen as insufficient to develop a communicative ability. In this context, a learner-centred communicative approach was recommended, accompanied by realistic and obtainable objectives and appropriate materials for implementation. Despite this understanding, the Buntús programme continued to form the basis of instruction in the years ahead.

Report on Primary Education

The most important discussion document of the CEB in terms of the primary school curriculum was entitled *Primary Education*, with terms of reference to review the existing research on the primary curriculum, to identify problems in implementation and to propose appropriate strategies to solve them.[27] The ensuing report published in 1985 analysed over 100 studies on the curriculum, the majority of which were small scale and local in nature. The report looked at the provisions of the *Primary School Curriculum* (1971) in terms of aspirations, aims and objectives for education. It viewed the two aims of primary education stated in the handbooks to be essentially aspirations, and suggested in excess of twenty more appropriate aims for primary education. It further asserted the need to formulate a set of sequenced objectives, stated in terms of pupil behaviour and outcomes, for the different subjects of the curriculum. A number of constraints on implementing the curriculum was recognised by the CEB, including class size, the unsystematic nature of in-service education and the lack of equipment and resources. The lack of support services for schools in the form of remedial teachers, a psychological service, and ancillary services such as caretakers and secretarial staff, was also criticised as it placed great strain on principals and other teachers to fulfil multiple roles.

The report raised a number of issues for attention, including undertaking a more informal approach at infant level, better provision for meeting the needs of pupils with learning difficulties, the forging of improved home-school links, focusing on second language learning for communicative purposes, addressing the poor implementation of arts subjects, paying closer attention to pupil transitions and the use of a wide array of assessment and evaluation techniques for educational purposes. Among the overall recommendations were a review of the aims and principles of the curriculum, the development of specific objectives for each subject, a review of the mathematics curriculum, improved in-service education and improved resources to support pupils with special educational needs and pupils affected by educational disadvantage.

Mathematics Education

In 1986, the CEB produced a discussion paper on mathematics at primary and junior cycle levels, with particular emphasis on the principles underpinning the mathematics curriculum. It found the research base for mathematics to be weak, with a limited number of studies focusing on attainment and little emphasis on infant classes. While the CEB was in agreement with the principles underpinning the mathematics curriculum, it noted that they had little influence at a practical level. Overall, a number of considerations were raised, including the need for more specific objectives at each class level, increased use of concrete materials and the local environment in teaching, the development of mathematical skills and concepts as opposed to focusing primarily on computational skills, the greater use of formal and informal assessment and greater continuity in curriculum content and methodologies. Teacher in-service training was also cited as a means to disseminate new methodologies and approaches and to lessen dependence on textbooks:

> Too frequently the textbook dictates the quality and pace of the teaching and denies the pupils the chance to explore their immediate environment to seek practical applications of the mathematical concepts they are expected to learn.[28]

In Our Schools – A Framework for Curriculum and Assessment

In Our Schools – A Framework for Curriculum and Assessment (1986) set out the CEBs thinking on curriculum and assessment and placed an emphasis on value for money in public services. A total of nine overarching aims for primary education were set forth.[29] It also stressed the need for constant review to detect differences in relation to the curriculum as written, as received and as implemented. Among the recommendations to the Minister, of which there were forty-five in total, were the need for evolution in curriculum and assessment planning, the importance of consultation with stakeholders and the need to promote creativity in schools.

Social, Political and Environmental Education

A report on social, political and environmental education by the CEB in 1987 stressed the importance of relationships in life and the need to understand community and society structure in an era of rapid change.[30] Civics was noted to be the most neglected subject in this area of the curriculum. In addition, the report called for greater continuity between curriculum provision at primary and post-primary levels.

The myriad of reports from the CEB between 1984 and 1986 provides a valuable insight into the implementation of the curriculum. Reports noted the poor research base on curriculum implementation, with little emphasis placed on classroom practice or pupil outcomes. The CEB analysed the aims and objectives for education within the handbooks and proposed a revision of these to be stated in terms of pupil outcomes and behaviour, wherein implementation could be more easily assessed. In essence, the work of the CEB repeated or reinforced many of the findings and recommendations of earlier reports and was influential in catalysing curriculum reforms in the 1990s.

9.2.7 Reports by the Department of Education

White Paper on Educational Development

A *White Paper on Educational Development* was published in 1980. In relation to the curriculum, the White Paper largely summarised its content and the evaluations on the curriculum in the 1970s. It made four, largely insignificant, recommendations in relation to the curriculum, as follows; the production of booklets on the local environment, a greater focus on the principle of integration, continued evaluation of the curriculum by the Curriculum Unit and an examination of alignment with post-primary curricula. The White Paper cited the main impediments to the successful implementation of the Irish curriculum to be the lack of interest in the subject outside schools, the inadequate use of Irish as a medium of instruction or communication in schools, teachers' competence and the teaching methods used. It also called for 'an entire aspect or part thereof of the curriculum [to be] taught through Irish in every primary school.'[31] It advocated increased levels of in-service training on teaching methods and the provision of materials and resources. Moreover, colleges of education were called on to dedicate more time to the teaching of Irish and to provide opportunities for all students to teach through Irish. In general, the White Paper neglected to address many of the implementation issues raised in studies in the 1970s regarding the curriculum and did little to advance curriculum implementation one decade after its introduction.

Programme for Action in Education

In 1984, the Department issued a *Programme for Action in Education*. The four-year programme was pragmatic as opposed to aspirational in nature, taking into account the challenging economic situation. However, the programme made little mention of the curriculum beyond committing to its ongoing evaluation by the Curriculum Unit and improving resources to national schools, prioritising those most disadvantaged.[32] It is noteworthy that a four-year educational strategy in the 1980s paid so little attention to the fundamental aspect of the curriculum, considering the concerns many reports were raising in relation to its implementation.

Review Body on the Primary Curriculum

Two major reviews of the primary education system were undertaken concurrently in the late 1980s, one relating specifically to the curriculum (Review Body on the Primary Curriculum) and the other to the system as a whole (Primary Education Review Body). It is surprising that two completely separate entities were considered necessary to perform this review, given the integral nature of the curriculum within primary education.

The Review Body on the Primary Curriculum was established in October 1987 to examine aspects of the implementation of the *Primary*

School Curriculum (1971), to identify weaknesses in design and implementation and to recommend amendments for the future implementation of the curriculum.[33] The Review Body was representative in nature and its terms of reference placed a particular focus on Irish, English and mathematics, on assessment within the curriculum, on the aims and objectives of primary education and on alignment with post-primary curricula. The Review Body received eighty-five written submissions, took a number of oral submissions and established five sub-committees to further its work. It issued its report in December 1990.

The Review Body endorsed the two general aims of primary education as posited in 1971 but proposed a slight rewording. It also felt that the curriculum was weakened by not including a number of more specific aims and it put forward nine such aims based on the development of the physical, social, emotional, spiritual and creative aspects of the child. It also offered a long list of twenty-four general objectives for education, based largely on the subject areas of the curriculum. The five principles underpinning the curriculum were endorsed by the Review Committee, while noting the distinction between their acceptance and implementation among teachers.

In relation to the English language, the Review Body agreed with the aims and content of the English curriculum in general but felt it was necessary to make certain aims and objectives more systematic, sequenced and explicit. Other aspects that needed to be addressed were the development of guidelines on pedagogic options, assessment methods and the planning of listening and speaking activities. It recommended an overall review of English, placing a particular focus on oral language learning of the child's vernacular, on reading to learn, greater provision for children with learning difficulties and an emphasis on promoting creativity and imagination.

The Review Body noted that the handbooks did not contain specific aims for the teaching of Irish beyond the aspiration that pupils would have the ability to communicate and to discuss items of interest in the language. It recommended that the general aim for Irish in Galltacht areas should be to develop systematically the communication skills of pupils at a level appropriate to their ability and environment, followed by more general objectives. In the Gaeltacht, the Review Body recommended a flexible curriculum to meet the language needs of all pupils, the provision of a set of readers and the adequate supply of textbooks, library books and reference books in the Irish language. These recommendations took cognisance of many of the recurring complaints regarding the Irish syllabus.

The Review Body proposed a restatement of the aims for mathematics learning to include more specific aims such as developing a positive attitude to mathematics, promoting understanding of key mathematical concepts and the application of mathematics to everyday situations. It also recommended the inclusion of specific objectives for each area of the curriculum, a reduction in focus on computation and an increased emphasis on concepts, the use of calculators, greater alignment between primary and post-primary curricula and the adequate supply of resources, equipment and materials. These proposals encapsulated a myriad of concerns regarding the mathematics curriculum that had been raised following 1971.

In relation to social and environmental studies, the Review Body proposed closer integration of history, geography and civics with this subject. It also recommended greater planning for social and environmental studies at school level, outlining general aims and objectives, skills and attitudes to be acquired. It further advocated an increased emphasis on activity and discovery methods, a revision of the handbooks to contain a range of teaching strategies and approaches, and resources and grants to equip schools with materials. Specifically in relation to history, the Review Body recommended continuing the focus on social history and retaining the concern for the cultural and religious traditions of all communities. The specific recommendations for geography included an emphasis on local aspects and to introduce geography into junior classes. The importance of integrating civics with other curriculum areas was stressed, with an emphasis on attitudinal as opposed to cognitive outcomes.

The Review Body noted the absence of a rationale for the teaching of the arts in the Teacher's Handbooks, recommending a statement of aesthetic principles from which the aims and objectives for the arts could be derived. The potential of drama as a methodology was also considered and its use advocated across all aspects of the curriculum. In relation to music, the absence of specific objectives was noted and the Review Body recommended a formal statement of aims and objectives, a more balanced treatment of performance and appreciation, a more varied repertoire of songs, the provision of materials for music appreciation, a review of pre-service and in-service training and the appointment of seconded teachers as specialist advisors. It recommended the devising of more specific aims and objectives for physical education also, including details on the skills, attitudes and knowledge expected. It also proposed that health education not be included as a subject owing to curriculum overload, proposing that it be treated as a cross-curriculum theme.

In general, the Review Body endorsed the length of the school day and year and recommended increased time be made available for in-service training. The use of Information Technology in schools was viewed as a resource to enrich the learning process, rather than an end in itself. The introduction of a modern language in primary schools was not recommended owing to curriculum overload and by virtue of the fact that pupils already learned two languages. It also addressed the issue of access to the curriculum for those affected by educational disadvantage, in both urban and rural contexts. It acknowledged the difficulty in identifying those who were disadvantaged, admitting 'not all disadvantaged children live in disadvantaged areas.'[34] It recognised the limited value of school-based interventions alone and called for wider government action to address the issue, with a specific focus on preschool interventions.

Evaluation and assessment were key features within the terms of reference of the Review Body. It identified a number of reasons for evaluation and assessment, including the provision of feedback to pupils and parents, for diagnostic purposes, to inform policy and planning and to indicate overall progress of the system. Overall, the Review Body recommended the use of both informal and formal assessment based on the objectives of the curriculum, with a focus on more formal assessment in senior classes. Formal assessment techniques proposed included criterion-referenced, norm-referenced and self-referenced tests. Information emanating from assessments would be communicated to parents and other professionals as appropriate, while a summative evaluation would be forwarded to post-primary schools. This was a significant shift from the existing practice in primary schools. First, the curriculum in 1971 did not contain specific objectives that could be assessed in this manner and before this was feasible, the work of the Review Body would have to be extended to provide such objectives. Second, there was no tradition of using standardised tests in schools following 1971, with a general dearth of available tests suitable for the Irish context.

By virtue of Circular 31/82, *Inspection of Schools*, the Review Body viewed the Inspectorate as the main agent of evaluation of the work of teachers and schools. The primary focus in the 1980s was on the working of the school as a whole. In general, the Review Body proposed a continuation of the external system of evaluation, complemented by internal school self-evaluation. It noted the work of the Inspectorate to be central to the school and called for the appointment of additional inspectors to ensure their duties were fulfilled. School self-evaluation was to be co-ordinated by the principal through the School Plan, based on the curriculum and devised in consultation with parents and managers. At system level, the Review Body asserted that evaluation needed to be based on curriculum objectives and conducted on an ongoing and regular basis, leading to the publication of concise national statistical abstracts.

The Review Body bemoaned the inadequate nature of the funding for primary schools, with 38 per cent of the education budget assigned to primary education. It asserted that this paucity of funding had impacted on the implementation of the curriculum and the Review Body prioritised an improvement in class sizes, the provision of in-service training and improved grants for equipment as the most pressing.

Two reservations were lodged by members of the Review Body. Dr Daniel Murphy, a ministerial nominee, felt the report did not stress adequately or propose solutions for the literacy problems of primary school leavers. The NPC-P objected to the short length of the school year, the decision not to introduce a foreign language and the lack of priority afforded to parental involvement in the final report.

Overall, the Review Body report endorsed the underlying philosophy and principles of the curriculum but asserted it required 'revision and reformulation in its aims, scope and content, in the manner in which it is implemented and in the way pupil progress is assessed and recorded and the way overall effectiveness of the system is evaluated.'[35] It also proposed the inclusion of more general aims and specific objectives to clarify what was expected and to assist evaluation. This represented a shift from the initial handbooks and one of the main motivations in this regard was to facilitate a higher degree of assessment and evaluation of curriculum implementation. The report of the Review Body acted as a springboard and catalyst for curriculum change throughout the 1990s.

Primary Education Review Body

The Primary Education Review Body was established in February 1988 and was representative of the education sector. Its terms of reference were 'to review the primary sector of education',[36] including the structures of primary education, demographic trends, quality of primary education and school organisation. The report produced consisted of forty-three short chapters and 107 recommendations. Among the recommendations were a review of the training of teachers, improved in-service education, a revised role for the Inspectorate, training for boards of management, supports for children with special educational needs and school buildings. It proposed the standardisation of practice and the clarification of rules regarding the school year, calling for 184 school days and an additional six days for school-related activities. The Primary Education Review Body recommended five main areas that were in need of increased funding, namely staffing, capitation, in-service training, building grants and provision for pupils with special educational needs. While this Review Body report did not impact directly on the curriculum, it addressed many issues of a structural and resource nature that impacted on its implementation and formed part of the evidence-base of the need for reform in the 1990s.

9.3 Subject-specific Studies regarding Implementation

In this period, a number of smaller scale studies and theses by individuals and groups with an interest in various aspects of the primary school curriculum were completed. Collectively, these studies provide a rich source of data in relation to curriculum implementation at practice level in the period under review. These are classified below under the main subject areas and are generally analysed chronologically within these categories.

9.3.1 English

The Teachers' Study Group initiated the first of a series of studies regarding reading attainment in 1964, a study replicated at five-year intervals until the 1980s. In 1974, it found an improvement across the whole range of reading ability and the gap between ability of Irish and British pupils had reduced considerably.[37] This could be attributed to a number of factors, including the increased emphasis on English in the curriculum, the availability of more reading materials in schools, the increased prominence of remedial teachers and new attitudes to reading promoted in the curriculum. A fourth replication of the study in 1979 once again found a significant improvement in attainment across the whole range of reading ability.[38] At this point, the attainment gap between Irish and British pupils had reduced further and there was little difference in attainment between boys and girls. Improvements were less marked in the 1980s.[39]

However, there were also a number of reports in the 1970s that pointed to growing illiteracy among entrants to post-primary education. This was exacerbated by the increasing numbers of pupils of all abilities transferring to post-primary schools following the advent of free post-primary education and improved screening and testing facilities. The Association of Remedial Teachers of Ireland asserted that a disproportionate number of pupils over the age of thirteen were experiencing reading difficulties on entry to post-primary education, with boys scoring considerably lower than girls.[40] Kellaghan and Fontes reported that approximately 6 per cent of sixth class primary pupils and first year post-primary students were unable to cope with the reading and writing demands of the curriculum.[41] In 1978, Swan noted that 16 per cent of first year students in post-primary schools were 'backward in reading', predominantly boys.[42] A study by Connaughton and Mahoney in the mid-1980s reported that 30 per cent of pupils entering the first year of post-primary education were in need of remedial attention.[43] Forde argued that the main underdeveloped aspect of English language teaching related to oral language, especially evident in senior classes where more formal teaching styles were in evidence. This led Forde to conclude that:

> Clearly much remains to be done; the ideals set forth in the 1971 curriculum, ideals regarded as being, on the whole, forward-looking and worthwhile, are by no means fully realised in practice.[44]

Forde further asserted that textbooks 'still reign supreme in reading classes' and lamented the limited range of books used to supplement such texts.[45] Killeen posited that while English standards were improving in general, the main focus was still on reading, writing and speaking, to the neglect of important aspects such as drama, literature, poetry and fiction.[46]

In a study by Fontes *et al.*, 80 per cent of time during English lessons was found to be teacher directed, with 60 per cent of time spent on whole-class discussions, 23 per cent on individual work and 17 per cent on group work.[47] This was a particularly worrying finding and highlighted a formal and didactic approach to English teaching among teachers who responded, in conflict with the methods espoused in the curriculum. Motherway argued that the teaching of poetry as envisaged in the handbooks did not materialise, particularly that it be enjoyable and related to the interests of the child.[48] Archer and O'Flaherty found the reading levels of pupils in the inner-city of Dublin to be much lower than national standards.[49]

In general, standards in English reading improved following the introduction of the curriculum. Certain studies point to a formal and didactic approach to the teaching of English, with a reliance on textbooks evident. The research also reports an emphasis on the traditional aspects of English such as reading and writing, with a concomitant neglect of important aspects prominent within the curriculum, such as oral work, poetry, dramatic activities and recreational reading.

9.3.2 Irish

In 1972, a Committee chaired by Mr Ó Murchú of University College Cork found little continuity in teaching content and methods in the Irish language between primary and post-primary levels. It called for an increased emphasis on written work at primary level and oral work at post-primary level to bridge the divide.[50] This evidences the fact the Department was aware of the mismatch between the Buntús programme and the post-primary curriculum from the early 1970s, yet little was undertaken to bridge the divide.

In 1974, Comhairle na Gaeilge published *Irish in Education*. It asserted that the introduction of the 1971 curriculum had a negative impact on standards in Irish as it reduced the time allocation to Irish, resulting in the fact 'that the standard of Irish teaching has already dropped considerably in some schools.'[51] The report recommended that at least one subject (apart from Irish) should be taught through the medium of Irish, to enable pupils to leave school with sufficient competence to communicate, read or watch programmes in the language. Another aspect highlighted to be in need of attention was the provision of textbooks and reference books in Irish.

Lindsey reported that 74 per cent of teachers believed the five-hour allocation for Irish was being observed, while 62 per cent found this time to be sufficient.[52] While 33 per cent of teachers felt parents were supportive of the teaching of Irish, 47 per cent perceived mixed support or apathy on the part of parents and a further 18 per cent noted negativity. Greaney administered three separate attainment tests to measure reading, usage and spelling ability in Irish. The results showed an improvement in third, fourth and fifth class between 1973–1974 and 1976–1977, but a decrease in all aspects except spelling for pupils in sixth class.[53] This led to optimism in relation to improving standards in the lower classes, which were being taught using methods and approaches advocated in the curriculum. The report produced by the INTO following the second curriculum day in schools in 1976 called for greater congruence between Irish readers and the Buntús programme, noting that while reading had improved, there was a general acceptance that overall standards in Irish had disimproved. Furthermore, a revision of the Buntús programme was called for in order to shorten lessons, to make the content more interesting and relevant to children's lives and to improve the resources accompanying the programme.[54]

In 1980, the Minister for Education formed An Chomhchoiste um Oideachas sa Ghaeltacht (Joint Committee on Education in the Gaeltacht) to examine educational issues in the Gaeltacht. The Committee outlined a multiplicity of deficiencies in the education system regarding Irish, such as small and ill-equipped schools, poor training for teaching in Gaeltacht regions and the dearth of suitable textbooks and resources in Irish.[55] The report's recommendations included the appointment of a specialist Inspectorate for the Gaeltacht, providing training in modern language teaching methods, strengthening the position of Irish within the colleges of education and the preparation of suitable readers and resources in Irish. The report also called for an entirely different curriculum to be devised for the Gaeltacht:

> Ó tharla gur ceantar teanga ar leith í an Ghaeltacht molann an tÚdarás go gceapfaí Curaclam ar leith do na Scoileanna atá ag múineadh trí Ghaeilge.[56][†]

A separate report by Comhar na Múinteoirí Gaeilge on education in the Gaeltacht noted similar reservations in relation to the poor quality of the Irish books available, asserting that the majority were 'lochtach agus thar a bheith mí-oiriúnach do pháistí na Gaeltachta.'[57][‡] Similarly, the Irish syllabus was asserted to be unsuitable for pupils with a command of the language and modifications proposed included a specific reading series and oral language programme for Gaeltacht areas. No concerted action was taken on foot of the recommendations of either report.

The ERC, Institiúid Teangeolaíochta Éireann and the Department undertook the task of devising criterion-referenced tests for second, fourth and sixth class pupils based on the content of the Buntús programme. At sixth class level, less than one-third of pupils mastered each objective, a

---

†   As the Gaeltacht is a distinct linguistic region, the authority recommends that a distinct curriculum be devised for the schools that are teaching through the medium of Irish.

‡   … defective and highly unsuitable for children in the Gaeltacht.

further two-fifths made minimal progress and the remaining third had made no worthwhile progress in Irish on transfer to post-primary. Similar findings were evident for pupils in second and fourth class, with pupils in Gaeltacht areas and attending Gaelscoileanna attaining higher standards.[58] Harris also examined Canadian research, which stated that 1,200 hours of instruction were required to acquire a basic competence in a second language, 2,100 hours for a middle competence and 5,000 hours for top-level competence. Based on previous studies, Harris estimated that approximately 1,728 hours of instruction in Irish were imparted over eight years, providing for between basic and middle competency.[59] It should be remembered that a much reduced allocation of time was made available for the teaching of Irish post-1971 and the number of schools using Irish as the sole medium of instruction had reduced greatly from 620 in 1946 to 199 in 1980 (see tables 6.1 and 7.9). Consequently, Harris surmised that the mismatch was 'primarily due to the performance expectations of the Nua Chúrsaí themselves being unrealistic rather than to factors such as inadequate teaching or unsuitable courses or methods.'[60] Consonant with the findings of Ó Domhnalláin and Ó Gliasáin,[61] Harris noted higher attainment for teachers using the traditional A.B.C. approach. This substantiated the concerns of many teachers that there was an inadequate emphasis on spelling, grammar and other basics of the Irish language in the Buntús programme. While modifying the syllabus and teaching methods could achieve improvements within the existing time allocation, these alone would not close the expectation gap. Cummins also confirmed the greater tendency in other jurisdictions to teach a number of subjects through the second language, owing to greater prestige of the language and strong parental support.[62]

Bord na Gaeilge, which superseded Comhairle na Gaeilge in 1978, published a four-year *Action Plan for Irish* in 1983. In relation to education, the report asserted that insufficient time was spent teaching the language in primary schools to lead to communicative ability, having reduced from approximately 45 per cent prior to 1971 to 25 per cent of total teaching time since the curriculum was introduced. To this end, the report recommended the use of Irish as a medium of instruction for certain subjects and as a language of communication within the school.[63] A review of the syllabus to ensure an emphasis on the spoken language was proposed, as were supports for teachers to use Irish as a medium of instruction in other subjects. The training of teachers to ensure better proficiency in the language was recommended, as was a review of the provisions of the professional Irish course in the colleges of education. Again, the recommendations remained unimplemented, with the difficulties inherent in the Irish curriculum, identified since the early 1970s, continuing to hamper its delivery in schools.

Norton outlined a number of weaknesses inherent in the Buntús approach. These included the fact that it was language-centred as opposed to child-centred and that it followed the structure and grammar of the language rather than the needs and interests of the child. As it was based excessively on dialogue, it remained contrived and poorly adapted for the communicative approach. The over-reliance on the audiovisual approach did not take account of methodological advances from the 1960s and the structure allowed little time for children to use the language.[64] This finding was echoed in the CEB report, *Language in the Curriculum* (1985).[65] Ní Argáin examined three textbooks for Irish classes and concluded that all were too difficult for pupils, recommending '*tá géarghá le hathruithe sna téascleabhair Ghaeilge a sholáthraítear do pháistí bunscoile*.'[66][†]

In 1985, the INTO issued a discussion document on the Irish language. It listed impediments to the successful teaching of Irish, including state apathy, lack of public support, the unsuitability of the syllabus, the lack of suitable textbooks, the dearth of teaching aids and audiovisual equipment, the absence of a broadcasting service, the lack of in-service training, the non-alignment with the post-primary curriculum and the difficulties with dialects.[67] In 1989, the INTO issued a further discussion document on the Irish language, reiterating the call for a radical revision of the Irish curriculum, with a greater emphasis on oral Irish and on Irish culture and traditions.[68]

Attitudinal surveys of the general public became a popular monitor of the position of the Irish language in the 1970s and 1980s.[69] Overall,

---

†   … there is an urgent need for changes in the Irish textbooks provided for primary school children.

these surveys reported a growing positive attitude towards the Irish language among the Irish population over time, of support for the teaching of Irish in schools, the importance of the language as a cultural and ethnic symbol and support for providing increased state investment for the Irish language. However, the CLÁR report found that between 60 and 75 per cent of respondents were dissatisfied with the teaching of Irish within the system, as it impacted on educational progress and equipped few with a communicative ability in the language.[70] Despite this and other research into difficulties in teaching and learning the Irish language, provision continued largely unaltered in the period under review.

The overall picture regarding the implementation of Irish from this research was one of concern for the suitability of the curriculum and of falling standards. Many of the studies reported similar findings and recommendations in relation to the revision of the Buntús programme, yet no action was taken. There was an overwhelming consensus as to the need for an increased focus on oral language, to review the suitability of the objectives for each class and to ensure the programme was child- as opposed to language-centred. The unrealistic expectations of what could be achieved in the Irish language engendered a sense of failure among pupils, teachers and the public in relation to progress. Moreover, there was no action taken based on research from the early 1970s that elucidated the negative impact of the lack of alignment of primary and post-primary curricula in Irish. The recurring recommendation to teach another aspect of the curriculum through Irish was never championed and this could have added value to pupils' learning experiences with little additional cost implications. The necessity for reform of the Buntús programme was reiterated by both state and non-government organisations from the early 1970s, yet the Buntús programme as devised in the 1960s remained the core approach in Irish for both Gaeltacht and Galltacht pupils. Considering the reliance placed on the Buntús programme by the majority of teachers, the failure to act on the outcomes of numerous studies undoubtedly impacted negatively on Irish language teaching and learning during the period.

9.3.3 Mathematics

Kellaghan *et al.* looked at the mathematical achievements of entrants to post-primary education in the mid-1970s based on objectives from the mathematics curriculum. They found significant areas of weakness in relation to attainment on decimals, percentages, operations with fractions and arithmetic problems, most notably among boys. They concluded that many pupils entered post-primary schools without mastering objectives within the primary school curriculum.[71] Close *et al.* found a wide variation in achievement among fifth and sixth class pupils, with approximately half of all pupils in both classes mastering curriculum objectives.[72] Pupils scored well on computation but scored poorly on problem solving, showing this emphasis in the curriculum was not being achieved in practice.

Mulryan asserted in 1984 that there was no seismic shift to experiential aspects of mathematics learning, while computational skills did not always follow understanding.[73] Mulryan and Close found that difficult vocabulary in mathematics textbooks militated against implementation of the curriculum, with little systematic planning for the introduction or consolidation of new vocabulary.[74] In 1989, Greaney and Close reported on research in relation to mathematical attainment since 1971 and noted that while pupils showed high levels of mastery in computation, there were poorer results in relation to geometry and problem solving.[75]

In an international comparative study of nine- and thirteen-year-old pupils in 1988, Ireland attained an average score showing strengths in numbers and operations and weakness in the areas of data organisation, interpretation, measurement, geometry and abstraction.[76] Greaney and Close attributed these weaknesses to a tendency to focus on the routine aspects of mathematics as opposed to the abstract, open-ended, problem-solving and representative elements of the subject.[77] Martin reported a wide range of outcomes among sixth class pupils on a criterion-referenced test, with the median representing mastery of 52 per cent of the forty-one skills tested.[78] Consequently, many pupils were completing primary education without mastering many of the objectives of the mathematics curriculum. Consonant with other studies, the main weaknesses related to problem solving, metric measure and geometry, with high standards evident in relation to operations with whole numbers, fractions and decimals.

Collectively, these studies point to success in the mechanical and routine elements of mathematics that were emphasised prior to 1971, while aspects prioritised within the curriculum such as the development of concepts, skills and problem solving were not well implemented in practice. Moreover, great reliance continued to be placed on the textbook, while concrete materials and activity methods received less attention. Consequently, many pupils failed to master key objectives, thus highlighting a mismatch between the rhetoric of the curriculum and the reality of mathematics teaching and learning.

9.3.4 Social and Environmental Studies, History, Geography and Civics

Following the second curriculum day in schools in 1976, teachers called for more supports and resources that focused on local aspects and the provision of a graded science syllabus for use in schools.[79] Gilligan surveyed teachers in senior classes of schools in Co. Meath and found that their methodologies had changed little following 1971, with a great reliance still placed on textbooks to determine both the content and the method. Furthermore, only one-third of respondents undertook fieldwork with their pupils.[80] The main reasons cited in this regard were lack of transport, large class sizes, lack of local knowledge and time pressures. Cregan noted that the readability of history textbooks used by sixth class pupils was impaired by inappropriate style and content, compromising the ability of weaker pupils to access or enjoy the history curriculum.[81] Motherway noted that a heavy reliance was placed on the use of textbooks following 1971 in the delivery of the history curriculum, concluding that:

> In practice, therefore, the history textbook is more than a teaching aid; rather it constitutes the history curriculum. The textbook provides the content; it structures and sequences this content; it provides the assignments and forms the basis of the methodology; implicitly it provides the aims.[82]

Beggan examined the implementation of the science aspect of the curriculum and noted that it was impeded by inadequate resources, teacher apathy, inspection difficulties and an over-crowded curriculum.[83] Bennett observed that history textbooks following 1971 contained more illustrations, photographs, extracts from primary sources, elements of social history and pupil activities, yet a focus on chronology remained.[84] He also submitted that geography textbooks gradually returned to an emphasis on the learning of facts as opposed to discovery methods.[85] In 1986, the Department issued guidelines to publishers on geography, stressing the importance of ensuring textbooks were readable for mixed ability pupils, that a focus be placed on the locality of the school and that enquiry-based methods be emphasised.[86]

The Department commissioned a survey on the implementation of the social and environmental studies curriculum among a cohort of teachers who had attended in-service training on the subject in 1989. The study found overall satisfaction with the syllabus but noted a number of aspects that impacted negatively on implementation, including a dearth of school-based resources, a lack of knowledge on local areas and difficulties in conducting field trips.[87] The report also placed a major emphasis on the importance of pre-service and in-service education in relation to both content and methodologies.

These studies show a discrepancy between the curriculum as envisaged and as implemented. The textbook remained a dominant force in the teaching of history and geography, with a consequent neglect of aspects of local importance within the range of experiences afforded to pupils. This was also apparent in relation to social and environmental studies, with little evidence of the use of field trips or studies on the immediate environment of pupils. Local history was often supported in theory, although practical implementation was not a widespread feature of practice. There were no significant studies relating to the implementation of civics, highlighting the low importance attached to the subject in practice.

9.3.5 The Arts

The paucity of research in relation to music, and particularly art and craft, is indicative of the low priority afforded to these subjects within schools throughout this period. In 1971, Fleischmann lauded the provisions of the music curriculum introduced but noted the impracticability in relation to implementation, asserting that only 500 to 1,000 teachers would be capable of immediate implementation, while for the remainder, 'it would take a major effort and some drastic changes to bring them about.'[88] At the second curriculum day in schools in 1976, teachers reported a lack of confidence in the teaching of music and art and craft, requesting in-service courses, improved equipment and resources, specialist teachers and a series of graded lessons to assist implementation.[89]

Benson argued in 1979 that the potential benefits of the arts sub-jects in the curriculum were not being realised due to a lack of training and confidence on the part of teachers as identified by major evaluations of the curriculum in the 1970s.[90] Herron conducted a study for the Arts Council into the provision of music education in schools in the mid-1980s. Among the overarching defects noted were the lack of alignment between the music curriculum at primary and post-primary levels, the paucity of money for equipment, the dearth of musical expertise among teachers and inspectors, and the lack of use of educational broadcasting.[91] In the introduction to the report, Benson stated the research outcomes provided a conclusive judgement that the overall situation in relation to music was 'little short of appalling.'[92]

In a study by Meany on the music curriculum, pupils were found to be experiencing difficulty in singing in intervals and in reading pitch, rhyme and rhythm.[93] Barriers to implementation of the curriculum identified included lack of time, lack of resources, an absence of in-service training and a lack of confidence and competence, with only 50 per cent of respond-ents to her survey considering themselves to be musically literate. O'Flynn reported similar results in relation to the experiences of pupils in music, including a paucity of musical materials and a lack of variety in the way pupils experienced music.[94] The INTO Education Committee produced a *Discussion Paper on the Arts in Education* in 1989, proposing a number of recommendations, such as in-service education for teachers, the appointment of peripatetic teachers and the provision of financial resources and facilities to schools.[95]

The overall findings from the limited research available reveal a certain lack of implementation in relation to music and art and craft. Studies report that teachers felt the curriculum in these subjects was too complex and in the absence of in-service training and supports, proved too difficult for many to implement. Consequently, the full range of experiences as envisaged in the curriculum was not provided to all pupils in either subject area.

9.3.6 Physical Education

There was limited research into the position of physical education in schools. Cotter investigated the implementation of the physical education curriculum in 1978 with a nationwide sample of 10 per cent of national schools. He found a large disparity in the availability of physical education equipment, with smaller rural schools the least well equipped.[96] Seventy per cent of schools surveyed had no general purpose room and lacked necessary equipment. Approximately 50 per cent of teachers expressed dissatisfaction with the quality of the training they received in the colleges of education. Less than 3 per cent of teachers surveyed followed the syllabus for physical education provided in the handbooks, while close to 74 per cent of respondents believed the syllabus was unrealistic. The element of the syllabus most taught was games, while orienteering and dance featured least prominently. The overall analysis led Cotter to conclude there was significant divergence between the theory and practice of the curriculum and that 'only half of the children in our National Schools are exposed to regular weekly Physical Education lessons.'[97] Donoghue listed a number of challenges in relation to the implementation of health education, including a lack of focus on the subject in pre-service and in-service training, a lack of resources and facilities, and large class sizes.[98]

The one significant study by Cotter in relation to physical education shows a huge dichotomy between the syllabus advocated in the handbooks and its actual implementation. The syllabus was not accompanied by a strategy to improve facilities and equipment in schools or a concerted effort to upskill teachers. The majority of teachers surveyed ignored the official curriculum in the absence of materials and confidence to implement it, while other teachers operated the least complex elements of its provisions within the confines of available facilities and expertise. In reality, most pupils did not receive a comprehensive physical education programme as envisaged in the curriculum during the period.

9.4 Thematic Studies regarding Implementation

A number of studies that span a range of subject areas and themes, such as infant education, methodologies, equipment and materials, and the alignment of primary and post-primary curricula, are detailed in this section. In tandem with other studies, these provide a vivid insight into the implementation of particular aspects of the curriculum.

9.4.1 Evaluations of Infant Education

The INTO held discussions with the Inspectorate in 1983–1984 regarding complaints from teachers that inspectors were demanding more formal teaching practices in infant classes than the curriculum envisaged.[99] The INTO also criticised the common practice of using infant classes as 'training grounds for young and inexperienced teachers', with 69 per cent of new graduates teaching infants in their first year in 1983–1984.[100]

Ní Mhaoldomhnaigh conducted a study on the implementation of the mathematics curriculum at infant level, based on a test designed from the curriculum. Approximately half of the classrooms examined used ability grouping for the teaching of mathematics. Ní Mhaoldomhnaigh found that two-thirds of pupils had mastered two-thirds of the objectives, with the areas of sorting, addition, time and pictograms scoring high, while performance was poorer on length, weight and capacity.[101] The question-naires revealed that few teachers spent the recommended three hours per week on mathematics, with a significant focus on written work as opposed to oral work.

In 1987, O'Rourke and Archer conducted a questionnaire study of teaching practices in infant classes and first class. The 581 questionnaires returned revealed that language teaching was formal, especially beyond junior infants. Most time was dedicated to reading and writing, with many teachers using a graded reading scheme.[102] A similar trend was also evident in relation to mathematics, with the emphasis on developing mathematical concepts reducing from 85 per cent of teachers in junior infants to 48 per cent of teachers in first class. While approximately 80 per cent of teachers surveyed grouped their pupils for certain subjects, they spent little time in meaningful group work and there was little opportunity for child-initiated activity. This was evidenced by the fact 45 per cent of time was allocated to whole-class teaching, with only 11 per cent of time allowed for child-led activities. This led the authors to conclude that 'the junior classes in Irish primary schools are, to a large extent, teacher-directed and "traditional."'[103] Higgins surveyed infant class teachers in Dublin in relation to their atti-tudes to the infant curriculum in 1987. Respondents reported large class sizes and the brevity of the two-year infant cycle as the main impediments to implementing the infant curriculum.[104]

Stapleton expressed concern at the involvement of children as young as four years of age in formal learning within the school system. Furthermore, methods used in Ireland did not compare well to the activity, discovery and play-based approaches used in other jurisdictions, or as proposed in the 1971 curriculum.[105] Her research with a sample of infant teachers in Dublin found support for change within infant education, with 72 per cent asserting the need for a new syllabus for infants. In addition, 97 per cent agreed the first year in infant classes should be more informal in nature, with 65 per cent espousing the view that the curriculum was too academic in nature. Furthermore, the organisation and provisions of infant classrooms did not facilitate a play-based and informal approach to learning, with 77 per cent of classrooms having no sand tray and 79 per cent having no play area. Moreover, 65 per cent of teachers agreed infants were confined to their seats for most parts of the day. However, it is arguable that the curriculum already allowed and even promoted a more informal approach in infant classes, yet many teachers showed a reluctance to embrace new methodologies that promoted such informal and active learning. Kelleher investigated the implementation of the curriculum in infant classes in South Dublin schools. She found that infant teachers did not generally understand the curriculum and called for a revision of the handbooks, considering their lack of influence on classroom practice.[106]

Horgan studied the degree of implementation of the 1971 curriculum in infant classes through the use of an observational schedule and interviews. This methodology is noteworthy and offers an insight into practice that many questionnaire studies do not reveal. The study focused on the use of play for developing cognitive, social, linguistic, creative and physical aspects of the child. Horgan found few instances of stimulating free play for pupils, while 70 per cent of school time was devoted to 'empty, waiting or watching activities.'[107] There was also a low incidence of pupils speaking in the classrooms observed, with teachers speaking for 56 per cent of the time, children for 15 per cent of the time and silence pertaining for 19 per cent of the time. Pupil-pupil interactions in pairs and small groups remained infrequent, with most tasks being teacher directed and requiring low levels of movement from pupils. This resulted in 47 per cent of time being spent passively in large groups, 16 per cent interacting within large groups, 15 per cent passive in small groups, 2 per cent interacting in small groups, 15 per cent interacting in pairs and 5 per cent alone. The majority of desks were arranged in traditional rows, despite the fact that 70 per cent of classrooms had modern, moveable furniture. The main obstacles to teachers making more use of play were found to be the attitude of the teacher, high pupil-teacher ratios and availability of equipment. This observational study corroborated previous research findings in relation to the formal and didactic nature of infant class teaching during the period.

While many evaluations asserted that the principles of the *Primary School Curriculum* (1971) were best implemented in the infant and junior classes, studies that focused specifically on these classes recorded a high degree of formality in teaching and learning. Pupils in infant classes were found to spend long periods of time being taught formally in whole-class contexts, with little engagement in purposeful activity. Furthermore, the tendency to appoint young and inexperienced teachers to infant classes continued throughout this period, a practice that reduced the experience and expertise available in these critical years of formation. While many impediments to implementation were reported such as the overcrowded nature of the infant curriculum, the low level of facilities, equipment and materials available to support an informal approach to teaching, and the preponderance of large classes, teachers' dispositions and attitudes were arguably an important factor in preventing a more progressive and child-centred approach within infant classes. The handbooks were seen to have little impact on practice and the full potential of the curriculum for infant classes was not realised.

9.4.2 Methodologies

Cloonan investigated teachers' practice in relation to the aims of the curriculum among a cohort of teachers in Galway in 1981. Most teachers felt they were implementing most features of the curriculum but a low incidence of use of nature walks and project-work was reported. Moreover, the majority of teachers expressed satisfaction with the Teacher's Handbooks, especially in relation to mathematics and English, while they also reported that the curriculum had led to a more child-centred approach.[108]

Egan investigated the incidence of using informal approaches, which were a key feature of the 1971 curriculum. The study found, consonant with other studies, widespread acceptance of this principle underpinning the curriculum, yet only two-thirds of teachers in junior classes and one-third of teachers in senior classes used an informal approach.[109] Conversely, there was a prevalence of didactic teaching, especially in the middle and senior grades, particularly among older teachers and by male teachers. In a follow-up study in 1982, Egan found that teachers who used an informal approach were less successful in achieving high results in both Irish and English in standardised tests. However, he cautioned that informal methods could teach aspects not assessed by such tests, which put a great emphasis on spelling, grammar and punctuation.[110] Gash asserted that based on the research conducted in relation to the implementation of the curriculum and teachers' attitudes towards it, 'there is not much which is radically progressive going on in Irish classes.'[111]

Burke and Fontes analysed the educational beliefs and teaching practices of sixth class teachers in the mid-1980s. They concluded from their analysis that many sixth class pupils experienced a highly structured, teacher-controlled and traditional education.[112] This was evidenced by the fact the majority of pupils were assigned seats and were not permitted to move freely around the classroom, while 86 per cent of teachers expected silence most of the time. Further evidence of the formal approach to teaching was substantiated by the fact that only 29 per cent of teachers took their pupils on trips and 66 per cent taught basic skills through textbooks. Teachers in the study spent the majority of their time on whole-class teaching, 18 per cent on teacher-directed individual work, 15 per cent on teacher-directed group work and only 7 per cent on individual work based on the child's choice. Overall, eighteen of the twenty-five hours were spent on instruction in Irish, English, mathematics and religion, with 93 per cent of time being teacher-directed.

This level of formality was higher than that found in previous studies and was consistent across all types and locations of schools, especially boys' schools. The study also revealed an inconsistency between expressed beliefs and practice, as many respondents expressed their support for an integrated curriculum, a child-centred approach and discovery learning. Sugrue made a comparison of teacher styles between the Burke and Fontes study in the Irish context and a Bennett study in the UK, concluding that Irish teachers were consistently more formal in their teaching approaches.[113] This study confirmed the mismatch between teachers' expressed values and actions in relation to the curriculum and portrayed a highly structured and formal approach to learning for sixth class pupils. Sugrue argued in 1990 that education in Ireland was more 'child-conscious' than child-centred in relation to its application.[114]

The INTO Education Committee conducted a study on school texts in 1989. It evidenced the inordinate influence of the textbook on teachers, with textbooks in use by over 90 per cent of teachers for all subjects except social and environmental studies. Workbooks were also employed for an array of subjects. Textbooks and workbooks exceeded by far the impact of the Teacher's Handbooks and the School Plan on the curriculum.[115]

Overall, these studies corroborated earlier findings of the prevalence of formal and didactic approaches to teaching in both infant and senior classes, despite an acceptance in theory by teachers responding to the principles integral to the *Primary School Curriculum* (1971). This provides a picture of the reality of practice in classrooms, which lacks resonance with the rhetoric of the curriculum or with the reported endorsement of its principles by teachers.

9.4.3 Equipment and Materials

A survey by Kellaghan and Gorman in 1968 revealed the poor availability of equipment and materials in schools, albeit a small improvement on that reported in *Investment in Education* in 1965. While 66 per cent of schools had a library, the majority were inadequately stocked, with an average of one book per child in towns and cities and considerably less provision in rural areas (where access to public library facilities was also more difficult). Only 16 per cent of schools had mathematics equipment, while 20 per cent had materials to teach art and craft.[116] McMahon found a similar paucity of equipment and materials in a Dublin school in 1973, concluding that:

> Though the curriculum advocates discovery and exploration by the children, there is no desk equipment for the children to use.[117]

Despite the importance attached to the school library within the curriculum, grant provision in the mid-1980s rested at a mere 25p per book, when the average cost of a library book was £3.75.[118] An INTO study in 1982 reported the majority of schools did not have adequate library facilities, a general-purpose room or adequate playing areas.[119] Even in 1990, the provision of equipment and materials to schools was not uniform. In a representative sample of 11 per cent of primary schools, the NPC-P found that 53 per cent of schools had televisions, 51 per cent had videos, 48 per cent had computers, 89 per cent had a projector, 95 per cent had a tape recorder, 81 per cent had a photocopier and 68 per cent had a telephone.[120]

9.4.4 Alignment between Primary and Post-primary Curricula

The lack of alignment between primary and post-primary curricula became a recurrent complaint from many quarters during this period. Even close to the inception of the curriculum, Sr Columba, President of the Conference of Convent Primary Schools, noted the 'traumatic' experience transfer from primary to post-primary education involved for many pupils and advocated greater communication to ensure a smooth transition.[121] At the 1972 Conference of Convent Secondary Schools, Minister Faulkner asserted the need to revise the system of entrance examinations to post-primary schools to ensure improved equality of opportunity for pupils.[122] From 1967, pupils were transferring to post-primary schools at a younger age, those of lower ability were also attending and their preparation for the format and content of the curriculum at second level was seen to be inadequate. Murphy also raised the question of continuity between primary and post-primary education, asserting the impossibility of attaining uniform standards in a context where 'the child works at his own pace and "discovers" for himself, where how children learn is more important than what they learn and where they explore their environment and rejoice in a flexible timetable.'[123] He criticised the notion of extending the primary school philosophy into post-primary education, asserting its inappropriateness even for the senior classes of primary schools.

The INTO submitted a report to the Department entitled *Educational Alignment* in 1973, asserting that a pupil taught meticulously under the 1971 curriculum would fail an entrance examination to a post-primary school, calling for a revision or abolition of such examinations to prevent a reversion to traditional methods of teaching in senior classes.[124] The necessity of examining curriculum alignment was also raised in the INTO submission to the White Paper in 1979, when the establishment of a council for curriculum studies was proposed.[125]

Crooks and Griffin addressed the transitional difficulties for primary pupils entering post-primary education owing to the differences in content and methodologies, and in the absence of effective communication and information sharing.[126] Rather than allocating sole responsibility to the introduction of the 1971 curriculum for the perceived decline in standards, Murphy posited that the increased tendency for pupils who traditionally would not have transferred to post-primary schools to continue their education affected overall standards.[127] Crooks and McKernan found that 40 per cent of post-primary principals in a study asserted the need to raise the age of transfer to post-primary schools, while 87 per cent felt the need for closer alignment between the two curricula through improved communication.[128] A seminar was held in 1979 to articulate some of the challenges inherent in the mismatch between the primary and post-primary curricula. O'Connor, Head of Education at Mary Immaculate College, noted the reciprocal lack of awareness on the part of primary and post-primary teachers, accentuated by the differences in the underlying philosophy of education at each level.[129] Barry asserted that the nature of post-primary education provided was unsuitable for the majority of pupils who transferred and called for greater communication and harmonisation between primary and post-primary curricula.[130]

In 1981, a Ministerial Committee reported 'on the problems of transition from child-centred primary to subject-centred post-primary schools.'[131] This committee investigated and made recommendations on three main aspects, namely, curriculum content and methodology, professional and in-service training and communication between the various levels. In relation to the curriculum, the report asserted, somewhat surprisingly, that curriculum continuity was already a feature of the system, identifying some slight problems in Irish, geography and mathematics:

> In fact, most of the syllabi on either side which are prescribed by the Department of Education seem to fit in very well with each other. Where they may not appear to do so, it is easy for a school, as it sees fit, to make the necessary adjustments.[132]

This conclusion is surprising considering the underlying inherent difference in the child-centred philosophy of education at primary level and the subject-centred approach at second level. The report recommended that the Department ensure representation of post-primary interests in the review of aspects of the primary curriculum, and *vice versa*, to ensure improved alignment. The report further proposed a special focus around the transition of pupils with emotional, intellectual, social or physical problems, for improved communication between both levels at transfer time and for the issue to be addressed within pre-service and in-service teacher training.

Continuity between primary and post-primary curricula was also cited as an issue in the CEB publication, *Primary Education*, which identified the need for greater alignment between primary and post-primary curricula and for the transfer of data on pupils from primary to post-primary schools.[133] Burke traced the separate traditions and philosophies within which primary and post-primary education had developed in Ireland, with their own structures, curriculum, teacher qualifications, salaries, Inspectorates and management structures.[134] He attributed a wash-back effect from post-primary education as the main factor for using a more formal approach in senior classes of primary schools. The Primary Education Review Body report recommended greater alignment between the two curricula and that entrance examinations should not be held while pupils were in primary school.[135] In 1991, the OECD commented on the separate treatment of curricula at primary and post-primary level and the need for greater planning to reduce problems upon transition.[136]

The lack of congruence was a result of the compartmentalised nature of devising the curriculum for primary and post-primary schools, even though both were devised by the same Department and over the same period of time. Studies from the early 1970s identified the problems this posed for implementation of the curriculum and commentators continued to reiterate these challenges over the next two decades. Despite this, no affirmative action was taken to reduce the barriers or to ameliorate the situation, which arguably contributed to the formal nature of the teaching methodologies used in senior classes of primary schools and to the qualitative difference in the experience of pupils upon transition to post-primary schooling.

9.4.5 Miscellaneous Thematic Studies

Research in relation to the public's attitudes to education in the mid-1970s reported that 80 per cent of respondents believed schools had improved since their schooldays.[137] However, there was agreement that there was still a greater emphasis on cognitive goals to the neglect of cultural, aesthetic and personal elements of education. Kellaghan *et al.* conducted a further attitudinal survey in 1980 to determine public opinion on the reforms in education since the 1960s. The majority of respondents were in favour of the changes introduced, especially the raising of the school leaving age and the changes in school management.[138]

McMahon, in a case study of one school in Dublin in 1973, noted parental preference for focusing on the essentials of literacy and numeracy within the curriculum, with a disregard for affective-oriented subjects.[139] The pressure on teachers to focus on the cognitive domain in the absence of parental understanding of the underlying philosophy of the curriculum was also noted. In McMahon's research, teachers felt largely unsupported in relation to the implementation of the curriculum, noting that while principals attended in-service courses, many teachers (most particularly those trained in traditional methods) received the Teacher's Handbooks without mediation in the form of a structured and universally available in-service programme. A further problem regarding implementation was posited as being an absence of ways in which to evaluate progress in the new methods, with many teachers and inspectors still using traditional methods to assess the new approach. Horgan reviewed the curriculum in 1973, stating it had assumed a low profile following its introduction in 1971. He outlined many of the challenges facing the implementation of the vision of the curriculum. He called for the necessary investment for its implementation to be made available, especially in relation to in-service education for teachers, as otherwise, the educational reform 'is doomed to failure, or, at best, stagnation.'[140]

Walsh conducted a questionnaire study to assess implementation of the curriculum based on the 'knowledge', 'acceptance' and 'action' of teachers in thirty schools in Wicklow.[141] An overwhelming majority of teachers felt the need for and welcomed the curriculum changes introduced in

1971. Overall, a high level of 'knowledge' of the principles was reported but respondents were somewhat uncertain as to what exactly the curriculum demanded of them. A total of 87 per cent of teachers also reported a high degree of 'acceptance' of using the local environment and 65 per cent agreed group work was more productive than classroom teaching. In relation to 'action', teachers reported less impact on their practice than on their knowledge and acceptance of the curriculum. This illustrates the mismatch between the endorsement of curriculum principles and their implementation, a feature of many of the attitudinal surveys conducted during this period.

Walsh also examined the relationship between the amount of in-service training attended and found no significant correlation to the knowledge, acceptance or action of teachers. While older teachers attended more in-service, they still reported the least feeling of success in implementing the curriculum. This highlights the difficulty teachers trained in traditional methodologies experienced in undertaking more progressive methods in the absence of a comprehensive support system. Walsh concluded that teachers' planning and recording of progress remained largely unaffected following the introduction of the 1971 curriculum. It is interesting that in this study, similar to the INTO (1976), the curriculum itself was not perceived to be a resource of ideas. In general, teachers were content with their level of implementing the curriculum, with 4 per cent believing they had been very successful, 49 per cent rating themselves as successful and 8 per cent as unsuccessful. Thirty-four per cent were unable to judge their performance in implementation, which is interesting and may be related to the absence of specific objectives within the curriculum.

Walsh's findings mirror those already analysed in the 1970s. While teachers were generally aware of the principles of the curriculum and agreed with them, the reality of their practice did not bear this out and many lacked the competence and confidence to implement core aspects of the curriculum. While the lack of resources and in-service training legitimately did hinder aspects of implementation, they cannot be held responsible for the lack of progress in relation to planning, recording and introducing certain elements of the curriculum. It is arguable that considering the high calibre of teachers in the era, other factors such as teacher conservatism and a reluctance to extend habitual practices impacted negatively on the introduction of certain aspects of the curriculum.

9.5 Overview of the Subject Areas

Evaluations of the implementation of English were practically unanimous in agreeing that the standard in English improved following the introduction of the *Primary School Curriculum* (1971). This is particularly evident in the areas of reading, while there was some concern about the maintenance of standards in pupils' written work and attainment in spelling. Research continued to evidence improved reading standards in comparative tests throughout the 1970s, reducing previously wide gaps between Irish pupils' reading ability and that of their British counterparts. However, there is evidence that the main focus in English remained on the core areas of reading and writing, with little emphasis on oral work, dramatic activities and poetry for the majority of pupils. Improved diagnostic testing and a concern for pupils that were under-achieving led to a greater focus on pupils who were not attaining basic literacy in primary schools. However, despite increased provision of remedial teachers and ancillary supports, studies revealed that many pupils continued to transfer to post-primary schools with literacy difficulties that would impede their subsequent educational progress.

A converse picture is evident for the progress of Irish in the same period, for which concerns were raised and doubts cast in relation to pupil progress. Evaluations overwhelmingly pointed to a disimprovement in many elements of the language, especially written work and particularly in senior classes. Reading was seen to have improved somewhat, while the position of oral language ability was ambiguous following conflicting evaluations, where pupils scored better on listening as opposed to speaking skills. Numerous commentators questioned the suitability of the standards expected from the study of Irish in primary schools, the effectiveness of the methodologies in use, the appropriateness of the language-centred Buntús programme within the child-centred curriculum, and the usefulness of many of the resources available for teaching Irish. A large minority of pupils failed to master the objectives of the Buntús programme and many left primary school without mastering the rudimentary elements of the language. The limitations of the Buntús programme were cited from its inception by its devisers, while numerous reports in the 1970s provided recommendations for its revision to ensure greater success in practice. The overemphasis on dialogue as opposed to narrative, the time constraints on implementing the five steps on a weekly basis, the lack of emphasis on grammar and other structures of the language and the rarity of using ancillary resources such as tapes and filmstrips, reduced the potential of the method to improve standards in practice. The Buntús programme was never revised or modernised in light of experience so that by 1990, it proved to be outdated, uninteresting and sexist in the contemporary context.

Mathematics education in this period produced mixed results. There was some consensus that pupils' understanding of mathematical concepts improved during the period, yet this was accompanied by a disimprovement in aspects such as computation and memorisation. Despite these findings, there was still concern in the 1980s about an overemphasis on the routine aspects of mathematics learning such as computation and mechanical operations, with a consequent neglect of elements such as problem solving, interpretation and abstraction emphasised in the curriculum. There were numerous calls in the period for more emphasis to be placed on the use of concrete materials, activity methods and interactive oral work in teaching mathematics, while the inordinate influence of the textbook was bemoaned by many commentators. Overall, studies showed that many pupils transferred to post-primary education without having mastered numerous skills and objectives inherent in the primary school mathematics curriculum.

There was an improved emphasis on social and environmental studies, history, geography and civics following 1971. While there was an enhanced focus on social history in this period, many evaluations lamented the chronological approach to history still pursued and the excessive reliance placed on the textbook for the presentation of material. Similarly, the increased prominence attached to human geography as opposed to the recall of facts was praised, yet the over-reliance on textbooks was seen to cause reversion to rote learning and memorisation. Another unanimous grievance with both history and geography was the neglect of the local environment of the pupil and school, which the curriculum stressed as being of paramount importance in setting the agenda for much of the content in these subjects. Numerous studies evidenced that fieldwork or trips beyond the immediate environs of the classroom were not a regular feature of either subject. Civics was noted to be particularly neglected in practice. In addition, many evaluations signalled the integration of social and environmental studies with other aspects of the curriculum, yet acknowledged that there was little incidence of linkage within subjects such as history, geography and civics.

The implementation of the music curriculum remained a recurrent difficulty following 1971. Evaluations noted teachers' perceptions that the syllabus was designed for music specialists as opposed to ordinary teachers, causing a lack of competence and confidence in implementation. Despite this, studies confirmed some degree of success in relation to aspects such as song singing and pitch. However, accomplishment in many aspects such as sight-reading and mastery of intervals remained low, while many other elements of the prescribed syllabus were not attempted widely in practice. Moreover, many evaluations pointed to an overemphasis on the expressive aspects of the subject, with little time afforded to the appreciation of music. Recurrent concerns and complaints of teachers regarding the implementation of music included the lack of expertise they held in the subject and the paucity of funding for musical equipment and materials.

The implementation of physical education posed many challenges for teachers, despite the laudable aims and guidelines in the handbooks. Studies almost unanimously evidenced poor levels of implementation of this subject in primary schools. The principal explanation for this situation was the unrealistic nature of the physical education programme relative to the available facilities and equipment in schools and teacher expertise in the area. The physical reality of many schools was that they lacked either indoor or outdoor facilities for physical education and few schools had an adequate supply of equipment and materials to implement the ambitious syllabus. Coupled with this was the poor knowledge base and proficiency of the majority of teachers in the subject. This led to a situation whereby routine and standard aspects of the curriculum were implemented in some schools, primarily games, with few teachers attempting core areas suggested such as dance or orienteering. Overall, the syllabus as defined in the handbooks was largely ignored by teachers. Health education was an element of the physical education syllabus that also remained perennially neglected during this period.

The inclusion of art and craft activities represented one of the most novel elements of the 1971 curriculum from its predecessor. While teachers generally welcomed its presence within the curriculum, many lacked the confidence and felt unprepared for its implementation. This led to a preponderance of activities in routine aspects such as painting, with few instances of implementing aspects such as construction and appreciation. Teachers also complained about the lack of facilities and materials provided for implementing this subject, which further restricted the range of elements attempted. Similar to the experience in music, evaluations signalled a focus on the expressive as opposed to appreciative elements of the subject. Moreover, little use was made of local and national resources such as museums and galleries to extend pupils' appreciation of the arts in wider society.

9.6 Summary and Conclusion

The *Primary School Curriculum* (1971) represented a radical difference in nature and content from its predecessor. Its five principles were widely endorsed by teachers throughout this period. However, there was a dichotomy between their endorsement in theory and their implementation in practice and the evidence points to a low level of practical implementation of these curriculum principles. As Sugrue stated, while teachers endorsed progressive ideology, 'when data on actual practice are isolated from these studies teachers seem to endorse a child-centred rhetoric while practising a more formal pedagogical style.'[142] This dichotomy between teachers' perceptions that they were implementing the curriculum and the reality of their practice remained an issue throughout the period from 1971 to 1990. As O'Leary concluded:

> Consciously or unconsciously, therefore, what has been happening in Irish Primary schools over the past nineteen years is not what was intended in 1971.[143]

This related not only to the emphasis placed on subjects within the curriculum, but also to the failure to employ many of the newer methodologies and teaching strategies advocated by the curriculum. One immediately evident example was the neglect to use the local environment as a basis of or resource for learning, with few incidences of pupils being facilitated to engage or interact with the wider environs of the school. Furthermore, the shift in teaching methodologies from rote learning and didactic methods in a class situation to one of activity and discovery learning in groups and individually did not become common practice, with the majority of pupils continuing to be taught in a structured and formal manner. While there is some evidence of cross-curriculum work being implemented, the level of integration advocated by the handbooks was never achieved and the curriculum remained in essence subject-based rather than an integrated entity. The vision in the handbooks for subjects such as art and craft, music and physical education, was not realised, despite the support for the principle of full and harmonious development. Moreover, there was a low incidence of the use of individual and group work in classrooms and an over-reliance on textbooks, despite an endorsement of the principle of individual difference. A didactic method of teaching predominated with little opportunity for time spent outside the classroom, despite support for the principle of activity and discovery learning. As the OECD concluded in 1991:

> Despite the vision and thoroughness of the 1971 primary schools curriculum proposals and the many practical innovations since carried through by dedicated teachers, the evidence suggests that emphasis is still largely on a didactic approach and often, in later primary years, in a relatively narrow range of subject matter.[144]

Some wider developments within the education system impacted positively on the implementation of the curriculum, including longer pre-service training and some provision of in-service education, the allocation of posts of responsibility and improvements in school buildings and environments. Moreover, there were more remedial teachers and single stream classes, and increased provision for pupils with special educational needs and for those affected by disadvantage.

Despite these many positive advances, the level of implementation varied from school to school. While it is not surprising or indicative of failure that all aspects of the curriculum were not implemented from 1971, it is of concern that so many aspects of its provisions did not become common practice in classrooms in the subsequent decades. Many constraints on implementation were in evidence prior to the introduction of the curriculum and communicated in submissions by a multiplicity of organisations to the Department. From 1971, these impeded the full implementation of the curriculum and diluted the aspirations of the curriculum designers as outlined in the handbooks. Impediments that recurred in much of the research throughout the era included large classes, the small number of ancillary staff, the under-resourcing of the Inspectorate, the inadequate provision of equipment and materials, the poor provision of psychological and remedial services, the dated nature of many school buildings, the lack of facilities and materials for many subject areas, and the inadequate and uncoordinated nature of in-service education. Problems in the implementation of the core traditional subjects were also evident, as many teachers found it difficult to modify their teaching styles and methodologies in line with the vision of the curriculum. A number of other pertinent factors included the lack of alignment with post-primary education, the lack of information for parents and the public on the nature and content of the curriculum, the paucity of information available on the local environment of schools, the failure to evaluate comprehensively the overall implementation of the curriculum on an ongoing basis and to act on such findings, and the lack of clarity in relation to aims and objectives for various subject areas within the curriculum. These were exacerbated by the fact there was no concerted plan for implementing the curriculum, with some of its provisions unrealistic in the societal and educational context of the time.

Drafting a curriculum is the first stage in the implementation process. The content of the curriculum had implications for the provision of necessary resources to ensure implementation. While some progress on these aspects was evident between 1968 and 1973, funding for such resources remained contingent on the economic situation, which was largely characterised by retrenchment and regression in the period. Furthermore, the lack of provision of equipment and materials for subjects focusing on the creative, aesthetic and physical aspects of development was a critical reason for their lack of implementation in practice. The lack of basic requisites, including library books, concrete materials and physical space, impacted negatively on the introduction of certain elements of subjects or prevented the use of more progressive methodologies for their implementation. Furthermore, this often affected rural schools, considering the capitation basis on which grants were paid, and disadvantaged schools, owing to the difficulty of raising funds locally to purchase such equipment, thus exacerbating inequalities within the system. In the absence of such materials, an inordinate reliance was placed on textbooks as a resource, which consequently affected the envisaged implementation of the curriculum.

Unequivocally, the nature of teacher education and the provision of in-service education was a major constraint on the implementation of the curriculum. With the inception of a degree course for teachers in the mid-1970s, pre-service training was considered adequate, albeit with some complaints such as a lack of focus on certain subjects within the colleges of education. It was the demand for in-service education that remained an ongoing entreaty throughout the period, a request that was never addressed in any co-ordinated or comprehensive manner. The absence of a strategic national policy for in-service education perpetuated the lack of expertise and confidence among teachers in implementing certain aspects of the curriculum, most notably music, physical education and art and craft. Moreover, Teachers' Centres never fulfilled their envisaged role in the provision of in-service education. Furthermore, in-service education was not always successful in changing teaching styles and approaches, and many teachers did not succeed in deviating from their traditional methods.

As 'experts' designed many of the syllabi, there was a high or even unrealistic expectation regarding the ability and expertise of generalist teachers in their implementation. The feeling of inadequacy this lack of confidence engendered affected the morale of many teachers in relation to their overall capacity, and may have tainted their general attitude towards the curriculum. In turn, there was a dearth of objective criteria for teachers to evaluate their own performance, which led to uncertainty and unease about their own professional performance. Consequently, the Teacher's Handbooks became redundant in the practice of many teachers and did not act as a resource in curriculum implementation on a daily basis as envisaged. This, allied with the inordinate influence and reliance on the textbook in classroom teaching, meant it was the textbook and publishers rather than the handbooks and the Department that determined the nature and content of the curriculum in practice.

However, the paucity of in-service training and resources alone does not explain why many aspects of the curriculum were not implemented, especially around the introduction of certain subject areas. Based on the findings of studies, it is probable that many teachers reverted to traditional methods and approaches in the core subjects and failed to embrace the implementation of newly introduced subjects. It is arguable that intelligent and interested professionals need not have depended so largely on external provision of in-service education. Indeed, the residential courses in 1973 provided a cohort of teachers in each inspection district with the skills to upskill other teachers through study groups and lectures at a local level. It is likely that other factors such as professional conservatism and a lack of confidence to engage with new ideas and processes also impacted negatively on implementation.

The issue of large class sizes was a recurrent theme following the introduction of the curriculum. A considerable proportion of pupils was also taught in multi-class contexts, militating further against implementation. Considering the importance assigned within the Teacher's Handbooks to individual and group work, to catering for individual differences and to using activity- and discovery-based methods, it was unrealistic to expect the widespread adoption of such methodologies in the context of such high pupil-teacher ratios. The educational demographics of the period resulted in a large increase in the pupil population, making it difficult to target money towards educational improvement in an era that was primarily characterised by economic recession.

The lack of alignment between the curriculum at primary and post-primary level was raised from the inception of the 1971 curriculum through to 1990, with little resolution of the issue achieved in the interim. The omission of post-primary representation from consultation with interested parties in the late 1960s limited the understanding of post-primary interests of the rationale or nature of curriculum reforms, broke the link in curriculum continuity and exacerbated the perception of falling standards. The problem arose as a child-centred curriculum, proposing a focus on individual needs and abilities up to sixth class, was followed by a subject-centred and exam-focused system at post-primary level. Post-primary educationalists perceived a decline in standards from the early 1970s and attributed the responsibility to the new curriculum, when arguably the enrolment of cohorts of pupils that previously would not have transferred to post-primary education was a major factor. Despite a changed focus within the curriculum, numerous evaluations pointed to the ongoing use of formal styles of teaching in both junior and senior classes of primary schools.

Beyond the booklet issued to parents in 1969, there was little ongoing effort on the Department's part to inform and educate parents and the general public as to the provisions of the curriculum. Many of the principles and concepts were new to parents and the wider public in the 1970s and communication could have led to a better understanding of the rationale and nature of the changes and fostered a more positive attitude to implementation. In the absence of information, predictably, parents relied on their knowledge and experiences of the education system to frame expectations for their children's progress. This led to much criticism and concern regarding perceived falling standards in the core areas and a disregard for many of the additional subjects, such as music, art and craft, social and environmental studies and physical education. To some extent, parental demands for an education more congruent with their expectations and experiences flavoured teachers' attitudes and impacted on classroom practice, leading to an increased emphasis on cognitive aspects of the curriculum and to a more formal approach to teaching.

The absence of ancillary and periphery supports for teachers in the implementation of the curriculum proved detrimental. In an increasingly complex educational environment, expectations were placed on teachers to introduce additional subject areas, to cater for pupils with special educational needs and to alleviate the effects of disadvantage on pupils. This was particularly true of principal teachers, who were allocated a myriad of additional functions. These were unrealistic in a context where the vast majority were teaching principals. The focus within the curriculum on the child's environment and locality placed an onus on teachers and schools to gather and document information locally. This was a challenging task as there was a paucity of data available and its amassing required in-depth personal research and analysis on the part of the teacher. Consequently, unless teachers were inherently interested in such matters, this did not occur. Accordingly, there was a neglect of many aspects espoused within the curriculum, such as a focus on the local history and geography of the area, the flora and fauna of the school and home locality, and sites of local interest and importance. Furthermore, the Inspectorate was under-resourced and understaffed throughout this period, and its involvement in a multiplicity of educational endeavours reduced the quantity of time spent in schools.

The absence of a systematic and comprehensive evaluation of the curriculum in the two decades following its implementation was a major weakness in determining its success in practice. Arguably, this was contributed to by the disbanding of the Development Unit of the Department of Education in the mid-1970s that had been established to co-ordinate and instigate policy development. In the absence of rigorous evaluation and revision of the curriculum, stagnation occurred and practice became detached from the intentions of the policy developers. While there was a multiplicity of studies examining various aspects of practice, teacher attitudes and pupil progress, their *ad hoc* and unco-ordinated nature resulted in a fragmented understanding of the nature of implementation. Research methodologies were restricted in nature, focusing largely on attitudes and opinions rather than analysing practice regarding implementation and learning outcomes. There was also a dearth of qualitative and empirical research on implementation, which weakened the findings in many of the evaluations. The majority of evaluations related to progress in Irish, English and mathematics, with little emphasis on the wider aspects of the curriculum that were projected as being of equal importance. Key evaluations by the Curriculum Unit were not published and so contributed little to educational debate at the time, reducing their capacity to inform educationalists' and the public's understanding of the nature of implementation. In the absence of baseline data on progress regarding the preceding curriculum, it was impossible to determine accurately the differences between the two in practice or to determine the characteristics that improved or disimproved curriculum delivery. Furthermore, there was little concerted action taken on the evaluations by the Department or other stakeholders in relation to ameliorating implementation. As a consequence, the effectiveness of much of the research undertaken in the period was negated owing to the lack of action on its findings.

Despite much goodwill towards the *Primary School Curriculum* (1971), the radical change it represented from its predecessor proved challenging to implement. As the OECD stated in 1991, twenty years following the introduction of the curriculum:

> As in many other countries, the aspirations and language of the reformers outstripped the readiness and willingness of the system as a whole to respond.[145]

Conclusion

This book has provided a detailed examination of the context, development, content and implementation of successive primary school curricula in Ireland from 1897 to 1990. Comprehensive summaries and conclusions have accompanied each chapter and section. These reviewed and analysed the pertinent characteristics of the development and implementation process and examined the impact of the wider societal and educational context during each phase. This concluding chapter is reserved to distil the key learning from this analysis of a century of curriculum development and implementation in Ireland and presents this under three overarching themes. The first theme relates to the impact of wider societal factors on the development and implementation of successive curricula. Second, the radical nature of curriculum change attempted at each juncture is analysed and implications drawn for the contemporary context. The final theme relates to implementation and contains three inter-related sub-themes, namely the insufficient focus on implementation during the development phase, the inadequate support for schools and school personnel to introduce reforms and the lack of provision for the systematic and continuous evaluation of implementation. The thematic analysis is also informed by engagement with modern national and international literature on effecting educational change, including the work of Fullan, Callan, Sarason, Hargreaves and Sugrue. Individually and collectively, these themes provide not only a review of past experiences but afford insights for the future development and implementation of curricula.

Impact of Wider Societal Factors

Schools exist within a wider societal context and their operation is tempered by political, social, economic, cultural and religious influences. This has been detailed for the various epochs in chapters 1, 4 and 7. Curriculum development and implementation at each juncture was affected by this wider milieu, with certain aspects playing a more considerable role at various times. This was evident, for example, when the cultural and ideological context of the 1920s impacted considerably on the programme devised. In the 1960s, the impact of economic thinking and social developments occupied a more prominent position. The political climate in 1900 when Ireland was a colony of the British Empire was materially different to that obtaining after independence and this contextual factor impacted significantly on what was considered important for inclusion in the curricula of schools. International influences also played an important part in curriculum development at various junctures, albeit for different and even contradictory reasons. In 1922, a reaction to the perceived over-dependence on international influences in the past was to neglect such influences in the devising of the curriculum and this practice continued for decades owing to Catholic Church and state fears of the omnipresence of secularism, the English language and other perceived negative influences in the wider world. The international influence and optimism of the 1960s was inherent in the *Primary School Curriculum* (1971) but many of its provisions proved challenging to implement owing to economic and social constraints in the 1970s and 1980s.

The power and influence of the Catholic Church in the development and implementation of curriculum policy cannot be understated. From the 1800s, the Catholic Church positioned itself as one of the key stakeholders in the arena of education and exercised power at proprietorial, managerial and consultative levels. The antagonism between the Catholic Church and the colonial power in the early part of the twentieth century was replaced with a strong symbiotic relationship between the Catholic Church and the state following independence. This bolstered further the predominant influence of the Catholic Church and its central influence in Irish society was reinforced by its key role in the provision and management of education throughout the country. In many ways, the deference shown by the state to the Catholic Church and the reluctance of both church and state to upset the *status quo* impeded reform and contributed to the stagnation in educational development for long periods in the twentieth century.

It is interesting to note the critical influence that key individuals, organisations and movements can have on the development of curricula at various times. Dr Starkie, by virtue of his appointment to the role of Resident Commissioner, had a profound impact on the education system between 1900 and 1920. In 1922, the influence of organisations such as the Gaelic League and individuals such as Rev. Corcoran proved decisive in devising the curriculum. They were instrumental in embedding cultural and nationalistic goals at the core of the primary school programme in an attempt to promote a distinct identity for Ireland. Of greater significance in this period was the fact that once these goals were incorporated within the programme, they influenced policy and practice long after societal developments would have warranted necessary or advisable. The framing of the programme in terms of these goals reduced the significance of educational aims in terms of the child's needs and arguably impacted on the quality of education provided to successive generations during this period.

Governments use the education system to impart what they deem to be the necessary knowledge, attitudes and skills to upcoming generations in order that they become educated and productive citizens. The focus of this preparation changes over time and a particular emphasis can become embedded in the system to respond to perceived needs. The impact of societal factors can be traced, somewhat, in the title of the Department responsible for education. Upon independence, the state placed a great emphasis on the promotion of the Irish language within the education system and responsibility for education was subsumed within Aireacht na Gaeilge, the Ministry for Irish, before the creation of a separate Department of Education in 1924. In 1997, in line with a greater focus on science and technology in schools, the name was changed to the Department of Education and Science. In 2010, it was renamed the Department of Education and Skills to reflect the emphasis on developing the necessary skills among young people to ameliorate the challenging economic condition of the country. While these name changes mattered little in the daily operation of the Department, they provide an insight into what government and society considered to be a priority at various junctures.

The wider societal context also impacted on the implementation of successive curricula. From an economic perspective, the Boer War in the early 1900s affected significantly the resources made available for the implementation of the *Revised Programme* (1900). Upon independence, the fledgling new state had little material resources to support comprehensively the programme reforms introduced in the 1920s. The introduction of the *Primary School Curriculum* (1971) was followed by an international oil crisis and this impacted significantly on the proposed initiatives to support implementation. Thus, at each juncture of curriculum change in the twentieth century, economic conditions deteriorated from the phase of curriculum development to the phase of curriculum implementation. Therefore, the aspirations of curriculum developers in relation to the resources available to introduce change did not materialise and undoubtedly, this affected the implementation of ambitious policies.

Radical Nature of Reforms

While curriculum planning must be aspirational in tone and content, it cannot neglect the societal and educational context in which it will be implemented. Each major curriculum reform between 1897 and 1990 represented a dramatic change from its predecessor in terms of its philosophy, methodologies and content. Indeed, greater continuity is evident between the curricula of 1900 and 1971 than with programme provisions in the 1920s. Furthermore, the cyclical nature of curriculum policy is evident as the underlying principles and philosophy of the 1900 and 1948 curricula are inherent in the *Primary School Curriculum* (1971) and indeed in the curriculum introduced at the start of the new millennium, the *Primary School Curriculum* (1999).

Throughout the twentieth century, curriculum development in Ireland was characterised by fundamental changes rather than a gradual evolution in policy and practice. Such an approach did not facilitate the necessary ongoing adaptability and responsiveness to changes in the wider societal context. Change in revolutionary format does not work well within a conservative and complex education system – implementation proves more steadfast when there is gradual change and evolution. For the most part, the revolutionary changes did not represent an organic development of the curriculum and were often motivated by non-educational reasons and driven by political or wider societal interest groups. Wide-ranging supports would have been a prerequisite to support the successful implementation of curriculum reform considering the radical nature of proposals at each juncture. An alternative that may yield better results would be the gradual and ongoing introduction of change rather than the development of discrete, over-arching innovations at periodic intervals.

Educational change often occurred on a sporadic basis, following long periods of neglect or apathy, and the reforms introduced were often multifaceted in nature. In most instances, there was a lack of focus on providing a theoretical framework or rationale for change within curriculum documents, which did little to imbue stakeholders with the knowledge or motivation for such radical adjustments. In 1900 and 1922, organisational and structural reforms were implemented in tandem with curriculum change which had the effect of placing the system in a state of flux. At a curriculum level, each reform was accompanied by the inclusion or exclusion of a wide range of subjects and the content, methodologies and approaches advocated for traditional core subjects often changed concurrently. Following attempts to introduce fundamental changes, there was often a reorientation by individuals and the system towards the *status quo*.

One of the most radical attempts at curriculum change was the predominant focus placed on the teaching and use of Irish as a medium of instruction from 1922. This took place in a context where a minority of teachers had proven competence in the language and was not supported with any concerted parallel movements in wider society to revive the language. Such an approach greatly overestimated the power of schools to instigate such a societal change and underestimated the complexity of effecting a change in the vernacular of a country. The curriculum generally tends to mirror and follow societal developments and the school-based language restoration project initiated in the 1920s ultimately failed in its attempt to encourage a society to follow a curriculum-based initiative.

The conceptualisation of childhood as portrayed within curricula oscillated throughout the period and impacted significantly on what and how children learned. This changed from the period after 1900 when heuristic methods were advocated to a more formal 'moulding' of the child between 1922 and 1971 in line with Catholic ideology. In this period following independence, it could be argued that pedagogical goals and the needs of the child became subservient to more nationalistic, religious and political aims. The *Revised Programme for Infants* (1948) and the *Primary School Curriculum* (1971) reverted to the activity-based and experiential principles and methodologies of the *Revised Programme* (1900). These placed a distinct value on the period of childhood and focused on the needs, interests and abilities of the child in the present. A focus was also placed on the holistic development of the child and the focus on cognitive development was complemented by a greater emphasis on aesthetic, physical, creative and emotional aspects.

Focus on Implementation

Curriculum Development Process

Arguably, a significant oversight with each revision of the curriculum rested with the lack of a strategic focus on implementation aligned to the societal and educational context of the time. In general, policies focused on principles and ideologies as opposed to practicalities, with policymakers erroneously believing that a change in policy would automatically translate into a change in practice. Historically, the main emphasis to effect curriculum change was placed on the production of curriculum documents that were subsequently disseminated to teachers for implementation. When policies were devised and disseminated, the work of the central authority was seen to be largely complete. Indeed, there was little understanding inherent in successive curricula of the need to plan for the process of implementation on an ongoing basis. There is often a large gap and complex relationship between policy developers and those with a direct remit for policy implementation. In this way, curriculum innovation or introducing change was largely perceived to be an event as opposed to a process, a destination rather than a journey. In reality, policy development represented the first, and arguably the least complex, step in effecting change in practice. What was absent in much of the policy development was the journey required to move from the contemporary practice to the policy aspiration. In the absence of a road map, many journeys were never commenced or lacked the focus to reach the desired destination.

Curriculum documents until the 1970s were generally short in nature, containing little detail on the rationale for reform or the inclusion of subjects, the principles, the time allocations, specific aims and objectives for the various subjects, the content to be covered for each class in each subject or the criteria for evaluation. This absence of clarity in relation to what was to be generally expected at each class level or the anticipated learning outcomes led to difficulties for those implementing the curriculum and for those evaluating the degree of implementation. While various curricula were introduced immediately, the conditions laid out in successive curriculum documents for successful implementation were addressed in a haphazard and tardy manner. At no juncture was curriculum reform accompanied by a comprehensive or systematic support infrastructure in the form of in-service training in the new philosophy, methodologies and content, the provision of equipment and resources or support to mediate the curriculum for implementation in individual school contexts. Even when limited supports were made available, they were often inadequate and a sense of inaction or lethargy surrounded their delivery, leaving a void in supports at arguably the most critical point of implementation. For example, the specimen *Notes for Teachers* for the 1900 programme did not become available until 1904, while most of the *Notes for Teachers* for the

1926 reform did not materialise until 1933. This left many teachers unsure as to what was expected of them at a critical point of implementation. Even when there was some level of consultation prior to the introduction of the *Primary School Curriculum* (1971), little action was taken to alter curriculum policy to address practical concerns around implementation raised by stakeholders.

There was little emphasis placed on the gradual roll out of new curriculum provisions to allow them to become embedded incrementally in practice. A further challenge was the lack of differentiation of curriculum provisions for the various contexts in which implementation would take place. Despite the latitude afforded to school management and teachers to adapt curricula for specific contexts, this facility was rarely used in the absence of training and support for managers, principals and teachers.

A lack of emphasis on the educational context was a recurring feature of curriculum development and aspirational policies often perished in the reality of this context. In general, policy was overly aspirational for the practical context in which it was to be implemented. Some of this may be attributed to the fact that curricula were generally designed by 'experts' with a particular interest or expertise in a curriculum area and set out high expectations for the generalist teacher. In the absence of a focus on supporting implementation, teachers often reverted to a focus on the core subjects and the use of traditional methods. There was a failure to realise that curriculum content and policy had implications for issues such as the resourcing of education. Circumstances within schools were less than conducive or propitious for educational change throughout much of the century. Such circumstances included the large classes in which many pupils were taught, the low attendance rates, the material condition of schools in terms of facilities and resources, a mismatch between curriculum provisions and parental expectations, the predominance of small schools, the dearth of suitable resources and educational materials, poor provision for teacher in-service training and the lack of alignment between school design and proposed methodologies. This often resulted in a tacit support in principle for reforms, yet existing school practice and culture proved more steadfast than proposed curriculum provisions.

Schools and School Personnel

In the implementation of curriculum change, principals and teachers are the key agents in the translation of the policy vision into reality in schools. There is growing consensus that the school as an institution represents the locus of change and it is there that reform must begin and end. In the period under review, this certainly was not the case in relation to curriculum innovation, with schools oftentimes being the last to become aware of the curriculum reforms proposed. Teachers occupy a pivotal position in curriculum implementation, acting as the conduit between aspiration and reality, between policy and practice. Historically, an inadequate emphasis was placed on supporting this key professional and in promoting the importance of each individual teacher in the successful implementation of curriculum change. Effecting curriculum change relates not only to changing the content – some of the most difficult challenges relate to the change of attitudes, motivation, philosophies, beliefs and practices of teachers. A lack of consultation on, and subsequently ownership of, curriculum change led teachers to view successive curricula as impositions and reduced teachers' zeal to lead change in their individual classrooms.

Change challenges the individual and institution to do things in a different way. When change is introduced, even if teachers are broadly supportive of its thrust in theory, it is considerably more difficult to effect a change in their practice. In other words, in the absence of ownership of change, teachers will portray an image of reform to satisfy policymakers and external educationalists, while in reality, practice changes little. This was certainly evidenced in the Irish context by teachers endorsing the principles underpinning the *Primary School Curriculum* (1971), while doing little to alter their practice to align with this. Successful change only becomes a reality when new practices are internalised and integrated with teachers' existing attitudes and practices. Systematic supports are required to enable teachers to incorporate new content and methodologies within their practice. In the absence of comprehensive supports for curriculum implementation throughout the twentieth century, much of the momentum and buoyancy for reform dissipated and, when eventually provided, their impact on practice was less effective than if they had been provided in tandem with the change process.

The highly structured nature of pre-service training, focusing on routine and didactic aspects of teaching, did little to prepare teachers to innovate in their subsequent careers. Throughout the period under review, teachers had difficulty adapting to and accommodating changes within their practice. Owing to the poor provision for training of teachers in the earlier part of the twentieth century and the absence of a co-ordinated system of in-service education throughout the century, teachers often lacked the ability or confidence to implement curriculum reforms. There was inadequate consideration given to the provision of support to teachers around the junctures of change in the form of in-service training in the new content and methodologies. While support was sometimes provided for newly-introduced subjects, little advice was given in the traditional subjects and it was often the changed content and methodologies in these familiar subjects that teachers found most difficult to implement.

Until 1971, there was little time afforded to teachers and schools to become familiar or engage with curriculum change, or to gain an element of understanding of the educational reforms introduced – they were disseminated for immediate implementation. This method of devising curricula did little to engender a sense of ownership or understanding on the part of teachers for the rationale or content of the proposed reforms. This was particularly acute in relation to the Irish language provisions from the 1920s, especially its use as a medium of instruction. Despite evidence of lack of competence in Irish, the programme was not altered adequately to reflect this reality and a sense of failure was engendered among teachers who felt unable to meet the high standards expected. The forced nature of implementation, especially in the earlier part of the century by linking performance in subject areas to salaries and promotional prospects, did little to inculcate enthusiasm among teachers for curriculum reform. Little emphasis was placed on winning over the hearts and minds of teachers at the junctures of curriculum change. Parents and managers too were dubious about the value of some of the educational reforms and undoubtedly influenced teachers in their implementation of the curriculum.

The *Primary School Curriculum* (1971) differed somewhat in this regard as it allowed for a period of piloting in a substantial number of schools, which led to a general awareness among principals and teachers as to its philosophy and content. During this phase, in-service training was undertaken by many teachers in the form of lectures and workshops and there was much discourse in educational journals on the nature of the proposed changes. Despite the many limitations of the process, this allowed for a more gradual implementation and consolidation of change in schools and for teachers to introduce the provisions of the curriculum in a more incremental way. Despite this, fundamental elements of the curriculum's content, principles and methodologies were not implemented. Teacher conservatism and resistance to change must also be considered as factors in this non-implementation.

A number of constraints on the role of the principal as a leader of change was evident in the Irish context, such as the previous training and experience for a leadership position and the range of roles and responsibilities that were beyond the personal knowledge and expertise of many principals. Given the importance of instructional leadership in the implementation of curriculum change, an insufficient focus was placed on the critical role of the principal as a driving force of innovation within schools. The transformation of the role in 1971 from one of administration to that of leadership and management proved challenging for many. Considering the majority of principals in Ireland were, and continue to be, teaching principals, the impact of this dual role should be a major consideration in future curriculum development and implementation.

Evaluating Curriculum Implementation

In the period prior to independence, a significant focus was placed on evaluating, reviewing and documenting curriculum implementation. Indeed, such reviews led to a number of revisions to address identified deficiencies in implementation. This approach was not as prevalent following independence, when there was a lack of focus on evaluating implementation and a reluctance to publish the findings of such research when available. This impacted negatively on the discourse on curriculum policy and on ensuring the education system remained current to the needs of the society it served. Indeed, the process of developing curriculum policy became more centralised and little was published around the process of its development, including the research informing policy decisions or submissions from organisations or individuals in response to proposed policies.

While there was some improvement from the 1970s, there was still low state investment in educational research and it remained difficult to attain timely data on the education system. Some research on curriculum implementation in the period 1971–1990 lacked breadth and rigour, particularly research that examined perception as opposed to actual practices in relation to curriculum implementation. Most research focused on the implementation of Irish, English and mathematics, neglecting the implementation of other aspects of the curriculum. When empirical and observational research was undertaken, it often found a dichotomy between endorsement of the curriculum in principle and the application of these principles in practice.

In the absence of a systematic approach to evaluation and reform, the system stagnated and the philosophy and content of the curriculum became mal-aligned with the community and society within which it was being implemented. The absence of clear objectives or outcomes in each subject within the 1971 curriculum made the process of evaluating implementation more difficult for teachers, schools, inspectors and researchers. In the absence of clear guidance, the Teacher's Handbooks became redundant and a greater focus was placed on textbooks, which came to have an inordinate influence on the curriculum as delivered in schools. Moreover, there was a dearth of information or knowledge as to exactly what was happening in classrooms and schools which led to a fragmented understanding of curriculum implementation. A clear and coherent picture must be established before the necessity for, or path to, reform can be delineated. There was also a reluctance to acknowledge when initiatives were not successful and to revise curricula. Even when research was undertaken that pointed to the need for a new direction or modification of policy, little timely and concerted action was undertaken to improve curriculum implementation in practice. The reluctance by the Department to publish reports on curriculum implementation, even up to the 1980s, reduced the impact of research when it was undertaken and it contributed little to public debate or understanding on curriculum implementation at the time. In the absence of systematic evaluation, which characterised much of the twentieth century in Ireland, the curriculum failed to react to the need for change and general evolution in a systematic or responsive way.

Evaluating the historical evolution of the primary school curriculum has much to offer current understandings in relation to effecting curriculum change in the Irish context. In the period examined, the cyclical focus on various educational principles, methodologies and content is evident and it is arguable that similar cycles will continue into the future. While the development of the education system in the period under review has been difficult at times, the achievements in relation to the quality, breadth and outcomes of pupils' learning experiences in the contemporary context are significant. A more democratic and participatory approach to the development of education policy is evident from the end of the twentieth century and the quality of policy has been enhanced by the involvement of key stakeholders.

This comprehensive evaluation of the experience of devising and implementing successive curricula over a century provides a useful case study of how aspirations for curriculum change can fall well short of realisation when insufficient attention is paid to the range of inter-locking factors that affect the successful implementation of policy. Such awareness is a prerequisite for not repeating past mistakes and is necessary in order to learn from previous responses, both successful and unsuccessful, to curriculum implementation. While the multiplicity of factors impacting on implementation have been elucidated, the nature of achieving educational change is infinitely more complex than ensuring a checklist of ingredients are provided for. It is the interplay of these factors at a particular point in time that impacts on translating curriculum policy into a practical reality in schools. An awareness of this complexity guides implementation and provides an awareness of the need for ongoing evaluation and revision to ensure practice matches policy. In the twentieth century, the journey of curriculum development and implementation was characterised by a lack of appreciation for the intricacy of effecting curriculum change. With this and other research, there is now a greater, and still growing, understanding of the process of achieving curriculum change. It is hoped this will inform the journey of ongoing curriculum development and implementation into the future.

Notes

Introduction

1   Department of Education (1995). *Charting our Education Future – White Paper on Education*. Dublin: The Stationery Office, p. 18.
2   Department of Education (1990). *Report of the Primary Education Review Body*. Dublin: The Stationery Office.
3   Review Body on the Primary Curriculum (1990). *Report of the Review Body on the Primary Curriculum*. Dublin: Department of Education.

Chapter 1

1   CSO (1974). *Statistical Abstract of Ireland 1970–1971*. Dublin: CSO, p. 20.
2   Plunkett, H. (1905). *Ireland in the New Century*. London: John Murray, p. 129.
3   Coolahan, J. (1973). *A Study of Curricular Policy for the Primary and Secondary Schools of Ireland 1900–1935, with Special Reference to the Irish Language and Irish History*. PhD Thesis. Dublin: Trinity College Dublin, p. 37.
4   Cullen, L. (1968). Irish Economic History: Fact and Myth (in) Cullen, L. (Ed.) (1968). *The Formation of the Irish Economy*. Cork: Mercier Press, pp. 113–124.
5   Nic Ghiolla Phádraig, M. (1990). *Childhood as a Social Phenomenon – National Report Ireland. European Centre for Social Welfare Policy and Research*. Eurosocial Report 36/8. Vienna: European Centre for Social Welfare Policy and Research.
6   Ó Loinsigh, P. (1975). The Irish Language in the Nineteenth Century. *Oideas*, Spring 1975, Volume 14, pp. 5–21.
7   Wall, M. (1969). The Decline of the Irish Language (in) Ó Cuív, B. (Ed.) (1969). *A View of the Irish Language*. Dublin: The Stationery Office, pp. 81–90.

8   O'Donoghue, T. (2000). *Bilingual Education In Ireland 1904–1922 – The Case of the Bilingual Programme of Instruction*. Centre for Irish Studies Monograph Series, No. 1 2000. Perth: Murdoch University, p. 23.

9   Ó Buachalla, S. (Ed.) (1980). *A Significant Irish Educationalist – The Educational Writings of P.H. Pearse*. Dublin: Mercier Press.

10   Ó Buachalla, S. (1981). The Irish Language in the Classroom. *The Crane Bag*, Volume 5, No. 2, pp. 849–862, p. 853.

11   For example, see Ó Tailliúr, P. (1964). Ceartliosta de Leabhar, Paimfléid, etc. Foilsithe in Éirinn ag Conradh na Gaedhilge 1893–1918. *Comhar*, Feabhra 1964, pp. 1–4; Márta 1964, pp. 5–8; Aibreán 1964, pp. 17–20; Bealtaine 1964, pp. 13–16; Meitheamh 1964, pp. 17–20; Iúil 1964, pp. 21–24; Lúnasa 1964, pp. 25–26.

12   Ó hAilín, T. (1969). Irish Revival Movements (in) Ó Cuív, B. (Ed.) (1969). *A View of the Irish Language*. Dublin: The Stationery Office, pp. 91–100, p. 97.

13   Ó Tuathaigh, G. (1993). The Irish State and Language Policy (in) The Future of Irish – Ten Essays Celebrating One Hundred Years of the Irish Language Movement, issued with *Fortnight* (April 1993), No. 316, pp. 3–5, p. 4.

14   Ó hAilín, T. (1969). Irish Revival Movements ..., p. 96.

15   Akenson, D. (1975). *A Mirror to Kathleen's Face – Education in Independent Ireland 1922–1960*. London: McGill-Queen's University Press; Titley, B. (1983). Church, State and the Control of Schooling in Ireland 1900–1944. Dublin: Gill and Macmillan Ltd.

16   Miller, D. (1973). *Church, State and Nation in Ireland 1898–1921*. Dublin: Gill and Macmillan, p. 4.

17   Inglis, T. (1998). *Moral Monopoly – The Rise and Fall of the Catholic Church in Modern Ireland*. Dublin: University College Dublin Press, p. 151.

18   Commissioners of National Education in Ireland [CNEI] (1902). *68th Report ... for 1901*, p. 17.

19   The Recent Pastoral of the Catholic Hierarchy. *Irish Teachers' Journal*, 6 October 1900, pp. 4–5, p. 4.

20   Royal Commission on Technical Instruction (1884). *Second Report of the Royal Commission on Technical Instruction – Volume IV: Evidence, &c Relating to Ireland*.

21   Selleck, R. (1968). *The New Education – The English Background 1870–1914*. Melbourne: Sir Isaac Pitman and Sons Ltd., p. 338.

22   CNEI (1892). *58th Report ... for 1891*, Appendix B, Rules and Regulations of the CNEI, Rule 1, p. 2.

23   Tussing, D. (1978). *Irish Educational Expenditures – Past, Present and Future*. Dublin: Economic and Social Research Institute, p. 11.

24   CNEI (1869). *35th Report ... for 1868*, Appendix B, pp. 191–224.

25   Coolahan, J. (1981). *Irish Education – History and Structure*. Dublin: Institute of Public Administration, p. 3.

26   Burke, A. (1994). *Teaching – Retrospect and Prospect*. Dublin: Brunswick Press.

27   Royal Commission of Inquiry into Primary Education (Ireland) (1870). *Conclusions and Recommendations Contained in the General Report*, Volume 1.

28   Commission on Manual and Practical Instruction [CMPI] (1898). *Appendices to the Reports of the Commissioners*. Dublin: Alexander Thom. and Co. Ltd., Appendix A (IX–1) – Subjects of Instruction in Irish National Schools, pp. 32–33.

29   CNEI (1904). *70th Report ... for 1903*, p. 2.

30   Hyland, A. (1983). The Treasury and Irish Education 1850–1922: The Myth and the Reality. *Irish Educational Studies*, Volume 3, No. 2, pp. 57–82, p. 70.

31   Coolahan, J. (1993). The Irish and Others in Irish Nineteenth-century Textbooks (in) Mangan, J. (Ed.) (1993). *The Imperial Curriculum*. London: Routledge, pp. 54–63.

32   Circular; *New Permanent Scales of Salaries for National Teachers*, December 1920.

33   CNEI (1871). *37th Report ... for 1870*, p. 5.

34   CNEI (1905). *71st Report ... for 1904*, p. 28.

35   *Ibid.*

36   CNEI (1921). *86th Report ... for 1919–1920*, p. 12.

37   CNEI (1871). *37th Report ... for 1870*, p. 3.

38   National Education (Ireland) Bill 1892. Bills, Public 1892, Volume 4, Bill 420, p. 647.

39   Coolahan, J. (1981). *Irish Education ...*, p. 15.

40   Coolahan, J. (1981). '*Education' in the Training Colleges – Carysfort 1877–1977: Two Centenary Lectures*. Blackrock: Our Lady of Mercy College, pp. 20–52, p. 20.

41   Mescal, J. (1957). *Religion in the Irish System of Education*. Dublin: Clonmore and Reynolds, p. 85.

42   Royal Commission of Inquiry into Primary Education (Ireland) (1870). *Conclusions and Recommendations ...*, Recommendations No. 99–104, p. 531.

43   CNEI (1902). *68th Report ... for 1901*, p. 6.

44   Magee, J. (1982). *The Master – A Social History of the Irish National Teacher 1831–1921*. Paper delivered at the Canon Rogers Memorial Lecture, St Joseph's College of Education Belfast, November 1982, p. 4. (Unpublished).

45   Coolahan, J. with O'Donovan, P. (2009). *A History of Ireland's School Inspectorate 1831–2008*. Dublin: Four Courts Press, pp. 19–21.

46 CNEI (1869). *35th Report ... for 1868*, Appendix A, Rules and Regulations of the CNEI, pp. 47–75, p. 53.

47 Vice-Regal Committee of Inquiry into Primary Education (Ireland) 1913, *Appendix to the First Report of the Committee*, Appendix 1, Growth of the System of National Education, Mr W.J. Dilworth, M.A., p. 129.

48 Royal Commission on Technical Instruction (1884). *Second Report of the Royal Commission ...*

49 Joyce, P.W. (1892). *The Teaching of Manual Work in Schools*. Dublin: M.H. Gill and Son, p. 12.

50 Walsh, W. (1928). *William J. Walsh, Archbishop of Dublin*. Dublin: The Talbot Press, p. 221; 505–507.

51 CNEI (1900). *66th Report ... for 1899–1900*, Appendix, Section 1, Mr Bonaparte-Wyse, District Inspector, p. 16.

52 CNEI (1897). *63rd Report ... for 1896–1897*, Appendix, Section 1, Mr Purser, Head Inspector, p. 61; Mr Sullivan, Head Inspector, p. 81; Mr Eardley, Head Inspector, p. 93; Dr Alexander, Head Inspector, p. 96; Dr Moran, Head Inspector, p. 105; Mr Tibbs, District Inspector, p. 207; Dr Bateman, District Inspector, p. 225.

53 CNEI (1898). *64th Report ... for 1897–1898*, Appendix, Section 1, Mr Sullivan, Head Inspector, p. 75; Dr Alexander, Head Inspector, p. 94.

54 CNEI (1896). *62nd Report ... for 1895*, Appendix A, p. 10.

55 CNEI (1898). *64th Report ... for 1897–1898*, Appendix, Section 1, Mr Stronge, Head Inspector, p. 84; Dr Alexander, Head Inspector, p. 98.

56 CNEI (1896). *62nd Report ... for 1895*, Appendix B, Mr Purser, Head Inspector, pp. 18–24.

57 CNEI (1905). *71st Report ... for 1904*, p. 28.

Chapter 2

1 Commission on Manual and Practical Instruction [CMPI] (1898). *Appendices to the Reports of the Commissioners*, Appendix A (I), Memorandum of the Commissioners of National Education on the Subject of Manual Instruction. Dublin: Printed for her Majesty's Stationery Office by Alexander Thom and Co. (Limited), pp. 5–6, p. 5.

2 *Ibid.*, p. 5.

3 *Ibid.*, p. 6.

4   CMPI (1898). *Final Report of the Commissioners*. Dublin: Alexander Thom and Co. (Limited), p. v.

5   *Ibid.*, p. 2.

6   CMPI (1897). *Second Volume of Minutes of Evidence ...*, Mr Bevis, p. 6, Column 3159; Mr Robinson, p. 17, Column 3487; Sir Philip Magnus, p. 43, Column 4172; Mr Stanley, p. 54, Column 4402; Sir Joshua Fitch, p. 128, Column 6498; *Third Volume of Minutes of Evidence ...*, Mr Salomon, pp. 143–144, Column 14222–14245; CMPI (1898). *Fourth Volume of Minutes of Evidence ...*, Rev. Brother Gogarty, p. 19, Column 14744; Brother Burke, p. 35, Column 15054; Mr Eardley, p. 234, Column 20920.

7   CMPI (1898). *Final Report of the Commissioners ...*, p. 5.

8   *Ibid.*, p. 13.

9   Commissioners of National Education in Ireland [CNEI] (1901). *67th Report ... for 1900*, p. 8.

10   CMPI (1898). *Final Report of the Commissioners ...*, p. 9.

11   *Ibid.*, p. 11.

12   O'Connor, M. (2010). *The Development of Infant Education in Ireland, 1838–1948: Epochs and Eras*. Bern: Peter Lang, p. 182.

13   CMPI (1898). *Final Report of the Commissioners ...*, p. 5.

14   *Ibid.*, p. 4.

15   *Ibid.*, p. 22.

16   *Ibid.*, p. 35.

17   *Ibid.*, p. 39.

18   *Ibid.*, p. 3.

19   *Ibid.*, p. 42.

20   *Ibid.*, p. 50.

21   CMPI (1897). *Second Volume of Minutes of Evidence ...*, Mr Taylor, p. 18, Column 3509; Sir Philip Magnus, p. 51, Column 4353; Mr Stanley, p. 55, Column 4443.

22   CMPI (1897). *First Report of the Commissioners ...*, Mr Stronge, p. 25, Column 900; Mr Cooke p. 57, Column 1861; *Second Volume of Minutes of Evidence ...*, Sir Philip Magnus, p. 44, Column 4183; *Fourth Volume of Minutes of Evidence ...*, Brother Burke, p. 34, Column 15051; J.J. Doherty, p. 351, Column 24192.

23   CMPI (1898). *Appendices to the Reports of the Commissioners*, Appendix C – Suggestions by Inspectors in Irish National Schools as to Modification of the Present Programme of Instruction in National Schools, pp. 269–288.

24   CMPI (1898). *Final Report of the Commissioners ...*, p. 4.

25   *Ibid.*

26   *Ibid.*, p. 59.

27   Coolahan, J. (1981). '*Education' in the Training Colleges – Carysfort 1877–1977: Two Centenary Lectures.* Blackrock: Our Lady of Mercy College, pp. 20–52, p. 30.

28   CMPI (1897). *First Report of the Commissioners ...*, Dr Moran, p. 48, Column 1617; Mr Cooke, p. 55, Column 1789.

29   CMPI (1898). *Final Report of the Commissioners ...*, p. 56.

30   Coolahan, J. (2005). The Schoolmaster in the New State (in) Fitzmaurice, G. (Ed.) (2005). *The World of Bryan MacMahon.* Cork: Mercier Press, pp. 163–192, p. 171.

31   Coolahan, J. (1981). '*Education' in the Training Colleges ...*, p. 31.

32   Vice-Regal Committee of Inquiry into Primary Education (Ireland) 1913, *Appendix to the Second Report of the Committee* – Minutes of Evidence, 13 March–25 June 1913, Mr P.E. Lemass, p. 266, Column 10891.

33   *Ibid.*, Appendix XXVIII, Report of the Board of National Education, made for the Information of his Excellency the Lord Lieutenant, in Reference to the Recommendations of the Commission on Manual and Practical Instruction, pp. 490–495.

34   *Ibid.*, p. 421, Column 13760.

35   *Abstracts of the Board's [Commissioners of National Education] Proceedings*, 28 March 1899, p. 3. National Library of Ireland, LO 2351.

36   Vice-Regal Committee of Inquiry into Primary Education (Ireland) 1913, *Appendix to the Second Report of the Committee ...*, Mr P.E. Lemass, p. 266, Column 10990.

37   *Ibid.*, Appendix XXVIII ..., p. 493.

38   *Ibid.*, p. 494.

39   *Abstracts of the Board's Proceedings*, 14 November 1899, p. 2.

40   Vice-Regal Committee of Inquiry into Primary Education (Ireland) 1913, *Appendix to the Second Report of the Committee ...*, Appendix XXX, The Revision of the School Curriculum and System of School Organisation, pp. 502–505, p. 502.

41   *Ibid.*, p. 503.

42   Vice-Regal Committee of Inquiry into Primary Education (Ireland) 1913, *Appendix to the Second Report of the Committee ...*, Dr Starkie, p. 284, Column 11266–11290.

43   *Ibid.*, Mr P.E. Lemass, p. 278, Column 11166.

44   Vice-Regal Committee of Inquiry into Primary Education (Ireland) 1913, *Final Report of the Committee*, p. 6.

45   Vice-Regal Committee of Inquiry into Primary Education (Ireland) 1913, *Appendix to the Second Report of the Committee* – Appendix XXVII, Downing, E.

and Purser, A., *Observations on the New School Programme* 16/07/1900, pp. 489–490, p. 489.

46 *Ibid.*, p. 490.

47 CNEI (1902). *67th Report … for 1900*, Appendix, Section II (F), Revised Programme of Instruction in National Schools – Notes, Hints and Observations for the Information of Managers and Teachers, Rule 52, p. 106.

48 CNEI (1902). *67th Report … for 1900*, Appendix, Section 1, Mr Downing, Chief Inspector, p. 7.

49 CNEI (1902). *67th Report … for 1900*, Appendix, Section II (F), Revised Programme of Instruction in National Schools …, p. 66.

50 *Ibid.*, p. 68.

51 CNEI (1901). *67th Report … for 1900*, p. 37.

52 CNEI (1902). *67th Report … for 1900*, Appendix, Section II (F), Revised Programme of Instruction in National Schools …, p. 69.

53 *Ibid.*, p. 72.

54 *Ibid.*

55 CNEI (1902). *68th Report … for 1901*, p. 6.

56 Dale, F.H. (1904). *Report of Mr F.H. Dale, His Majesty's Inspector of Schools, Board of Education, on Primary Education in Ireland*. Printed for His Majesty's Stationery Office by Alexander Thom and Co. (Limited) Abbey Street, p. 52.

57 Starkie, W.J.M. (1911). *The History of Irish Primary and Secondary Education During the Last Decade – An Inaugural Address*. Belfast, p. 17.

58 CNEI (1902). *67th Report … for 1900*, Appendix, Section II (F), Revised Programme of Instruction in National Schools …, p. 75.

59 *Ibid.*, p. 68.

60 *Ibid.*, p. 79.

61 *Ibid.*, p. 68.

62 *Ibid.*, p. 72.

63 *Ibid.*, p. 68.

64 *Brief Outline of the History of the Inspectorate in the National Schools of Ireland*, p. 3. (Unpublished).

65 *Abstracts of the Board's Proceedings*, 10 April 1900, p. 3.

66 *Brief Outline of the History of the Inspectorate …*, p. 4.

67 Vice-Regal Committee of Inquiry into Primary Education (Ireland) 1913, *Final Report of the Committee*, p. 5.

68 Meeting of National Teachers at Tramore – The New Rules. *The Freeman's Journal*, 7 September 1900, p. 2.

69 INTO (1901). *Congress Programme for 1901 – The Thirty-Fourth Annual Congress*, Royal University Buildings Dublin. Dublin: Oraham, p. 36.

70 *Ibid.*, p. 20.
71 National Education – The New Programme from the Teachers' Point of View. *Irish Teachers' Journal*, 27 October 1900, Volume XXXIV, No. 43, pp. 4–6, p. 4.
72 Our Aims and Objectives. *The Irish School Monthly – A Magazine of Practical School Work*, September 1900, Volume 1, No. 1. Dublin: Blackie and Son Limited, pp. 3–4, p. 3.
73 Starkie, W.J.M. (1902). *Recent Reforms in Irish Education.* An Address read before the British Association Belfast, 11 September 1902. Dublin: Blackie and Son Limited, p. 24.
74 Starkie, W.J.M. (1911). *The History of Irish Primary and Secondary Education ...,* p. 17.
75 CNEI (1902). *67th Report ... for 1900,* Appendix, Section 1, Mr Goodman, General Report on Musical Instruction, p. 81.

Chapter 3

1   Heller, W.M. (1902). The Introduction of Practical Instruction into Irish National Schools. *The Irish School Monthly – A Magazine of Practical School Work*, October 1902, Volume 3, No. 2. Dublin: Blackie and Son Limited, pp. 35–40, p. 35.
2   Commissioners of National Education in Ireland [CNEI] (1902). *68th Report ... for 1901,* pp. 38–39.
3   CNEI (1902). *68th Report ... for 1901,* p. 8; Appendix, Section 1, Mr Downing, Chief Inspector, p. 34; CNEI (1905). *70th Report ... for 1903,* Appendix, Section 1, Mr M'Elwaine, Senior Inspector, p. 69; CNEI (1905). *71st Report ... for 1904,* Appendix, Section 1, Mr Dewar, Senior Inspector, p. 24; Mr Ross, Senior Inspector, p. 79.
4   CNEI (1902). *68th Report ... for 1901,* Appendix, Section 1, Mr Ross (quoted in) Mr Purser, Chief Inspector, p. 95; CNEI (1904). *69th Report ... for 1902,* Appendix, Section 1, Mr Stronge, Senior Inspector, p. 12; Mr Craig, Senior Inspector, p. 165; CNEI (1905). *71st Report ... for 1904,* p. 3; Appendix, Section 1, Mr Cox, Senior Inspector, p. 51.
5   CNEI (1902). *68th Report ... for 1901,* Appendix, Section 1, Mr Stronge (quoted in) Mr Downing, Chief Inspector, p. 34; Mr Hughes (quoted in) Mr Downing,

Chief Inspector, p. 49; Mr Purser, Chief Inspector, p. 97; CNEI (1905). *71st Report ... for 1904*, Appendix, Section 1, Mr Daly, Senior Inspector, p. 104.

6   CNEI (1902). *67th Report ... for 1900*, Appendix, Section 1, Mr Downing, Chief Inspector, p. 8; CNEI (1904). *69th Report ... for 1902*, Appendix, Section 1, Dr Alexander, Senior Inspector, p. 17; Mr Pedlow, Senior Inspector, p. 72; CNEI (1905). *70th Report ... for 1903*, Appendix, Section 1, Mr Headen, Senior Inspector, p. 103.

7   CNEI (1902). *68th Report ... for 1901*, Appendix, Section 1, Mr O'Connor (quoted in) Mr Purser, Chief Inspector, p. 102; CNEI (1904). *69th Report ... for 1902*, Appendix, Section 1, Mr Dewar, Senior Inspector, p. 24; CNEI (1905). *71st Report ... for 1904*, p. 3; Appendix, Section 1, Mr Dewar, Senior Inspector, p. 26.

8   CNEI (1902). *68th Report ... for 1901*, Appendix, Section 1, Mr Kelly (quoted in) Mr Purser, Chief Inspector, p. 101; CNEI (1905). *70th Report ... for 1903*, Appendix, Section 1, Mr Dalton, Senior Inspector, p. 149.

9   CNEI (1902). *67th Report ... for 1900*, Appendix, Section 1, Mr Craig (quoted in) Mr Downing, Chief Inspector, p. 12; CNEI (1902). *68th Report ... for 1901*, Appendix, Section 1, Mr Worsely (quoted in) Mr Downing, Chief Inspector, p. 45; Mr Goodman, General Report on Musical Instruction, p. 147.

10   CNEI (1902). *68th Report ... for 1901*, Appendix, Section 1, Mr Murphy (quoted in) Mr Purser, Chief Inspector, p. 100; CNEI (1905). *71st Report ... for 1904*, p. 3; Appendix, Section 1, Dr Alexander, Senior Inspector, p. 17; Mr Headen, Senior Inspector, p. 71.

11   CNEI (1902). *68th Report ... for 1901*, Appendix, Section 1, Mr Purser, Chief Inspector, p. 97; CNEI (1905). *70th Report ... for 1903*, Appendix, Section 1, Mr Hynes, Senior Inspector, p. 61.

12   CNEI (1902). *68th Report ... for 1901*, Appendix, Section 1, Mr FitzGerald (quoted in) Mr Purser, Chief Inspector, p. 101; CNEI (1904). *69th Report ... for 1902*, Appendix, Section 1, Mr Stronge, Senior Inspector, p. 12; Mr Hynes, Senior Inspector, p. 45.

13   CNEI (1902). *67th Report ... for 1900*, Appendix, Section 1, Mr Downing, Chief Inspector, p. 7; CNEI (1902). *68th Report ... for 1901*, Appendix, Section 1, Mr Connelly (quoted in) Mr Downing, Chief Inspector, p. 44.

14   CNEI (1902). *67th Report ... for 1900*, Appendix, Section 1, Mr Purser, Chief Inspector, p. 43; Mr Murphy (quoted in) Mr Purser, Chief Inspector, p. 59; CNEI (1905). *71st Report ... for 1904*, p. 3; Appendix, Section 1, Mr Headen, Senior Inspector, p. 71; CNEI (1906). *72nd Report ... for 1905–1906*, Appendix, Section 1, Mr M'Elwaine, Senior Inspector, p. 33; Mr O'Riordan, Senior Inspector, p. 173.

15   The New Programme. *The Irish School Weekly*, 6 February 1904, Volume 1, No. 1,
      pp. 19–20; Educational Topics of the Month – Decline of Manual Training. *The
      Irish School Monthly – A Magazine of Practical School Work*, June 1905, Volume
      5, No. 10. Dublin: Blackie and Son Limited, pp. 343–345.
16   CNEI (1902). *68th Report ... for 1901*, Appendix, Section 1, Dr Alexander
      (quoted in) Mr Downing, Chief Inspector, p. 35; Dr Skeffington (quoted in)
      Mr Downing, Chief Inspector, p. 35; Mr Headen (quoted in) Mr Downing,
      Chief Inspector, p. 38; Mr Coyne (quoted in) Mr Downing, Chief Inspector,
      p. 49; CNEI (1905). *71st Report ... for 1904*, Appendix, Section 1, Dr Alexander,
      Senior Inspector, p. 15; CNEI (1906). *72nd Report ... for 1905–1906*, Appendix,
      Section 1, Mr Stronge, Senior Inspector, p. 20.
17   CNEI (1914). *79th Report ... for 1912–1913*, Appendix, Section 1, Mr M'Elwaine,
      Senior Inspector, p. 53.
18   CNEI (1904). *69th Report ... for 1902*, Appendix, Section 1, Mr Stronge, Senior
      Inspector, p. 11.
19   CNEI (1902). *68th Report ... for 1901*, Appendix, Section 1, Mr Cox (quoted in)
      Mr Downing, Chief Inspector, p. 56; Mr Hughes (quoted in) Mr Downing,
      Chief Inspector, p. 57; Mr Hogan (quoted in) Mr Purser, Chief Inspector, p. 92;
      CNEI (1904). *69th Report ... for 1902*, Appendix, Section 1, Mr Stronge, Senior
      Inspector, p. 13; Dr Beatty, Senior Inspector, p. 110.
20   Vice-Regal Committee of Inquiry into Primary Education (Ireland) 1913,
      Appendix to the First Report of the Committee, Appendix II (16), The School
      Curriculum – Circular to Inspectors, Organisers and their Officers, pp. 146–147,
      p. 146.
21   Hyland, A. (1973). *Educational Innovation – A Case Study. An Analysis of the
      Revised Programme of 1900 for National Schools in Ireland*. M.Ed. Thesis. Dublin:
      Trinity College Dublin, p. 63.
22   Dale, F.H. (1904). *Report of Mr F.H. Dale, His Majesty's Inspector of Schools,
      Board of Education, on Primary Education in Ireland*. Printed for His Majesty's
      Stationery Office by Alexander Thom and Co. (Limited) Abbey Street,
      Preface.
23   *Ibid.*, p. 68.
24   Vice-Regal Committee of Inquiry into Primary Education (Ireland) 1913,
      Appendix to the Second Report of the Committee – Minutes of Evidence, 13
      March–25 June 1913, Mr J. Hynes, p. 101, Column 6607.
25   Vice-Regal Committee of Inquiry into Primary Education (Ireland) 1913,
      Appendix to the First Report of the Committee ..., Mr J. McNeill, p. 54, Column
      1498.; *Appendix to the Second Report of the Committee* ..., Rev. C. Grierson, p. 79,

Column 5895; *Appendix to the Third Report of the Committee* ..., Rev. E.D. Crowe, p. 11, Column 14914.

26   Vice-Regal Committee of Inquiry into Primary Education (Ireland) 1913, *Appendix to the First Report of the Committee* ..., Mr W. Dilworth, p. 4, Column 85.

27   *Ibid.*, Mr A.N. Bonaparte Wyse, p. 81, Column 2160–2168.

28   Vice-Regal Committee of Inquiry into Primary Education (Ireland) 1913, *Appendix to the Second Report of the Committee* ..., Mr F.H. Dale, p. 252, Column 10717–10724.

29   CNEI (1902). *67th Report ... for 1900*, Appendix, Section 1, Mr Downing, Chief Inspector, p. 8. CNEI (1902). *68th Report ... for 1901*, Appendix, Section 1, Mr Downing, Chief Inspector, p. 22; Mr Purser, Chief Inspector, p. 78; CNEI (1905). *71st Report ... for 1904*, Appendix, Section 1, Dr Alexander, Senior Inspector, p. 13; Mr Headen, Senior Inspector, p. 66; Mr Ross, Senior Inspector, p. 79; Mr Murphy, Senior Inspector, p. 94; CNEI (1906). *72nd Report ... for 1905–1906*, Appendix, Section 1, Mr Stronge, Senior Inspector, p. 21.

30   CNEI (1905). *71st Report ... for 1904*, Appendix, Section 1, Dr Skeffington, Senior Inspector, p. 33; CNEI (1906). *72nd Report ... for 1905–1906*, Appendix, Section 1, Mr M'Elwaine, Senior Inspector, p. 32.

31   Vice-Regal Committee of Inquiry into Primary Education (Ireland) 1913, *Final Report of the Committee*, p. 14.

32   Vice-Regal Committee of Inquiry into Primary Education (Ireland) 1913, *Appendix to the Third Report of the Committee* ..., Miss Mahon, p. 327, Column 23236.

33   See Ní Chuinneagáin, S. (1995). The Irish National Teachers' Organisation (INTO) and the Deputation Crisis of 1910. *Oideas*, Summer 1995, Volume 43, pp. 94–110.

34   Vice-Regal Committee of Inquiry into Primary Education (Ireland) 1913, *Final Report of the Committee*, pp. 50–52.

35   CNEI (1903). *68th Report ... for 1901*, Appendix, Section II (G), Revised Instructions to Inspectors, p. 79.

36   Vice-Regal Committee of Inquiry into Primary Education (Ireland) 1913, *Appendix to the First Report of the Committee*, Appendix II, Circulars Issued by the National Board of Education, pp. 134–150.

37   CNEI (1903). *68th Report ... for 1901*, Appendix, Section II (G), Revised Instructions to Inspectors, p. 80.

38   Vice-Regal Committee of Inquiry into Primary Education (Ireland) 1913, *Appendix to the Third Report of the Committee* ..., Mr Carter, p. 102, Column 17598.

39 CNEI (1905). *71st Report ... for 1904*, p. 2.
40 CNEI (1902). *67th Report ... for 1900*, Appendix, Section 1, Mr Bevis, Head Organiser of Hand and Eye Training and Drawing, p. 101.
41 *Ibid.*, Mr Downing, Chief Inspector, p. 14.
42 CNEI (1908). *74th Report ... for 1907–1908*, p. 12.
43 CNEI (1905). *71st Report ... for 1904*, p. 7.
44 CNEI (1902). *68th Report ... for 1901*, Appendix, Section 1, Mr Headen (quoted in) Mr Downing, Chief Inspector, p. 39; CNEI (1905). *71st Report ... for 1904*, Appendix, Section 1, Mr Dalton, Senior Inspector, p. 88.
45 CNEI (1911). *76th Report ... for 1909–1910*, Appendix, Section 1, Messrs. Purser and Hynes, General Report on the Training Colleges, p. 7.
46 CNEI (1921). *86th Report ... for 1919–1920*, p. 28.
47 Starkie, W.J.M. (1911). *The History of Irish Primary and Secondary Education During the Last Decade – An Inaugural Address*. Belfast, p. 3.
48 CNEI (1903). *68th Report ... for 1901*, Section II, Elementary Science and Manual Instruction in National Schools – Circular to Managers, p. 55.
49 Keogh, H. (1976). Some Aspects of the Starkie Era: The System of National Education in Ireland 1899–1922. *Proceeding of ESAI*, Galway, pp. 63–66, p. 66.
50 *Circular to Managers of National Schools*, May 1903 (quoted in) Vice-Regal Committee of Inquiry into Primary Education (Ireland) 1913, *Appendix to the Second Report of the Committee ...*, Dr Starkie, p. 292, Column 11318.
51 CNEI (1902). *Building Grants for National Schools in Ireland – Report of Committee 1902*. Printed for Her Majesty's Stationery Office by Alexander Thom and Co., p. 8.
52 Dale, F.H. (1904). *Report of Mr F.H. Dale ...*, p. 15.
53 CNEI (1905). *71st Report ... for 1904*, p. 3.
54 CNEI (1902). *68th Report ... for 1901*, p. 14.
55 Dale, F.H. (1904). *Report of Mr F.H. Dale ...* p. 53.
56 CNEI (1908). *74th Report ... for 1907–1908*, p. 17.
57 CNEI (1902). *68th Report ... for 1901*, Appendix, Section 1, Mr McEnery (quoted in) Mr Downing, Chief Inspector, p. 52.
58 Confidential Letter Book of the CNEI, letter dated 10 June 1903 (quoted in) Hyland, A. (1973). *Educational Innovation ...*, p. 273.
59 CNEI (1906). *72nd Report ... for 1905–1906*, Appendix, Section II (K), pp. 191–212.
60 *Agricultural Instruction in the System of Primary Education from the establishment of the Commissioners of National Education up to the Present Day*. National Archives, File 14395A, p. 5.
61 CNEI (1904). *70th Report ... for 1903*, p. 12.

62 Plunkett, H. (1905). *Ireland in the New Century*. London: John Murray, p. 152.
63 CNEI (1899). *65th Report ... for 1898–1899*, p. 34.
64 CNEI (1902). *67th Report ... for 1900*, Appendix, Section II (F), Revised Programme of Instruction in National Schools ..., p. 68.
65 Pearse, P. (1904). Bilingual Education 2.1.1904 (in) Ó Buachalla, S. (Ed.) (1980). *A Significant Irish Educationalist – The Educational Writings of P.H. Pearse.* Dublin: Mercier Press, pp. 24–26, p. 25.
66 Pearse, P. (1903). The New Coisde Gnótha : Its Work 9.5.1903 (in) Ó Buachalla, S. (Ed.) (1980). *A Significant Irish Educationalist ...*, pp. 5–7.
67 O'Donoghue, T. (2000). *Bilingual Education In Ireland 1904–1922 – The Case of the Bilingual Programme of Instruction*. Centre for Irish Studies Monograph Series, No. 1 2000. Perth: Murdoch University, p. 49.
68 CNEI (1908). *73rd Report ... for 1906–1907*, Appendix, Section 1, Dr Skeffington, Senior Inspector, p. 50.
69 CNEI (1910). *75th Report ... for 1908–1909*, Appendix, Section 1, Mr Mangan, Examiner and Inspector of Irish, pp. 136–143.
70 Fitzpatrick, B. (1918). *Bilingualism as a Factor in Education with Application to the Language Question in Ireland*. M.A. Thesis. Dublin: University College Dublin.
71 Ó Buachalla, S. (1981). *The Irish Language in the Classroom. The Crane Bag*, Volume 5, No. 2, pp. 849–862, p. 852.
72 Department of Education (1926). *Report of the Department of Education for the School Year 1924–1925 and the Financial and Administrative Years 1924–25–26.* Dublin: The Stationery Office, p. 31.

Chapter 4

1 Democratic Programme. *Dáil Debates*, 21 January 1919, Volume F, Column 23.
2 Barrington, T. (1967). Public Administration 1927–36 (in) McManus, F. (Ed.) (1967). *The Years of the Great Test 1926–39*. Cork: Mercier Press, pp. 80–91.
3 *Times Educational Supplement*, 30 December 1922, p. 567; Deputy O'Connell, *Dáil Debates*, 3 July 1924, Volume 8, Column 407; Irish Labour Party and Trade Union Congress (1925). *Labour's Policy on Education – Being the Report of a Special Committee of the National Executive of the Irish Labour Party and Trade Union Congress*. Dublin: Irish Labour Party and Trade Union Congress, p. 10;

Deputy Concannon, *Seanad Debates*, 22 January 1941, Volume 25, Column 12; INTO (1943). *Annual Directory and Irish Educational Year Book for 1943*. Dublin: Cahill and Co. Ltd, p. 39; A Council of Education. *Irish Independent*, 13 September 1944, p. 2; Deputy Corish, *Dáil Debates*, 20 May 1947, Volume 106, Column 408; INTO (1947). *A Plan for Education*. Dublin: INTO, p. 20.

4 *Draft for an Act to make Further Provision with respect to Education in Saor-Stát Éireann and for purposes connected therewith – Part 1: Advisory Council*. UCD Archives, Eoin MacNeill Papers, LA1/P/41.

5 Akenson, D. (1975). *A Mirror to Kathleen's Face – Education in Independent Ireland 1922–1960*. London: McGill-Queen's University Press, p. 107.

6 Proposed Council of Education in Éire. *Times Educational Supplement*, 24 December 1938, p. 462.

7 Provisional Government of Ireland (1922). *Draft Constitution of the Irish Free State*. Dublin: Eason and Son.

8 Lynch, P. (1984). The Irish Free State and the Republic of Ireland, 1921–1966 (in) Moody, T. and Martin, F. (Eds) (1984). *The Course of Irish History*. Cork: Mercier Press, pp. 324–341, p. 324.

9 Murphy, J. (1975). *Ireland in the Twentieth Century*. Dublin: Gill and Macmillan, p. 64.

10 *Na Coláistí Ullmhucháin*, July 1931. UCD Archives, Blythe Papers, P24/302; *Memorandum re Preparatory Colleges*. UCD Archives, Blythe Papers, P24/302, p. 2; *Scheme of Scholarships in Secondary Schools for Pupils from the Fíor-Ghaeltacht*, July 1931. UCD Archives, Blythe Papers, P24/303; *Fees for Instruction through Irish*, 19 December 1930. UCD Archives, Blythe Papers P24/345.

11 Programme of Fianna Fáil (1926) (quoted in) Mitchell, A. and Ó Snodaigh, P. (1985). *Irish Political Documents 1916–1949*. Dublin: Irish Academic Press, p. 175.

12 Keogh, D. (1994). *Twentieth-century Ireland – Nation and State*. Dublin: Gill and Macmillan, p. 172.

13 Ó Buachalla, S. (1988). *Education Policy in Twentieth Century Ireland*. Dublin: Wolfhound Press, p. 251.

14 Peillon, M. (1982). *Contemporary Irish Society – An Introduction*. Dublin: Gill and Macmillan, p. 172.

15 Deputy de Valera, *Dáil Debates*, 6 June 1940, Volume 80, Column 1631.

16 O'Carroll, M. (1998). Inspired Educator and Ecumenist of Sorts. *Studies*, Winter 1998, Volume 87, No. 348, pp. 365–371, p. 365.

17 Bunreacht na hÉireann (1937). *Constitution of Ireland*. Dublin: The Stationery Office.

18 Deputy Mulcahy, *Dáil Debates*, 19 July 1956, Volume 159, column 1494.

19   Whyte, J. (1984). Ireland 1966–82 (in) Moody, T. and Martin, F. (Eds) (1984). *The Course of Irish History*. Cork: Mercier Press, pp. 342–362.

20   Deputy Hillery, *Dáil Debates*, 30 May 1963, Volume 203, Column 598; Dr Hillery, Address to Dublin Comhairle of Fianna Fáil, 28 February 1964 (quoted in) O'Connor, S. (1986). *A Troubled Sky – Reflections on the Irish Educational Scene 1957–1968*. Dublin: ERC, p. 78.

21   Organisation Jottings – The New Programme: Summary of Reply given by Mr J.J. O'Kelly (Sceilg) to Deputation from Programme Conference re New Programme. *The Irish School Weekly*, 28 January 1922, Volume LXXI, No. 4, p. 77.

22   Brown, T. (1981). *Ireland: A Social and Cultural History 1922–1979*. Glasgow: Fontana, p. 247.

23   CSO (1965). *Statistical Abstract of Ireland 1965*. Dublin: The Stationery Office, p. 53.

24   *Level of Living in Ireland: Measurement and Index of. Ireland – Health, including Demographic Conditions*. National Archives, File S15733.

25   McCartney, D. (1969). Education and the Language, 1938–1951 (in) Nowlan, K. and Williams, T. (Eds) (1969). *Ireland in the War Years and After 1939–51*. Dublin: Gill and Macmillan, pp. 80–94, p. 91.

26   Ferriter, D. (2003). Suffer Little Children? The Historical Validity of Memoirs of Irish Childhood (in) Dunne, J. and Kelly, J. (Eds) (2003). *Childhood and its Discontents – The First Seamus Heaney Lectures*. Dublin: The Liffey Press, pp. 69–106; McMahon, S. and O'Donoghue, J. (Eds) (1993). *Tales out of School*. Dublin: Poolbeg.

27   Kelleher, J. (1957). Ireland ... And Where Does She Stand? *Foreign Affairs*, Volume 35, No. 3, pp. 485–495, p. 495.

28   Kiernan, G. and Walsh, T. (2004). The Changing Nature of Early Childhood Care and Education in Ireland. *Irish Educational Studies*, Volume 23, No. 2, pp. 1–18.

29   Farren, S. (1995). *The Politics of Irish Education 1920–1965*. Belfast: Institute of Irish Studies, p. 225.

30   Curtin, C. (1986). Marriage and the Family (in) Clancy, P., Drudy, S., Lynch, K. and O'Dowd, L. (Eds) (1986). *Ireland – A Sociological Profile*. Dublin: Institute of Public Administration in association with the Sociological Association of Ireland, pp. 155–172.

31   Curtin, C. and Varley, A. (1984). Children and Childhood in Rural Ireland: A Consideration of the Ethnographic Literature (in) Curtin, C., Kelly, M. and O'Dowd, L. (1984). *Culture and Ideology in Ireland*. Galway: Officina Typographica, Galway University Press. pp. 30–45.

32   Devine, D. (1999). Children: Rights and Status in Education – A Socio-historical Analysis. *Irish Educational Studies*, Spring 1999, Volume 18, pp. 14–28.

33   Devlin, B. (1972). The Gaelic League – A Spent Force? (in) Ó Tuama, S. (Ed.) (1972). *The Gaelic League Idea*. Cork: Mercier Press, pp. 87–97, p. 91.

34   MacNamara, J. (1971). Successes and Failures in the Movement for the Restoration of Irish (in) Rubin, J. and Jernudd, B. (Eds) (1971). *Can Language be Planned?* Hawaii: East-West Center Press, pp. 65–94, p. 81.

35   Akenson, D. (1975). *A Mirror to Kathleen's Face ...*, p. 39.

36   *Level of Living in Ireland ...*, National Archives, File S15733.

37   Murphy, J. (1975). *Ireland in the Twentieth Century ...*, p. 65.

38   Meenan, J. (1970). *The Irish Economy since 1922*. Liverpool: University Press, p. 92.

39   De Valera, E. (1943). The Ireland we Dreamed of, 17 March 1943 (in) Moynihan, M. (Ed.) (1980). *Speeches and Statements by Eamon de Valera 1917–1973*. Dublin: Gill and Macmillan, p. 466.

40   Lee, J. (1970). Continuity and Change in Ireland, 1945–70 (in) Lee, J. (Ed.) (1970). *Ireland 1945–1970*. Dublin: Gill and Macmillan, pp. 166–177, p. 169.

41   Kennedy, K., Giblin, T. and McHugh, D. (1988). *The Economic Development of Ireland in the Twentieth Century*. London: Routledge, p. 55.

42   Department of Finance (1958). *Economic Development*. Dublin: The Stationery Office, p. 238.

43   Department of Finance (1958). *Programme for Economic Expansion*. Dublin: The Stationery Office.

44   Department of Finance (1964). *Second Programme for Economic Expansion – Part 2*. Dublin: The Stationery Office, p. 197.

45   Department of Finance (1969). *Third Programme – Economic and Social Development 1969–1972*. Dublin: The Stationery Office, p. 193.

46   Halloran, J. (1962). The New Society: Community and Social Change. *Doctrine and Life*, July 1962, Volume 12, No. 7, pp. 365–378, p. 374.

47   Government of Ireland (1969). *Ireland Tomorrow*. Dublin: The Stationery Office, p. 7.

48   Kennedy, K., Giblin, T. and McHugh, D. (1988). *The Economic Development of Ireland ...*, p. 55.

49   O'Malley, D. (1967). University Education in Dublin – Statement of Minister for Education, 18 April 1967. *Studies*, Summer 1967, Volume LVI, No. 222, pp. 113–121, p. 115.

50   An Roinn Oideachais (1962). *Tuarascáil 1960–61*. Baile Átha Cliath: Oifig an tSoláthair, p. 123.

51 An Roinn Oideachais (1974). *Tuarascáil – Táblaí Staitistic 1968/69–1971/72*. Baile Átha Cliath: Oifig an tSoláthair, p. 23.

52 NESC (1975). *Educational Expenditure in Ireland*. Dublin: NESC, p. 8.

53 Tussing, D. (1978). *Irish Educational Expenditures – Past, Present and Future*. Dublin: Economic and Social Research Institute, p. 164.

54 Akenson, D. (1975). *A Mirror to Kathleen's Face ...*, p. 89.

55 Mescal, J. (1957). *Religion in the Irish System of Education*. Dublin: Clonmore and Reynolds Ltd., p. 143; Whyte, J. (1990). *Church and State in Modern Ireland 1923–1979 – Second Edition*. Dublin: Gill and Macmillan, p. 21.

56 Department of Education (1926). *Report of the Department of Education for the School Year 1924–1925 and the Financial and Administrative Years 1924–25–26*. Dublin: The Stationery Office, p. 7.

57 Drudy, S. and Lynch, K. (1993). *Schools and Society in Ireland*. Dublin: Gill and Macmillan, p. 74.

58 Deputy MacNeill, *Dáil Debates*, 1 December 1922, Volume 1, Columns 2577–78; Deputy Derrig, *Dáil Debates*, 20 May 1947, Volume 106, Columns 409; Deputy Mulcahy, *Dáil Debates*, 4 May 1948, Volume 110, Column 1093.

59 Record of Irish Ecclesiastical Events for the Year 1921. *Irish Catholic Directory*, 20 October 1921, pp. 577–578.

60 Titley, B. (1983). *Church, State and the Control of Schooling in Ireland 1900–1944*. Dublin: Gill and Macmillan Ltd., p. 158.

61 Inglis, T. (1998). *Moral Monopoly – The Rise and Fall of the Catholic Church in Modern Ireland*. Dublin: University College Dublin Press, p. 191.

62 Archbishop John Charles McQuaid (1945). *Irish Catholic Directory*, 20 February 1944, p. 674.

63 Abbott, W. (Ed.) (1966). *The Documents of Vatican II*. London: Geoffrey Chapman.

64 Whyte, J. (1979). Church, State and Society 1950–1970 (in) Lee, J. (Ed.) (1979). *Ireland 1945–1970*. Dublin: Gill and Macmillan, pp. 73–82, p. 82.

65 An Roinn Oideachais (1968). *Tuarascáil 1965–66*. Baile Átha Cliath: Oifig an tSoláthair, p. 23.

66 McCracken, J. (1958). *Representative Government in Ireland: A Study of Dáil Éireann, 1919–1948*. London: Oxford University Press, p. 92.

67 *The Commissioners of National Education*. National Archives, File 14395A, p. 12.

68 Department of Education (1925). *Statistics relating to National Education in Saorstát for the Year 1922–1923*. Dublin: The Stationery Office, p. 6.

69 Barrington, T. (1980). *The Irish Administrative System*. Dublin: Institute of Public Administration, pp. 31–32.

70   Circular 10/67; *Promotion of Pupils in National Schools*, March 1967.

71   Commission on School Accommodation (2001). *Amalgamation of First Level Schools*. Dublin: Department of Education and Science, p. 7.

72   Department of Education (1929). *Amalgamation of Schools – Revision of Rules and Regulations*. Dublin: Department of Education, p. 2.

73   Deputy Lenihan, *Dáil Debates*, 5 December 1968, Volume 237, Column 2075; Deputy Faulkner, *Dáil Debates*, 22 April 1970, Volume 245, Column 1875.

74   Department of Education (1965). *Investment in Education – Report of the Survey Team appointed by the Minister for Education in October 1962*. Dublin: The Stationery Office, p. 55.

75   Keegan, F. (1996). The Role of Amalgamation within the National Primary Education System, 1831–1994. *Irish Educational Studies*, Spring 1996, Volume 15, pp. 291–298, p. 295.

76   An Roinn Oideachais (1974). *Tuarascáil – Táblaí Staitistic 1968/69–1971/72 ...*, p. 69.

77   Department of Education (1928). *Report of the Department of Education for the School Years 1925–26–27 and the Financial and Administrative Year 1926–27*. Dublin: The Stationery Office, p. 6.

78   O'Connor, S. (1986). *A Troubled Sky ...*, p. 182.

79   Department of Education (1924). *Scholarships from Primary School*. Dublin: The Stationery Office, p. 5.

80   An Roinn Oideachais (1963). *Tuarascáil 1961–62*. Baile Átha Cliath: Oifig an tSoláthair, p. 44.

81   Department of Education (1930). *Report of the Department of Education 1928–1929*. Dublin: The Stationery Office, p. 22.

82   Department of Education (1937). *Report of the Department of Education 1935–1936*. Dublin: The Stationery Office, p. 29.

83   Circular 7/43; *Revised Regulations for the Primary School Certificate Examination*.

84   INTO (1967). *Reports of the Central Executive Committee and Finance Committee for the Year 1966–1967, together with Accounts and Statistics and Resolutions on Organisation Matters*. Dublin: INTO, p. 23.

85   Department of Education (1926). *Report of the Department of Education for the School Years 1924–25 ...*, p. 35; Department of Education (1928). *Report of the Department of Education for the School Years 1925–26–27 ...*, p. 187.

86   Department of Education (1928). *Report of the Department of Education for the School Years 1925–26–27 ...*, p. 7.

87   Department of Education (1933). *Report of the Department of Education 1931–1932*. Dublin: The Stationery Office, p. 4.

88 Hyland, A. (1979). Shared Areas in Irish National Schools. *Proceedings of ESAI 1979*, Dublin, pp. 175–199, p. 184.

89 INTO (1947). *A Plan for Education* ..., p. 86.

90 Department of Education (1965). *Investment in Education* ..., pp. 259–260.

91 Department of Education (1969). *Ár nDaltaí Uile – All our Children*. Dublin: Department of Education, p. 15.

92 Department of Education (1965). *Rules for National Schools under the Department of Education*. Dublin: The Stationery Office, p. 12.

93 *Ibid.*, p. 26.

94 *Publications in Irish, An Gúm.* Memorandum on the 'Gúm' prepared by Publications Officer, Department of Education, 8 August 1947. National Archives, File S9538A.

95 Publications in Irish, An Gúm. *An Gúm – Publications up to 28 July 1951*. National Archives, File S9538A.

96 Publications in Irish – General. *Leabhair de Chuid An Ghúm a Díoladh mar Bhrus-pháipéar*. National Archives, File S9538B.

97 Coolahan, J. (2003). Unrealised Potential: The Relationship of Schools with the Library Service (in) McDermott, N. (Ed.) (2003). *The University of the People: Celebrating Ireland's Public Libraries – The Thomas Davis Lecture Series*. Dublin: The Library Council, pp. 143–166.

98 Department of Education (1967). *Towards a White Paper on Education*, p. 8. (Unpublished).

99 Deputy Hillery, *Dáil Debates*, 29 April 1964, Volume 209, Column 630.

100 INTO (1969). *Reports of the Central Executive Committee and Finance Committee for the Year 1968–1969, together with Accounts and Statistics and Resolutions on Organisation Matters*. Dublin INTO, pp. 1–2.

101 Bennett, J. (1992). *Culture, Curriculum and Primary Education in Ireland 1920–1970*. PhD Thesis. Kildare: National University of Ireland, Maynooth, p. 104.

102 *Ibid.*, p. 243.

103 MacNeill, E. (1925) Irish Educational Policy II. *Irish Statesman*, 24 October 1925, p. 200.

104 Hyde, D. (n.d.) The Necessity for de-Anglicising Ireland (in) Ó Conaire, B. (Ed.) (1986). *Language, Love and Lyrics, Essays and Lectures of Douglas Hyde*. Dublin: Academic Press, pp. 153–170.

105 De Valera, E. (1937). The Constitution of Ireland, Radio Broadcast 29 December 1938 (in) Moynihan, M. (Ed.) (1980). *Speeches and Statements by Eamon de Valera* ..., p. 365.

106 O'Doherty, E. (1958). Bilingualism: Educational Aspects. *Advancement of Science*, March 1958, Volume 14, No. 56, pp. 282–287, p. 287.

107 Kelly, A. (2002). *Compulsory Irish: Language and Education in Ireland 1870s–1970s.* Dublin: Irish Academic Press, p. 141.

108 Department of Education (1936). *Report of the Department of Education 1934–1935.* Dublin: The Stationery Office p. 2.

109 Coimisiún na Gaeltachta (1926). *Report of Coimisiún na Gaeltachta.* Dublin: The Stationery Office.

110 Commission on the Restoration of the Irish Language (1963). *Summary, in English, of the Final Report.* Dublin: The Stationery Office.

111 Kelly, A. (2002). *Compulsory Irish* ..., p. 92.

112 Ó Baoill, D. (1988). Language Planning in Ireland: The Standardisation of Irish (in) Ó Riagáin, P. (Ed.) (1988). *International Journal of the Sociology of Language – Language Planning in Ireland.* Amsterdam: Mouton de Gruyter, pp. 109–126, p. 114.

113 Ó Cuív, B. (1969). Irish in the Modern World (in) Ó Cuív, B. (Ed.) (1969). *A View of the Irish Language.* Dublin: The Stationery Office, pp. 122–132, p. 131.

114 Circular; *Revival of Irish – What Children Can do?* March 1941, p. 7.

115 *Ibid.*

116 Jones, V. (1996). Coláiste Moibhí – The Last Preparatory College. *Irish Educational Studies,* Spring 1996, Volume 15, pp. 101–112, p. 103.

117 Department of Education (1926). *Report of the Department of Education for the School Year 1924–25* ..., p. 17.

118 Department of Education (1934). *Revision of Rules and Regulations for National Schools under the Department of Education with an Explanatory Note on the Revised Salary Scales and the New Pension Scheme.* Dublin: Department of Education, p. 3.

119 Moroney, M. (2004). *An Analysis of the Development of Salaries and Pensions of National Teachers and of the Role of the Irish National Teachers' Organisation in their Progression, 1831 to 2000.* PhD Thesis. Kildare: National University of Ireland, Maynooth, pp. 336–337.

120 An Roinn Oideachais (1968). *Tuarascáil 1965–66* ..., p. 24.

121 An Roinn Oideachais (1974). *Tuarascáil – Táblaí Staitistic 1968/69–1971/72* ..., p. 17.

122 Department of Education (1926). *Report of the Department of Education for the School Year 1924–25* ..., p. 41.

123 Corcoran, T. (1923). The Native Speaker as Teacher. *Irish Monthly,* April 1923, Volume 51, pp. 187–190, p. 187.

124 Department of Education (1926). *Report of the Department of Education for the School Year 1924–25* ..., p. 41.

125 Department of Education (1934). *Report of the Department of Education 1932–1933*. Dublin: The Stationery Office, p. 12.

126 Department of Education (1937). *Report of the Department of Education 1935–36* ..., p. 9.

127 Deputy Lynch, *Dáil Debates*, 22 May 1958, Volume 168, Column 640–41.

128 Deputy Hillery, *Dáil Debates*, 24 May 1960, Volume 182, Column 72–73.

129 St Patrick's College (1975). *St Patrick's College, Drumcondra: Centenary Booklet 1875–1975*. Dublin: Beacon Printing Co. Ltd, p. 23.

130 *Ibid.*, p. 24.

131 Training Colleges – *Instruction of Students through the Medium of Irish*. Letter to Our Lady of Mercy Training College, July 1931. National Archives, Box 355, File 17131.

132 Department of Education (1930). *Report of the Department of Education 1928–29* ..., p. 17.

133 Parkes, S. (1984). *Kildare Place – The History of the Church of Ireland Training College 1811–1969*. Dublin: Church of Ireland College of Education, p. 145.

134 Department of Education (1926). *Report of the Department of Education for the School Year 1924–25* ..., p. 40.

135 Coolahan, J. (1981). '*Education' in the Training Colleges – Carysfort 1877–1977: Two Centenary Lectures*. Blackrock: Our Lady of Mercy College, pp. 20–52, p. 37.

136 *Ibid.*, p. 41.

137 Coolahan, J. (1998). Educational Studies and Teacher Education in Ireland, 1965–1995. *Paedagogica Historica*: Supplementary Series, Volume III, Gent, Belgium, pp. 431–445, p. 433.

138 Department of Education (1929). *Report of the Department of Education 1927–1928*. Dublin: The Stationery Office, p. 15.

139 Department of Education (1925). *Report and Statistics relating to National Education in Saorstát for the Year 1923–1924*. Dublin: The Stationery Office, p. 26.

140 Irish Courses for Teachers and Irish Colleges. *Memorandum – The Training of Teachers in Irish*. National Archives, Box 298, File 14806, p. 2.

141 Department of Education (1928). *Report of the Department of Education for the School Years 1925–26–27* ..., p. 122.

142 *Ibid.*

143 *Teachers' Qualifications in Irish*, June 1928. National Archives, Box 342, File 16610.

144 Office of National Education (1931). *Qualifications of Teachers – Classes of Persons Eligible for Recognition as Teachers: Revision of Rules and Regulations, September 1931*. National Archives, Box 727, File 31752.

145 Department of Education (1930). *Report of the Department of Education 1928–29 ...*, p. 21.

146 *Control of Primary Teachers in their Capacity as Members of that Profession.* National Archives, File 14395A, p. 1.

147 *Circular to Inspectors*, November 1922, p. 1.

148 Visits of Organisers to Irish Speaking Districts during July 1924. *Circular to Inspectors and Organisers.* National Archives, Box 364, File 17397.

149 *Letter from Irish National Teachers' Organisation. Circular to Inspectors – Programme 1923–1924, February 1924.* National Archives, Box 624, File 27513, p. 4.

150 *Ibid.*, p. 1.

151 Department of Education (1927). *Report presented by the Committee on Inspection of Primary Schools to the Minister for Education.* Dublin: The Stationery office, p. 5.

152 *Ibid.*, p. 7.

153 *Appeals against Inspectors' Reports of General Inspections and Regulations for the Award of Primary School Certificate, Revised Instructions to Inspectors.* National Archives, Box 575, File 25629.

154 Revised Instructions to Inspectors (in) Department of Education (1928). *Report of the Department of Education for the School Years 1925–26–27 ...*, p. 11.

155 *Circulars and Memoranda to Inspectors including 'Teachers' Rating.' Questions of Conditions for rating 'Highly Efficient' and 'Efficient.'* July 1929. National Archives, Box 471, File 21432.

156 Circular 11/31; *Circular to Managers, Teachers and Inspectors on Teaching through the Medium of Irish*, p. 2.

157 Circular 12/31; *Circular to Inspectors on the Award of Highly Efficient and Efficient Ratings*, p. 2.

158 *Brief Outline of the History of the Inspectorate in the National Schools of Ireland*, p. 6 (Unpublished).

159 Barrington, T. (1980). *The Irish Administrative System ...*, p. 113.

160 Coolahan, J. (1984). The Fortunes of Education as a Subject of Study and of Research in Ireland. *Irish Educational Studies*, Volume 4, No. 1, pp. 1–34, p. 16.

161 Sheehan, J. (1979). Education and Society in Ireland, 1945–70 (in) Lee, J. (Ed.) (1979). *Ireland 1945–1970.* Dublin: Gill and Macmillan, pp. 61–72, p. 63.

162 Coolahan, J. (1984). The Fortunes of Education ..., p. 20.

163 United Nations Declaration on the Rights of the Child (1959) (quoted in) Wilkerson, A. (1973). *The Rights of Children – Emergent Concepts of Law and Society.* Philadelphia: Temple University Press, pp. 3–6, p. 5.

164 Department of Health (1960). *The Problem of the Mentally Handicapped*. Dublin: The Stationery Office; Commission of Inquiry on Mental Handicap (1965). *Report of the Commission of Inquiry on Mental Handicap*. Dublin: The Stationery Office.

165 O'Sullivan, N. (1984). *Remedial Reading Education in the Primary School*. M.Ed. Thesis. Kildare: National University of Ireland, Maynooth, p. 24.

166 Commission on Itinerancy (1963). *Report of the Commission on Itinerancy*. Dublin: The Stationery Office, p. 65.

167 Committee on the Provision of Educational Facilities for the Children of Itinerants (1970). Educational Facilities for the Children of Itinerants. *Oideas*, Autumn 1970, Volume 5, pp. 44–53, p. 44.

168 NIEC (1966). *Comments on 'Investment in Education.'* Dublin: NIEC, p. 5.

169 Tuairim (1962). *Educating Towards a United Europe – Pamphlet 8*. Dublin: Tuairim, p. 6.

170 Hurley, K. (1977). Primary School: Whither the Curriculum. *Compass*, Volume 6, No. 2, pp. 15–25, p. 16.

171 Keogh, D. (1994). *Twentieth-century Ireland* ..., p. 253.

172 Whyte, J. (1984). Ireland 1966–82 ..., p. 354.

173 Akenson, D. (1975). *A Mirror to Kathleen's Face* ..., p. 143.

174 Labour Party (1963). *Challenge and Change in Education – Policy Document issued by the Labour Party*. Dublin: The Labour Party; Fine Gael (1966). *Policy for a Just Society – Education*. Dublin: Fine Gael.

175 Fine Gael (1966). *Policy for a Just Society – Irish Language Preservation*. Dublin: Fine Gael, p. 1.

176 Lynch, P. (1984). The Irish Free State and the Republic of Ireland, 1921–1966 ..., p. 337.

177 Dr Hillery (1962). Irish Education for the New Europe. *European Teacher – Journal of the Irish Section of the European Association of Teachers*, Volume 1, No. 1, pp. 4–6, p. 6.

178 Atkinson, N. (1964). The School Structure in the Republic of Ireland. *Comparative Education Review*, Volume 8, pp. 276–280, p. 279.

179 Big Changes to be Made in Education. *The Irish Times*, 21 May 1963, p. 1.

180 O'Connor, S. (1968). Post-Primary Education in Ireland: Now and in the Future. *Studies*, Autumn 1968, Volume 57, No. 227, pp. 233–251, p. 234.

181 Department of Education (1965). *Investment in Education* ...

182 *Ibid.*, p. 145.

183 OECD (1969). *Reviews of National Policies for Education – Ireland*. Paris: OECD, p. 47.

Chapter 5

1   Programme of Reorganised Sinn Féin (1917) (quoted in) Mitchell, A. and Ó Snodaigh, P. (1985). *Irish Political Documents 1916–1949*. Dublin: Irish Academic Press, p. 36.

2   Kelly, A. (1993). The Gaelic League and the Introduction of Compulsory Irish into the Free State Education System. *Oideas*, Winter 1993, Volume 41, pp. 46–57, p. 55.

3   The Education Programme of the Gaelic League (quoted in) Hyland, A. and Milne, K. (1987). *Irish Educational Documents – Volume 1. Selection of Extracts from Documents relating to the History of Irish Education from the Earliest Times to 1922*. Dublin: Church of Ireland College of Education, p. 190.

4   O'Connell, T. (1968). *100 Years of Progress – The Story of the Irish National Teachers' Organisation 1868–1968*. Dublin: Dakota Press, p. 342.

5   National Programme Conference (1922). *National Programme of Primary Instruction*. Dublin: The Educational Company of Ireland, p. 3.

6   Farren, S. (1995). *The Politics of Irish Education 1920–1965*. Belfast: Institute of Irish Studies, p. 116.

7   National Programme Conference (1922). *National Programme of Primary Instruction* ..., p. 2.

8   Coolahan, J. (1973). *A Study of Curricular Policy for the Primary and Secondary Schools of Ireland 1900–1935, with Special Reference to the Irish Language and Irish History*. PhD Thesis. Dublin: Trinity College Dublin, p. 285.

9   National Programme Conference (1922). *National Programme of Primary Instruction* ..., p. 4.

10 Coolahan, J. (1973). *A Study of Curricular Policy* ..., p. 257.

11 National Programme Conference (1922). *National Programme of Primary Instruction* ..., p. 4.

12 *Ibid.*

13 Akenson, D. (1975). *A Mirror to Kathleen's Face – Education in Independent Ireland 1922–1960*. London: McGill-Queen's University Press, p. 43.

14 Lyons, F.S.L. (1971). *Ireland Since the Famine*. London: Fontana Press, p. 637.

15 National Programme Conference (1922). *National Programme of Primary Instruction* ..., p. 3.

16 *Ibid.*, p. 15.

17 Akenson, D. (1975). *A Mirror to Kathleen's Face* ..., p. 44.

18 Ó Cuív, B. (1966). Education and Language (in) Williams, D. (Ed.) (1969). *The Irish Struggle 1916–1926*. London: Routledge and Kegan Paul, pp. 153–166, p. 162.

19 Pearse, P. (1915). The Murder Machine (in) Ó Buachalla, S. (Ed.) (1980). *A Significant Irish Educationalist – The Educational Writings of P.H. Pearse*. Dublin: Mercier Press, p. 384.

20 National Programme Conference (1922). *National Programme of Primary Instruction* ..., p. 5.

21 *Ibid.*, p. 10.

22 *Ibid.*, p. 5.

23 Coolahan, J. (1982). Developments in English Reading in the Irish National Schools, 1937–1977 (in) Swan, D. (Ed.) (1982). *Perspectives on Reading – A Symposium on the Theory and Teaching of Reading*. Dublin: The Glendale Press, pp. 168–181, p. 179; Farren, S. (1995). *The Politics of Irish Education* ..., p. 56.

24 National Programme Conference (1922). *National Programme of Primary Instruction* ..., p. 5.

25 Corcoran, T. (1923). How English may be Taught without Anglicising. *Irish Monthly*, June 1923, Volume 51, pp. 269–273, p. 269.

26 National Programme Conference (1922). *National Programme of Primary Instruction* ..., p. 5.

27 *Ibid.*, p. 14.

28 *Ibid.*, pp. 23–24.

29 *Ibid.*, p. 30.

30 *Ibid.*

31 Circular; *New Programme of Instruction in National Schools*, April 1922.

32 National Programme Conference (1922). *National Programme of Primary Instruction* ..., p. 13.

33 The National Programme Conference. *The Irish School Weekly*, 13 August 1921, Volume XLIX, No. 51, pp. 1246–1261.

34 O'Neill, J. (1943). The Educationalist. *Studies*, June 1943, Volume XXXII, No. 126, pp. 157–160, p. 158.

35 Corcoran, T. (1930). The Catholic Philosophy of Education. *Studies*, June 1930, Volume XIX, No. 74, pp. 199–210, p. 204.

36 Corcoran, T. (1925). Class Examinations. *Irish Monthly*, June 1925, Volume 53, pp. 286–289, p. 286.

37 See for example: Corcoran, T. (1923). An Infant Language Method Wanted. *Irish Monthly*, October 1923, Volume 51, pp. 489–490, p. 490; Corcoran, T. (1924). Is the Montessori Method to be Introduced into our Schools?, I, – The Montessori Principles. *Irish Monthly*, April 1924, Volume 52, pp. 118–124; Corcoran, T. (1926).

The True Children's Garden. *Irish Monthly*, May 1926, Volume 54, pp. 229–233; Corcoran, T. (1927). Pestalozzi and the Catholic Orphans. *Irish Monthly*, March 1927, Volume 55, pp. 118–124.

38   Corcoran, T. (1925). The Irish Language in the Irish Schools. *Studies*, September 1925, Volume XIV, No. 55, pp. 377–388, p. 385.

39   Rev. Corcoran, Professor of Education at UCD. National Archives, Box 130, File 8536, Part 2.

40   Corcoran, T. (1923). How the Irish Language can be Revived. *Irish Monthly*, January 1923, Volume 51, pp. 26–30, p. 27; Corcoran, T. (1924). The Language Campaigns in Alsace-Lorraine. *Studies*, June 1924, Volume XIII, No. 50, pp. 201–213, p. 209.

41   Corcoran, T. (1923). How the Irish Language can be Revived ..., p. 27.

42   Corcoran, T. (1925). The Irish Language in the Irish Schools ..., p. 386.

43   Corcoran, T. (1923). The Native Speaker as Teacher. *Irish Monthly*, April 1923, Volume 51, pp. 187–190, p. 190.

44   O'Connor, M. (2004). The Theories on Infant Pedagogy of Dr Timothy Corcoran, Professor of Education, University College, Dublin. *Irish Educational Studies*, Spring/Summer 2004, Volume 23, No. 1, pp. 35–47.

45   Educational Topics. *The Irish School Weekly*, 5 April 1924, Volume LXXV, No. 13, p. 425.

46   The School Programme – Deputation to the Minister for Education. *The Irish School Weekly*, 8 November 1924, Volume LXXV, No. 44, p. 1315.

47   Report of the Central Executive Committee for the Year 1924–1925 – The School Programme. *The Irish School Weekly*, 28 February 1925, Volume LXXVI, No. 9, pp. 251–254.

48   National Programme Conference (1926). *Report and Programme presented by the National Programme Conference to the Minister for Education*. Dublin: The Stationery Office, p. 4.

49   McKenna, L. (1912). The Educational Value of Irish. *Studies*, June 1912, Volume 1, No. 2, pp. 307–326, p. 308.

50   *Letter from Seosamh O'Neill to the Department of Finance*, 19 May 1925. National Archives, Box 130, File 8536, Part 1.

51   *National Programme Conference – Minutes 9 June 1925*. National Archives, Box 244, File 12842.

52   *Report and Programme submitted by The National Programme Conference to the Minister for Education*. National Archives, Box 250, File 12848, p. 2.

53   *List of Points on which Information is Specifically Desired by the National Programme Conference*. National Archives, Box 244, File 12842.

54 *Digest of the Replies received in relation to the Points on which Information is Specifically Desired by the National Programme Conference. Question 1–8.* National Archives, File 12850.

55 National Programme Conference (1926). *Report and Programme presented ...*, p. 7.

56 *National Programme Conference, Examining Sub-committee of National Programme Conference.* National Archives, Box 245, File 12850.

57 *Report and Programme submitted by The National Programme Conference ...*, p. 4.

58 National Programme Conference (1926). *Report and Programme ...*, p. 8.

59 *Agenda for Meeting on 10 November.* National Archives, Box 130, File 8536, Part 2.

60 *National Programme Conference, Minutes of Second Meeting of Sub-Committee*, 25 July 1925. National Archives, Box 245, File 12850.

61 Mr MacEnrí, Principal, Bangor Erris Boys' N.S., Co. Mayo; Cáit Nic Fhlanchuidhe, Assistant Teacher, Mulnahona Girls' School, Ring; Mr Timothy O'Brien, Principal, St Michael and John's School, Dublin; Michael Moriarity, Letterleague National School, Letterkenny. National Archives, Box 130, File 8536, Part 2.

62 Máire Ní Cheallacháin, Scoil Bhríde. National Archives, Box 130, File 8536, Part 2.

63 Máire Ní Ghallachobhair, Teacher of Day Pupils in Eccles Street Convent, Dublin. National Archives, Box 130, File 8536, Part 2.

64 Cáit Nic Fhlanchuidhe ..., Box 130, File 8536, Part 2.

65 Miss Heagen, Central Infant Model School; Mr Bohan, Principal, Cloonteagh N.S., Longford; Michael Moriarity ... Box 130, File 8536, Part 2.

66 Michael Moriarity ...; Mr MacEnrí ..., Box 130, File 8536, Part 2.

67 Mr Bohan ...; Mr MacEnrí ...; Cáit Nic Fhlanchuidhe ...; Mr Timothy O'Brien ...; Michael Moriarity ..., Box 130, File 8536, Part 2.

68 Cáit Nic Fhlanchuidhe ...; Máire Ní Ghallachobhair ..., Box 130, File 8536, Part 2.

69 Mr Liam Mac Fhachtna, Inspector of Irish in the National Schools. National Archives, Box 130, File 8536, Part 2.

70 Mr Joseph Hanly, General Organising Inspector of Rural Science. National Archives, Box 130, File 8536, Part 2.

71 Mr Liam Ó Ceallaigh, District Inspector; Mr F. O'Tierney, Divisional Inspector. National Archives, Box 130, File 8536, Part 2.

72 Inspector's Conference on the National Programme, June 1925. *Conference of the Divisional Inspectors on the National Conference Programme.* National Archives, Box 244, File 12845, p. 3.

73 Little, R. (1925). *General Report on the State of Education in Division V.* National Archives, File 12850, p. 4; O'Tighearnaigh, P. (1925). *Report of State of Education in Galway Division.* National Archives, File 12850, p. 15.

74 FitzGerald, P. (1925). *Report of State of Education in the Dublin Division.* National Archives, File 12850, p. 8.

75 Rev. Corcoran, Professor of Education at UCD. National Archives, Box 130, File 8536, Part 2.

76 *Ibid.*

77 *Ibid.*

78 Mr E. Culverwell, Professor of Education, Trinity College Dublin. National Archives, Box 130, File 8536, Part 2.

79 Rev. Phelan, Master of Method, Christian Brothers' Training College, Dublin. National Archives, Box 130, File 8536, Part 2.

80 Rev. T. O'Rahilly, National School Manager, Presentation Schools, Dublin. National Archives, Box 130, File 8536, Part 2.

81 *Views of Catholic Clerical School Managers' Association in detail on the points submitted by the National Programme Conference.* National Archives, Box 246, File 12852.

82 *Views of the Chamber of Commerce,* Dublin. National Archives, Box 246, File 12852.

83 *Views of the Association of Training College Teachers. National Archives,* Box 246, File 12852.

84 *Views of the Education Committee, Galway County Council.* National Archives, Box 246, File 12852.

85 *Office of Adjutant General – Memo re Programme of Primary Education.* National Archives, Box 246, File 12852.

86 *Submission of Aodh O'Neill,* Ministry of Defence. National Archives, Box 246, File 12852; *Programme Conference 1925 – Church of Ireland General Synod's Board of Education.* National Archives, Box 246, File 12852.

87 Office of National Education: National Programme Conference – Views of Office in relation to Reviewing the Programme (1925). *Albert Agricultural College – Reply to your G.1689/25.* National Archives, File AG1/G1689/25, p. 1.

88 Office of National Education: National Programme Conference – Views of Office in relation to Reviewing the Programme (1925). *Memorandum furnished by the Department of Lands and Agriculture for the Information of the National Programme Conference.* National Archives, File AG1/G1689/25, p. 6.

89 *Recommendations and Suggested Changes in the Present Primary Programme for Schools, Adopted and Approved by the Protestant Teachers' Union at a Meeting held on 3 September 1925.* National Archives, Box 245, File 12849.

90 *Programme Conference 1925 – Church of Ireland General Synod's Board of Education …*

91 *Programme Conference 1925 – Statement submitted by the Central Executive Committee of the Irish National Teachers' Organisation.* National Archives, Box 246, File 12852.

92 *Extracts from National Programme Conference Discussion – Infant Standards.* National Archives, Box 244, File 12847, p. 1.

93 Rule 127 – Recommendation of Programme. *Extracts from National Programme Conference Discussion – Infant Standards.* National Archives, Box 410, File 19168, p. 3.

94 National Programme Conference (1926). *Report and Programme …*, p. 9.

95 *Ibid.*, p. 14.

96 *National Programme Conference – Meeting on 10 November 1925.* National Archives, Box 130, File 8536, Part 2, p. 9.

97 National Programme Conference (1926). *Report and Programme …*, p. 11.

98 *Ibid.*, p. 12.

99 *Ibid.*, p. 10.

100 *Ibid.*

101 *Ibid.*

102 *Ibid.*, p. 12.

103 *Ibid.*, p. 36.

104 *Ibid.*, p. 40.

105 *Ibid.*, p. 42.

106 *Ibid.*, p. 14.

107 *Ibid.*, p. 43.

108 *Ibid.*, p. 52.

109 *Ibid.*, p. 21.

110 *Ibid.*, p. 53.

111 Deputy O'Sullivan, *Dáil Debates*, 7 May 1926, Volume 15, Column 1313.

112 Circular; *Programme of Instruction for National Schools*, July 1926.

113 Department of Education (1927). *Regulations and Explanatory Notes for the Teaching of Rural Science and Nature Study in Primary Schools.* Dublin: The Stationery Office, p. 3.

114 Department of Education (1930). *Rural Science and Nature Study – Suggested Demonstrations for the Illustration of Lessons.* Dublin: Government Publications Sales Office, p. 3.

115   Department of Education (1933). *Notes for Teachers – Irish*. Dublin: The Stationery
      Office, p. 1.
116   Department of Education (1933). *Notes for Teachers – English*. Dublin: The
      Stationery Office, p. 3.
117   Department of Education (1933). *Notes for Teachers – History*. Dublin: The
      Stationery Office, p. 3.
118   *Ibid.*, p. 14.
119   Department of Education (1934). *National Tradition and Folklore*. Dublin: The
      Stationery Office, p. 1.
120   Department of Education (1933). *Notes for Teachers – Physical Training*. Dublin:
      The Stationery Office.
121   Department of Education (1933). *Notes for Teachers – Geography*. Dublin: The
      Stationery Office, p. 1.
122   Department of Education (1933). *Notes for Teachers – Music*. Dublin: The
      Stationery Office, p. 3.
123   Department of Education (1935). *Notes for Teachers – Mathematics*. Dublin: The
      Stationery Office, p. 1.
124   INTO (1933). *Official Programme of the Sixty-Fifth Annual Congress*. Dublin:
      Educational Company of Ireland, p. 54; Resolutions Passed at 1934 Congress.
      The Irish School Weekly, 21 April 1934, Volume XXXVI, No. 16, p. 397.
125   Department of Education (1927). *Report presented by the Committee on Inspection
      of Primary Schools to the Minister for Education*. Dublin: The Stationery office,
      pp. 21–61.
126   Report of CEC Representatives on Programme Conference (appendix to) INTO
      (1934). *Annual Directory and Irish Educational Year Book for 1934*. Dublin: Wood
      Printing Works Limited, p. 43.
127   Deputy Derrig, *Dáil Debates*, 11 April 1934, Volume 51, Column 1604.
128   Department of Education (1934). *Revised Programme of Primary Instruction*.
      Dublin: The Wood Printing Works, p. 3.
129   *Ibid.*
130   O'Connor, M. (2010). *The Development of Infant Education in Ireland, 1838–1948:
      Epochs and Eras*. Bern: Peter Lang, pp. 227–250.
131   Department of Education (1948). *Revised Programme for Infants*. Dublin: The
      Stationery Office; Department of Education (1951). *The Infant School – Notes
      for Teachers*. Dublin: The Stationery Office.
132   Department of Education (1945). *Report of the Department of Education 1943–
      1944*. Dublin: The Stationery Office, p. 21.
133   Department of Education (1948). *Revised Programme for Infants ...*, p. 5.
134   *Ibid.*

135 Department of Education (1951). *The Infant School ...*, p. 3.
136 *Ibid.*, p. 4.
137 *Ibid.*, p. 45.
138 O'Connor, M. (1987). Infant Education in Independent Ireland 1922–1971. *An Múinteoir*, Autumn 1987, Volume 2, No. 1, pp. 5–7, p. 6.

Chapter 6

1 Department of Education (1928). *Report of the Department of Education for the School Years 1925–26–27 and the Financial and Administrative Year 1926–1927.* Dublin: The Stationery Office, p. 43.
2 Department of Education (1926). *Report of the Department of Education for the School Year 1924–1925 and the Financial and Administrative Years 1924–25–26.* Dublin: The Stationery Office, p. 42; Department of Education (1928). *Report of the Department of Education for the School Years 1925–26–27 ...*, p. 25, p. 36, p. 187; Department of Education (1931). *Report of the Department of Education 1929–1930.* Dublin: The Stationery Office, p. 47.
3 Department of Education (1929). *Report of the Department of Education 1927–1928.* Dublin: The Stationery Office, p. 23.
4 Department of Education (1928). *Report of the Department of Education for the School Years 1925–26–27 ...*, p. 25, p. 44; Department of Education (1931). *Report of the Department of Education 1929–30 ...*, p. 26.
5 Department of Education (1928). *Report of the Department of Education for the School Years 1925–26–27 ...*, p. 40; Department of Education (1930). *Report of the Department of Education 1928–29 ...*, p. 32.
6 Department of Education (1930). *Report of the Department of Education 1928–1929.* Dublin: The Stationery Office, p. 31.
7 Department of Education (1929). *Report of the Department of Education 1927–28 ...*, p. 34.
8 Teaching through Irish – *Reports from Divisional Inspectors. Statement based on the Special Confidential Reports of the Divisional Inspectors on the present position as regards Teaching through the Medium of Irish.* National Archives, Box 665, File 28933, p. 2.
9 *Ibid.*, p. 6.

10 Department of Education (1929). *Report of the Department of Education 1927–28* ..., p. 25.

11 Department of Education (1928). *Report of the Department of Education for the School Years 1925–26–27* ..., p. 36.

12 Department of Education (1934). *Report of the Department of Education 1932–1933*. Dublin: The Stationery Office, p. 22.

13 *Ibid.*, p. 24; Department of Education (1937). *Report of the Department of Education 1935–1936*. Dublin: The Stationery Office, p. 22; Department of Education (1946). *Report of the Department of Education 1944–1945*. Dublin: The Stationery Office, p. 18.

14 Department of Education (1936). *Report of the Department of Education 1934–1935*. Dublin: The Stationery Office, p. 24; Department of Education (1937). *Report of the Department of Education 1935–36* ..., p. 22.

15 Derrig, T. (1941). Opening of Congress – Minister Disappointed at Slow Progress of Revival. *The Irish School Weekly*, 19 April 1941, Volume LXIII, No. 16, p. 278.

16 Department of Education (1932). *Report of the Department of Education 1930–1931*. Dublin: The Stationery Office, p. 23.

17 *Ibid.*, p. 24; Deputy Derrig, *Dáil Debates*, 2 November 1932, Volume 44, Column 850–851.

18 Department of Education (1932). *Report of the Department of Education 1930–31* ..., p. 23.

19 Circular 11/60; *Teaching of Irish*.

20 Department of Education (1946). *Report of the Department of Education 1944–45* ..., p. 93.

21 Deputy O'Connell, *Dáil Debates*, 21 May 1930, Volume 34, Column 2168; Labour Party (1943). *Labour's Programme for a Better Ireland*. Dublin: Labour Party, p. 17; Deputy Dillon, *Dáil Debates*, 11 April 1934, Volume 51, Column 1573; Deputy Corry, *Dáil Debates*, 13 June 1944, Volume 94, Column 368; Deputy Keane, *Seanad Debates*, 18 June 1947, Volume 33, Column 1961; McElligott, T. (1955). Some Thoughts on our Educational Discontents. *University Review*, Volume 1, No. 5, pp. 27–36, p. 28.

22 Department of Education (1928). *Report of the Department of Education for the School Years 1925–26–27* ..., p. 44.

23 *Ibid.*, p. 41; Department of Education (1934). *Report of the Department of Education 1932–33* ..., p. 23; Department of Education (1935). *Report of the Department of Education 1933–1934*. Dublin: The Stationery Office, p. 22.

24 Department of Education (1930). *Report of the Department of Education 1928–29* ..., p. 221.

25 Department of Education (1928). *Report of the Department of Education for the School Years 1925–26–27* ..., p. 29; Department of Education (1929). *Report of the Department of Education 1927–28* ..., p. 31.
26 Department of Education (1928). *Report of the Department of Education for the School Years 1925–26–27* ..., p. 38.
27 *Ibid.*, p. 35.
28 Department of Education (1936). *Report of the Department of Education 1934–35* ..., p. 27.
29 Department of Education (1937). *Report of the Department of Education 1935–36* ..., p. 25.
30 An Roinn Oideachais (1963). *Tuarascáil 1961–62*. Baile Átha Cliath: Oifig an tSoláthair, p. 51.
31 Department of Education (1926). *Report of the Department of Education for the School Years 1924–25* ..., p. 68; Department of Education (1928). *Report of the Department of Education for the School Years 1925–26–27* ..., p. 25; Department of Education (1929). *Report of the Department of Education 1927–28* ..., p. 23; Department of Education (1930). *Report of the Department of Education 1928–29* ..., p. 50.
32 Department of Education (1930). *Report of the Department of Education 1928–29* ..., p. 59.
33 *Ibid.*, p. 221.
34 Department of Education (1929). *Report of the Department of Education 1927–28* ..., p. 38.
35 Department of Education (1928). *Report of the Department of Education for the School Years 1925–26–27* ..., p. 41; Department of Education (1934). *Report of the Department of Education 1932–33* ..., p. 25; Department of Education (1935). *Report of the Department of Education 1933–34* ..., p. 23.
36 An Roinn Oideachais (1964). *Tuarascáil 1962–63*. Baile Átha Cliath: Oifig an tSoláthair, p. 52.
37 Department of Education (1928). *Report of the Department of Education for the School Years 1925–26–27* ..., p. 41; Department of Education (1929). *Report of the Department of Education 1927–28* ..., p. 23; Department of Education (1930). *Report of the Department of Education 1928–29* ..., p. 43.
38 Department of Education (1929). *Report of the Department of Education 1927–28* ..., p. 38.
39 Department of Education (1930). *Report of the Department of Education 1928–29* ..., p. 65; Department of Education (1937). *Report of the Department of Education 1935–36* ..., p. 24; Department of Education (1955). *Report of the Department of Education 1953–1954*. Dublin: The Stationery Office, p. 7.

40 An Roinn Oideachais (1965). *Tuarascáil 1963–64*. Baile Átha Cliath: Oifig an tSoláthair, p. 51.

41 Department of Education (1930). *Report of the Department of Education 1928–29* ..., p. 61; Department of Education (1934). *Report of the Department of Education 1932–33* ..., p. 25.

42 Department of Education (1928). *Report of the Department of Education for the School Years 1925–26–27* ..., p. 26; Department of Education (1935). *Report of the Department of Education 1933–34* ..., p. 24.

43 Department of Education (1934). *Report of the Department of Education 1932–33* ..., p. 26; Department of Education (1957). *Report of the Department of Education for the Year 1955–1956*. Dublin: The Stationery Office, p. 8.

44 Department of Education (1928). *Report of the Department of Education for the School Years 1925–26–27* ..., p. 30.

45 Department of Education (1929). *Report of the Department of Education 1927–28* ..., p. 38.

46 An Roinn Oideachais (1963). *Tuarascáil 1961–62* ..., p. 51.

47 Department of Education (1934). *Report of the Department of Education 1932–33* ..., p. 25.

48 Department of Education (1928). *Report of the Department of Education for the School Years 1925–26–27* ..., p. 41; Department of Education (1930). *Report of the Department of Education 1928–29* ..., p. 51.

49 Department of Education (1928). *Report of the Department of Education for the School Years 1925–26–27* ..., p. 26.

50 Department of Education (1934). *Report of the Department of Education 1932–33* ..., p. 31.

51 Department of Education (1929). *Report of the Department of Education 1927–28* ..., p. 40.

52 *Ibid.*, p. 23; Department of Education (1930). *Report of the Department of Education 1928–29* ..., p. 65; Department of Education (1931). *Report of the Department of Education 1929–30* ..., p. 25.

53 Department of Education (1930). *Report of the Department of Education 1928–29* ..., p. 53.

54 Department of Education (1939). *Report of the Department of Education 1937–1938*. Dublin: The Stationery Office, p. 21.

55 An Roinn Oideachais (1960). *Tuarascáil 1958–59*. Baile Átha Cliath: Oifig an tSoláthair, p. 8.

56 An Roinn Oideachais (1964). *Tuarascáil 1962–63* ..., p. 51.

57 Department of Education (1930). *Report of the Department of Education 1928–29* ..., p. 61.

58 Department of Education (1934). *Report of the Department of Education 1932–33* ..., p. 26.

59 Circular 2/39; *Instruction in Cookery and Laundry Work (or Domestic Economy) in National Schools.*

60 Circular 6/43; *Arrangements and Suggestions regarding Written Exercises, Home Work, and the Teaching of Needlework and Cookery and Laundry, in the existing Emergency.*

61 Department of Education (1930). *Report of the Department of Education 1928–29* ..., p. 63.

62 Department of Education (1926). *Report of the Department of Education for the School Year 1924–25* ..., p. 22; Department of Education (1928). *Report of the Department of Education for the School Years 1925–26–27* ..., p. 31; Department of Education (1929). *Report of the Department of Education 1927–28* ..., p. 25; Department of Education (1930). *Report of the Department of Education 1928–29* ..., p. 32; Department of Education (1931). *Report of the Department of Education 1929–30* ..., p. 25.

63 Department of Education (1928). *Report of the Department of Education for the School Years 1925–26–27* ..., p. 26.

64 Department of Education (1928). *Report of the Department of Education for the School Years 1925–26–27* ..., p. 28. Department of Education (1930). *Report of the Department of Education 1928–29* ..., p. 49; Department of Education (1931). *Report of the Department of Education 1929–30* ..., p. 25.

65 Department of Education (1930). *Report of the Department of Education 1928–29* ..., p. 32.

66 An Roinn Oideachais (1963). *Tuarascáil 1961–62* ..., p. 52.

67 Department of Education (1928). *Report of the Department of Education for the School Years 1925–26–27* ..., p. 187.

68 Department of Education (1928). *Report of the Department of Education for the School Years 1925–26–27* ..., p. 41; An Roinn Oideachais (1962). *Tuarascáil 1960–61*. Baile Átha Cliath: Oifig an tSoláthair, p. 56.

69 Department of Education (1928). *Report of the Department of Education for the School Years 1925–26–27* ..., p. 31.

70 *Ibid.*, p. 41.

71 Department of Education (1953). *Report of the Department of Education 1951–1952*. Dublin: The Stationery Office, p. 8.

72 An Roinn Oideachais (1962). *Tuarascáil 1960–61* ..., p. 56; An Roinn Oideachais (1964). *Tuarascáil 1962–63* ..., p. 50.

73 An Roinn Oideachais (1962). *Tuarascáil 1960–61* ..., p. 56.

74 An Roinn Oideachais (1964). *Tuarascáil 1962–63* ..., p. 51.

75   Department of Education (1930). *Report of the Department of Education 1928–*
      29 ..., p. 37.

76   *Memorandum from the Minister for Education Enclosing an Account of the Activities*
      of the Department since the Election of the Dáil in August 1923, 26 April 1927.
      National Archives, File S5360/6.

77   *Ibid.*

78   *Education in the Irish Free State – General Statement*, December 1931. National
      Archives, File S2223.

79   *Ibid.*

80   *Results Achieved During Year 1930–1931.* National Archives, File S2223.

81   Department of Education (1927). *Commission on Technical Education – Report.*
      Dublin: The Stationery Office, p. 38.

82   Commission on Emigration (1956). *Commission on Emigration 1948–1954.*
      Dublin: The Stationery Office, p. 177.

83   Commission on Youth Unemployment (1951). *Report*, paragraph 51, p. 23.
      (Unpublished).

84   INTO (1936). *Annual Directory and Irish Educational Year Book for 1936.* Dublin:
      Wood Printing Works Limited, p. 56.

85   INTO (1941). *Report of Committee of Inquiry into the Use of Irish as a Teaching*
      Medium to Children whose Home Language is English. Dublin: INTO, p. 18.

86   Deputy Derrig, *Dáil Debates*, 1 June 1942, Volume 87, Column 734.

87   Deputy Derrig, *Seanad Debates*, 23 July 1942, Volume 26, Column 1877.

88   Pollak, J. (1943). *Irish Language: Development in Schools – On Teaching Irish.*
      National Archives, File S7801.

89   Church of Ireland (1936). *Journal of the Third Session of the Twenty-Fourth General*
      Synod of the Church of Ireland. Dublin: Hodges and Figgis, p. LXXVI.

90   Church of Ireland (1939). *Sixty-ninth Report of Proceedings of the Representative*
      Body laid before the General Synod of the Church of Ireland. Dublin: Hodges and
      Figgis, p. 232.

91   Church of Ireland (1950). *Seventy-Seventh General Synod of the Church of Ireland*
      – Report of the Board of Education on Teaching through the Medium of Irish.
      Dublin: Association for Promoting Christian Knowledge, pp. 183–188, p. 187.

92   Report of Departmental Committee to Examine the Educational System, estab-
      lished in March 1945. *Final Report*, 1 December 1947. National Archives, File
      S18921B.

93   *Ibid.*, p. 2.

94   *Ibid.*, p. 7.

95   O'Connell, T. (1968). *100 Years of Progress – The Story of the Irish National*
      Teachers' Organisation 1868–1968. Dublin: Dakota Press, p. 377.

96 INTO (1947). *A Plan for Education*. Dublin: INTO, p. 53.
97 *Ibid.*, p. 10.
98 *Ibid.*, p. 48.
99 *Ibid.*, p. 104.
100 The Editor's Page. *The Irish School Weekly*, 19 and 26 March 1949, Volume LI, No. 11–12, p. 133; The Editor's Page. *The Irish School Monthly*, May 1955, Volume LVII, No. 5, p. 110.
101 A Plan for Education. *The Irish School Weekly*, 3 and 10 May 1947, Volume LXIX, No. 17 and 18, p. 195.
102 Education Council Members Named. *The Irish Times*, 5 April 1950, p. 1.
103 Department of Education (1954). *Report of the Council of Education*. Dublin: The Stationery Office, p. 1.
104 *Ibid.*, Appendix 2, pp. 314–318.
105 *Ibid.*, paragraph 128.
106 *Ibid.*, paragraph 194.
107 *Ibid.*, paragraph 159.
108 *Ibid.*, paragraph 352.
109 *Ibid.*, paragraph 10.
110 Council of Education (in) INTO (1951). *Reports of the Central Executive Committee, Northern Committee and Finance Committee for the Year 1949*. Dublin: Wood Printing Works, pp. 48–55, p. 48.
111 Memo from INTO to Council of Education (in) INTO (1951). *Reports of the Central Executive Committee ...*, pp. 29–32, p. 30.
112 Department of Education (1954). *Report of the Council of Education ...*, paragraph 5.
113 Birch, P. (1955). The Report of the Council of Education. *Irish Ecclesiastical Record*, January 1955, Volume 83, pp. 1–11.
114 Ó Catháin, S. (1954). The Report of the Council of Education. *Studies*, Winter 1954, Volume 43, No. 172, pp. 361–374, p. 363.
115 Resolutions Adopted at kilkee Congress 1955. *The Irish School Monthly*, May 1955, Volume LVII, No. 5, pp. 107–108, p. 107.
116 Dent, C. (1969). *The Education Act, 1944 – Provisions, Regulations, Circulars, Later Acts – Twelfth Edition*. London: University of London Press Ltd.; Government of Northern Ireland Ministry of Education (1956). *Programme for Primary Schools*. Belfast: Her Majesty's Stationery Office.
117 Circular 8/54; *Scheme for the Provision of 'Free' Instruction in National Schools on One Half Day per Week*.
118 Department of Education (1956). *Report of the Department of Education 1954–1955*. Dublin: The Stationery Office, p. 8.

119 Department of Education – *Memorandum for the Government*, 29 October 1956. National Archives, File S15015A.

120 Department of Education (1956). *Programme of Primary Instruction*. Dublin: The Stationery Office.

121 MacNamara, J. (1966). *Bilingualism and Primary Education – A Study of Irish Experience*. Great Britain: T. and A. Constable Limited, p. 135.

122 *Ibid.*, p. 137.

123 FitzGerald, G. (1966). The Primary School Curriculum – Economic Comment. *The Irish Times*, 4 May 1966, p. 15.

124 Tuairim (1962). *Irish Education – Pamphlet 9*. London: Tuairim-London Research Group, pp. 25–37, p. 25.

125 McGee, P. (1977). An Examination of Trends in Reading Achievement in Dublin over a Ten-Year Period (in) Greaney, V. (Ed.) (1977). *Studies in Reading*. Dublin: Dublin Educational Company, pp. 27–35, p. 33.

126 Kelly, S. and McGee, P. (1967). Survey of Reading Comprehension – A Study in Dublin City National Schools. *New Research in Education*, June 1967, Volume I, pp. 131–134.

127 Kellaghan, T., MacNamara, J. and Neuman, E. (1969). Teachers' Assessments of the Scholastic Progress of Pupils. *Irish Journal of Education*, Volume 3, No. 2, pp. 95–104, p. 95.

Chapter 7

1 Harris, J. (1989). The Policy-making Role of the Department of Education (in) Mulcahy, D. and O'Sullivan, D. (Eds) (1989). *Irish Educational Policy – Process and Substance*. Dublin: Institute of Public Administration, pp. 7–25, p. 11.

2 Fine Gael (1980). *Action Programme for Education in the '80s: A Fine Gael Policy Document*. Dublin: Fine Gael, p. 33; Fianna Fáil (1981). *Our Programme for the '80s*. Dublin: Fianna Fáil, p. 50; Fine Gael (1981). *A Better Future – Let the Country Win*. Dublin: Fine Gael, p. 23.

3 Labour Party (1975). *Education at First Level: A Policy for our Children's Future*. Dublin: Labour Party, p. 6; Fine Gael (1980). *Action Programme for Education in the '80s ...*, p. 26; Fine Gael Ard Fheis (1980). *Education Discussion Document*. Dublin: Fine Gael; Fianna Fáil (1987). *The Programme for National Recovery*. Dublin: Fianna Fáil, p. 53.

4   Department of Education (1990). *Report of the Primary Education Review Body.* Dublin: The Stationery Office, p. 85.
5   *Ibid.*, p. 86.
6   Mulcahy, D. (1992). Promoting the European Dimension in Irish Education. *Irish Educational Studies*, Spring 1992, Volume 11, pp. 179–190.
7   Breen, R., Hannan, D., Rottman, D. and Whelan, T. (1990). *Understanding Contemporary Ireland. State, Class and Development in the Republic of Ireland.* Dublin: Gill and Macmillan, p. 1.
8   CSO (2003). *Census 2002: Volume 2 – Ages and Marital Status.* Dublin: CSO, pp. 9–10.
9   Department of Education (1990). *Report of the Primary Education Review Body* ..., p. 13.
10 Walshe, J. (1999). *A New Partnership – From Consultation to Legislation in the Nineties.* Dublin: Institute of Public Administration, p. 1.
11 Kennedy, S. (1981). Introduction (in) Kennedy, S. (Ed.) (1981). *One Million Poor? The Challenge of Irish Inequality.* Dublin: Turoe Press, pp. 7–11, p. 8.
12 Circular 9/82; *The Abolition of Corporal Punishment in National Schools.*
13 Devine, D. (1999). Children: Rights and Status in Education – A Socio-historical Analysis. *Irish Educational Studies*, Spring 1999, Volume 18, pp. 14–28, p. 22.
14 Coolahan, J. (1981). *Irish Education – History and Structure.* Dublin: Institute of Public Administration, p. 178.
15 CSO (2003). *Census 2002 – Principal Socio-economic Results.* Dublin: CSO, p. 33.
16 McKenna, A. (1988). *Childcare and Equal Opportunities – Policies and Services for Childcare in Ireland.* Dublin: Employment Equality Agency, p. 38.
17 O'Neill, A. (1993). Adapting the *Stay Safe* Programme for Special Education. *Reach*, Volume 6, No. 2, pp. 96–100, p. 96.
18 Keogh, D. (1994). *Twentieth-century Ireland – Nation and State.* Dublin: Gill and Macmillan, p. 347.
19 Hussey, G. (1990). *At the Cutting Edge – Cabinet Diaries 1982–1987.* Dublin: Gill and Macmillan, p. 69.
20 Fianna Fáil (1987). *The Programme for National Recovery* ..., p. 5.
21 Circular 20/87; *Average Enrolments Required for the Appointment and Retention of Assistant Teachers in National Schools.*
22 Ward, N. (1986). The Church and the I.N.T.O. in the National School System – A Brief Look at the Basic Positions, and at some Points of Compliance and Conflict (in) INTO – District XV (1986). *Proceedings of the Third Annual Drumcondra Education Conference.* Dublin: INTO – District XV, pp. 3–8.

23   Tussing, D. (1978). *Irish Educational Expenditures – Past, Present and Future.*
     Dublin: Economic and Social Research Institute, p. 13.
24   An Roinn Oideachais (1974). *Tuarascáil – Táblaí Staitistic 1968/69–1971/72.* Baile
     Átha Cliath: Oifig an tSoláthair, p. 23; ... (1991). *Tuarascáil Staitistiúil 1989–90.*
     Baile Átha Cliath: Oifig an tSoláthair, p. 11.
25   Review Body on the Primary Curriculum (1990). *Report of the Review Body on
     the Primary Curriculum.* Dublin: Department of Education, p. 93.
26   Tussing, D. (1981). Equity and the Financing of Education (in) Kennedy, S. (Ed.)
     (1981). *One Million Poor? ...*, pp. 201–216.
27   NESC (1975). *Educational Expenditure in Ireland.* Dublin: NESC, p. 76.
28   National Parents' Council – Primary (1990). *The Cost of Free Education – A Survey
     on the Cost to Parents of Free Primary Education in Ireland.* Dublin: National
     Parents' Council – Primary, p. 4.
29   Coolahan, J. (1987). The Changing Context for the Exercise of Professionalism
     in Teaching (in) Hogan, P. (1987). *Willingly to School? Perspectives on Teaching
     as a Profession in Ireland in the Eighties.* Dublin: ESAI, pp. 15–33, p. 23.
30   Flude, M. and Hammer, M. (Eds) (1990). *The Education Reform Act 1988 – Its
     Origins and Implications.* London: The Falmer Press.
31   Mac Gréil, M. and Ó Gliasáin, M. (1974). Church Attendance and Religious
     Practice of Dublin Adults. *Social Studies*, April 1974, Volume 3, No. 2, pp. 163–212,
     p. 176.
32   Nic Ghiolla Phádraig, M. (1990). *Childhood as a Social Phenomenon – National
     Report Ireland.* European Centre for Social Welfare Policy and Research.
     Eurosocial Report 36/8. Vienna: European Centre for Social Welfare Policy
     and Research.
33   *Report of the Working Party Established by the Education Committee of the
     Hierarchy and the Conference of Major Religious Superiors to Examine the Future
     Involvement of Religious in Education* (1973). (Unpublished).
34   O'Flaherty, L. (1994). Religious Control of Schooling in Ireland: Some Policy
     Issues in Review. *Irish Educational Studies*, Spring 1994, Volume 13, pp. 62–70,
     p. 63.
35   Clancy, P. (1999). Education Policy (in) Quin, S., Kennedy, P., O'Donnell, A.
     and Kiely, G. (Eds) (1999). *Contemporary Irish Social Policy.* Dublin: University
     College Dublin Press, pp. 72–107, p. 79.
36   Drudy, S. and Lynch, K. (1993). *Schools and Society in Ireland.* Dublin: Gill and
     Macmillan, p. 79.
37   Department of Education (1980). *White Paper on Educational Development.*
     Dublin: The Stationery Office, p. 34.

38 Hyland, A. (1989). The Multi-denominational Experience in the National School System in Ireland. *Irish Educational Studies*, Volume 8, No. 1, pp. 89–114, p. 98.

39 NESC (1975). *Educational Expenditure in Ireland ...*, p. 58.

40 An Roinn Oideachais (1991). *Tuarascáil Staitistiúil 1989–90*. Baile Átha Cliath: Oifig an tSoláthair, p. 17.

41 *Ibid.*, p. 3.

42 *Ibid.*, p. 26.

43 Department of Education (1965). *Investment in Education – Report of the Survey Team appointed by the Minister for Education in October 1962*. Dublin: The Stationery Office, p. 7.

44 An Roinn Oideachais (1980). *Tuarascáil Staitistiúil 1978–79*. Baile Átha Cliath: Oifig an tSoláthair, p. 4.

45 Hart, I. (1975). Absenteeism at National Schools – Educational, Medical and Social Aspects. *Economic and Social Review*, Volume 6, No. 3, pp. 313–335.

46 Hyland, A. (1980). Current Trends in the Design of National Schools in Ireland. *Compass*, Volume 9, No. 1, pp. 31–41, p. 33.

47 Coolahan, J. (1981). *Irish Education ...*, p. 179.

48 CEB (1985). *Primary Education – A Curriculum and Examinations Board Discussion Paper*. Dublin: CEB, p. 13.

49 Kavanagh, J. (1985). The Design of Irish Primary School Buildings in the Era of the New Curriculum. *Irish Educational Studies*, Volume 5, No. 1, pp. 102–120, p. 114.

50 Deputy Faulkner, *Dáil Debates*, 9 July 1970, Volume 248, Column 869.

51 De Buitléar, S. (1971). *The Role of the Primary Schools' Inspector*, p. 2. (Unpublished).

52 Deputy Faulkner, *Dáil Debates*, 2 March 1972, Volume 259, Column 882.

53 Preas-Agallamh – An Curaclam Nua – *Focal ón Aire*, May 1971. (Unpublished).

54 Circular 14/71; *Grants for the Provision of Audio-visual Teaching Equipment for National Schools*.

55 Minister Faulkner, *Dáil Debates*, 15 April 1970, Volume 245, Column 1312.

56 Department of Education (1990). *Report of the Primary Education Review Body ...*, p. 103.

57 O'Connell, F. (1993). Male/Female Imbalance in Primary Teaching: An Analysis of Recruitment Statistics. *Oideas*, Winter 1993, Volume 41, pp. 138–147, p. 146.

58 Herron, D. (1985). Principals' Delegation and Posts of Responsibility in Dublin National Schools. *Irish Educational Studies*, Volume 5, No. 2, pp. 118–136, p. 118.

59   Government of Ireland (1980). *Review Body on Teachers' Pay – Interim Report.*
      Dublin: The Stationery Office.
60   Higher Education Authority (1970). *Report on Teacher Education.* Dublin:
      Stationery Office, p. 14.
61   I.N.T.O. Comments on the Higher Education Authority Report on Teacher
      Education (in) INTO (1971). *Reports of the Central Executive Committee and
      Finance Committee for the Year 1970–1971, together with Accounts and Statistics
      and Resolutions on Organisation Matters.* Dublin: INTO, p. 57.
62   Symposium: Report on Teacher Training. *Oideas*, Spring 1971, Volume 6,
      pp. 4–32.
63   Coolahan, J. (1981). *'Education' in the Training Colleges – Carysfort 1877–1977:
      Two Centenary Lectures.* Blackrock: Our Lady of Mercy College, pp. 20–52,
      p. 44.
64   Department of Education (1990). *Report of the Primary Education Review
      Body ...*, p. 8.
65   Greaney, V., Burke, A. and McCann, J. (1987). Entrants to Primary Teacher
      Education in Ireland. *European Journal of Teacher Education*, Volume 10, No.
      2, pp. 127–140, p. 127.
66   Comhairle na Gaeilge (1974). *Irish in Education.* Dublin: The Stationery Office,
      p. 44.
67   Ó Buachalla, S. (1981). The Irish Language in the Classroom. *The Crane Bag*,
      Volume 5, No. 2, pp. 849–862, p. 860.
68   ERC (1982). *An Evaluation of the Three-year Course Leading to the Bachelor of
      Education (B.Ed) Degree.* Dublin: ERC, p. 132.
69   In-service Training Courses for National Teachers – First Meeting of Steering
      Committee held on 10 Samhain, 1970 (in) INTO (1971). *Reports of the Central
      Executive Committee ...*, pp. 77–82, p. 78.
70   INTO (1972). *Reports of the Central Executive Committee and Finance Committee
      for the Year 1971–1972, together with Accounts and Statistics and Resolutions on
      Organisation Matters.* Dublin: INTO, p. 8.
71   Ó Suilleabháin, S. (1973). Teachers' Centres: Theory and Practice. *Oideas*, Summer
      1973, Volume 10, pp. 13–17.
72   O'Reilly, Y. (1985). *A Study of Teachers' Centres in the Republic of Ireland, with
      Particular Reference to their Role in In-service Education.* M.Ed. Thesis. Dublin:
      Trinity College Dublin, p. 216.
73   Coolahan, J. (1989). Educational Policy for National Schools, 1960–1985
      (in) Mulcahy, D. and O'Sullivan, D. (Eds) (1989). *Irish Educational Policy ...*,
      pp. 27–76, p. 52.

74 Carr, J. (1992). Professional Development and Training (in) Council of Teachers' Unions (1992). *Education Conference*. Dublin: Council of Teachers' Unions, pp. 13–18, p. 14.

75 Department of Education (1990). *Report of the Primary Education Review Body* ..., p. 25.

76 Committee on In-service Education (1984). *Report of the Committee on In-service Education*. Dublin: The Stationery Office, p. 1.

77 Department of Education (1984). *Programme for Action in Education 1984–1987*. Dublin: The Stationery Office, p. 35.

78 OECD (1991). *Reviews of National Policies for Education – Ireland*. Paris: OECD, p. 99.

79 Sugrue, C. (2003). Principal's Professional Development: Realities, Perspectives and Possibilities. *Oideas*, Spring 2003, Volume 50, pp. 8–39.

80 Circular 16/73; *Responsibilities and Duties of Principal Teachers and Teachers in Charge of National Schools*.

81 Department of Education (1990). *Report of the Primary Education Review Body* ..., p. 45.

82 OECD (1991). *Reviews of National Policies for Education* ..., p. 110.

83 Department of Education (1990). *Report of the Primary Education Review Body* ..., p. 18.

84 *Ibid.*, p. 28.

85 See for example: Department of Education (1972). *The Education of Children who are Handicapped by Impaired Hearing – Report of a Committee Appointed by the Minister for Education*. Dublin: The Stationery Office; Department of Education (1982). *The Education of Physically Handicapped Children – Report of a Committee appointed by John Bruton T.D., Parliamentary Secretary to the Minister for Education*. Dublin: The Stationery Office; Review Group on Mental Handicap Services (1990). *Needs and Abilities – A Policy for the Intellectually Disabled*. Dublin: The Stationery Office.

86 Department of Education (1988). *Guidelines on Remedial Education*. Dublin: The Stationery Office.

87 O'Sullivan, N. (1984). *Remedial Reading Education in the Primary School*. M.Ed. Thesis. Kildare: National University of Ireland, Maynooth; Lynch, P. and O'Sullivan, A. (1986). Remedial Teaching in Primary Schools (in) Greaney, V. and Molloy, B. (Eds) (1986). *Dimensions of Reading*. Dublin: The Educational Company of Ireland, pp. 88–105, p. 99.

88 Department of Education (1990). *Report of the Primary Education Review Body* ..., p. 62.

89   CEB (1985). *Primary Education ...*, p. 13; Department of Education (1985). *Report of the Committee on Discipline in Schools*. Dublin: The Stationery Office, p. 42; INTO (1986). *Towards a Primary Schools' Psychological Service*. Dublin: INTO, p. 3.

90   Department of Education (1992). *Annual Report of the Primary Inspectorate for the Year 1990–1991 to the Minister for Education*, p. 14. (Unpublished).

91   Dwyer, C. (1981). *Seven Years of Progress? Third Report on the Educational Needs of Travelling People*. Submitted by the National Coordinator for the Education of Travelling People, p. 2. (Unpublished).

92   Department of Education (1985). *Páistí an Lucht Taistil; Dréacht Curaclaim*. Dublin: Department of Education.

93   Review Body of the Travelling People (1983). *Report of the Review Body of the Travelling People*. Dublin: The Stationery Office, p. 62.

94   Department of Education (1984). *Programme for Action in Education 1984–87 ...*, p. 20.

95   Cronin, B. (1990). Educational Provision for the Children of Travelling Families: A Survey. *Reach*, Volume 4, No. 1, pp. 24–28.

96   Deputy Faulkner, *Dáil Debates*, 22 April 1970, Volume 245, Column 1868.

97   Hussey, G. (1990). *At the Cutting Edge ...*, p. 66.

98   CSO (2004). *Census 2002 – Irish Language: Volume 11*. Dublin: CSO, p. 11.

99   CLÁR (1975). *Report*. Dublin: The Stationery Office, p. 307.

100 Department of Education (1969). *Ár nDaltaí Uile – All our Children*. Dublin: Department of Education, p. 52.

101 An Roinn Oideachais (1966). *Buntús Gaeilge: Réamhthuarascáil ar Thaighde Teangeolaíochta a Rinneadh an Teanglann*. Baile Átha Cliath: Oifig an tSoláthair.

102 Ó Domhnalláin, T. and Ó Gliasáin, M. (1976). *Audiovisual Methods v A.B.C. Methods in the Teaching of Irish*. Dublin: Institiúid Teangeolaíochta Éireann, p. 6.

103 Ó Domhnalláin, T. (1981). Buntús Gaeilge – Cúlra, Cur le Chéile, Cur i Bhfeidhm. *Teangeolas*, Geimhreadh 1981, No. 13, pp. 24–32, p. 29.

104 *Ibid.*

105 Mac Aogáin, E. (1990). *Teaching Irish in the Schools: Towards a Language Policy for 1992*. Dublin: Institiúid Teangeolaíochta Éireann, p. 20.

106 Cummins, J. (1978). Immersion Programs: the Irish Experience. *International Review of Education*, Volume 24, No. 3, pp. 273–282, p. 273; Cummins, J. (1982). Reading Achievement in Irish and English Medium Schools. *Oideas*, Summer 1982, Volume 26, pp. 21–26.

107 Cummins, J. (1977). A Comparison of Reading Achievement in Irish and English-medium Schools (in) Greaney, V. (Ed.) (1977). *Studies in Reading*. Dublin: Educational Company of Ireland, pp. 128–133.

108 Ó Ciaráin, G. (1982). *The Effects of all-Irish Primary Schooling on Cognitive and Academic Development*. M.Ed. Thesis. Maynooth: National University of Ireland, Maynooth, p. 213.

109 The Growth of Irish Medium Schools outside the Gaeltacht: 1972–2004. Accessed at: <http://www.gaelscoileanna.ie/documents/GrowthofGaelscoileanna1072–2004.doc>, 24 January 2004.

110 Department of Education (1984). *Léas – A Department of Education Information Bulletin*. Winter 1984, No. 1, p. 1.

111 Circular 12/76; *Inspection of Schools*; Circular 31/82; *Inspection of Schools*.

112 Department of Education (1981). *Report of the Committee on Primary Schools Inspection*, p. 90. (Unpublished).

113 Department of Education (1992). *Annual Report of the Primary Inspectorate for the Year 1990–91 ...*, p. 19.

114 Department of Education (1981). *Report of the Committee on Primary Schools Inspection ...*, pp. 114–115.

115 *Inspectorate Statistics* – Personal Communication from the Personnel Section of the Department of Education and Science, 16 May 2006.

116 Kellaghan, T. (1973). Evaluation in Schools. *Oideas*, Autumn 1973, Volume 11, pp. 4–19, p. 4.

117 Greaney, V. (1979). Developing National Attainment Measures: A Study of the Irish Experience. *Proceedings of ESAI 1979*, Dublin, pp. 209–223, p. 210.

118 Walshe, J. (1987). Parents Hit at Drop in Basic Skills of Students. *Irish Independent*, 17 June 1987, p. 5.

119 INTO (1989). *Assessment – A Report by the Education Committee*. Dublin: INTO, p. 10.

120 Sanders, J. and Greaney, V. (1986). Self-evaluation of the Irish Primary School. *Oideas*, Autumn 1986, Volume 29, pp. 41–51.

121 Grant, C. (1986). Initiating and Sustaining Staff Development through the Medium of the Plean Scoile (in) INTO – District XV (1986). *Proceedings of the Third Annual Drumcondra Education Conference*. Dublin: INTO – District XV, pp. 42–50.

122 Kellaghan, T. (1971). Educational Research (in) Murphy, M. (Ed.) (1971). *Education in Ireland 2 – What Should Students Learn?* Cork: Mercier Press, pp. 17–39, p. 20.

123 *Ibid.*, p. 19.

124 Coolahan, J. (1981). *Irish Education ...*, p. 150.

125 Department of Education (1981). *Report of the Committee on Primary Schools Inspection* ..., p. 74.
126 Kellaghan, T. (1976). Paper delivered to the Primary Inspectors' Conference in January 1976 (quoted in) de Buitléar (1978). *A National Educational Policy Review – Ireland.* (Unpublished).
127 CEB (1985). *Primary Education* ..., p. 40.
128 Department of Education (1990). *Report of the Primary Education Review Body* ..., p. 96.
129 Kellaghan, T. (1989). The Interface of Research, Evaluation, and Policy in Irish Education (in) Mulcahy, D. and O'Sullivan, D. (Eds) (1989). *Irish Educational Policy* ..., pp. 191–218, p. 202.
130 Hogan, P. and Herron, D. (1992). *Register of Theses on Educational Topics in Universities in Ireland – Volume Two 1980–1990.* Dublin: ESAI, Preface.
131 ESAI (1980). *Register of Theses on Educational Topics in Universities in Ireland 1911–1979.* Dublin: ESAI.
132 Fontes, P. (1983). Theses on Educational Topics in Universities in Ireland: Their Distribution by University, Topic and Degree. *Irish Journal of Education*, Volume 17, No. 2, pp. 80–104, p. 80.
133 Harris, J. (1972). The Irish Association for Curriculum Development. *Compass*, May 1972, Volume 1, No. 1, pp. 4–7, p. 4.
134 Tussing, D. (1978). *Irish Educational Expenditures* ..., p. 177.
135 Colgan, J. (1991). Minimum Requirements for an Education Act(s). *Church and State*, Spring 1991, No. 37, pp. 16–19, p. 16.

Chapter 8

1 Deputy Colley, *Dáil Debates*, 16 June 1965, Volume 216, Column 958–959.
2 De Buitléar, S. (n.d.). *The New Curriculum.* (Unpublished).
3 *Letter from Domhnall Ó hUallacháin to Roinnchigire and Cigirí Ceantair on 13 January 1967.* (Unpublished).
4 Department of Education (1967). *Towards a White Paper on Education*, p. 1. (Unpublished).
5 *Ibid.*, p. 3.
6 *Ibid.*, p. 4.
7 *Ibid.*, p. 16.

8 *Ibid.*

9 *Ibid.*, p. 31.

10 *Ibid.*, p. 33.

11 *Ibid.*, p. 40.

12 *Ibid.*

13 *Ibid.*, p. 77.

14 *Ibid.*, p. 84.

15 *Ibid.*, p. 94.

16 O'Connor, S. (1986). *A Troubled Sky – Reflections on the Irish Educational Scene 1957–1968.* Dublin: ERC, p. 191.

17 Coolahan, J. (1989). Educational Policy for National Schools, 1960–1985 (in) Mulcahy, D. and O'Sullivan, D. (Eds) (1989). *Irish Educational Policy – Process and Substance.* Dublin: Institute of Public Administration, pp. 27–76, p. 63.

18 *Dréacht Curaclaim do na Bunscoileanna – Ceisteanna ina Thaobh.* Attachment to Letter on 13 December 1967 from Domhnaill Ó hUallacháin to Seamus de Buitléar. (Unpublished).

19 Department of Education (1968). *Primary Education New Curriculum – A Working Document.* Department of Education Files, File 11357. (Unpublished).

20 *Ibid.*, p. 1.

21 Deputy O'Malley, *Dáil Debates*, 8 February 1968, Volume 232, Column 774.

22 INTO (1969). *Reports of the Central Executive Committee and Finance Committee for the Year 1968–1969, together with Accounts and Statistics and Resolutions on Organisation Matters.* Dublin INTO, p. 36.

23 Major Educational Reforms Suggested – Plan for Primary System. *The Irish Times*, 14 December 1968, p. 12.

24 Primary Education – New Curriculum: A Working Document. *An Múinteoir Náisiúnta*, February 1969, Volume 13, No. 9, pp. 5–39.

25 INTO (1970). *Reports of the Central Executive Committee and Finance Committee for the Year 1969–1970, together with Accounts and Statistics and Resolutions on Organisation Matters.* Dublin: INTO, pp. 13–26, p. 13.

26 *Ibid.*, p. 25.

27 Teachers' Study Group (1969). *Reports on the Draft Curriculum for Primary Schools.* Dublin: Teachers' Study Group, p. 5.

28 *Digest of Responses to the Working Document, 1969–1970.* (Unpublished).

29 The End of the Murder Machine? *The Irish Times*, 1 July 1969, p. 10.

30 Heney, M. (1970). H.E.A. Asserts its Hand in the Power Game. *The Irish Times Annual Review*, 1 January 1970, p. 5.

31 *Letter from John at Oxfordshire County Council to James Butler, Inspector of Schools*, 1 April 1969, p. 1. (Unpublished).

32 *Ibid.*
33 Department of Education (1969). *Ár nDaltaí Uile – All our Children*. Dublin: Department of Education, p. 8.
34 Ó Floinn, T. (1969). New Curriculum for the Primary Schools. *An Múinteoir Náisiúnta*, December 1969, Volume 14, No. 6, pp. 5–9, p. 5.
35 *Ibid.*, p. 8.
36 *Ibid.*
37 Mac Donnchadha, M. (1969). New Approaches to Mathematics – Part 1: Mathematics at First level. *Oideas*, Spring 1969, Volume 2, pp. 4–8, p. 8.
38 *Ibid.*
39 De Buitléar, S. (1969). Curaclam Nua le hAghaidh na Buncsoile. *Oideas*, Autumn 1969, Volume 3, pp. 4–12, p. 4.
40 De Buitléar, S. (1969). *Notes for Talk by Mr T. Ó Floinn, M.A., Assistant Secretary, Department of Education on the New Curriculum for the Primary Schools*. October 1969, p. 4. (Unpublished).
41 *Ibid.*, p. 9.
42 *Address by Minister Brian Lenihan to Congress of INTO*, Hydro Hotel, Kilkee, Tuesday 8 April 1969. National Archives, File GIS 1/231.
43 *Ibid.*
44 Deputy Faulkner, *Dáil Debates*, 22 April 1970, Volume 245, Column 1873.
45 Circular 15/71; *Study Day for New Curriculum*.
46 Mac Cathmhaoil, S. (1972). Lá an Churaclaim i nGaillimh. *An Múinteoir Náisiúnta*, January 1972, Volume 16, No. 1, p. 22.
47 Circular issued in 1969 (quoted in) CEB (1985). *Primary Education – A Curriculum and Examinations Board Discussion Paper*. Dublin: CEB, p. 8.
48 Circular 20/71; *New Curriculum – Pilot Schools*.
49 *New Curriculum Pilot Schemes*. Department of Education Files, File 11403.
50 Walsh, M. (1980). *A Study of the Implementation of the 1971 Curriculum for Irish Primary Schools*. M. Litt Thesis. Dublin: Trinity College Dublin, p. 110.
51 O'Connell, N. (1979) (in) Seminar Proceedings – Bridging the Gap (1979). *Oideas*, Spring 1979, Volume 20, pp. 25–29, p. 26.
52 Gillespie, F. (1971). A 'Pilot School' at Work. *Oideas*, Spring 1971, Volume 6, pp. 53–56, p. 53.
53 *Ibid.*, p. 55.
54 Whelan, M. (1970). Glenanaar – An Experiment in Integration. *Oideas*, Autumn 1970, Volume 5, pp. 30–37, p. 35.
55 INTO (1971). *Reports of the Central Executive Committee and Finance Committee for the Year 1970–1971, together with Accounts and Statistics and Resolutions on Organisation Matters*. Dublin: INTO, p. 75.

56 Walsh, M. (1980). *A Study of the Implementation of the 1971 Curriculum* ..., p. 110.

57 Ó Suilleabháin, G. (1969). Srac Fhéacaint ar an gCuraclaim Nua – A Report on a Recent Course for Primary Teacher's in Saint Patrick's Training College. *An Múinteoir Náisiúnta*, October 1969, Volume 14, No. 4, p. 16.

58 Hyland, A. (1987). The Process of Curriculum Change in the Irish National School System. *Irish Educational Studies*, Volume 6, No. 2, pp. 17–38, p. 28.

59 Deputy Faulkner, *Dáil Debates*, 22 April 1970, Volume 245, Column 1873–1874.

60 INTO (1971). *Reports of the Central Executive Committee* ..., p. 75.

61 De Buitléar, S. (1973). *New Primary School Curriculum (1971)*, p. 2. (Unpublished).

62 Deputy Faulkner, *Dáil Debates*, 15 April 1970, Volume 245, Column 1312.

63 Circular 8/71; *New Curriculum – Handbook for Teachers*; Circular 22/71; *New Curriculum – Handbook for Teachers – Volume II*.

64 Department of Education (1971). *Primary School Curriculum: Teacher's Handbook – Part 1*. Dublin: Department of Education, p. 12.

65 *Ibid.*

66 *Ibid.*, p. 13.

67 *Ibid.*, p. 19.

68 *Ibid.*, p. 20.

69 *Ibid.*

70 *Ibid.*, p. 18.

71 *Ibid.*, p. 15.

72 *Ibid.*, p. 22.

73 *Ibid.*, p. 13.

74 *Ibid.*, p. 14.

75 *Ibid.*, p. 23.

76 Department of Education (1965). *Rules for National Schools under the Department of Education*. Dublin: The Stationery Office, p. 8.

77 Abbott, W. (Ed.) (1966). *The Documents of Vatican II*. London: Geoffrey Chapman, p. 635.

78 Glendenning, D. (1999). *Education and the Law*. Dublin: Butterworths, p. 97.

79 Department of Education (1971). *Primary School Curriculum: Teacher's Handbook – Part 1* ..., p. 30.

80 *Ibid.*, p. 81.

81 *Ibid.*

82 *Ibid.*, p. 125.

83 *Ibid.*, p. 126.

84   *Ibid.*, p. 266.
85   *Ibid.*, p. 268.
86   *Ibid.*, p. 279.
87   Department of Education (1971). *Primary School Curriculum: Teacher's Handbook – Part 2*. Dublin: Department of Education, p. 12.
88   *Ibid.*, p. 87.
89   *Ibid.*, pp. 87–88.
90   *Ibid.*, p. 115.
91   *Ibid.*, p. 133.
92   *Ibid.*
93   *Ibid.*, p. 134.
94   *Ibid.*, p. 207.
95   *Ibid.*, p. 211.
96   *Ibid.*, p. 214.
97   *Ibid.*, p. 322.
98   See for example: Montessori, M. (1917). *The Advanced Montessori Method*. London: William Heinemann; Dewey, J. (1956). *The Child and the Curriculum – The School and Society*. Chicago: The University of Chicago Press; Bruner, J. (1960). *The Process of Education*. Cambridge, Massachusetts: Harvard University Press; Dewey, J. (1963). *Experience and Education*. New York: Collier Books; Piaget, J. and Inhelder, B. (1969). *The Psychology of the Child*. London: Routledge and Kegan Paul.
99   Central Advisory Council for Education (England) (1967). *Children and their Primary Schools – A Report of the Central Advisory Council for Education (England). Volume 1: Report*. London: Her Majesty's Stationery Office.
100 Hurley, K. (1977). Primary School: Whither the Curriculum. *Compass*, Volume 6, No. 2, pp. 15–25, p. 16.
101 Scottish Education Department (1965). *Primary Education in Scotland*. Edinburgh: Her Majesty's Stationery Office.
102 Government of Northern Ireland Ministry of Education (1956). *Programme for Primary Schools*. Belfast: Her Majesty's Stationery Office, p. 7.
103 Stenhouse, L. (1975). *An Introduction to Curriculum Research and Development*. London: Heinemann; Gordon, P. and Lawton, D. (1978). *Curriculum Change in the Nineteenth and Twentieth Centuries*. London: Hodder and Stoughton Educational.

Chapter 9

1   Walsh, M. (1980). *A Study of the Implementation of the 1971 Curriculum for Irish Primary Schools*. M. Litt Thesis. Dublin: Trinity College Dublin, p. 126.

2   Ó Domhnalláin, T. and Ó Gliasáin, M. (1976). *Audiovisual Methods v A.B.C. Methods in the Teaching of Irish*. Dublin: Institiúid Teangeolaíochta Éireann, p. 15.

3   Conference of Convent Primary Schools in Ireland (1975). *Evaluation of the New Curriculum for Primary Schools*. Dublin: Conference of Convent Primary Schools in Ireland, p. 27.

4   INTO (1976). *Primary School Curriculum: Curriculum Questionnaire Analysis by Education Committee*. Dublin: INTO.

5   INTO (1985). *The Irish Language in Primary Education – Summary of INTO Survey of Teachers' Attitudes to the Position of Irish in Primary Education*. Dublin: INTO.

6   MRBI (1985). *The Irish Language in Primary Schools. – Survey Report*. Dublin: INTO.

7   INTO (1988). *Primary School Curriculum – Report and Discussion Papers*. Dublin: INTO, p. 5.

8   Fontes, P. and Kellaghan, T. (1977). *The New Primary School Curriculum, its Implementation and Effects*. Dublin: ERC.

9   Department of Education (1984). *Programme for Action in Education 1984–1987*. Dublin: The Stationery Office, p. 16.

10   Tuairisc ar Theagasc an Chorpoideachais sna Bunscoileanna (1979) (in) An Roinn Oideachais – An tAonad Curaclaim (1988). *Synthesis of Reports 1977–1987*, p. 22. (Unpublished).

11   Department of Education Curriculum Unit (1982). *English in the Primary School – Survey Report*, p. 3. (Unpublished).

12   Department of Education (1992). *Annual Report of the Primary Inspectorate for the Year 1990–1991 to the Minister for Education*, p. 10. (Unpublished).

13   An Roinn Oideachais – An tAonad Curaclaim (1983). *A Report on the Teaching of Music in Primary Schools*, p. 6. (Unpublished).

14   An Roinn Oideachais – An tAonad Curaclaim (1983). *Daoneolas agus Eolas Imshaoil – Tuairisc ar Fheidhmiú an Churaclaim sna Bunscoileanna*, p. 32. (Unpublished).

15   De Buitléar (1978). *A National Educational Policy Review – Ireland*, p. 111. (Unpublished).

16   CEB (1985). *Primary Education – A Curriculum and Examinations Board Discussion Paper.* Dublin: CEB, Appendix, p. 160.

17   Tuairisc ar an Mhatamitic i Rang VI (1984) (in) An Roinn Oideachais – An tAonad Curaclaim (1988). *Synthesis of Reports 1977–1987*, p. 12. (Unpublished).

18   Department of Education Curriculum Development Unit (1984). *Report on the Implementation of Art and Craft Activities in Primary Schools*, p. 13. (Unpublished).

19   Harris, J. (1984). *Spoken Irish in Primary Schools: An Analysis of Achievement.* Dublin: Institiúid Teangeolaíochta Éireann.

20   An Roinn Oideachais – An tAonad Curaclaim (1985). *An Ghaeilge – Tuairisc ar Fheidhmiú an Churaclaim sna Bunscoileanna*, p. 4. (Unpublished).

21   *Ibid.*, p. 24.

22   An Roinn Oideachais – An tAonad Curaclaim (1987). *The Implementation of the Principles of the Primary School Curriculum – Perceptions of Teachers and Principals: Survey Report*, p. 4. (Unpublished).

23   Report on the Pilot Project on Computers in the Primary School (1987) (in) An Roinn Oideachais – An tAonad Curaclaim (1988). *Synthesis of Reports 1977–1987*, p. 24. (Unpublished).

24   Report on the Pilot Project on Science in the Primary School (1987) (in) An Roinn Oideachais – An tAonad Curaclaim (1988). *Synthesis of Reports 1977–1987*, p. 32. (Unpublished).

25   CEB (1985). *The Arts in Education – A Curriculum and Examinations Board Discussion Paper.* Dublin: CEB, p. 20.

26   CEB (1985). *Language in the Curriculum – A Curriculum and Examinations Board Discussion Paper.* Dublin: CEB, p. 28.

27   CEB (1985). *Primary Education ...*, p. 6.

28   CEB (1986). *Mathematics Education: Primary and Junior Cycle Post-primary – A Curriculum and Examinations Board Discussion Paper.* Dublin: CEB, p. 17.

29   CEB (1986). *In Our Schools – A Framework for Curriculum and Assessment.* Dublin: CEB.

30   CEB (1987). *Social, Political and Environmental Education – Report of the Board of Studies.* Dublin: CEB, p. 2.

31   Department of Education (1980). *White Paper on Educational Development.* Dublin: The Stationery Office, p. 116.

32   Department of Education (1984). *Programme for Action in Education 1984–1987 ...*

33   Review Body on the Primary Curriculum (1990). *Report of the Review Body on the Primary Curriculum.* Dublin: Department of Education, p. 5.

34   *Ibid.*, p. 75.

35   *Ibid.*, p. 97.
36   Department of Education (1990). *Report of the Primary Education Review Body.* Dublin: The Stationery Office, p. IX.
37   Travers, M. (1976). A Second Replication of a Survey of Reading Comprehension in Dublin City Schools. *Irish Journal of Education*, Volume 10, No. 1, pp. 18–22.
38   Ward, N. (1982). A Fourth Survey of Reading Comprehension in Dublin City National Schools. *Irish Journal of Education*, Volume 16, No. 1, pp. 56–61, p. 57.
39   Forde, P. and Shiel, G. (1993). Assessment of English Reading in Primary Schools. *Oideas*, Spring 1993, Volume 40, pp. 5–20, p. 6.
40   Association of Remedial Teachers of Ireland (1976). *A Priority in Education.* Dublin: Association of Remedial Teachers of Ireland, p. 14.
41   Kellaghan, T. and Fontes, P. (1977). Incidence and Correlates of Illiteracy in Irish Primary Schools. *Irish Journal of Education*, Volume 11, No. 1, pp. 5–20, p. 18.
42   Swan, D. (1978). *Reading Standards in Irish Schools.* Dublin: The Educational Company, p. 69.
43   Connaughton, U. and Mahoney, M. (1985). Post-primary Remedial Teaching: A Survey. *Learn*, Volume 7, pp. 2–7.
44   Forde, P. (1979). The Teaching of English in Dublin Primary Schools (in) Reading Association of Ireland (1979). *Proceedings of the Fourth Annual Conference.* Dublin: Reading Association of Ireland, pp. 104–111, p. 111.
45   *Ibid.*, p. 104.
46   Killeen, J. (1986). Approaches to the Teaching of English in Dublin City Schools (in) Greaney, V. and Molloy, B. (Eds) (1986). *Dimensions of Reading.* Dublin: The Educational Company of Ireland, pp. 73–76.
47   Fontes, P., Kellaghan, T. and O'Brien, M. (1983). Relationships between Time Spent Teaching, Classroom Organisation, and Reading Achievement. *Irish Journal of Education*, Volume 15, No. 2, pp. 79–91, p. 88.
48   Motherway, A. (1987). Poetry in the Primary School. *Oideas*, Spring 1987, Volume 30, pp. 37–47, p. 40.
49   Archer, P. and O'Flaherty, B. (1991). Literacy Problems among Primary School Leavers in Dublin's Inner City. *Studies in Education*, Autumn 1991, Volume 7, No. 2, pp. 7–13, p. 12.
50   Torthaí Staidéir: Leanúnachas i Múineadh na Gaeilge ó Bhunscoil go hIarbhunscoil. *Oideas*, Autumn 1972, Volume 9, pp. 18–21, p. 20.
51   Comhairle na Gaeilge (1974). *Irish in Education.* Dublin: The Stationery Office, p. 35.
52   Lindsey, J. (1975). Irish Language Teaching: A Survey of Teacher Perceptions. *Irish Journal of Education*, Volume 9, No. 2, pp. 97–107, p. 103.

53   Greaney, V. (1978). Trends in Attainment in Irish from 1973 to 1977. *Irish Journal of Education*, Volume 7, No. 1, pp. 22–35.

54   INTO (1978). *Reports of the Central Executive Committee and Finance Committee for the Year 1977–1978, together with Accounts and Statistics and Resolutions on Organisation Matters*. Dublin: INTO, p. 58.

55   An Roinn Oideachas (1982). *Tuarascáil an Chomhchoiste um Oideachas sa Ghaeltacht*. Baile Átha Cliath: Oifig an tSoláthair, p. 17.

56   *Ibid.*, p. 69.

57   Comhar na Múinteoirí Gaeilge (1981). *Bunoideachas trí Ghaeilge sa Ghaeltacht – Tuarascáil*. Baile Átha Cliath: Comhar na Múinteoirí Gaeilge, p. 5.

58   Harris, J. (1984). *Spoken Irish in Primary Schools* ..., p. 8.

59   *Ibid.*, p. 4.

60   *Ibid.*, p. 139.

61   Ó Domhnalláin, T. and Ó Gliasáin, M. (1976). *Audiovisual Methods v A.B.C. Methods* ...

62   Cummins, J. (1978). Immersion Programs: the Irish Experience. *International Review of Education*, Volume 24, No. 3, pp. 273–282, p. 273.

63   Bord na Gaeilge (1983). *Action Plan for Irish 1983–1986*. Dublin: Bord na Gaeilge, p. 5.

64   Norton, S. (1984). A Communicative Syllabus for Irish in the Primary School: Arguments and Practical Proposals (in) INTO – District XV (1984). *Proceedings of the First Annual Drumcondra Education Conference*. Dublin: INTO – District XV, pp. 110–123, p. 111.

65   CEB (1985). *Language in the Curriculum* ...

66   Ní Argáin, C. (1990). Soléite nó Doléite? Staidéar ar Sholéiteacht Théascleabhar Gaeilge sa Bhunscoil. *Oideas*, Spring 1983, Volume 35, pp. 35–55, p. 48.

67   INTO (1985). *The Irish National Teachers' Organisation and the Irish Language – Discussion Document*. Dublin: Irish INTO, p. 2.

68   The Irish National Teachers' Organisation and the Irish Language. *Tuarascáil*, March 1989, No. 3, pp. 29–31, p. 31.

69   Ó Riagáin, P. (1988). Public Attitudes towards Irish in the Schools: A Note on Recent Surveys. *Teangeolas*, Geimhreadh 1988, No. 25, pp. 19–21.

70   CLÁR (1975). *Report*. Dublin: The Stationery Office, p. 292.

71   Kellaghan, T., Madaus, G., Airasian, P. and Fontes, P. (1976). The Mathematical Attainments of Post-primary Entrants. *Irish Journal of Education*, Volume 10, No. 1, pp. 3–17.

72   Close, S., Kellaghan, T., Madaus, G. and Airasian, P. (1978). Growth in Mathematical Attainments of Pupils. *Irish Journal of Education*, Volume 7, No. 1, pp. 3–21, p. 14.

73 Mulryan, C. (1984). Effective Communication of Mathematics at Primary Level: Focus on the Textbooks. *Irish Educational Studies*, Volume 4, No. 2, pp. 62–81, p. 62.

74 Mulryan, C. and Close, S. (1982). A Study of the Mathematical Vocabulary of Primary School Mathematics Textbooks. *Irish Educational Studies*, Volume 2, pp. 305–321.

75 Greaney, V. and Close, S. (1989). Mathematics Achievement in Irish Primary Schools. *Irish Journal of Education*, Volume 22, No. 2, pp. 51–64, p. 51.

76 Martin, M., Hickey, B. and Murchan, D. (1992). Educational Progress in Ireland: Maths and Science. *Irish Journal of Education*, Volume 26, pp. 105–116.

77 Greaney, V. and Close, S. (1992). Mathematics in Irish Primary Schools: A Review of Research. *Oideas*, Spring 1992, Volume 38, pp. 41–61, p. 55.

78 Martin, M. (1990). Mathematics Achievement in Sixth Class in Irish Primary Schools. *Irish Journal of Education*, Volume 24, No. 1, pp. 27–39, p. 34.

79 INTO (1978). *Reports of the Central Executive Committee* ..., p. 64.

80 Gilligan, J. (1982). *Teaching of History in Senior Standards in the Curriculum of Irish National Schools 1961–1981*. M.Ed. Thesis. Dublin: University College Dublin, p. 246.

81 Cregan, A. (1983). A Study of the Readability of Four History Textbooks in Use in Sixth Class in Irish Primary Schools. *Irish Educational Studies*, Volume 3, No. 1, pp. 166–185.

82 Motherway, A. (1986). The Textbook Curriculum: The Status and Role of the Textbook in the Teaching of History and English at Senior Primary Level. *Irish Educational Studies*, Volume 6, No. 1, pp. 193–204, p. 195.

83 Beggan, G. (1988). A Profile of the Progress of Science in Primary Education in Ireland, 1837–1986. *Oideas*, Spring 1988, Volume 32, pp. 36–50.

84 Bennett, J. (1994). History Textbooks in Primary Schools in the Republic of Ireland, 1971–1993. *Oideas*, Summer 1994, Volume 42, pp. 26–38, p. 28.

85 Bennett, J. (1993). Geography Textbooks in the Republic of Ireland, 1973–1993. *Irish Journal of Education*, Volume 27, No. 1 and 2, pp. 25–35, p. 26.

86 Department of Education (1986). *Geography Textbooks for Primary Schools: Suggestions for Publishers*, p. 3. (Unpublished).

87 Department of Education (1994). *Report of the Inter-Departmental Working Group on Environmental Awareness*. Dublin: The Stationery Office, p. 13.

88 Fleischmann, A. (1971). Music in Education (in) Murphy, M. (Ed.) (1971). *Education in Ireland 2 – What Should Students Learn*. Cork: Mercier Press, pp. 68–88, p. 72.

89 INTO (1978). *Reports of the Central Executive Committee* ..., pp. 63–71.

90 Benson, C. (1979). The Arts in the Primary School. *An Múinteoir Náisiúnta*, October 1979, Volume 23, No. 3, pp. 9–13.

91 Herron, D. (1985). *Deaf Ears? A Report on the Provision of Music Education in Irish Schools*. Dublin: The Arts Council, pp. V–VI.

92 Benson, C. (1985). Introduction (in) Herron, D. (1985). *Deaf Ears?* ..., pp. V–VI, p. VI.

93 Meany, M. (1986). Aspects of Music Education in the Primary School. *Irish Educational Studies*, Volume 6, No. 1, pp. 172–179, p. 174.

94 O'Flynn, J. (1990). The Selection and Organisation of Musical Materials in Irish Schools. *Oideas*, Spring 1990, Volume 35, pp. 56–73, p. 68.

95 INTO (1989). *The Arts in Education – A Report by the Education Committee*. Dublin: INTO.

96 Cotter, M. (1978). *An Investigation into the Teaching of Physical Education in National Schools in the Republic of Ireland*. M.Ed. Thesis. Dublin: Trinity College Dublin, p. 187.

97 *Ibid.*, p. 177.

98 Donoghue, E. (1981). Health Education in Schools. *Compass*, Volume 10, No. 2, pp. 7–14, p. 8.

99 INTO (1984). *C.E.C and E.C. Reports 1983–1984*. Dublin: INTO, p. 20.

100 INTO (1984). *Ages of Entry – Report of the Education Committee*. Dublin: INTO, p. 15.

101 Ní Mhaoldomhnaigh, S. (1985). The Infant Mathematics Curriculum in Practice – A Study (in) INTO – District XV (1985). *Proceedings of the Second Annual Drumcondra Education Conference*. Dublin: INTO – District XV, pp. 12–23, p. 12.

102 O'Rourke, B. and Archer, P. (1987). A Survey of Teaching Practices in the Junior Grades of Irish Primary Schools. *Irish Journal of Education*, Volume 21, No. 2, pp. 53–79, p. 57.

103 *Ibid.*, p. 77.

104 Higgins, M. (1987). *Infant Education in the Republic of Ireland – A Critique*. M.Ed. Thesis. Kildare: National University of Ireland, Maynooth, p. 168.

105 Stapleton, G. (1988). *Infant Education and the Irish Primary School*. M.Ed. Thesis. Dublin: Trinity College Dublin, p. 212.

106 Kelleher, A. (1990). *Infant Education and the 1971 Curriculum*. M.Ed. Thesis. Dublin: University College Dublin, p. 139.

107 Horgan, M. (1991). Aspects of Play in the Junior Infant Classroom. *Irish Educational Studies*, Volume 10, No. 1, pp. 67–81, p. 70.

108 Cloonan, T. (1981). *Primary School Curriculum and Teachers' Attitudes*. M.Ed. Thesis. Galway: University College Galway, p. 56.

109 Egan, O. (1981). Informal Teaching in the Primary School: Characteristics and Correlates. *Irish Journal of Education*, Volume 15, No. 1, pp. 5–22, p. 16.

110 Egan, O. (1982). Informal Teaching in the Primary School: Effects on Pupil Achievement. *Irish Journal of Education*, Volume 16, No. 1, pp. 16–26, p. 22.

111 Gash, H. (1985). Foundations and Practice of the New Curriculum. *Irish Educational Studies*, Volume 5, No. 1, pp. 86–101, p. 99.

112 Burke, A. and Fontes, P. (1986). Educational Beliefs and Practices of Sixth-class Teachers in Irish Primary Schools. *Irish Journal of Education*, Volume 20, No. 2, pp. 51–77.

113 Sugrue, C. (1990). Child-centred Education in Ireland since 1971: An Assessment. *Oideas*, Spring 1990, Volume 35, pp. 5–21, p. 16.

114 *Ibid.*, p. 5.

115 INTO (1989). *School Texts – A Report by the Education Committee*. Dublin: INTO, p. 6.

116 Kellaghan, T. and Gorman, L. (1968). A Survey of Teaching Aids in Irish Primary Schools. *Irish Journal of Education*, Volume 2, No. 1, pp. 32–40, p. 36.

117 McMahon, E. (1975). *A Study of a Primary School*. M.Ed. Thesis. Kildare: National University of Ireland, Maynooth, p. 2.

118 Department of Education (1985). *Report of the Primary Inspectorate to the Minister for Education on the Year 1 September 1983 – 31 August 1984*, p. 12. (Unpublished).

119 INTO (1982). *An Examination of the Educational Implications of School Size 1981–1982*. Dublin: INTO, p. 5.

120 National Parents' Council – Primary (1990). *The Cost of Free Education – A Survey on the Cost to Parents of Free Primary Education in Ireland*. Dublin: National Parents' Council – Primary, p. 20.

121 Columba, M. (1973). The Primary School Curriculum. *Compass*, February 1973, Volume 2, No. 1, pp. 4–9, p. 9.

122 *Address of Mr Pádraig Faulkner, T.D., Minister for Education at the Annual General Meeting of the Conference of Convent Secondary Schools at University College Belfield on Wednesday 28 June, 1972*. National Archives, File GIS 1/149.

123 Murphy, D. (1972). The New Primary School Curriculum. *Studies*, Autumn 1972, Volume LXI, No. 243, pp. 199–218, p. 211.

124 INTO (1973). *Reports of the Central Executive Committee and Finance Committee for the Year 1972–1973, together with Accounts and Statistics and Resolutions on Organisation Matters*. Dublin: INTO, p. 38.

125 INTO (1979). *Proposals to the Minister for Education in Connection with the White Paper on Education*. Dublin: INTO, p. 8.

126 Crooks, T. and Griffin, K. (1978). Editorial. *Compass*, Volume 7, No. 1, pp. 4–12.

127 Murphy, C. (1980). *School Report – The Guide to Irish Education for Parents, Teachers and Students.* Dublin: Ward River Press, p. 57.

128 Crooks, T. and McKernan, J. (1984). *The Challenge of Change: Curriculum Development in Irish Post-primary Schools 1970–1984.* Dublin: Institute of Public Administration, pp. 89–90.

129 O'Connor, D. (1979). Seminar Proceedings – Bridging the Gap (1979). *Oideas,* Spring 1979, Volume 20, pp. 5–8, p. 8.

130 Barry, T. (1979). Seminar Proceedings – Bridging the Gap ..., pp. 29–32, p. 32.

131 Department of Education (1981). *Report of the Pupil Transfer Committee.* Dublin: The Stationery Office, p. 1.

132 *Ibid.,* p. 42.

133 CEB (1985). *Primary Education ...,* p. 6.

134 Burke, A. (1987). From Primary to Post-primary: Bridge or Barrier. *Oideas,* Spring 1987, Volume 30, pp. 5–23, p. 5.

135 Department of Education (1990). *Report of the Primary Education Review Body ...,* p. 75.

136 OECD (1991). *Reviews of National Policies for Education – Ireland.* Paris: OECD, p. 72.

137 Madaus, G., Fontes, P., Kellaghan, T. and Airasian, P. (1979). Opinions of the Irish Public on the Goals and Adequacy of Education. *Irish Journal of Education,* Volume 13, No. 2, pp. 87–125, p. 119.

138 Kellaghan, T., Madaus, G., Airasian, P. and Fontes, P. (1981). Opinions of the Irish Public on Innovations in Education. *Irish Journal of Education,* Volume 15, No. 1, pp. 23–40, p. 23.

139 McMahon, E. (1975). *A Study of a Primary School ...,* p. 74.

140 Horgan, J. (1973). The New Curriculum – A Review. *Primary News.* Dublin: Gill and Macmillan, p. 1.

141 Walsh, M. (1980). *A Study of the Implementation of the 1971 Curriculum ...*

142 Sugrue, C. (1997). *Complexities of Teaching: Child-centred Perspectives.* London: Falmer, p. 25.

143 O'Leary, M. (1991). The Primary Curriculum. *Studies in Education,* Autumn 1991, Volume 7, No. 2, pp. 58–61, p. 61.

144 OECD (1991). *Reviews of National Policies for Education ...,* p. 67.

145 *Ibid.,* p. 63.

Bibliography

Arrangement of Bibliography

Manuscript and Unpublished Source Material
    National Archives
    UCD Archives
    Other Unpublished Material

British Parliamentary Reports and Sources
    Commission on Manual and Practical Instruction (CMPI)
    Reports of the Commissioners of National Education
    Reports Emanating from Britain, Pre-1922
    Reports Relating to Britain, Post-1922

Publications of the Government of Ireland
    Annual Reports of the Department of Education
    Occasional Reports of the Department of Education
    Department of Education Circulars
    Other Government Reports and Documents

Irish Parliamentary Debates
    Dáil and Seanad Debates

Chapters in Books

Articles in Journals and Periodicals

Articles in Conference Proceedings

Books Relating to the Subject and Period

Reports, Pamphlets and Political Programmes

Newspapers, Annual Reports and Year books

INTO Journals

Unpublished Theses

Manuscript and Unpublished Source Material

National Archives

Address by Minister Brian Lenihan to Congress of INTO, Hydro Hotel, Kilkee, Tuesday 8 April 1969. National Archives File GIS 1/231.

Address of Mr Pádraig Faulkner, T.D., Minister for Education at the Annual General Meeting of the Conference of Convent Secondary Schools at University College Belfield on Wednesday 28 June, 1972. National Archives, File GIS 1/149.

Agenda for Meeting on 10 November. National Archives, Box 130, File 8536, Part 2.

Agricultural Instruction in the System of Primary Education from the establishment of the Commissioners of National Education up to the Present Day. National Archives, File 14395A.

Appeals against Inspectors' Reports of General Inspections and Regulations for the Award of Primary School Certificate, Revised Instructions to Inspectors. National Archives, Box 575, File 25629.

Circulars and Memoranda to Inspectors including 'Teachers' Rating.' Questions of Conditions for Rating 'Highly Efficient' and 'Efficient.' July 1929. National Archives, Box 471, File 21432.

Control of Primary Teachers in their Capacity as Members of that Profession. National Archives, File 14395A.

Department of Education – *Memorandum for the Government,* 29 October 1956. National Archives, File S15015A.

Digest of the Replies received in relation to the Points on which information is specifically desired by the National Programme Conference. Question 1–8. National Archives, File 12850.

Education in the Irish Free State – General Statement, December 1931. National Archives, File S2223.

Evidence of Cáit Nic Fhlanchuidhe to Second National Programme Conference, Assistant Teacher, Mulnahona Girls' School, Ring. National Archives, Box 130, File 8536, Part 2.

… *Máire Ní Cheallacháin* …, Scoil Bhríde. National Archives, Box 130, File 8536, Part 2.

… *Máire Ní Ghallachobhair* …, Teacher of Day Pupils in Eccles Street Convent, Dublin. National Archives, Box 130, File 8536, Part 2.

… *Michael Moriarity* …, Letterleague National School, Letterkenny. National Archives, Box 130, File 8536, Part 2.

... *Miss Heagen* ..., Central Infant Model School. National Archives, Box 130, File 8536, Part 2.

... *Mr Bohan* ..., Principal, Cloonteagh N.S., Longford. National Archives, Box 130, File 8536, Part 2.

... *Mr E. Culverwell* ..., Professor of Education, Trinity College Dublin. National Archives, Box 130, File 8536, Part 2.

... *Mr F. O'Tierney* ..., Divisional Inspector. National Archives, Box 130, File 8536, Part 2.

... *Mr Joseph Hanly* ..., General Organising Inspector of Rural Science. National Archives, Box 130, File 8536, Part 2.

... *Mr Liam Mac Fhachtna* ..., Inspector of Irish in the National Schools. National Archives, Box 130, File 8536, Part 2.

... *Mr Liam Ó Ceallaigh* ..., District Inspector. National Archives, Box 130, File 8536, Part 2.

... *Mr MacEnrí* ..., Principal, Bangor Erris Boys' N.S., Co. Mayo. National Archives, Box 130, File 8536, Part 2.

... *Mr Timothy O'Brien* ..., Principal, St. Michael and John's School, Dublin. National Archives, Box 130, File 8536, Part 2.

... *Rev. Corcoran* ..., Professor of Education at UCD. National Archives, Box 130, File 8536, Part 2.

... *Rev. Phelan* ..., Master of Method, Christian Brothers' Training College, Dublin. National Archives, Box 130, File 8536, Part 2.

... *Rev. T. O'Rahilly* ..., National School Manager, Presentation Schools, Dublin. National Archives, Box 130, File 8536, Part 2.

Extracts from National Programme Conference Discussion – Infant Standards. National Archives, Box 244, File 12847.

FitzGerald, P. (1925). *Report of State of Education in the Dublin Division*. National Archives, File 12850.

Inspector's Conference on the National Programme, June 1925. *Conference of the Divisional Inspectors on the National Conference Programme*. National Archives, Box 244, File 12845.

Irish Courses for Teachers and Irish Colleges. *Memorandum – The Training of Teachers in Irish*. National Archives, Box 298, File 14806.

Letter from Irish National Teachers' Organisation. Circular to Inspectors – Programme 1923–1924, February 1924. National Archives, Box 624, File 27513.

Letter from Seosamh O'Neill to the Department of Finance, 19 May 1925. National Archives, Box 130, File 8536, Part 1.

Level of Living in Ireland: Measurement and Index of. Ireland – Health, including Demographic Conditions. National Archives, File S15733.

List of Points on which Information is Specifically Desired by the National Programme Conference. National Archives, Box 244, File 12842.

Little, R. (1925). *General Report on the State of Education in Division V*. National Archives, File 12850, p. 4.

Memorandum from the Minister for Education Enclosing an Account of the Activities of the Department since the Election of the Dáil in August 1923, 26 April 1927. National Archives, File S5360/6.

National Programme Conference, Examining Sub-committee of National Programme Conference. National Archives, Box 245, File 12850.

National Programme Conference – Meeting on 10 November 1925. National Archives, Box 130, File 8536, Part 2.

National Programme Conference – Minutes 9 June 1925. National Archives, Box 244, File 12842.

National Programme Conference, Minutes of Second Meeting of Sub-Committee, 25 July 1925. National Archives, Box 245, File 12850.

O'Tighearnaigh, P. (1925). *Report of State of Education in Galway Division*. National Archives, File 12850.

Office of Adjutant General – Memo re Programme of Primary Education. National Archives, Box 246, File 12852.

Office of National Education (1931). *Qualifications of Teachers – Classes of Persons Eligible for Recognition as Teachers: Revision of Rules and Regulations*, September 1931. National Archives, Box 727, File 31752.

Office of National Education: National Programme Conference – Views of Office in relation to Reviewing the Programme (1925). *Albert Agricultural College – Reply to your G.1689/25*. National Archives, File AG1/G1689/25.

Office of National Education: National Programme Conference – Views of Office in relation to Reviewing the Programme (1925). *Memorandum furnished by the Department of Lands and Agriculture for the Information of the National Programme Conference*. National Archives, File AG1/G1689/25.

Pollak, J. (1943). *Irish Language: Development in Schools – On Teaching Irish*. National Archives, File S7801.

Programme Conference 1925 – Church of Ireland General Synod's Board of Education. National Archives, Box 246, File 12852.

Programme Conference 1925 – Statement submitted by the Central Executive Committee of the Irish National Teachers' Organisation. National Archives, Box 246, File 12852.

Publications in Irish, An Gúm. Memorandum on the 'Gúm' prepared by Publications Officer, Department of Education, 8 August 1947. National Archives, File S9538A.

Publications in Irish, An Gúm. *An Gúm – Publications up to 28 July 1951*. National Archives, File S9538A.

Publications in Irish – General. *Leabhair de Chuid An Ghúm a Díoladh mar Bhruspháipéar*. National Archives, File S9538B.

Recommendations and Suggested Changes in the Present Primary Programme for Schools, Adopted and Approved by the Protestant Teachers' Union at a Meeting held on 3 September 1925. National Archives, Box 245, File 12849.

Report and Programme submitted by The National Programme Conference to the Minister for Education. National Archives, Box 250, File 12848.

Report of Departmental Committee to Examine the Educational System, established in March 1945. *Final Report*, 1 December 1947. National Archives, File S18921B.

Results Achieved During Year 1930–1931. National Archives, File S2223.

Rule 127 – Recommendation of Programme. *Extracts from National Programme Conference Discussion – Infant Standards*. National Archives, Box 410, File 19168.

Statistics relative to the Position of Irish in the National Schools (prior to 1922). National Archives, Box 367, File 17511.

Submission of Aodh O'Neill, Ministry of Defence. National Archives, Box 246, File 12852.

Teachers' Qualifications in Irish, June 1928. National Archives. Box 342, File 16610.

Teaching through Irish – *Reports from Divisional Inspectors. Statement based on the Special Confidential Reports of the Divisional Inspectors on the present position as regards Teaching through the Medium of Irish*. National Archives, Box 665, File 28933.

The Commissioners of National Education. National Archives, File 14395A.

Training Colleges – *Instruction of Students through the Medium of Irish*. Letter to Our Lady of Mercy Training College, July 1931. National Archives, Box 355, File 17131.

Views of Catholic Clerical School Managers' Association in detail on the points submitted by the National Programme Conference. National Archives, Box 246, File 12852.

Views of the Association of Training College Teachers. National Archives, Box 246, File 12852.

Views of the Chamber of Commerce, Dublin. National Archives, Box 246, File 12852.

Views of the Education Committee, Galway County Council. National Archives, File 12852.

Visits of Organisers to Irish Speaking Districts during July 1924. *Circular to Inspectors and Organisers*. National Archives, Box 364, File 17397.

UCD Archives

Draft for an Act to make Further Provision with respect to Education in Saor-Stát Éireann and for purposes connected therewith – Part 1: Advisory Council. UCD Archives, Eoin MacNeill Papers, LA1/P/41.

Fees for Instruction through Irish, 19 December 1930. UCD Archives, Blythe Papers P24/345.

Memorandum re Preparatory Colleges. UCD Archives, Blythe Papers, P24/302.

Na Coláistí Ullmhucháin, July 1931. UCD Archives, Blythe Papers, P24/302.

Scheme of Scholarships in Secondary Schools for Pupils from the Fíor-Ghaeltacht, July 1931. UCD Archives, Blythe Papers, P24/303.

Other Unpublished Material

An Roinn Oideachais – An tAonad Curaclaim (1983). *A Report on the Teaching of Music in Primary Schools.* (Unpublished).

An Roinn Oideachais – An tAonad Curaclaim (1985). *An Ghaeilge – Tuairisc ar Fheidhmiú an Churaclaim sna Bunscoileanna.* (Unpublished).

An Roinn Oideachais – An tAonad Curaclaim (1983). *Daoneolas agus Eolas Imshaoil – Tuairisc ar Fheidhmiú an Churaclaim sna Bunscoileanna.* (Unpublished).

An Roinn Oideachais – An tAonad Curaclaim (1987). *The Implementation of the Principles of the Primary School Curriculum – Perceptions of Teachers and Principals: Survey Report.* (Unpublished).

Brief Outline of the History of the Inspectorate in the National Schools of Ireland. (Unpublished).

Commission on Youth Unemployment (1951). *Report.* (Unpublished).

Curaclam do na Bunscoileanna, December 1967. (Unpublished).

De Buitléar, S. (1969). *Notes for Talk by Mr T. Ó Floinn, M.A., Assistant Secretary, Department of Education on the New Curriculum for the Primary Schools.* October 1969. (Unpublished).

De Buitléar, S. (1971). *The Role of the Primary Schools' Inspector.* (Unpublished).

De Buitléar, S. (1973). *New Primary School Curriculum (1971).* (Unpublished).

De Buitléar (1978). *A National Educational Policy Review – Ireland.* (Unpublished).

De Buitléar, S. (n.d.). *The New Curriculum.* (Unpublished).

Department of Education (1967). *Towards a White Paper on Education.* (Unpublished).

Department of Education (1968). *Primary Education New Curriculum – A Working Document*. Department of Education Files, File 11357. (Unpublished).

Department of Education (1981). *Report of the Committee on Primary Schools Inspection*. (Unpublished).

Department of Education (1985). *Report of the Primary Inspectorate to the Minister for Education on the Year 1 September 1983 – 31 August 1984*. (Unpublished).

Department of Education (1986). *Geography Textbooks for Primary Schools: Suggestions for Publishers*. (Unpublished).

Department of Education (1992). *Annual Report of the Primary Inspectorate for the Year 1990–1991 to the Minister for Education*. (Unpublished).

Department of Education Curriculum Development Unit (1984). *Report on the Implementation of Art and Craft Activities in Primary Schools*. (Unpublished).

Department of Education Curriculum Unit (1982). *English in the Primary School – Survey Report*. (Unpublished).

Digest of Responses to the Working Document, 1969–1970. (Unpublished).

Dréacht Curaclaim do na Bunscoileanna – Ceisteanna ina Thaobh. Attachment to Letter on 13 December 1967 from Domhnaill Ó hUalacháin to Seamus de Buitléar. (Unpublished).

Dwyer, C. (1981). *Seven Years of Progress? Third Report on the Educational Needs of Travelling People*. Submitted by the National Coordinator for the Education of Travelling People. (Unpublished).

Inspectorate Statistics – Personal Communication from the Personnel Section of the Department of Education and Science, 16 May 2006. (Unpublished).

Letter from Domhnall Ó hUallacháin to Roinnchigire and Cigirí Ceantair on 13 January 1967. (Unpublished).

Letter from John at Oxfordshire County Council to James Butler, Inspector of Schools, 1 April 1969, p. 1. (Unpublished).

Magee, J. (1982). *The Master – A Social History of the Irish National Teacher 1831–1921*. Paper delivered at the Canon Rogers Memorial Lecture, St. Joseph's College of Education Belfast, November 1982. (Unpublished).

New Curriculum Pilot Schemes. Department of Education Files, File 11403. (Unpublished).

Preas-Agallamh – An Curaclam Nua – *Focal ón Aire*, May 1971. (Unpublished).

Report on the Pilot Project on Computers in the Primary School (1987) (in) An Roinn Oideachais – An tAonad Curaclaim (1988). *Synthesis of Reports 1977–1987*. (Unpublished).

Report on the Pilot Project on Science in the Primary School (1987) (in) An Roinn Oideachais – An tAonad Curaclaim (1988). *Synthesis of Reports 1977–1987*. (Unpublished).

Report of the Working Party Established by the Education Committee of the Hierarchy and the Conference of Major Religious Superiors to Examine the Future Involvement of Religious in Education (1973). (Unpublished).

Tuairisc ar Theagasc an Chorpoideachais sna Bunscoileanna (1979) (in) An Roinn Oideachais – An tAonad Curaclaim (1988). *Synthesis of Reports 1977–1987.* (Unpublished).

Tuairisc ar an Mhatamitic i Rang VI (1984) (in) An Roinn Oideachais – An tAonad Curaclaim (1988). *Synthesis of Reports 1977–1987.* (Unpublished).

British Parliamentary Reports and Sources

Commission on Manual and Practical Instruction

Commission on Manual and Practical Instruction in Primary Schools under the Board of National Education in Ireland (1897). *First Report of the Commissioners and Minutes of the Evidence taken at the First Seven Public Sittings.* Dublin: Alexander Thom and Co. (Limited). [C. 8383] [C. 8384].

... (1897). *Second Volume of Minutes of Evidence, comprising that taken in England between March 18 and April 9, 1897, being a supplement to the Second Report of the Commissioners* ... [C. 8532].

... (1897). *Third Volume of Minutes of Evidence, comprising that taken in England between April 29 and July 31, 1897, being a supplement to the Third Report of the Commissioners* ... [C. 8619].

... (1898). *Fourth Volume of Minutes of Evidence comprising that taken between September 29 and December 17, 1897, being a supplement to the Final Report of the Commissioners* ... [C. 8924].

... (1898). *Final Report of the Commissioners* ... [C. 8923].

... (1898). *Appendices to the Reports of the Commissioners* ... [C. 8925].

Reports of the Commissioners of National Education

Commissioners of National Education (1869). *35th Report of the Commissioners of National Education for 1868.* Dublin: Alexander Thom. and Co. [4193] XXI.

... (1871). *37th Report ... 1870* [C. 360] XXLL.
... (1892). *58th Report ... for 1891 – Appendices* [C. 6788–I] XXX.
... (1896). *62nd Report ... for 1895 – Appendices* [C. 8185] XXVIII.
... (1897). *63rd Report ... for 1896–1897* [C. 8600] XXVIII.
... (1897). *63rd Report ... for 1896–1897 – Appendices* [C. 8601] XXVIII.
... (1898). *64th Report ... for 1897–1898 – Appendices* [C. 9039] XXVII.
... (1899). *65th Report ... for 1898–1899* [C. 9446] XXIV.
... (1900). *66th Report ... for 1899–1900 – Appendix 1* [Cd. 286] XXIII.
... (1901). *67th Report ... for 1900* [Cd. 704] XXI.
... (1902). *67th Report ... for 1900 – Appendix 1* [Cd. 954] XXX.
... (1902). *67th Report ... for 1900 – Appendix II* [Cd. 872] XXX.
... (1902). *68th Report ... for 1901* [Cd. 1198] XXX.
... (1902). *68th Report ... for 1901 – Appendix, Section 1* [Cd. 997] XXX.
... (1903). *68th Report ... for 1901 – Appendix, Section 1* [Cd. 1444] XXI.
... (1904). *69th Report ... for 1902 – Appendix, Section 1* [Cd. 1890] XX.
... (1904). *70th Report ... for 1903* [Cd. 2230] XX.
... (1905). *70th Report ... for 1903 – Appendix, Section 1* [Cd. 2373] XXVII.
... (1905). *71st Report ... for 1904* [Cd. 2567] XXVIII.
... (1905). *71st Report ... for 1904 – Appendix, Section 1* [Cd. 2654] XXVIII.
... (1906). *72nd Report ... for 1905–1906* [Cd. 3154] XXIX.
... (1906). *72nd Report ... for 1905–1906 – Appendices* [Cd. 3185] XXIX.
... (1908). *73rd Report ... for 1906–1907 – Appendix, Section 1* [Cd. 3861] XXVII.
... (1908). *74th Report ... for 1907–1908* [Cd. 4291] XXVII.
... (1910). *75th Report ... for 1908–1909 – Appendix 1* [Cd. 5062] XXV.
... (1911). *76th Report ... for 1909–1910 – Appendix, Section 1* [Cd. 5491] XXI.
... (1914). *79th Report ... for 1912–1913 – Appendix, Section 1* [Cd. 7382] XXVII.
... (1921). *86th Report ... for 1919–1920* [Cmd. 1476] XI.

Reports Emanating from Britain, Pre-1922

Abstracts of the Board's [Commissioners of National Education] Proceedings 1898–1900.
LO 2351, National Library of Ireland.
CNEI (1902). *Building Grants for National Schools in Ireland – Report of Committee
1902.* Printed for Her Majesty's Stationery Office by Alexander Thom and Co.
Dale, F.H. (1904). *Report of Mr F.H. Dale, His Majesty's Inspector of Schools, Board of
Education, on Primary Education in Ireland.* Printed for His Majesty's Stationery
Office by Alexander Thom and Co. (Limited) Abbey Street [Cd. 1981].

National Education (Ireland) Bill 1892. Bills, Public 1892, Volume 4, Bill 420, p. 647.

Royal Commission of Inquiry into Primary Education (Ireland) (1870). *Conclusions and Recommendations Contained in the General Report*, Volume 1. [C. – 6].

Royal Commission on Technical Instruction (1884). *Second Report of the Royal Commission on Technical Instruction – Volume IV: Evidence, &c Relating to Ireland*. [c. 3981–III].

Vice-Regal Committee of Inquiry into Primary Education (Ireland) 1913, *Appendix to the First Report of the Committee* – Minutes of Evidence, 13 February–12 March 1913. [Cd. 6829].

Vice-Regal Committee of Inquiry into Primary Education (Ireland) 1913, *Appendix to the Second Report of the Committee* – Minutes of Evidence, 13 March–25 June 1913. [Cd. 7229].

Vice-Regal Committee of Inquiry into Primary Education (Ireland) 1913, *Appendix to the Third Report of the Committee* – Minutes of Evidence 26 June–17 September 1913. [Cd. 7480].

Vice-Regal Committee of Inquiry into Primary Education (Ireland) 1913, *Final Report of the Committee*. [Cd. 7235].

Reports Relating to Britain, Post-1922

Central Advisory Council for Education (England) (1967). *Children and their Primary Schools – A Report of the Central Advisory Council for Education (England). Volume 1: Report*. London: Her Majesty's Stationery Office.

Government of Northern Ireland Ministry of Education (1956). *Programme for Primary Schools*. Belfast: Her Majesty's Stationery Office, p. 5.

Scottish Education Department (1965). *Primary Education in Scotland*. Edinburgh: Her Majesty's Stationery Office.

Publications of the Government of Ireland

Annual Reports of the Department of Education

Annual Reports/Tuarascáil Staitistiúil of the Department of Education/An Roinn Oideachais (1925–1991).

Occasional Reports of the Department of Education

An Roinn Oideachais (1966). *Buntús Gaeilge: Réamhthuarascáil ar Thaighde Teangeolaíochta a Rinneadh an Teanglann.* Baile Átha Cliath: Oifig an tSoláthair.

An Roinn Oideachas (1982). *Tuarascáil an Chomhchoiste um Oideachas sa Ghaeltacht.* Baile Átha Cliath: Oifig an tSoláthair.

Commission on School Accommodation (2001). *Amalgamation of First Level Schools.* Dublin: Department of Education and Science.

Department of Education (1924). *Scholarships from Primary School.* Dublin: The Stationery Office.

Department of Education (1925). *Statistics relating to National Education in Saorstát for the Year 1922–1923.* Dublin: The Stationery Office.

Department of Education (1925). *Report and Statistics relating to National Education in Saorstát for the Year 1923–1924.* Dublin: The Stationery Office.

Department of Education (1927). *Commission on Technical Education – Report.* Dublin: The Stationery Office.

Department of Education (1927). *Regulations and Explanatory Notes for the Teaching of Rural Science and Nature Study in Primary Schools.* Dublin: The Stationery Office.

Department of Education (1927). *Report presented by the Committee on Inspection of Primary Schools to the Minister for Education.* Dublin: The Stationery office.

Department of Education (1929). *Amalgamation of Schools – Revision of Rules and Regulations.* Dublin: Department of Education.

Department of Education (1930). *Rural Science and Nature Study – Suggested Demonstrations for the Illustration of Lessons.* Dublin: Government Publications Sales Office.

Department of Education (1933). *Notes for Teachers – English.* Dublin: The Stationery Office.

Department of Education (1933). *Notes for Teachers – Geography.* Dublin: The Stationery Office.

Department of Education (1933). *Notes for Teachers – History.* Dublin: The Stationery Office.

Department of Education (1933). *Notes for Teachers – Irish.* Dublin: The Stationery Office.

Department of Education (1933). *Notes for Teachers – Music.* Dublin: The Stationery Office.

Department of Education (1933). *Notes for Teachers – Physical Training.* Dublin: The Stationery Office.

Department of Education (1934). *National Tradition and Folklore*. Dublin: The Stationery Office.

Department of Education (1934). *Revised Programme of Primary Instruction*. Dublin: The Wood Printing Works.

Department of Education (1934). *Revision of Rules and Regulations for National Schools under the Department of Education with an Explanatory Note on the Revised Salary Scales and the New Pension Scheme*. Dublin: Department of Education.

Department of Education (1935). *Notes for Teachers – Mathematics*. Dublin: The Stationery Office.

Department of Education (1948). *Revised Programme for Infants*. Dublin: The Stationery Office.

Department of Education (1951). *The Infant School – Notes for Teachers*. Dublin: The Stationery Office.

Department of Education (1954). *Report of the Council of Education*. Dublin: The Stationery Office.

Department of Education (1956). *Programme of Primary Instruction*. Dublin: The Stationery Office.

Department of Education (1965). *Investment in Education – Report of the Survey Team appointed by the Minister for Education in October 1962*. Dublin: The Stationery Office.

Department of Education (1965). *Investment in Education – Report of the Survey Team appointed by the Minister for Education in October 1962 – Annexes and Appendices*. Dublin: The Stationery Office.

Department of Education (1965). *Rules for National Schools under the Department of Education*. Dublin: The Stationery Office.

Department of Education (1969). *Ár nDaltaí Uile – All our Children*. Dublin: Department of Education.

Department of Education (1971). *Primary School Curriculum: Teacher's Handbook – Part 1*. Dublin: Department of Education.

Department of Education (1971). *Primary School Curriculum: Teacher's Handbook – Part 2*. Dublin: Department of Education.

Department of Education (1972). *The Education of Children who are Handicapped by Impaired Hearing – Report of a Committee Appointed by the Minister for Education*. Dublin: The Stationery Office.

Department of Education (1980). *White Paper on Educational Development*. Dublin: The Stationery Office.

Department of Education (1981). *Report of the Pupil Transfer Committee*. Dublin: The Stationery Office.

Department of Education (1982). *The Education of Physically Handicapped Children – Report of a Committee appointed by John Bruton T.D., Parliamentary Secretary to the Minister for Education.* Dublin: The Stationery Office.

Department of Education (1984). *Programme for Action in Education 1984–1987.* Dublin: The Stationery Office.

Department of Education (1985). *Páistí an Lucht Taistil; Dréacht Curaclaim.* Dublin: Department of Education.

Department of Education (1985). *Report of the Committee on Discipline in Schools.* Dublin: The Stationery Office.

Department of Education (1988). *Guidelines on Remedial Education.* Dublin: The Stationery Office.

Department of Education (1990). *Report of the Primary Education Review Body.* Dublin: The Stationery Office.

Department of Education (1994). *Report of the Inter-Departmental Working Group on Environmental Awareness.* Dublin: The Stationery Office.

Department of Education (1995). *Charting our Education Future – White Paper on Education.* Dublin: The Stationery Office.

Review Body on the Primary Curriculum (1990). *Report of the Review Body on the Primary Curriculum.* Dublin: Department of Education.

Department of Education Circulars (in chronological order)

Circular; *New Permanent Scales of Salaries for National Teachers,* December 1920.

Circular; *New Programme of Instruction in National Schools,* April 1922.

Circular to Inspectors, November 1922.

Circular; *Programme of Instruction for National Schools,* July 1926.

Circular 11/31; *Circular to Managers, Teachers and Inspectors on Teaching through the Medium of Irish.*

Circular 12/31; *Circular to Inspectors on the Award of Highly Efficient and Efficient Ratings.*

Circular 2/39; *Instruction in Cookery and Laundry Work (or Domestic Economy) in National Schools.*

Circular; *Revival of Irish – What Children Can do?* March 1941.

Circular 6/43; *Arrangements and Suggestions regarding Written Exercises, Home Work, and the Teaching of Needlework and Cookery and Laundry, in the existing Emergency.*

Circular 7/43; *Revised Regulations for the Primary School Certificate Examination.*

Circular 8/54; *Scheme for the Provision of 'Free' Instruction in National Schools on One Half Day per Week.*
Circular 11/60; *Teaching of Irish.*
Circular 10/67; *Promotion of Pupils in National Schools*, March 1967.
Circular 8/71; *New Curriculum – Handbook for Teachers.*
Circular 14/71; *Grants for the Provision of Audio-visual Teaching Equipment for National Schools.*
Circular 15/71; *Study Day for New Curriculum.*
Circular 20/71; *New Curriculum – Pilot Schools.*
Circular 22/71; *New Curriculum – Handbook for Teachers – Volume II.*
Circular 16/73; *Responsibilities and Duties of Principal Teachers and Teachers in Charge of National Schools.*
Circular 12/76; *Inspection of Schools.*
Circular 9/82; *The Abolition of Corporal Punishment in National Schools.*
Circular 31/82; *Inspection of Schools.*
Circular 20/87; *Average Enrolments Required for the Appointment and Retention of Assistant Teachers in National Schools.*

Other Government Reports and Documents

Bord na Gaeilge (1983). *Action Plan for Irish 1983–1986.* Dublin: Bord na Gaeilge.
Bunreacht na hÉireann (1937). *Constitution of Ireland.* Dublin: The Stationery Office.
CLÁR (1975). *Report.* Dublin: The Stationery Office.
CSO (1965). *Statistical Abstract of Ireland 1965.* Dublin: The Stationery Office.
CSO (1967). *Statistical Abstract of Ireland 1967.* Dublin: The Stationery Office.
CSO (1974). *Statistical Abstract of Ireland 1970–1971.* Dublin: CSO.
CSO (2003). *Census 2002: Volume 2 – Ages and Marital Status.* Dublin: CSO.
CSO (2003). *Census 2002 – Principal Socio-economic Results.* Dublin: CSO.
CSO (2004). *Census 2002 – Irish Language: Volume 11.* Dublin: CSO.
Coimisiún na Gaeltachta (1926). *Report of Coimisiún na Gaeltachta.* Dublin: The Stationery Office.
Comhairle na Gaeilge (1974). *Irish in Education.* Dublin: The Stationery Office.
Commission of Inquiry on Mental Handicap (1965). *Report of the Commission of Inquiry on Mental Handicap.* Dublin: The Stationery Office.
Commission on Emigration (1956). *Commission on Emigration 1948–1954.* Dublin: The Stationery Office.

Commission on Itinerancy (1963). *Report of the Commission on Itinerancy*. Dublin: The Stationery Office.

Commission on the Restoration of the Irish Language (1963). *Summary, in English, of the Final Report*. Dublin: The Stationery Office.

Committee on In-service Education (1984). *Report of the Committee on In-service Education*. Dublin: The Stationery Office.

Department of Finance (1958). *Economic Development*. Dublin: The Stationery Office.

Department of Finance (1958). *Programme for Economic Expansion*. Dublin: The Stationery Office.

Department of Finance (1964). *Second Programme for Economic Expansion – Part 2*. Dublin: The Stationery Office.

Department of Finance (1969). *Third Programme – Economic and Social Development 1969–1972*. Dublin: The Stationery Office.

Department of Health (1960). *The Problem of the Mentally Handicapped*. Dublin: The Stationery Office.

Department of Industry and Commerce (1949). *Ireland – Statistical Abstract 1947–1948*. Dublin: The Stationery Office.

Government of Ireland (1969). *Ireland Tomorrow*. Dublin: The Stationery Office.

Government of Ireland (1980). *Review Body on Teachers' Pay – Interim Report*. Dublin: The Stationery Office.

Higher Education Authority (1970). *Report on Teacher Education*. Dublin: Stationery Office.

National Council for Curriculum and Assessment (1999). *Primary School Curriculum*. Dublin: National Council for Curriculum and Assessment.

National Programme Conference (1922). *National Programme of Primary Instruction*. Dublin: The Educational Company of Ireland.

National Programme Conference (1926). *Report and Programme presented by the National Programme Conference to the Minister for Education*. Dublin: The Stationery Office.

Provisional Government of Ireland (1922). *Draft Constitution of the Irish Free State*. Dublin: Eason.

Review Body of the Travelling People (1983). *Report of the Review Body of the Travelling People*. Dublin: The Stationery Office.

Review Group on Mental Handicap Services (1990). *Needs and Abilities – A Policy for the Intellectually Disabled*. Dublin: The Stationery Office.

Irish Parliamentary Debates

Detailed references to Dáil and Seanad Debates referenced are listed in the
Endnotes.
Dáil and Seanad Debates were accessed at: <http://historical-debates.oireachtas.
ie/>.

Chapters in Books

Barrington, T. (1967). Public Administration 1927–36 (in) McManus, F. (Ed.) (1967).
The Years of the Great Test 1926–39. Cork: Mercier Press, pp. 80–91.
Benson, C. (1985). Introduction (in) Herron, D. (1985). *Deaf Ears? A Report on the
Provision of Music Education in Irish Schools.* Dublin: The Arts Council, pp.
V–VI.
Clancy, P. (1999). Education Policy (in) Quin, S., Kennedy, P., O'Donnell, A. and
Kiley, G. (Eds) (1999). *Contemporary Irish Social Policy.* Dublin: University
College Dublin Press, pp. 72–107.
Coolahan, J. (1982). Developments in English Reading in the Irish National Schools,
1937–1977 (in) Swan, D. (Ed.) (1982). *Perspectives on Reading – A Symposium on
the Theory and Teaching of Reading.* Dublin: The Glendale Press, pp. 168–181.
Coolahan, J. (1987). The Changing Context for the Exercise of Professionalism in
Teaching (in) Hogan, P. (1987). *Willingly to School? Perspectives on Teaching as
a Profession in Ireland in the Eighties.* Dublin: ESAI, pp. 15–33.
Coolahan, J. (1989). Educational Policy for National Schools, 1960–1985 (in) Mulcahy,
D. and O'Sullivan, D. (Eds) (1989). *Irish Educational Policy – Process and
Substance.* Dublin: Institute of Public Administration, pp. 27–76.
Coolahan, J. (1993). The Irish and Others in Irish Nineteenth-Century Textbooks
(in) Mangan, J. (Ed.) (1993). *The Imperial Curriculum.* London: Routledge,
pp. 54–63.
Coolahan, J. (2003). Unrealised Potential: The Relationship of Schools with the
Library Service (in) McDermott, N. (Ed.) (2003). *The University of the People:
Celebrating Ireland's Public Libraries – The Thomas Davis Lecture Series.* Dublin:
The Library Council, pp. 143–166.

Coolahan, J. (2005). The Schoolmaster in the New State (in) Fitzmaurice, G. (Ed.) (2005). *The World of Bryan McMahon*. Cork: Mercier Press, pp. 163–192.

Cullen, L. (1968). Irish Economic History: Fact and Myth (in) Cullen, L. (Ed.) (1968). *The Formation of the Irish Economy*. Cork: Mercier Press, pp. 113–124.

Cummins, J. (1977). A Comparison of Reading Achievement in Irish and English-medium Schools (in) Greaney, V. (Ed.) (1977). *Studies in Reading*. Dublin: Educational Company of Ireland, pp. 128–133.

Curtin, C. (1986). Marriage and the Family (in) Clancy, P., Drudy, S., Lynch, K. and O'Dowd, L. (Eds) (1986). *Ireland – A Sociological Profile*. Dublin: Institute of Public Administration in association with the Sociological Association of Ireland, pp. 155–172.

Curtin, C. and Varley, A. (1984). Children and Childhood in Rural Ireland: A Consideration of the Ethnographic Literature (in) Curtin, C., Kelly, M. and O'Dowd, L. (1984). *Culture and Ideology in Ireland*. Galway: Officina Typographica, Galway University Press. pp. 30–45.

Devlin, B. (1972). The Gaelic League – A Spent Force? (in) Ó Tuama, S. (Ed.) (1972). *The Gaelic League Idea*. Cork: Mercier Press, pp. 87–97.

Ferriter, D. (2003). Suffer Little Children? The Historical Validity of Memoirs of Irish Childhood (in) Dunne, J. and Kelly, J. (Eds) (2003). *Childhood and its Discontents – The First Seamus Heaney Lectures*. Dublin: The Liffey Press, pp. 69–106.

Fleischmann, A. (1971). Music in Education (in) Murphy, M. (Ed.) (1971). *Education in Ireland 2 – What Should Students Learn*. Cork: Mercier Press, pp. 68–88.

Harris, J. (1989). The Policy-making Role of the Department of Education (in) Mulcahy, D. and O'Sullivan, D. (Eds) (1989). *Irish Educational Policy – Process and Substance*. Dublin: Institute of Public Administration, pp. 7–25.

Hyde, D. (n.d.) The Necessity for de-Anglicising Ireland (in) Ó Conaire, B. (Ed.) (1986). *Language, Love and Lyrics, Essays and Lectures of Douglas Hyde*. Dublin: Academic Press, pp. 153–170.

Kellaghan, T. (1971). Educational Research (in) Murphy, M. (Ed.) (1971). *Education in Ireland 2 – What Should Students Learn*. Cork: Mercier Press, pp. 17–39.

Kellaghan, T. (1989). The Interface of Research, Evaluation, and Policy in Irish Education (in) Mulcahy, D. and O'Sullivan, D. (Eds) (1989). *Irish Educational Policy – Process and Substance*. Dublin: Institute of Public Administration, pp. 191–218.

Kennedy, S. (1981). Introduction (in) Kennedy, S. (Ed.) (1981). *One Million Poor? The Challenge of Irish Inequality*. Dublin: Turoe Press, pp. 7–11.

Killeen, J. (1986). Approaches to the Teaching of English in Dublin City Schools (in) Greaney, V. and Molloy, B. (Eds) (1986). *Dimensions of Reading*. Dublin: The Educational Company, pp. 73–76.

Lee, J. (1970). Continuity and Change in Ireland, 1945–70 (in) Lee, J. (Ed.) (1970). *Ireland 1945–1970*. Dublin: Gill and Macmillan, pp. 166–177.

Lynch, P. (1984). The Irish Free State and the Republic of Ireland, 1921–1966 (in) Moody, T. and Martin, F. (Eds) (1984). *The Course of Irish History*. Cork: Mercier Press, pp. 324–341.

Lynch, P. and O'Sullivan, A. (1986). Remedial Teaching in Primary Schools (in) Greaney, V. and Molloy, B. (Eds) (1986). *Dimensions of Reading*. Dublin: The Educational Company of Ireland, pp. 88–105.

MacNamara, J. (1971). Successes and Failures in the Movement for the Restoration of Irish (in) Rubin, J. and Jernudd, B. (Eds) (1971). *Can Language be Planned?* Hawaii: East-West Center Press, pp. 65–94.

McCartney, D. (1969). Education and the Language, 1938–1951 (in) Nowlan, K. and Williams, T. (Eds) (1969). *Ireland in the War Years and After 1939–51*. Dublin: Gill and Macmillan, pp. 80–94.

McGee, P. (1977). An Examination of Trends in Reading Achievement in Dublin over a Ten-Year Period (in) Greaney, V. (Ed.) (1977). *Studies in Reading*. Dublin: Educational Company of Ireland, pp. 27–35.

Ó Cuív, B. (1966). Education and Language (in) Williams, D. (Ed.) (1969). *The Irish Struggle 1916–1926*. London: Routledge and Kegan Paul, pp. 153–166.

Ó Cuív, B. (1969). Irish in the Modern World (in) Ó Cuív, B. (Ed.) (1969). *A View of the Irish Language*. Dublin: The Stationery Office, pp. 122–132.

Ó hAilín, T. (1969). Irish Revival Movements (in) Ó Cuív, B. (Ed.) (1969). *A View of the Irish Language*. Dublin: The Stationery Office, pp. 91–100.

Sheehan, J. (1979). Education and Society in Ireland, 1945–70 (in) Lee, J. (Ed.) (1979). *Ireland 1945–1970*. Dublin: Gill and Macmillan, pp. 61–72.

Tussing, D. (1981). Equity and the Financing of Education (in) Kennedy, S. (Ed.) (1981). *One Million Poor? The Challenge of Irish Inequality*. Dublin: Turoe Press, pp. 201–216.

Wall, M. (1969). The Decline of the Irish Language (in) Ó Cuív, B. (Ed.) (1969). *A View of the Irish Language*. Dublin: The Stationery Office, pp. 81–90.

Whyte, J. (1979). Church, State and Society 1950–1970 (in) Lee, J. (Ed.) (1979). *Ireland 1945–1970*. Dublin: Gill and Macmillan, pp. 73–82.

Whyte, J. (1984). Ireland 1966–82 (in) Moody, T. and Martin, F. (Eds) (1984). *The Course of Irish History*. Cork: Mercier Press, pp. 342–362.

Articles in Journals and Periodicals

Archbishop John Charles McQuaid (1945). *Irish Catholic Directory*, 20 February 1944, p. 674.

Archer, P. and O'Flaherty, B. (1991). Literacy Problems among Primary School Leavers in Dublin's Inner City. *Studies in Education*, Autumn 1991, Volume 7, No. 2, pp. 7–13.

Atkinson, N. (1964). The School Structure in the Republic of Ireland. *Comparative Education Review*, Volume 8, pp. 276–280.

Barry, T. (1979). Seminar Proceedings – Bridging the Gap (1979). *Oideas*, Spring 1979, Volume 20, pp. 29–32.

Beggan, G. (1988). A Profile of the Progress of Science in Primary Education in Ireland, 1837–1986. *Oideas*, Spring 1988, Volume 32, pp. 36–50.

Bennett, J. (1993). Geography Textbooks in the Republic of Ireland, 1973–1993. *Irish Journal of Education*, Volume 23, No. 1 and 2, pp. 25–35.

Bennett, J. (1994). History Textbooks in Primary Schools in the Republic of Ireland, 1971–1993. *Oideas*, Summer 1994, Volume 42, pp. 26–38.

Birch, P. (1955). The Report of the Council of Education. *Irish Ecclesiastical Record*, January 1955, Volume 83, pp. 1–11.

Burke, A. (1987). From Primary to Post-primary: Bridge or Barrier. *Oideas*, Spring 1987, Volume 30, pp. 5–23.

Burke, A. and Fontes, P. (1986). Educational Beliefs and Practices of Sixth-class Teachers in Irish Primary Schools. *Irish Journal of Education*, Volume 20, No. 2, pp. 51–77.

Close, S., Kellaghan, T., Madaus, G. and Airasian, P. (1978). Growth in Mathematical Attainments of Pupils. *Irish Journal of Education*, Volume 12, No. 1, pp. 3–21.

Colgan, J. (1991). Minimum Requirements for an Education Act(s). *Church and State*, Spring 1991, No. 37, pp. 16–19.

Columba, M. (1973). The Primary School Curriculum. *Compass*, February 1973, Volume 2, No. 1, pp. 4–9.

Committee on the Provision of Educational Facilities for the Children of Itinerants (1970). Educational Facilities for the Children of Itinerants. *Oideas*, Autumn 1970, Volume 5, pp. 44–53.

Connaughton, U. and Mahoney, M. (1985). Post-primary Remedial Teaching: A Survey, *Learn*, pp. 2–7.

Coolahan, J. (1984). The Fortunes of Education as a Subject of Study and of Research in Ireland. *Irish Educational Studies*, Volume 4, No. 1, pp. 1–34.

Coolahan, J. (1998). Educational Studies and Teacher Education in Ireland, 1965–1995. *Paedagogica Historica*: Supplementary Series, Volume III, Gent, Belgium, pp. 431–445.

Corcoran, T. (1923). An Infant Language Method Wanted. *Irish Monthly*, October 1923, Volume 51, pp. 489–490.

Corcoran, T. (1923). How English may be Taught without Anglicising. *Irish Monthly*, June 1923, Volume 51, pp. 269–273.

Corcoran, T. (1923). How the Irish Language can be Revived. *Irish Monthly*, January 1923, Volume 51, pp. 26–30.

Corcoran, T. (1923). The Native Speaker as Teacher. *Irish Monthly*, April 1923, Volume 51, pp. 187–190.

Corcoran, T. (1924). Is the Montessori Method to be Introduced into our Schools?, I, – The Montessori Principles. *Irish Monthly*, April 1924, Volume 52, pp. 118–124.

Corcoran, T. (1924). The Language Campaigns in Alsace-Lorraine. *Studies*, June 1924, Volume XIII, No. 50, pp. 201–213.

Corcoran, T. (1925). Class Examinations. *Irish Monthly*, June 1925, Volume 53, pp. 286–289.

Corcoran, T. (1925). The Irish Language in the Irish Schools. *Studies*, September 1925, Volume XIV, No. 55, pp. 377–388.

Corcoran, T. (1926). The True Children's Garden. *Irish Monthly*, May 1926, Volume 54, pp. 229–233.

Corcoran, T. (1927). Pestalozzi and the Catholic Orphans. *Irish Monthly*, March 1927, Volume 55, pp. 118–124.

Corcoran, T. (1930). The Catholic Philosophy of Education. *Studies*, June 1930, Volume XIX, No. 74, pp. 199–210.

Cregan, A. (1983). A Study of the Readability of Four History Textbooks in Use in Sixth Class in Irish Primary Schools. *Irish Educational Studies*, Volume 3, No. 1, pp. 166–185.

Cronin, B. (1990). Educational Provision for the Children of Travelling Families: A Survey. *Reach*, Volume 4, No. 1, pp. 24–28.

Crooks, T. and Griffin, K. (1978). Editorial. *Compass*, Volume 7, No. 1, pp. 4–12.

Cummins, J. (1978). Immersion Programs: the Irish Experience. *International Review of Education*, Volume 24, No. 3, pp. 273–282.

Cummins, J. (1982). Reading Achievement in Irish and English Medium Schools. *Oideas*, Summer, 1982, Volume 26, pp. 21–26.

De Buitléar, S. (1969). Curaclam Nua le hAghaidh na Buncsoile. *Oideas*, Autumn 1969, Volume 3, pp. 4–12.

Devine, D. (1999). Children: Rights and Status in Education – A Socio-historical Analysis. *Irish Educational Studies*, Volume 18, Spring 1999, pp. 14–28.

Donoghue, E. (1981). Health Education in Schools. *Compass*, Volume 10, No. 2, pp. 7–14.

Dr Hillery (1962). Irish Education for the New Europe. *European Teacher – Journal of the Irish Section of the European Association of Teachers*, Volume 1, No. 1, pp. 4–6.

Egan, O. (1981). Informal Teaching in the Primary School: Characteristics and Correlates. *Irish Journal of Education*, Volume 15, No. 1, pp. 5–22.

Egan, O. (1982). Informal Teaching in the Primary School: Effects on Pupil Achievement. *Irish Journal of Education*, Volume 16, No. 1, pp. 16–26.

Fontes, P. (1983). Theses on Educational Topics in Universities in Ireland: Their Distribution by University, Topic and Degree. *Irish Journal of Education*, Volume 17, No. 2, pp. 80–104.

Fontes, P., Kellaghan, T. and O'Brien, M. (1983). Relationships between Time Spent Teaching, Classroom Organisation, and Reading Achievement. *Irish Journal of Education*, Volume 15, No. 2, pp. 79–91.

Forde, P. and Shiel, G. (1993). Assessment of English Reading in Primary Schools. *Oideas*, Spring 1993, Volume 40, pp. 5–20.

Gash, H. (1985). Foundations and Practice of the New Curriculum. *Irish Educational Studies*, Volume 5, No. 1, pp. 86–101.

Gillespie, F. (1971). A 'Pilot School' at Work. *Oideas*, Spring 1971, Volume 6, pp. 53–56.

Greaney, V. (1978). Trends in Attainment in Irish from 1973 to 1977. *Irish Journal of Education*, Volume 12, No. 1, pp. 22–35.

Greaney, V. (1979). Developing National Attainment Measures: A Study of the Irish Experience. *Proceedings of ESAI 1979*, Dublin, pp. 209–223.

Greaney, V. and Close, S. (1989). Mathematics Achievement in Irish Primary Schools. *Irish Journal of Education*, Volume 22, No. 2, pp. 51–64.

Greaney, V. and Close, S. (1992). Mathematics in Irish Primary Schools: A Review of Research. *Oideas*, Spring 1992, Volume 38, pp. 41–61.

Greaney, V., Burke, A. and McCann, J. (1987). Entrants to Primary Teacher Education in Ireland. *European Journal of Teacher Education*, Volume 10, No. 2, pp. 127–140.

Halloran, J. (1962). The New Society: Community and Social Change. *Doctrine and Life*, July 1962, Volume 12, No. 7, pp. 365–378.

Harris, J. (1972). The Irish Association for Curriculum Development. *Compass*, Volume 1, No. 1, May 1972, pp. 4–7.

Hart, I. (1975). Absenteeism at National Schools – Educational, Medical and Social Aspects. *Economic and Social Review*, Volume 6, No. 3, pp. 313–335.

Herron, D. (1985). Principals' Delegation and Posts of Responsibility in Dublin National Schools. *Irish Educational Studies*, Volume 5, No. 2, pp. 118–136.

Horgan, M. (1991). Aspects of Play in the Junior Infant Classroom. *Irish Educational Studies*, Volume 10, No. 1, pp. 67–81.

Hurley, K. (1977). Primary School: Whither the Curriculum. *Compass*, Volume 6, No. 2, pp. 15–25.

Hyland, A. (1979). Shared Areas in Irish National Schools. *Proceedings of ESAI 1979*, Dublin, pp. 175–199.

Hyland, A. (1980). Current Trends in the Design of National Schools in Ireland. *Compass*, Volume 9, No. 1, pp. 31–41.

Hyland, A. (1983). The Treasury and Irish Education 1850–1922: The Myth and the Reality. *Irish Educational Studies*, Volume 3, No. 2, pp. 57–82.

Hyland, A. (1987). The Process of Curriculum Change in the Irish National School System. *Irish Educational Studies*, Volume 6, No. 2, pp. 17–38.

Hyland, A. (1989). The Multi-denominational Experience in the National School System in Ireland. *Irish Educational Studies*, Volume 8, No. 1, pp. 89–114.

Jones, V. (1996). Coláiste Moibhí – The Last Preparatory College. *Irish Educational Studies*, Spring 1996, Volume 15, pp. 101–112.

Kavanagh, J. (1985). The Design of Irish Primary School Buildings in the Era of the New Curriculum. *Irish Educational Studies*, Volume 5, No. 1, pp. 102–120.

Keegan, F. (1996). The Role of Amalgamation within the National Primary Education System, 1831–1994. *Irish Educational Studies*, Spring 1996, Volume 15, pp. 291–298.

Kellaghan, T. (1973). Evaluation in Schools. *Oideas*, Autumn 1973, Volume 11, pp. 4–19.

Kellaghan, T. and Fontes, P. (1977). Incidence and Correlates of Illiteracy in Irish Primary Schools. *Irish Journal of Education*, Volume 11, No. 1, pp. 5–20.

Kellaghan, T. and Gorman, L. (1968). A Survey of Teaching Aids in Irish Primary Schools. *Irish Journal of Education*, Volume 2, No. 1, pp. 32–40.

Kellaghan, T., MacNamara, J. and Neuman, E. (1969). Teachers' Assessments of the Scholastic Progress of Pupils. *Irish Journal of Education*, Volume 3, No. 2, pp. 95–104.

Kellaghan, T., Madaus, G., Airasian, P. and Fontes, P. (1976). The Mathematical Attainments of Post-primary Entrants. *Irish Journal of Education*, Volume 10, No. 1, pp. 3–17.

Kellaghan, T., Madaus, G., Airasian, P. and Fontes, P. (1981). Opinions of the Irish Public on Innovations in Education. *Irish Journal of Education*, Volume 15, No. 1, pp. 23–40.

Kelleher, J. (1957). Ireland ... And Where Does She Stand? *Foreign Affairs*, Volume 35, No. 3, pp. 485–495.

Kelly, A. (1993). The Gaelic League and the Introduction of Compulsory Irish into the Free State Education System. *Oideas*, Winter 1993, Volume 41, pp. 46–57.

Kelly, S. and McGee, P. (1967). Survey of Reading Comprehension – A Study in Dublin City National Schools. *New Research in Education*, June 1967, Volume I, pp. 131–134.

Keogh, H. (1976). Some aspects of the Starkie Era: The System of National Education in Ireland, 1899–1922. *Proceedings of ESAI 1976*, Galway, pp. 63–66.

Kiernan, G. and Walsh, T. (2004). The Changing Nature of Early Childhood Care and Education in Ireland. *Irish Educational Studies*, Volume 23, No. 2, pp. 1–18.

Lindsey, J. (1975). Irish Language Teaching: A Survey of Teacher Perceptions. *Irish Journal of Education*, Volume 9, No. 2, pp. 97–107.

Mac Donnchadha, M. (1969). New Approaches to Mathematics – Part 1: Mathematics at First level. *Oideas*, Spring 1969, Volume 2, pp. 4–8.

Mac Gréil, M. and Ó Gliasáin, M. (1974). Church Attendance and Religious Practice of Dublin Adults, *Social Studies*, April 1974, Volume 3, No. 2, pp. 163–212.

McElligott, T. (1955). Some Thoughts on our Educational Discontents. *University Review*, Volume 1, No. 5, pp. 27–36.

McKenna, L. (1912). The Educational Value of Irish. *Studies*, June 1912, Volume 1, No. 2, pp. 307–326.

Madaus, G., Fontes, P., Kellaghan, T. and Airasian, P. (1979). Opinions of the Irish Public on the Goals and Adequacy of Education. *Irish Journal of Education*, Volume 13, No. 2, pp. 87–125.

Martin, M. (1990). Mathematics Achievement in Sixth Class in Irish Primary Schools. *Irish Journal of Education*, Volume 24, No. 1, pp. 27–39.

Martin, M., Hickey, B. and Murchan, D. (1992). Educational Progress in Ireland: Maths and Science. *Irish Journal of Education*, Volume 26, pp. 105–116.

Meany, M. (1986). Aspects of Music Education in the Primary School. *Irish Educational Studies*, Volume 6, No. 1, pp. 172–179.

Motherway, A. (1986). The Textbook Curriculum: The Status and Role of the Textbook in the Teaching of History and English at Senior Primary Level. *Irish Educational Studies*, Volume 6, No. 1, pp. 193–204.

Motherway, A. (1987). Poetry in the Primary School. *Oideas*, Spring 1987, Volume 30, pp. 37–47.

Mulcahy, D. (1992). Promoting the European Dimension in Irish Education. *Irish Educational Studies*, Volume 11, Spring 1992, pp. 179–190.

Mulryan, C. (1984). Effective Communication of Mathematics at Primary Level: Focus on the Textbooks. *Irish Educational Studies*, Volume 4, No. 2, pp. 62–81.

Mulryan, C. and Close, S. (1982). A Study of the Mathematical Vocabulary of Primary School Mathematics Textbooks. *Irish Educational Studies*, Volume 2, pp. 305–321.

Murphy, D. (1972). The New Primary School Curriculum. *Studies*, Autumn 1972, Volume LXI, No. 243, pp. 199–218.

Ní Argáin, C. (1990). Soléite no Doléite? Staidéar ar Sholéiteacht Théascleabhar Gaeilge sa Bhunscoil. *Oideas*, Spring 1983, Volume 35, pp. 35–55.

Ní Chuinneagáin, S. (1995). The Irish National Teachers' Organisation (INTO) and the Deputation Crisis of 1910. *Oideas*, Summer 1995, Volume 43, pp. 94–110.

Ó Baoill, D. (1988). Language Planning in Ireland: The Standardisation of Irish (in) Ó Riagáin, P. (Ed.) (1988). *International Journal of the Sociology of Language – Language Planning in Ireland*. Amsterdam: Mouton de Gruyter, pp. 109–126.

Ó Buachalla, S. (1981). The Irish Language in the Classroom. *The Crane Bag*, Volume 5, No. 2, pp. 849–862.

O'Carroll, M. (1998). Inspired Educator and Ecumenist of Sorts. *Studies*, Winter 1998, Volume 87, No. 348, pp. 365–371.

Ó Catháin, S. (1954). The Report of the Council of Education. *Studies*, Winter 1954, Volume 43, No. 172, pp. 361–374.

O'Connell, F. (1993). Male/Female Imbalance in Primary Teaching: An Analysis of Recruitment Statistics, *Oideas*, Winter 1993, Volume 41, pp. 138–147.

O'Connell, N. (1979) (in) Seminar Proceedings – Bridging the Gap (1979). *Oideas*, Spring 1979, Volume 20, pp. 25–29.

O'Connor, D. (1979). Seminar Proceedings – Bridging the Gap (1979). *Oideas*, Spring 1979, Volume 20, pp. 5–8.

O'Connor, M. (2004). The Theories on Infant Pedagogy of Dr Timothy Corcoran, Professor of Education, University College, Dublin. *Irish Educational Studies*, Spring/Summer 2004, Volume 23, No. 1, pp. 35–47.

O'Connor, S. (1968). Post-Primary Education in Ireland: Now and in the Future. *Studies*, Autumn 1968, Volume 57, No. 227, pp. 233–251.

Ó Domhnalláin, T. (1981). Buntús Gaeilge – Cúlra, Cur le Chéile, Cur i Bhfeidhm. *Teangeolas*, Geimhreadh 1981, No. 13, pp. 24–32.

O'Doherty, E. (1958). Bilingualism: Educational Aspects. *Advancement of Science*, March 1958, Volume 14, No. 56, pp. 282–287.

O'Flaherty, L. (1994). Religious Control of Schooling in Ireland: Some Policy Issues in Review. *Irish Educational Studies*, Spring 1994, Volume 13, pp. 62–70.

O'Flynn, J. (1990). The Selection and Organisation of Musical Materials in Irish Schools. *Oideas*, Spring 1990, Volume 35, pp. 56–73.

O'Leary, M. (1991). The Primary Curriculum. *Studies in Education*, Autumn 1991, Volume 7, No. 2, pp. 58–61.

Ó Loinsigh, P. (1975). The Irish Language in the Nineteenth Century. *Oideas*, Spring 1975, Volume 14, pp. 5–21.

O'Malley, D. (1967). University Education in Dublin – Statement of Minister for Education, 18 April 1967. *Studies*, Summer 1967, Volume LVI, No. 222, pp. 113–121.

O'Neill, A. (1993). Adapting the *Stay Safe* Programme for Special Education. *Reach*, Volume 6, No. 2, pp. 96–100.

O'Neill, J. (1943). The Educationalist. *Studies*, June 1943, Volume XXXII, No. 126, pp. 157–160.

Ó Riagáin, P. (1988). Public Attitudes towards Irish in the Schools: A Note on Recent Surveys. *Teangeolas*, Geimhreadh 1988, No. 25, pp. 19–21.

O'Rourke, B. and Archer, P. (1987). A Survey of Teaching Practices in the Junior Grades of Irish Primary Schools. *Irish Journal of Education*, Volume 21, No. 2, pp. 53–79.

Ó Suilleabháin, S. (1973). Teachers' Centres: Theory and Practice. *Oideas*, Summer 1973, Volume 10, pp. 13–17.

Ó Tailliúr, P. (1964). Ceartliosta de Leabhar, Paimfléid, etc. Foilsithe in Éirinn ag Conradh na Gaedhilge 1893–1918. *Comhar*, Feabhra 1964, pp. 1–4; Márta 1964, pp. 5–8; Aibreán, pp. 17–20; Bealtaine 1964, pp. 13–16; Meitheamh 1094, pp. 17–20; Iúil 1964, pp. 21–24; Lúnasa, pp. 25–26.

Ó Tuathaigh, G. (1993). The Irish State and Language Policy (in) The Future of Irish – Ten Essays Celebrating One Hundred Years of the Irish Language Movement, issued with *Fortnight* (April 1993), No. 316, pp. 3–5.

Record of Irish Ecclesiastical Events for the Year 1921. *Irish Catholic Directory*, 20 October 1921, pp. 577–578.

Sanders, J. and Greaney, V. (1986). Self-evaluation of the Irish Primary School. *Oideas*, Autumn 1986, Volume 29, pp. 41–51.

Sugrue, C. (1990). Child-centred Education in Ireland since 1971: An Assessment. *Oideas*, Spring 1990, Volume 35, pp. 5–21.

Sugrue, C. (2003). Principal's Professional Development: Realities, Perspectives and Possibilities. *Oideas*, Spring 2003, Volume 50, pp. 8–39.

Symposium: Report on Teacher Training. *Oideas*, Spring 1971, Volume 6, pp. 4–32.

Torthaí Staidéir: Leanúnachas i Múineadh na Gaeilge ó Bhunscoil go hIarbhunscoil. *Oideas*, Autumn 1972, Volume 9, pp. 18–21.

Travers, M. (1976). A Second Replication of a Survey of Reading Comprehension in Dublin City Schools. *Irish Journal of Education*, Volume 10, No. 1, pp. 18–22.

Ward, N. (1982). A Fourth Survey of Reading Comprehension in Dublin City National Schools. *Irish Journal of Education*, Volume 16, No. 1, pp. 56–61.

Whelan, M. (1970). Glenanaar – An Experiment in Integration. *Oideas*, Autumn 1970, Volume 5, pp. 30–37.

Articles in Conference Proceedings

Carr, J. (1992). Professional Development and Training (in) Council of Teachers'
Unions (1992). *Education Conference.* Dublin: Council of Teachers' Unions,
pp. 13–18.

Coolahan, J. (1981). *'Education' in the Training Colleges – Carysfort 1877–1977: Two
Centenary Lectures.* Our Lady of Mercy College Blackrock. Blackrock: Our
Lady of Mercy College, pp. 20–52.

Forde, P. (1979). The Teaching of English in Dublin Primary Schools (in) Reading
Association of Ireland (1979). *Proceedings of the Fourth Annual Conference.*
Dublin: Reading Association of Ireland, pp. 104–111.

Grant, C. (1986). Initiating and Sustaining Staff Development through the Medium of
the Plean Scoile (in) INTO – District XV (1986). *Proceedings of the Third Annual
Drumcondra Education Conference.* Dublin: INTO – District XV, pp. 42–50.

Ní Mhaoldomhnaigh, S. (1985). The Infant Mathematics Curriculum in Practice
– A Study (in) INTO – District XV (1985). *Proceedings of the Second Annual
Drumcondra Education Conference.* Dublin: INTO – District XV, pp. 12–23.

Norton, S. (1984). A Communicative Syllabus for Irish in the Primary School:
Arguments and Practical Proposals (in) INTO – District XV (1984). *Proceedings
of the First Annual Drumcondra Education Conference.* Dublin: INTO – District
XV, pp. 110–123.

Ward, N. (1986). The Church and the I.N.T.O. in the National School System – A Brief
Look at the Basic Positions, and at some Points of Compliance and Conflict
(in) INTO – District XV (1986). *Proceedings of the Third Annual Drumcondra
Education Conference.* Dublin: INTO – District XV, pp. 3–8.

Books Relating to the Subject and Period

Abbott, W. (Ed.) (1966). *The Documents of Vatican II.* London: Geoffrey
Chapman.

Akenson, D. (1975). *A Mirror to Kathleen's Face – Education in Independent Ireland
1922–1960.* London: McGill-Queen's University Press.

Barrington, T. (1980). *The Irish Administrative System.* Dublin: Institute of Public
Administration.

Breen, R., Hannan, D., Rottman, D. and Whelan, T. (1990). *Understanding Contemporary Ireland. State, Class and Development in the Republic of Ireland.* Dublin: Gill and Macmillan.

Brown, T. (1981). *Ireland: A Social and Cultural History 1922–1979.* Glasgow: Fontana.

Bruner, J. (1960). *The Process of Education.* Cambridge, Massachusetts: Harvard University Press.

Burke, A. (1994). *Teaching – Retrospect and Prospect.* Dublin: Brunswick Press.

Coolahan, J. (1981). *Irish Education – History and Structure.* Dublin: Institute of Public Administration.

Coolahan, J. with O'Donovan, P. (2009). *A History of Ireland's School Inspectorate 1831–2008.* Dublin: Four Courts Press.

Crooks, T. and McKernan, J. (1984). *The Challenge of Change: Curriculum Development in Irish Post-primary Schools 1970–1984.* Dublin: Institute of Public Administration.

Dent, C. (1969). *The Education Act, 1944 – Provisions, Regulations, Circulars, Later Acts – Twelfth Edition.* London: University of London Press Ltd.

Dewey, J. (1956). *The Child and the Curriculum – The School and Society.* Chicago: The University of Chicago Press.

Dewey, J. (1963). *Experience and Education.* New York: Collier Books.

Drudy, S. and Lynch, K. (1993). *Schools and Society in Ireland.* Dublin: Gill and Macmillan.

Farren, S. (1995). *The Politics of Irish Education 1920–1965.* Belfast: Institute of Irish Studies.

Flude, M. and Hammer, M. (Eds) (1990). *The Education Reform Act 1988 – Its Origins and Implications.* London: The Falmer Press.

Fullan, M. (1993). *Change Forces: Probing the Depths of Educational Reform.* London: The Falmer Press.

Glendenning, D. (1999). *Education and the Law.* Dublin: Butterworths.

Gordon, P. and Lawton, D. (1978). *Curriculum Change in the Nineteenth and Twentieth Centuries.* London: Hodder and Stoughton Educational.

Hargreaves, A., Lieberman, A., Fullan, M. and Hopkins, D. (Eds) (1998). *The International Handbook of Educational Change.* London: Kluwer Academic Publishers.

Hussey, G. (1990). *At the Cutting Edge – Cabinet Diaries 1982–1987.* Dublin: Gill and Macmillan.

Hyland, A. and Milne, K. (1987). *Irish Educational Documents – Volume 1. Selection of Extracts from Documents relating to the History of Irish Education from the Earliest Times to 1922.* Dublin: Church of Ireland College of Education.

Inglis, T. (1998). *Moral Monopoly – The Rise and Fall of the Catholic Church in Modern Ireland.* Dublin: University College Dublin Press.

Joyce, P.W. (1892). *The Teaching of Manual Work in Schools.* Dublin: M.H. Gill and Son.

Kelly, A. (2002). *Compulsory Irish: Language and Education in Ireland 1870s–1970s.* Dublin: Irish Academic Press.

Kennedy, K., Giblin, T. and McHugh, D. (1988). *The Economic Development of Ireland in the Twentieth Century.* London: Routledge.

Keogh, D. (1994). *Twentieth-century Ireland – Nation and State.* Dublin: Gill and Macmillan.

Lyons, F.S.L. (1971). *Ireland Since the Famine.* London: Fontana Press.

MacNamara, J. (1966). *Bilingualism and Primary Education – A Study of Irish Experience.* Great Britain: T. and A. Constable Limited.

McCracken, J. (1958). *Representative Government in Ireland: A Study of Dáil Éireann, 1919–1948.* London: Oxford University Press.

McMahon, S. and O'Donoghue, J. (Eds) (1993). *Tales out of School.* Dublin: Poolbeg.

Meenan, J. (1970). *The Irish Economy Since 1922.* Liverpool: Liverpool University Press.

Mescal, J. (1957). *Religion in the Irish System of Education.* Dublin: Clonmore and Reynolds Ltd.

Miller, D. (1973). *Church, State and Nation in Ireland 1898–1921.* Dublin: Gill and Macmillan.

Mitchell, A. and Ó Snodaigh, P. (1985). *Irish Political Documents 1916–1949.* Dublin: Irish Academic Press.

Montessori, M. (1917). *The Advanced Montessori Method.* London: William Heinemann.

Moynihan, M. (Ed.) (1980). *Speeches and Statements by Eamon de Valera 1917–1973.* Dublin: Gill and Macmillan.

Murphy, J. (1975). *Ireland in the Twentieth Century.* Dublin: Gill and Macmillan.

Ó Buachalla, S. (Ed.) (1980). *A Significant Irish Educationalist – The Educational Writings of P.H. Pearse.* Dublin: Mercier Press.

Ó Buachalla, S. (1988). *Education Policy in Twentieth Century Ireland.* Dublin: Wolfhound Press.

O'Connell, T. (1968). *100 Years of Progress – The Story of the Irish National Teachers' Organisation 1868–1968.* Dublin: Dakota Press.

O'Connor, M. (2010). *The Development of Infant Education in Ireland, 1838–1948: Epochs and Eras.* Bern: Peter Lang.

O'Connor, S. (1986). *A Troubled Sky – Reflections on the Irish Educational Scene 1957–1968*. Dublin: ERC.

O'Donoghue, T. (2000). *Bilingual Education In Ireland 1904–1922 – The Case of the Bilingual Programme of Instruction*. Centre for Irish Studies Monograph Series, No. 1 2000. Perth: Murdoch University.

Parkes, S. (1984). *Kildare Place – The History of the Church of Ireland Training College 1811–1969*. Dublin: Church of Ireland College of Education.

Peillon, M. (1982). *Contemporary Irish Society – An Introduction*. Dublin: Gill and Macmillan.

Piaget, J. and Inhelder, B. (1969). *The Psychology of the Child*. London: Routledge and Kegan Paul.

Plunkett, H. (1905). *Ireland in the New Century*. London: John Murray.

Sarason, S. (1982). *The Culture of the School and the Problem of Change (Second Edition)*. Boston: Allyn and Bacon.

Selleck, R. (1968). *The New Education – The English Background 1870–1914*. Melbourne: Sir Isaac Pitman and Sons Ltd.

Stenhouse, L. (1975). *An Introduction to Curriculum Research and Development*. London: Heinemann.

Sugrue, C. (1997). *Complexities of Teaching: Child-centred Perspectives*. London: The Falmer Press.

Titley, B. (1983). *Church, State and the Control of Schooling in Ireland 1900–1944*. Dublin: Gill and Macmillan Ltd.

Tussing, D. (1978). *Irish Educational Expenditures – Past, Present and Future*. Dublin: Economic and Social Research Institute.

Walsh, W. (1928). *William J. Walsh, Archbishop of Dublin*. Dublin: The Talbot Press.

Walshe, J. (1999). *A New Partnership – From Consultation to Legislation in the Nineties*. Dublin: Institute of Public Administration.

Whyte, J. (1990). *Church and State in Modern Ireland 1923–1979 – Second Edition*. Dublin: Gill and Macmillan.

Wilkerson, A. (1973). *The Rights of Children – Emergent Concepts of Law and Society*. Philadelphia: Temple University Press.

Reports, Pamphlets and Political Programmes

Reports

Association of Remedial Teachers of Ireland (1976). *A Priority in Education*. Dublin: Association of Remedial Teachers of Ireland.

Callan, J. (2006). *Developing Schools: Enriching Learning – The SCD Experience*. Maynooth: Department of Education, National University of Ireland, Maynooth.

Comhar na Múinteoirí Gaeilge (1981). *Bunoideachas trí Ghaeilge sa Ghaeltacht – Tuarascáil*. Baile Átha Cliath: Comhar na Múinteoirí Gaeilge.

Conference of Convent Primary Schools in Ireland (1975). *Evaluation of the New Curriculum for Primary Schools*. Dublin: Conference of Convent Primary Schools in Ireland.

CEB (1985). *Language in the Curriculum – A Curriculum and Examinations Board Discussion Paper*. Dublin: CEB.

CEB (1985). *Primary Education – A Curriculum and Examinations Board Discussion Paper*. Dublin: CEB.

CEB (1985). *The Arts in Education – A Curriculum and Examinations Board Discussion Paper*. Dublin: CEB.

CEB (1986). *In Our Schools – A Framework for Curriculum and Assessment*. Dublin: CEB.

CEB (1986). *Mathematics Education: Primary and Junior Cycle Post-primary – A Curriculum and Examinations Board Discussion Paper*. Dublin: CEB.

CEB (1987). *Social, Political and Environmental Education – Report of the Board of Studies*. Dublin: CEB.

ERC (1982). *An Evaluation of the Three-year Course Leading to the Bachelor of Education (B.Ed) Degree*. Dublin: ERC.

ESAI (1980). *Register of Theses on Educational Topics in Universities in Ireland 1911–1979*. Dublin: ESAI.

Fontes, P. and Kellaghan, T. (1977). *The New Primary School Curriculum, its Implementation and Effects*. Dublin: ERC.

Harris, J. (1984). *Spoken Irish in Primary Schools: An Analysis of Achievement*. Dublin: Institiúid Teangeolaíochta Éireann.

Herron, D. (1985). *Deaf Ears? A Report on the Provision of Music Education in Irish Schools*. Dublin: The Arts Council.

Hogan, P. and Herron, D. (1992). *Register of Theses on Educational Topics in Universities in Ireland – Volume Two 1980–1990*. Dublin: ESAI.

INTO (1941). *Report of Committee of Inquiry into the Use of Irish as a Teaching Medium to Children whose Home Language is English*. Dublin: INTO.

INTO (1947). *A Plan for Education*. Dublin: INTO.

INTO (1976). *Primary School Curriculum: Curriculum Questionnaire Analysis by Education Committee*. Dublin: INTO.

INTO (1979). *Proposals to the Minister for Education in Connection with the White Paper on Education*. Dublin: INTO.

INTO (1982). *An Examination of the Educational Implications of School Size 1981–1982*. Dublin: INTO.

INTO (1984). *Ages of Entry – Report of the Education Committee*. Dublin: INTO.

INTO (1985). *The Irish National Teachers' Organisation and the Irish Language – Discussion Document*. Dublin: INTO.

INTO (1985). *The Irish Language in Primary Education – Summary of INTO Survey of Teachers' Attitudes to the Position of Irish in Primary Education*. Dublin: INTO.

INTO (1986). *Towards a Primary Schools' Psychological Service*. Dublin: INTO.

INTO (1988). *Primary School Curriculum – Report and Discussion Papers*. Dublin: INTO.

INTO (1989). *Assessment – A Report by the Education Committee*. Dublin: INTO.

INTO (1989). *School Texts – A Report by the Education Committee*. Dublin: INTO.

INTO (1989). *The Arts in Education – A Report by the Education Committee*. Dublin: INTO.

Mac Aogáin, E. (1990). *Teaching Irish in the Schools: Towards a Language Policy for 1992*. Dublin: Institiúid Teangeolaíochta Éireann.

McKenna, A. (1988). *Childcare and Equal Opportunities – Policies and Services for Childcare in Ireland*. Dublin: Employment Equality Agency.

MRBI (1985). *The Irish Language in Primary Schools. – Survey Report*. Dublin: INTO.

Murphy, C. (1980). *School Report – The Guide to Irish Education for Parents, Teachers and Students*. Dublin: Ward River Press.

NESC (1975). *Educational Expenditure in Ireland*. Dublin: NESC.

NIEC (1966). *Comments on 'Investment in Education.'* Dublin: NIEC.

National Parents' Council – Primary (1990). *The Cost of Free Education – A Survey on the Cost to Parents of Free Primary Education in Ireland*. Dublin: National Parents' Council – Primary.

Nic Ghiolla Phádraig, M. (1990). *Childhood as a Social Phenomenon – National Report Ireland*. European Centre for Social Welfare Policy and Research. Eurosocial Report 36/8. Vienna: European Centre for Social Welfare Policy and Research.

Ó Domhnalláin, T. and Ó Gliasáin, M. (1976). *Audiovisual Methods v A.B.C. Methods in the Teaching of Irish*. Dublin: Institiúid Teangeolaíochta Éireann.

OECD (1969). *Reviews of National Policies for Education – Ireland*. Paris: OECD.

OECD (1991). *Reviews of National Policies for Education – Ireland*. Paris: OECD.

St. Patrick's College (1975). *St. Patrick's College, Drumcondra: Centenary Booklet 1875–1975*. Dublin: Beacon Printing Co. Ltd.

Swan, D. (1978). *Reading Standards in Irish Schools*. Dublin: The Educational Company.

Teachers' Study Group (1969). *Reports on the Draft Curriculum for Primary Schools*. Dublin: Teachers' Study Group.

Pamphlets

Department of Education (1984). *Léas – A Department of Education Information Bulletin*. Winter 1984, No. 1.

Horgan, J. (1973). The New Curriculum – A Review. *Primary News*. Dublin: Gill and Macmillan.

Starkie, W.J.M. (1902). *Recent Reforms in Irish Education*. An Address read before the British Association Belfast, 11 September 1902. Dublin: Blackie and Son Limited.

Starkie, W.J.M. (1911). *The History of Irish Primary and Secondary Education During the Last Decade – An Inaugural Address*. Belfast.

Tuairim (1962). *Educating Towards a United Europe – Pamphlet 8*. Dublin: Tuairim.

Tuairim (1962). *Irish Education – Pamphlet 9*. London: Tuairim-London Research Group.

Political Programmes

Fianna Fáil (1981). *Our Programme for the '80s*. Dublin: Fianna Fáil.

Fianna Fáil (1987). *The Programme for National Recovery*. Dublin: Fianna Fáil.

Fine Gael (1966). *Policy for a Just Society – Education*. Dublin: Fine Gael.

Fine Gael (1966). *Policy for a Just Society – Irish Language Preservation*. Dublin: Fine Gael.

Fine Gael (1980). *Action Programme for Education in the '8os: A Fine Gael Policy Document*. Dublin: Fine Gael.

Fine Gael Ard Fheis (1980). *Education Discussion Document*. Dublin: Fine Gael.

Fine Gael (1981). *A Better Future – Let the Country Win*. Dublin: Fine Gael.

Irish Labour Party and Trade Union Congress (1925). *Labour's Policy on Education – Being the Report of a Special Committee of the National Executive of the Irish Labour Party and Trade Union Congress*. Dublin: Irish Labour Party and Trade Union Congress.

Labour Party (1943). *Labour's Programme for a Better Ireland*. Dublin: Labour Party.

Labour Party (1963). *Challenge and Change in Education – Policy Document issued by the Labour Party*. Dublin: The Labour Party.

Labour Party (1975). *Education at First Level: A Policy for our Children's Future*. Dublin: Labour Party.

Newspapers and Annual Reports

Newspapers

Fortnight
Freeman's Journal
Irish Independent
Irish Statesman
The Irish Times
Times Educational Supplement

Annual Reports

INTO (1901–1991)
General Synod of the Church of Ireland (1936–1950)

INTO Journals and Yearbooks

Annual Directory and Irish Educational Year Book
An Múinteoir
An Múinteoir Náisiúnta
Irish Teachers' Journal
The Irish School Monthly
The Irish School Weekly
Tuarascáil

Unpublished Theses

Bennett, J. (1992). *Culture, Curriculum and Primary Education in Ireland 1920–1970.* PhD Thesis. Kildare: National University of Ireland, Maynooth.

Cloonan, T. (1981). *Primary School Curriculum and Teachers' Attitudes.* M.Ed. Thesis. Galway: University College Galway.

Coolahan, J. (1973). *A Study of Curricular Policy for the Primary and Secondary Schools of Ireland 1900–1935, with Special Reference to the Irish Language and Irish History.* PhD Thesis. Dublin: Trinity College Dublin.

Cotter, M. (1978). *An Investigation into the Teaching of Physical Education in National Schools in the Republic of Ireland.* M.Ed. Thesis. Dublin: Trinity College Dublin.

Fitzpatrick, B. (1918). *Bilingualism as a Factor in Education with Application to the Language Question in Ireland.* M.A. Thesis. Dublin: University College Dublin.

Gilligan, J. (1982). *Teaching of History in Senior Standards in the Curriculum of Irish National Schools 1961–1981.* M.Ed. Thesis. Dublin: University College Dublin.

Higgins, M. (1987). *Infant Education in the Republic of Ireland – A Critique.* M.Ed. Thesis. Kildare: National University of Ireland, Maynooth.

Hyland, A. (1973). *Educational Innovation – A Case Study. An Analysis of the Revised Programme of 1900 for National Schools in Ireland.* M.Ed. Thesis. Dublin: Trinity College Dublin.

Kelleher, A. (1990). *Infant Education and the 1971 Curriculum*. M.Ed. Thesis. Dublin: University College Dublin.

McMahon, E. (1975). *A Study of a Primary School*. M.Ed. Thesis. Kildare: National University of Ireland, Maynooth.

Moroney, M. (2004). *An Analysis of the Development of Salaries and Pensions of National Teachers and of the Role of the Irish National Teachers' Organisation in their Progression, 1831 to 2000*. PhD Thesis. Kildare: National University of Ireland, Maynooth.

Ó Ciaráin, G. (1982). *The Effects of all-Irish Primary Schooling on Cognitive and Academic Development*. M.Ed. Thesis. Maynooth: National University of Ireland, Maynooth.

O'Reilly, Y. (1985). *A Study of Teachers' Centres in the Republic of Ireland, with Particular Reference to their Role in In-service Education*. M.Ed. Thesis. Dublin: Trinity College Dublin.

O'Sullivan, N. (1984). *Remedial Reading Education in the Primary School*. M.Ed. Thesis. Kildare: National University of Ireland, Maynooth.

Stapleton, G. (1988). *Infant Education and the Irish Primary School*. M.Ed. Thesis. Dublin: Trinity College Dublin.

Walsh, M. (1980). *A Study of the Implementation of the 1971 Curriculum for Irish Primary Schools*. M. Litt Thesis. Dublin: Trinity College Dublin.

Walsh, T. (2006). *A Critical Analysis of Curricular Policy in Irish Primary Schools, 1897–1990*. PhD Thesis. Kildare: National University of Ireland, Maynooth.

Appendix 1: Compulsory and Optional Subjects in the Primary School Curriculum, 1872–1999

Year	Compulsory Subjects	Optional/ Additional Subjects	Additional Notes
1872	Reading, writing, spelling, grammar, arithmetic, geography, needlework (girls), agriculture (boys).	Vocal music, book-keeping, Kindergarten, drawing, instrumental music, algebra, geometry and mensuration, trigonometry, navigation, mechanics, hydrostatics and pneumatics, light and sound, heat and steam engine, physical geography, heat and magnetism, botany, animal physiology and zoology, inorganic chemistry, geology; Latin, Greek, French, German, Irish, handicraft, hygiene, spinning, weaving, netmending, other cottage industries, type-writing, shorthand, bee-keeping, laundry work (girls), dressmaking (girls), practical cookery (girls), dairying (girls), management of poultry (girls), domestic economy (girls).	There was little uptake of this broad array of optional subjects in Irish primary schools between 1872 and 1900.
1900	English, arithmetic, Kindergarten methods, manual instruction, drawing, object lessons and elementary science, singing, school discipline and physical drill, cookery (girls), laundry (girls), needlework (girls).	French, Latin, mathematics, Irish, instrumental music.	English and arithmetic were the only 'compulsory subjects', with all other subjects to be taught if teachers were proficient and the necessary facilities and resources were available. Geography and history were taught through geographical and historical reading books. From 1904, manual instruction was discontinued in senior classes, geography was included as a separate subject, cookery applied in fifth and sixth classes only.

Year	Compulsory Subjects	Optional/ Additional Subjects	Additional Notes
1922	Religion (extra-curricular), Irish, English, mathematics (arithmetic, algebra and geometry), history and geography, singing, drill, needlework (girls).	Drawing, advanced algebra, advanced geometry and mensuration, French (or other continental language), Latin, nature study, book-keeping, elementary science (where a suitably equipped laboratory and trained teacher was available), cookery, rural science and school gardening, manual instruction (woodwork), domestic science.	All work in infant classes was to be through the medium of Irish. The work in infant classes was classified under language, drawing, numbers, Kindergarten gifts and occupations, songs and games. A veto was allowed to parents regarding the teaching of either the Irish or English language in schools. History and geography were to be taught as one subject.
1926	Religion (extra-curricular), Irish, English, mathematics, history, geography, music, rural science/ nature study, needlework (girls).	Drawing, domestic science, cookery and laundry, physical training, manual instruction.	All work in infant classes was to be through the medium of Irish, but allowing English to be used before 10:30 a.m. and after 2:00 p.m. The work in infant classes was classified under language, Kindergarten, songs, games, arithmetic and drawing. Higher and lower course were introduced in Irish and English, with the aim that the higher course in Irish would become the norm. Algebra and geometry (as part of mathematics) became optional in classes taught by women teachers and in one-teacher schools. History and geography were reconstituted as separate subjects.

Year	Compulsory Subjects	Optional/ Additional Subjects	Additional Notes
1934	Religion (extra-curricular), Irish, English, arithmetic, history, geography, music, needlework (girls), algebra or geometry (large boys' schools only).	English (first class), rural science/ nature study, domestic science, drawing, physical training, manual instruction, algebra and geometry (girls' schools and small schools).	All work in infant classes was to be through the medium of Irish. No English was allowed in infant classes, while English became an optional subject in first class. The higher course in Irish and the lower course in English was to be taught in all schools.
1948	Religion (extra-curricular), Irish, English, arithmetic, history, geography, music, needlework (girls), algebra or geometry (large boys' schools only).	English (first class), rural science/ nature study, domestic science, drawing, physical training, manual instruction, algebra and geometry (girls' schools and small schools).	*Revised Programme for Infants* allowed for a more child-centred and heuristic approach in infant classes. Optional thirty minutes of English allowed each day in infant classes.
1971	Religion (extra-curricular), language (Irish and English), mathematics, art and craft, social and environmental studies, history, geography, civics, music, physical education.	N/A	

Index

RETHINKING EDUCATION

Rethinking education has never been more important. While there are many examples of good, innovative practice in teaching and learning at all levels, the conventional education mindset has proved largely resistant to pedagogic or systemic change, remaining preoccupied with the delivery of standardised packages in a standardised fashion, relatively unresponsive to the diversity of learners' experiences and inclinations as well as to the personal perspectives of individual teachers. The challenge of our times in relation to education is to help transform that mindset.

This series takes up this challenge. It re-examines perennial major issues in education and opens up new ones. It includes, but is not confined to, pedagogies for transforming the learning experience, any-time-any-place learning, new collaborative technologies, fresh understandings of the roles of teachers, schools and other educational institutions, providing for different learning styles and for students with special needs, and adapting to changing needs in a changing environment.

This peer-reviewed series publishes monographs, doctoral dissertations, conference proceedings, edited books, and interdisciplinary studies. It welcomes writings from a variety of perspectives and a wide range of disciplines. Proposals should be sent to any or all of the series editors: Dr Marie Martin, mmartin@martech.org.uk; Dr Gerry Gaden, gerry.gaden@ucd.ie; and Dr Judith Harford, judith.harford@ucd.ie.